Seeing the Light

Seeing the Light

Samuel Schuman

Religious Colleges in Twenty-First-Century America

THE JOHNS HOPKINS UNIVERSITY PRESS | BALTIMORE

The Johns Hopkins University Press
2715 North Charles Street
Baltimore, Maryland 21218-4363
www.press.jhu.edu

Library of Congress Cataloging-in-Publication Data
Schuman, Samuel.
    Seeing the light : religious colleges in twenty-first-century
America / Samuel Schuman.
        p. cm.
    Includes bibliographical references and index.
    ISBN-13: 978-0-8018-9372-8 (hardcover : alk. paper)
    ISBN-10: 0-8018-9372-0 (hardcover : alk. paper)
    1. Church colleges—United States. I. Title.
    LC538.S38 2009
    378'.0710973—dc22   2009007057

A catalog record for this book is available from the British Library.

*Special discounts are available for bulk purchases of this book. For more information,
please contact Special Sales at 410-516-6936 or specialsales@press.jhu.edu.*

The Johns Hopkins University Press uses environmentally friendly book
materials, including recycled text paper that is composed of at least 30 percent
post-consumer waste, whenever possible. All of our book papers are acid-free,
and our jackets and covers are printed on paper with recycled content.

As always, for Nancy

Contents

Acknowledgments

To a degree that is unfamiliar to me, writing *Seeing the Light* has been a journey undertaken in company. I cannot begin to acknowledge and thank the hundreds of students, faculty, and staff at the colleges and universities I visited who have taken the time to respond to my queries and demonstrated the patience to help me understand the light they see at their schools. Some of those questions of mine must have seemed stupid or hostile, or both.

Three institutions—the University of Minnesota, Morris; the University of North Carolina–Asheville, and the University of New Mexico—have given gifts of time and money that made this project possible. In particular, President Robert Bruininks of the University of Minnesota awarded me a research grant that funded most of the (rather extensive) travel that provided the foundation for *Seeing the Light*. Anne Ponder and Rosalie Otero in North Carolina and New Mexico have been important friends and helpers.

I would not have known the institutions described in this book without the help of Andrew Wiseley, Anne Raia, John Korstad, John Doody, Ken Bratt, Dick Thomas, Jennifer Holberg, Walter Adamson, and Glen and Oree Robinson.

Thoughtful reactions from Pegge Saylor, Kathy Whatley, James Morales, and Don and Elaine Bailey sharpened my writing. Where it remains dull, the responsibility is all mine. Colleagues including Melody Veenendal, Gary Strei, Bob Yearout, Elaine Warren, and Carrie Grussing were more help than they knew. Jackie Wehmueller at the Johns Hopkins University Press has been a discerning, patient, and kind editor.

All of my family has given me more support than I deserve. Our children and their children are the brightest light I see in my life. My greatest gratitude is acknowledged in the dedication.

PART I

Introduction

Seeing the Light is a book about religious colleges, in particular evangelical Protestant institutions, and their place in contemporary American higher education. These schools are varied and, in many cases, flourishing, and their stories are worthy of attention by all of us interested in contemporary postsecondary institutions. My title makes reference, among other things, to James Burtchaell's work *The Dying of the Light*, which seeks to advance the proposition that religious colleges in contemporary American culture have lost that base in faith which brought them into existence and sustained them in their development. Although Burtchaell makes his argument with magisterial force and many of his observations are keen, I obviously disagree with his primary thesis. I believe that the light still shines brightly.

In chapter 1, which follows, I discuss why I undertook this project, why I think the subject merits consideration by those outside as well as within the world of faith-based higher education, and how this particular author came to this particular project. I also define some of the terms used on or about religious colleges and universities.

In chapter 2, I review briefly the history of American higher education from its beginnings in the colonial period to the present day, from the perspective of the evolving relationships between religion and American colleges and universities. All the institutions of higher education in our nation prior to the Revolutionary War were firmly grounded in both religion and public missions. Those core defining functions were clearly differentiated in the ninety years between the Revolution and the Civil War. From 1865 until 1944 and the end of World War II, American higher education grew explosively and changed almost as dramatically, taking a shape that is familiar today. In the second half of the twentieth century, many colleges and universities saw their religious connections weakened or broken; others struggled to maintain them in radically changed circumstances; and a third group of new religious institutions was born.

To establish a perspective for our specific focus on evangelical Christian institutions, the chapter concludes with an overview of the various religious institutions and religions across the spectrum of contemporary higher learning. I discuss a wide range of non-Christian colleges with religious connections.

In chapter 3, the final chapter of part I, we take a look at Roman Catholic higher education. I discuss not only its traditional colleges and comprehensive, graduate-level universities but also a group of "new Catholic" colleges, founded in the very recent past and often with unexpected links to the evangelical Christian colleges.

The core section of the book, presented in parts II–IV, is a more detailed look at a group of ten Christian colleges and universities, highlighting their similarities and differences, from each other and from other, more "mainstream" institutions. Recognizing the impossibility of a truly comprehensive survey of these institutions, I have chosen a small cluster of schools that seem both intrinsically interesting and broadly representative. Most are flourishing, but not necessarily in the same ways, and most are facing important challenges as well. I have clustered the portraits of these institutions into three smaller groups on the basis of some common denominator of interest, but in actuality, all ten of these schools merit comparison to each other. The subgroups are:

- Two Baptist universities (Baylor and Anderson)
- Three other denominational colleges (New Saint Andrews, Calvin, and North Park)
- Five nondenominational Christian institutions that seem to represent the dominant model of contemporary American religious collegiate education (George Fox, Westmont, Oral Roberts, Northwestern College, and Wheaton)

Finally, I conclude with some thoughts about what I believe the national higher education community as a whole can learn from the successes and trials of those institutions.

Appended to the text is a review of some of the key literature on religious colleges and universities. If this review is not particularly deep, it does aim to be rather broad, and at least touch upon most of the major topics and themes that have interested writers in this area.

1 | An Agenda for the Study of Religious Colleges and Universities

God clepeth folk to him in sundry wise.
CHAUCER, "The Wife of Bath's Prologue" (l. 108), from *The Canterbury Tales*

Two Introductory Stories

Several years ago, I was serving as the chief executive of the University of Minnesota, Morris, a liberal arts branch campus of the land-grant state university. Our small campus (about eighteen hundred students) was in the process of moving from Division II to Division III of the NCAA and was changing athletic conference affiliation at the same time. As a college in the rural upper Midwest, in the west-central region of our state far from the metropolitan Twin Cities area, a significant fraction of our students came from family backgrounds in which religion, primarily Lutheranism and Roman Catholicism, played an important role. In fact, the largest five student groups on our campus, out of a total of around eighty, were religious groups such as the Fellowship of Christian Athletes and the Lutheran Campus Ministry.

The Upper Midwest Athletics Conference we were joining consisted of a number of fairly nearby schools, with similar enrollment and fiscal profiles. Some of them were strongly religious colleges—Northwestern College (St. Paul) and Crown College, for example. Others were not—Northland and Rockford, among them. Our school had had a dismal record in Division II, and most agreed that the move to Division III was sensible. But some members of the faculty were less comfortable about the change of conference affiliation. This dissatisfaction reached a head at a meeting of the all-campus legislative body, the Campus Assembly, where one faculty member stood and asked, with some sarcasm and bitterness, whether we really wanted our institution to be affiliated with "a bunch of two-bit Bible colleges." Although the large majority of Campus Assembly members in fact *did* find the new conference affiliation desirable, a significant minority grumbled assent with this gloomy assessment.

Later, in a quiet, private conversation, I had the opportunity to ask the vocal faculty critic if she had ever actually been to any of the institutions with which she did not want to see us linked. She responded that she had never visited any of them and did not need to in order to know what kind of places they were. She might have been surprised at their popularity. Because of my work on the proposed conference change, I knew that, in one recent five-year period, Northwestern College had seen an enrollment increase of 28.7% and Crown of 48.7%. Our university did subsequently change conference affiliation; it worked out very well, both in terms of athletics and in the context of interinstitutional communication and cooperation. But the phrase "two-bit Bible colleges" remains in my memory as a truly distasteful example of the least enlightened view of religious colleges and universities sometimes entertained by otherwise clever academics in the secular sphere.

◆◆◆

At the 2006 annual meeting of the National Collegiate Honors Council, some two thousand undergraduates, faculty members, and honors administrators gathered to share with each other much of what is best about contemporary collegiate education. The conference included a handful of Student Interdisciplinary Research Panels, one of which focused on three presentations clustered under the heading "Religion's Influence on the Development of Personal and Public Attitudes." All three research reports were by women students, and all of the presenters identified themselves as evangelical or deeply committed Christian students. One attended a branch of a public university, one a Roman Catholic women's college (although the presenter was not herself Catholic), and one a Christian university.[1]

The first paper, by the student from the Christian college, presented that young woman's research and meditations on capital punishment. She described, with careful objectivity, the case for "an eye for an eye" retributive justice and the contrary argument for mercy and forgiveness, noting that there were biblical precedents for both. In the spirit of historic Calvinist Protestantism, it was clear that the student felt that she herself could read the relevant biblical passages, weigh them, and draw her own conclusions as to whether the Bible leaned more heavily for or against the death penalty. In the question period following her presentation, she responded to a direct question from the audience by affirming that she opposed capital punishment, concluding that the weight of biblical authority supported those who argued for God's infinite mercy.

The second paper was written by a student from a secular, public university. She opened her presentation by noting her strong evangelical position and faith. Her project had begun as an effort to reconcile her fervent and conservative Christianity with a nearly equally vigorous belief in the equality of the sexes. One the one hand, she believed that women deserved a liberated position both in the workplace and at home and, on the other, she understood the traditional conservative Christian injunction that husbands and fathers held a position of primacy over wives and mothers and was aware that many in her faith tradition believed that the only acceptable role for women was, in fact, as wives and mothers. She considered injunctions like that in 1 Timothy 2:11, "Let a woman learn in silence with full submission." But in the final analysis, the student (who was, in fact, a wife and a mother and whose husband was at home caring for their child while she was making her presentation at the conference) put greater authority on the well-known passage from Galatians: "There is no longer Jew nor Greek, there is no longer slave or free, there is no longer male and female; for all of you are one in Christ Jesus" (3:28). This student argued, finally, for what she termed a biblical or evangelical feminism.

The third presenter was a thoughtful and articulate young woman attending a small, traditionally female, Roman Catholic college. Her paper concerned the efforts of students at her school to stage a production of Eve Ensler's play *The Vagina Monologues,* an effort that had been prohibited by the senior administration of the college. This student made an unambiguous case for what she called collegiate liberty and First Amendment rights. She believed that the effort of her college's president to prevent the performance was nothing more or less than unwarranted censorship and that it had the anti-Christian effect of provoking hostility and misunderstanding.[2]

These three honors student research projects had been accepted for the program of the conference with no ideological filter in place (indeed, it was my impression that all papers offered by students with the support of their home institution honors programs had been accepted). All three were by students who made a clear point of their commitment to a Christian perspective. One argued for feminism, one against capital punishment, and one for the freedom to present a contemporary play about women's bodies.

•••

Religious students, religion on campus, and religious colleges are *not* simple or simple-minded, as too many secular academics seem to think. I would argue that my second story illustrates the invalidity of the opinion expressed in the first. As Paul A. Bramadat (himself a Unitarian) observes in his study of the InterVarsity Christian Fellowship at McMaster University, evangelical Christians are "not illiterate hillbillies" and do not merit "the profound condescension I have encountered when discussing evangelicals with liberal Christians, academics, and friends."[3] In a recent alumni publication of Grinnell College (no one's idea of a sectarian liberal arts college and, coincidentally, my alma mater), a current (class of 2010) student writes of finding at that institution "a large group of people who were deeply religious." These Grinnellian Christians, the writer finds, "never assume they know the perfect route to God. They constantly debate, argue, and redefine their views on Christ, God and what it means to be Christian. They're friends with Jews, Muslims, Hindus, Unitarians and yes, even atheists. They see a world not of one correct faith, but of many."[4] In the pages that follow, my aim is to present a view of religious colleges and universities that is neither condescending nor simple. These institutions merit thoughtful, serious, and respectful study, and there is much that the larger world of twenty-first-century American higher education can learn from them

Why Write about Religious Colleges?

When colleagues have discovered that I am working on a project that focuses upon religious colleges, the most common response has been, in one form or another, Why would you want to do that? Occasionally, this question carries a burden of scorn. Most often, though, it reflects genuine puzzlement. Religious colleges—their missions, operations, successes and failures, students, faculty, staffs, histories, futures—seem to many academics so peripheral to "mainstream" American higher education as to be virtually invisible. Just to cite, almost at random, one example: the otherwise instructive and enlightened winter 2008 issue of the Association of American Colleges and Universities periodical *Diversity and Democracy* is devoted to "Religious Diversity and the Making of Meaning." In addition to an introduction and bibliography, the issue featured nine articles on topics such as "Beyond Spirituality: A New Framework for Educators" and "Speaking of Religion: Facilitating Difficult Dialogues." But not once in the twenty-four-page journal devoted to religion in higher education is there even a hint that the American higher education community includes religious colleges. None of the essays focuses in a substantial way on those institutions. And none of the authors represented in the special number teaches at what would be identified as a Christian college.

For those of us who are not positioned within these institutions, there are at least three compelling reasons to study and seek to understand them: the very ignorance and occasional hostility with which nonreligious or secular academia approaches overtly religious institutions; the spectacular success that many of those schools are currently enjoying, a success from which the rest of us have much to learn; and the responsiveness of these religious colleges and universities to what we are discovering are the wants and needs of contemporary students. A good place to begin is with the last of these themes.

Student Spirituality

Had anyone else proposed a massive project to study the spiritual development of undergraduate students in twenty-first-century America, the building of credibility, participation, and attention would have been a difficult and long-drawn-out process. But when Alexander Astin, working with the Higher Education Research Institute (HERI) at UCLA, undertook such a project, with support from the John Templeton Foundation, interest was immediate and profound.[5] Astin is one of a very small group of contemporary students of American higher education with virtually universal name recognition and impeccable credibility. When he suggests that our institutions of higher education have neglected the "interior" understandings of students in favor of the outer aspects of life, colleges and universities, higher education associations, and media pay attention.[6] Astin recruited a national advisory board which included a broad cross section of higher education's leaders, including Arthur Levine, Nathan Hatch, Carol Geary Schneider, Huston Smith, and Diana Chapman Walsh. The Spirituality in Higher Education project is an ongoing enterprise, but its first results are impressive and clear. Astin, co–principal investigator Helen Astin, and their research team administered a survey to more than 110,000 entering students at 236 diverse institutions in the fall of 2004. Earlier, a smaller pilot survey of some 3,680 students in their third year had been administered. Plans call for continued longitudinal surveying.

The results of the survey revealed that 80% report an interest in spirituality and 76% describe themselves (to some or to a great extent) as searching for a meaning or purpose in life. Similarly, 74% have discussed these issues with their friends, and about half (47%) are actively seeking opportunities for spiritual growth. About eight in ten report that they believe in God, and the same number attended some sort of religious service in the previous year. About two-thirds pray. The HERI report measured both "spirituality" and "religiousness." Most who scored high on the latter index also scored high on the former, but there were also many students who described themselves as "spiritual" but not especially "religious." Students who described themselves as both religious and spiritual tended to be somewhat more conservative, politically and socially, than their peers, although on some contemporary issues, especially affirmative action and opposition to the death penalty, college students who are religious tend to espouse "liberal" positions. The students surveyed were asked to indicate their religious preferences: 26% self-identified as Roman Catholic, 17% as mainline Protestants, 13% as Baptist, and 11% as "other Christian." Perhaps most tellingly, 17% said their religious preference was "none," while 26% consider themselves to be "born-again Christians."[7] And nearly half (48%) of all the students surveyed said that it was essential or very important that college encourage their personal expression of spirituality. An important caveat is offered in a recent opinion piece by Stephen Prothero, a professor of religious studies, who notes that contemporary college students may value spirituality but, in his view, they are not actually knowledgeable about religion.[8]

The HERI team has also surveyed college professors about their attitudes toward spirituality, both personally and professionally. The results are fascinating to compare to those above for students. More than forty thousand professors at 421 colleges completed surveys. Like their students, 81% considered themselves to some or a great extent to be spiritual persons, and 70% have as a goal developing a meaningful philosophy of life. Faculty members are religious as well as spiritual: 64% consider themselves religious persons, and 61% pray. Only about one-third of faculty members, 37%, do not consider themselves at all religious.

The demographics of these results are significant. On all issues, women tend to score higher on measures of self-identified spirituality (generally in the range of 10% higher) than men. African Americans score higher than whites, who, in turn, see themselves as more spiritual than Asians. Not surprisingly, faculty members at religious colleges see themselves as more spiritual than those at nonsectarian colleges or public institutions.

Like students, faculty members who describe themselves as religious also describe themselves as spiritual, but some 13% of those who say they are spiritual also say they are not at all religious. A high correlation exists between faculty members who identify themselves as spiritual and those who focus on the personal development of students. This group also expresses a more positive attitude about their jobs and about their lives than their nonspiritual colleagues.

On a similar survey, undertaken by Neil Gross of Harvard University and Solon Simmons of George Mason University and sponsored by the Social Science Research Council, findings consistent with the HERI study prevail. More than half the faculty members at nonreligious institutions report that they believe in God, either without any doubt or despite some doubts (52%). The highest number of nonbelievers (still only about a third) work at elite doctoral institutions, the fewest at community colleges (15%). In this survey, 19% of all the professorate, and 17% of faculty members at secular institutions describe themselves as born-again Christians.[9]

The HERI survey also asked professors about the role of religion and spirituality in their work as faculty members. When asked if colleges should be engaged in helping with the spiritual development of students, only 30% agreed. Large differences exist on this issue by discipline: 41% in health sciences and 40% in humanities agreed, scaling down to 24% in physical sciences and only 22% in biological sciences. When categorized by type of institution, more than 60% agreed with this goal in Roman Catholic and "other religious" colleges, whereas only 18% in public universities and 23% in public colleges shared this view. Overall, a little more than half of the faculty members surveyed (57%) disagreed with the statement that the spiritual dimensions of faculty members' lives has no place in the academy.

Another ongoing study by Barbara E. Walvoord of the University of Notre Dame reveals similar results in the context of introductory religious study courses.[10] According to her research, 73% of students at religious colleges and 54% of their peers at secular colleges say that one of their goals in religious studies courses in college is to develop moral and ethical values; and 70% of students at religious institutions and 51% at secular schools want to develop their own religious beliefs in those courses. However, only 25% of faculty at secular colleges agrees with the first goal, and only 8% with the second. (Only 29% of faculty at religious institutions wants to strengthen students' commitment to a particular set of beliefs, although 63% of the students has that goal.) And a University of Pennsylvania study demonstrated that 86% of contemporary American twelve- to eighteen-year-olds believes religion (not "spirituality" but "religion") is important in life.[11]

There are, of course, some other desires and needs of college-age young women and men that religious colleges (and religious subgroups within secular colleges) are meeting. Bramadat notes what he calls the "psycho-spiritual needs" of college students.[12] These include the quests for a supportive community, for mystery, for unconditional divine love, and for answers to spiritual questions.

From this wealth of statistical data, the following conclusions emerge clearly: the overwhelming majority of today's undergraduate students see themselves as spiritual and religious individuals, and most of them seek to develop their spiritual selves in college. Similarly, the majority of college professors self-define as religious and spiritual, but significantly fewer of them, especially outside the realm of religious colleges, believe that spiritual development and religious growth have a place in their work. It would seem that most contemporary college students want from their collegiate years a kind of experience that most of their professors, particularly at secular colleges and universities, do not want to offer. The demand for spiritual development in college may exceed the supply. It should come as no shock that religious colleges, which are significantly more responsive to this goal of college students, are attractive to them, and are attracting them.

The Success of Religious Colleges

This brings us to the second reason I want to engage in this study—the success of many religious colleges in today's higher-education marketplace. I choose my words thoughtfully: "marketplace" is, alas, an appropriate description of the contemporary competition for student recruits, for philanthropic or public support, and for recognition among colleges and universities.

Certainly not all religious colleges are thriving in the student recruitment field, and not all secular ones are struggling. Many elite nonreligious institutions, public and private, still receive multiple applications from qualified prospective students for each available space in the first-year class. And some religious institutions face worrisome challenges in student recruitment. But the overall picture is one in which the religious

institutions, especially the evangelical Christian ones, are achieving a record of overwhelming success in the competition to recruit students, including students of exceptionally high promise. Consider, as a microcos-
mic example, these facts from the state of Minnesota, which are familiar
to me from my time serving as the chancellor of a nonreligious, public
liberal arts college there. During the period of 2001–5, the Minnesota Office of Higher Education reported that the average Minnesota private four-
year college increased in student enrollment by 7.2%. This figure *included*
the state's private religious schools. But the figures for just the latter institutions are staggering. Minnesota's four evangelical-oriented colleges
showed these increases: Bethany Lutheran College, 35%; Bethel University, 29.1%; Crown College, 48.7%; and Northwestern College, 28.7%.

The smallest of these colleges is Bethany Lutheran with just 582 students, while the largest, Bethel, has 3,860 enrolled. Administrators and
students at the four Minnesota evangelical colleges attribute this extraor-
dinary success to precisely the yearning for spiritual attentiveness recorded nationally by Astin. For example, the president of Bethel commented to
the *Minneapolis Star-Tribune,* "Every college and university has an impact
on values, but you get a more coherent package at a school like Bethel.
People know where you're coming from. We have commitment from
our core faith." A student at the same institution reports her frustration
with classes she took at a community college where "anything spiritual
was nonexistent," and she affirms that "spirituality is at the core of how
I act."[13]

Mainstream Protestant private colleges in Minnesota are also experiencing a surge of interest in religion and religious issues. Macalester
College in St. Paul, for example, which is affiliated with the Presbyterian
Church but is usually identified as a secularized institution, finds that it
is "experiencing a rising number of religious studies majors and all kinds
of different religious group activities."[14]

Minnesota's enrollment statistics, while slightly more dramatic than
average, are wholly in keeping with the national trends. The U.S. Department of Education, as summarized by the Council for Christian Colleges
and Universities (CCCU), noted these trends in increasing enrollment
during the reporting period 1990–98: all U.S. institutions, 5.3%; public
institutions, 3.0%; private institutions, 13.4%; religious-affiliated institutions, 15.6%; and CCCU institutions, 36.9%. The CCCU reported that
from 1990 to 2000 its member campuses experienced a 47.36% growth

increase.[15] These trends transcend the borders of the United States. *Inside Higher Ed* reports, "As in the United States, Christian higher education is booming in Canada, with the number of evangelical universities growing from 3 to 12 since 1972."[16]

Religious colleges, of course, vary not just in the numbers of students recruited but in their quality, as measured by the standard qualitative indices of entering members of the first year class. Like nonreligious colleges and universities, there are both "elite" and "less selective" institutions. Those at the top have a student profile of which any college or university would be proud. Wheaton College, for example, matriculated 572 students in the freshman class of fall 2006. The average high school GPA of that class was 3.73 and 57% graduated in the top 10% of their class. Using the conventional formula, the middle 50% of the class scored between 1240 and 1420 on the critical reasoning test of the SAT and between 27 and 31 on the ACT. Perhaps most impressively, National Merit Scholarship Finalists composed 36% of the class.[17] At Calvin College, the ACT of the middle 50% of the class of 2006 was 23–28, and the SAT combined score of that group was 1100–1310. Baylor University had 2,783 students in the entering class of fall 2006, with a mid-50%-SAT range of 1110–1310 (mean, 1213) and 23–28 (mean, 25) on the ACT.[18] And at the University of Notre Dame, 69% of the students who entered that same fall were in the top 5% of their high school class, with 86% in the top 10%. The range of SAT scores for the mid 50% of entering students at Notre Dame was 1340–1470 and the ACT range was 31–33.[19] Students with such academic qualifications would be eagerly sought after by the great majority of American colleges and universities.

One of the many ways in which students are of central importance to all colleges and universities is fiscal: their tuitions generate a substantial portion of annual operating funds at many private institutions. Public funding, state support (at public colleges and universities), corporate and foundation giving, and private philanthropy are the other major sources of collegiate funding. Tracking philanthropic success is more difficult at religious institutions than at nonreligious ones. But the evidence at individual institutions and some information about general trends suggest that here, too, religious colleges, especially conservative Christian institutions, are doing very well.

Thus, the National Committee for Responsive Philanthropy has studied giving and receiving patterns of "evangelical, conservative" organizations, including colleges and universities. It does so from an avowedly liberal perspective, one that is overt about the committee's mission to "help equalize the playing field that decades of economic inequality and pervasive discrimination had created." Its study documents the "sizable amount of grant dollars flowing from foundations to religious organizations advocating extreme socially conservative causes and policies."[20] While the primary interest and concern of the committee is political conservativism, it expresses clear discomfort about the level of support for evangelical Christian causes, including educational endeavors, and for evangelical leaders and organizations that support Christian colleges.

A similar general conclusion is reached in *Who Really Cares: The Surprising Truth about Compassionate Conservatism* by Arthur Brooks.[21] Brooks finds that religious conservatives are considerably more philanthropic than nonreligious liberals. He concludes that, in the year 2000, religious American adults gave on average $2,210, whereas secular donors averaged only $642. Religious donors even gave more to nonreligious causes than secular philanthropists. Religious liberals, Brooks affirms, gave at higher levels than nonreligious liberals, and religious conservatives gave at higher levels than nonreligious conservatives.

Philanthropy, then, is flourishing among conservative and religious American individuals and groups, and this is reflected in the fund-raising success of some religious colleges and universities.

A cautionary aside: certainly it is not the case that every religious college in contemporary America is fiscally flourishing. While studying Christian colleges for *Seeing the Light,* I had the misfortune to be present at one such school just as it failed. Sheldon Jackson College in Sitka, Alaska, was a Presbyterian institution founded in 1878 by its namesake, a missionary who became Alaska's first superintendent of education. Its students included a substantial number of Native Alaskans. Never wealthy, the financial fate of Sheldon Jackson took a catastrophic turn around the turn of the twenty-first century. The college fell into difficulties with the U.S. Department of Education and with its regional accreditor, the Northwest Association of Schools and Colleges, largely because of serious problems with internal handling of financial aid monies and inappropriately altering the allocation of funds from a FIPSE grant. In June 2007 some $6 million in debt, Sheldon Jackson announced its immediate closing, terminated all but two of its one hundred employees, and sought to dispose of its physical campus. A virtuous mission, a noble vision, and a valuable history cannot outweigh inadequate fiscal management, even at the most religious of institutions. Sheldon Jackson College is sad proof that doing good and doing well are very different things.[22]

Finally, the religious sector of American higher education has done well within the barometer of some significant segments of public opinion within American culture at large. Here, information is plentiful, although it needs to be understood contextually: Baylor is going to have a different reputation among Texas Baptists than with New England Unitarians. Many of the smaller religious colleges are known only within their denomination or their region. Certainly the same skepticism should reflect upon considerations of the reputations of nonreligious institutions: Texas A&M is going to have a higher standing relative to Bowdoin in the Southwest than in the Northeast. There are, of course, many collegiate ranking systems and publications available for public consumption. These are taken with different levels of seriousness within academe itself. Commonly, institutions that do well on a college ranking tend to assume that ranking system is valid and merits widespread dissemination. Those which fare poorly will suggest that the rating in question is dubious and of little significance. The nationally published and widely read *U.S. News* annual ratings of colleges and universities prompts such a response because they are based on a Byzantine set of scales, some of which have seemed to many rather arbitrary.[23] Perhaps most controversial is the heavily weighted scale based on reputational status. Because what we seek to examine here are precisely those widespread reputational issues, however, the *U.S. News* rankings are highly instructive in this particular context.

Many religious institutions rank in the upper tiers of the *U.S. News* annual reports. In the 2006 report, for example, in their respective categories:[24]

- The University of Notre Dame ranks number 20, just above the University of California at Berkeley and Carnegie Mellon University, just below Emory.
- Furman University follows Dickinson and is ahead of Franklin and Marshall.
- Wheaton College (Illinois) is ranked at number 61, ahead of Earlham, Willamette, Agnes Scott, and the College of Wooster.
- Westmont College (California) is ranked above Hampden-Sidney, Susquehanna, Washington and Jefferson, Augustana, and Hollins.

- Valparaiso is number 3 among "Master's Degree Granting Universities—Midwest."

In sum, the assumption I cited earlier that all religious institutions, including the strongly conservative evangelical Christian colleges, are "two-bit Bible colleges" is an irrational one, easily refuted by even the quickest survey of the quantitative evidence.

The Reputation and Image of Religious Institutions

Finally, that very irrationality among my academic colleagues, peers, and friends suggested to me that this study would be a worthwhile one. Surely, if there is a core value to be found in the world of scholarship, of academia, it is that conclusions should be based on demonstrable facts, if those facts are available and especially if they are unambiguous. Many of the harshest critics of religious colleges cite exactly this point as a linchpin of their criticism: they contend, not without some justification, that some of those colleges, in some areas, accept certain doctrines and understandings on the basis of faith, not evidence. Indeed, they argue, strong and compelling rational evidence is ignored, in order to reach institutional conclusions in conformity with religious doctrine. Certainly this is a theme in discussions of evolution, creationism, and intelligent design—and, within the bounds of reasoned academic discourse, it should be.[25] Yet those same critics themselves sometimes ignore some compelling evidence that argues for understanding religious colleges and universities complexly, thoughtfully, and nondismissively. It is ironic that one area in which presumed rational and objective academics and academic culture drifts rapidly into irrational and subjective opinion is within the realm of higher education itself.

Seeing the Light does not aim to offer a whitewashed, adulatory view of religious higher education in contemporary America, I see, and endeavor to demonstrate convincingly and explicitly, some weaknesses in this sector of our collegiate community, some disconcerting blind spots, some unsettling beliefs and practices. But I also see remarkable strengths, staggering diversity, and powerful attractions among those institutions, and it is my aim to present them accurately and with sincere appreciation.

Seeing the Light describes contemporary faith-based colleges and universities from the perspectives of the students, faculty, and administrators who study, teach, and work there. To me, this approach is appropriate, even necessary. There are, however, other ways of looking at these religious institutions. For example, some who have studied, written, and spoken about such institutions approach their investigation from the standpoint of theological measures rather than instructional effectiveness. From such a perspective, sometimes, quite different conclusions from mine are drawn. Where I am asking if these colleges meet the educational and spiritual needs of the students, sectarian purists might ask if the instructional and co-curricular programs of the college are uniformly designed to advance the tenets of a specific religious outlook. Consequently, where I am inclined to respond with admiration to a certain willingness to entertain diverse perspectives and opinions at faith-based schools, others may see such diversity as threatening or contrary to the religious missions that created and support these institutions. Similarly, I do not pay very much attention (although I do not ignore) some of the social issues which have become linked to some segments of the evangelical community in recent years: gay marriage, abortion, stem cell research, and the like. Examining religious colleges primarily as religious, not educational, places seems to me a legitimate enterprise. Just as one could study churches as social organizations, theological transmitters, teaching organizations, or even architectural statements, one can look at universities in a variety of ways. I choose to look at religious schools as schools. While I do not ignore or minimize the religious aspects of these places, I seek to study them, unambiguously and unapologetically, as first and foremost institutions created for and devoted to intellectual exploration and growth, places for learning.

Those of us who are not in the religious sector of contemporary higher education, who spend much time and energy seeking to recruit students, raise fiscal support, and improve the way in which we are perceived by the many publics we seek to serve have much to learn from our religious institutional peers. It is my strong wish that *Seeing the Light* will be a significant step in that learning.

Why Should *I* Study Religious Colleges?

There are good and even compelling reasons why religious colleges and universities merit study. But why should I do so? What qualifies this particular academic, with a career mostly in the public sector and an expertise in Renaissance literary studies, to write about such places?

I am not a Christian, and have never worked in an institution that would fit the definition that follows of a Christian college. To some, those two facts might immediately disqualify me from authorship of such a study. I would argue, however, exactly the opposite. An objective, fair, balanced, and accurate description of schools that are proud of their Christian zeal needs to be written by someone who is not a member of that faith and not a zealot. At the same time, it should not be written by an author who feels herself or himself in an oppositional relationship with these colleges. A sympathetic outsider, someone who is genuinely interested in such places, who is without strong negative biases toward such institutions, but could never be "of them" is required: I fit that description. A person of my background (Jewish faith, political liberal, theologically conflicted) would be disqualified, formally and officially, from employment at most of the more conservative evangelical institutions discussed on the pages that follow. At the same time, I have been welcomed cordially and openly and treated with thoughtful, humane colleagueship as an inquisitive visitor at exactly those same places. I have enjoyed visiting them and listening to those who live, work, and study there, even as I know that my status could never be other than "guest."

Additionally, I studied several religious colleges for an earlier book on small colleges and developed some sense of their character and the range of possibilities in them. That study, *Old Main: Small Colleges in Twenty-First Century America*, paid particular attention to twelve institutions. Two were Christian colleges, Westmont College and George Fox. One, the College of New Rochelle, was a Roman Catholic woman's institution. Of the remainder, about half retained a connection to their religious tradition, at a level that could be described as faith related but were no longer essentially religious institutions (e.g., Centenary College), and the rest were either overtly created as or had evolved into wholly secular institutions (e.g., University of Wisconsin at Superior, Grinnell College).

Further, as noted in my introductory sentences, in the role of chancellor I led my public campus of a major land-grant university (University of Minnesota, Morris) into an athletic conference dominated by Christian Colleges (Northwestern College of Minnesota, Crown College, Martin Luther College) and consequently have spent considerable time on the campuses of those institutions, interacting with their presidents, coaches, athletic directors, and, to a lesser extent, students and faculty.

Finally, I have worked at several institutions that have strong sectarian roots, although they have evolved in different directions: I taught for a decade at a historically Methodist college (Cornell, in Iowa) and served for a decade as the chief academic officer at a Quaker college (Guilford, in North Carolina). I began my teaching career at a Roman Catholic men's college (St. Mary's of California).

In short, I would describe myself as a moderate and a friend of religious higher education, but writing from a position external to that movement. I believe that religious colleges occupy a legitimate and valuable place within the wide and diverse spectrum of today's American higher education community. But at the same time, I recognize that those colleges and universities are, like all sublunar works of humankind, imperfect and limited.

How Does One Write about Religious Colleges?

This book is about contemporary educational institutions, not a theological dictionary or encyclopedia. However, by this point it should be obvious that it is time for a note on nomenclature. Words are never "just words," and nowhere is this truer than in the realm of religion and studies of religion.

What is a religious college or university and what is a *Christian* college or university? These terms are used slightly differently by different individuals and institutions, not infrequently depending upon the cultural history and theological perspective brought to the discussion.

This is probably a question no easier to answer than "what is a Christian?" In both cases, it is much easier to know "what isn't": Christians are not, for example, Jews, Muslims, or atheists. Religious colleges are not state universities, private nonsectarian colleges, community colleges, and the like.

A more positive working definition can be created: I use the words *religious colleges* for those institutions which overtly identify as a core, defining element of their mission an affirmation of their theist character. In the United States, these are overwhelmingly, but not unanimously, *Christian colleges,* by which I mean colleges or universities with an evangelical, Protestant Christian perspective. These institutions are not, however, *Bible colleges* (although the line can blur) or *seminaries.* The former focus primarily on teaching and learning scripture: students at Bible colleges will not have the option of majoring in physics or psychology, although there may be programs in religious education or sacred music. Seminaries, of course, have as their primary function the training of clergy. Some religious colleges have seminaries attached, but those two functions are commonly kept as distinct as, say, a College of Arts and Sciences and a College of Engineering at a major research university. Christian colleges likewise do not include mainstream, nonsectarian colleges or universities with a heritage of religious foundation but which are currently not, at their core, still fundamentally linked to their religious past. For such institutions, I use phrases such as *historically religious* or *traditionally Christian*. Cornell College, Warren Wilson, Duke, and Vanderbilt would be illustrations of these schools. *Catholic colleges and universities* are an important element in the tradition of American religious-linked higher learning. It can be argued vigorously, and has been, that all Catholic institutions are religious institutions, in the foregoing sense (having as a core defining element of their mission an affirmation of their sectarian, theist, character), and, conversely, that only some of them are. A new group of theologically conservative and often as well socially and curricularly conservative Catholic institutions have, as we shall see at some length, challenged the depth of religious commitment of the more traditional Catholic institutions such as Notre Dame, Georgetown, Villanova, or St. Mary's College of California. *Secular* schools are those which either were overtly founded without religious links, have evolved beyond the point where there is any discernable tie to a religious heritage whatsoever, or are public institutions. What that "point" *is* exactly is much debated and discussed, and will be revisited often in the pages which follow.

Students who graduate from religious schools can prepare for a variety of careers and further study, not just ministerial or religious vocations. They can choose a variety of majors, not just in religious subject matters. Such schools frequently ask a profession of faith, values, and behavior from students and/or faculty and/or staff. Their curriculum often includes faith-based courses, and their extracurriculum promotes an overtly religious, almost always Christian, set of activities. They do not cultivate religious diversity and commonly require (and universally promote) some sort of regular communal liturgical exercise (e.g., weekly chapel or daily prayer). They are often considerably more directive of student behavior and lifestyle issues than mainstream universities or colleges.

A few other terms need to be defined to make what follows clear. These are not precise or theologically nuanced definitions, but they should suffice for the purposes of our discussions.

Evangelicalism: The segment of the Protestant Christian world identified as evangelicalism includes a strong and central belief in biblical inerrancy; the necessity of a personal, saving, experience of Jesus Christ; and the desirability of actively seeking to bring others to Christianity. Evangelical Christians not infrequently use the term Christian to apply only to evangelicalism—for example, "She's either an Episcopalian or a Catholic, not a Christian."

Calvinism: Calvinists believe that people are predestined for salvation or damnation and that their eternal fate does not rest on the basis of any of their actions on earth.

Dispensationalism: According to dispensationalism, human history is divided into seven dispensations or periods, the last of which, "the kingdom," will soon arrive with the second coming of Christ.

Holiness Movement: Adherents of the holiness movement believe that the carnal nature of man can be cleansed by faith and the power of the Holy Spirit and by the forgiveness of sins through Jesus Christ. This purity of heart is called Christian Perfection. This movement consists of a revivalistic set of sects. Dwight Moody and the Wesleyan Church are examples of the Holiness tradition.

Fundamentalist: In use since the 1920s to describe a movement that began in the late nineteenth century, fundamentalism comes from the 1909 book *The Fundamentals*. Fundamentalists are strongly conservative in matters of religion and believe in biblical inerrancy, virgin birth, atonement through the Crucifixion, the Resurrection, and Second Coming. Fundamentalists also tend to be socially more conservative than other evangelical groups. The term has evolved a considerably different, almost always wholly negative, connotation when applied to non-Christian groups—for example, Islamic fundamentalists.

Pentecostal: The division of Protestant Christians known as Pentecostal is characterized by belief in "Holy Spirit baptism" of adults after they have had a personal experience of Jesus Christ; speaking in tongues; and highly emotional worship. Pentecostal sects include Assemblies of God and the Church of God in Christ.

Charismatic: Members of charismatic Protestant or Catholic groups believe in speaking in tongues, prophesying, and divine healing. Charismatic Christians emphasize the importance of the Holy Spirit.

A final defining note: the subject of this book is religious institutions, not religion in institutions. Although that subject is a fascinating one and overlaps this investigation, I do not plan to focus in a significant way on the religious lives of students at public or secular institutions (as, e.g., in the work of Alexander Astin and the HERI on college student spirituality).

2 | Contexts Historical and Denominational

Colleges are complex creatures. Individual institutions and the contexts of which they are a part are idiosyncratic, often ambiguous, nuanced. As we examine contemporary Christian colleges, it is worthwhile to recall the development over time of the links between religion and higher education in America. Francis Oakley, a past president of Williams College and a thoughtful student of our nation's postsecondary education, has remarked that, to understand the ethos of contemporary institutions, it is necessary to grasp "the dense particularities of their specific individual histories."[1] And John R. Thelin reminds us that "colleges and universities are historical institutions. . . . heritage is the lifeblood of our campuses."[2] It is as well a valuable contextualizing study to examine the range of today's colleges and universities with religious missions tied to traditions outside evangelical Protestantism.

Historical Contexts

The history of the educational development of the United States, including the development of collegiate-level learning, has been written often and well. Here, I scan the story of the development of higher learning in America, from its origins in the colonial period to the present day, looking through the lens of institutional religiosity.[3] This view provides not only a revealing perspective on our nation's colleges and universities but a necessary springboard into a discussion of the religious institutions that are the focus of *Seeing the Light*.

Colonial Colleges, 1636–1776

Before the Revolutionary War, nine collegiate institutions were founded in America. Although their founding dates span a period of more than a century and a quarter (1636–1769), these institutions have much in common. Their stories are also illuminating in the context of religious institutions in contemporary American higher education. As many students of higher education have pointed out, "To be a college in America before the Civil War was to be a Christian college."[4] Listed here with each institution are its founding date and initial religious affiliation:[5]

Harvard	1636	Puritan
William and Mary	1693	Episcopal (Anglican)
Yale	1701	Congregational
Princeton	1746	Presbyterian
Columbia	1754	Episcopal
University of Pennsylvania	1755	Episcopal
Brown	1765	Baptist
Rutgers	1766	Dutch Reformed
Dartmouth	1769	Protestant general/Congregational

Even among the Puritans, the impulse to found colleges was not always wholly pure. Puritans, urban and mercantile, were not fond of the Anglican agrarian gentry. Moreover, American dissenters were excluded entirely from the universities of England and, thus, of necessity had to create their own.

At the conclusion of the colonial period, the combined student population of these institutions was just under one thousand souls, and there were about 135 faculty altogether at the nine universities—that is to say, they were, together, about the size of one single small contemporary college. Today none of the colonial colleges, all of which began under some sort of sectarian sponsorship, proclaim a current religious affiliation. All of them offer students diverse opportunities for religious activities, but in no case are those part of the institutions' formal programs.

Colonial college curricula were universal and mandated: everyone studied the same subjects, at the same point in their college career (rather like Thomas Aquinas College today, which we shall examine in some depth later). Studies "centered on classical texts and the foundations of Christian doctrine."[6] Electives did not enter the American college curriculum until after the Civil War. Thus, the following description of the early Harvard curriculum can represent, with only slight variants, that of all the pre-Revolutionary institutions: "Aristotelian logic and physics, arithmetic, geometry, astronomy, grammar, rhetoric, dialectic, etymology, syntax and prosodia were taught for the purpose of disciplining the mind. Upperclassmen studied Greek and Hebrew grammar and there were occasional lectures in history and natural science. Students were expected to declaim once a month and great stress was placed on study of the Bible.

For a degree the student had to present evidence of his ability to read the Scriptures in Latin."[7]

The colonial colleges were of a mixed sectarian and public nature. In this characteristic, they embodied the perspective of their era, for "the idea that education and religion were inseparable was deeply ingrained in Calvinism."[8] They were chartered as public institutions and educated laypersons for secular vocations such as medicine and the law. Because of their religious ties, they also trained clergymen. As Arthur M. Cohen argues in *The Shaping of American Higher Education,* one of the three defining characteristics of the American colonies was their "religious spirit. . . . Protestantism and Anglicanism newly separated from Catholicism and continually reforming, yielding variations in patterns of observance from deism . . . to fervent sects devoted to emotional worship."[9] In a sense, these institutions were the seeds of several strands of American higher learning which, over our postcolonial history, separated and became distinct.

Harvard University famously began with an appropriation of four hundred pounds from the Massachusetts General Court in 1636. It reflected a strong Puritan belief in learning, as well as a dread "to leave an illiterate Ministry to the Churches, when our present Ministers shall lie in the Dust."[10] (That dread may have been somewhat overenthusiastically stated for public relations purposes, according to several historians of colonial American higher education.)[11] Harvard's Byzantine governing structure reveals its mixed secular and religious character. The college was to be governed by two boards, the Corporation and the Overseers. The Corporation consisted of five "fellows," the treasurer, and the president of the college. The Overseers consisted of ministers from Cambridge and surrounding towns. Student behavior codes were strict, and attendance not just at classes but at worship was required and, apparently, enforced.[12] About half of Harvard's graduates during the 1600s actually entered the ministry, the other half going into commercial or professional careers. Harvard set the model for its colonial peers in its mix of puritan and public oversight and mission. As Richard Hofstadter and Wilson Smith point out, it "did not distinguish sharply between secular and theological learning."[13] Indeed, the sharp distinction between secular and sectarian governance of higher education in American can be dated to the *Dartmouth College Case* of 1816 discussed below.

Several of the southern states sought to create collegiate institutions before the Revolution: Maryland attempted to found a Catholic college (Roman Catholics were excluded from most of the Protestant colonial colleges), South Carolina an Episcopal institution, and there were several efforts within North Carolina, Georgia, and the city of Charleston. But Virginia, after a few false starts, became home to the southernmost colonial college with the founding of William and Mary at Williamsburg in 1693. William and Mary was founded by the Reverend James Blair, who represented the Episcopal Commissary of Virginia. Like Harvard, William and Mary had as one core purpose the training of the clergy: Reverend Blair offered the rationale "that the Church of Virginia [Episcopal] may be furnished with a seminary of ministers of the Gospel."[14] But the college can also point to distinguished secular students such as Thomas Jefferson, John Marshall, and James Monroe. Students had to demonstrate competence in Latin and Greek to be admitted, the faculty had to affirm orthodox piety, and student behavior was strictly regulated. Also like Harvard, William and Mary was governed by a mixture of church and public authorities, the "Faculty," which consisted of the college president and the professors and the "Visitors," a board of fourteen laymen and four clerics chosen by the Virginia legislature. The original curriculum at the college was divided into grammar, philosophy, and sacred theology. By the time of the Revolution, students at William and Mary could study science, mathematics, and law, as well as religion and philosophy.

In 1701 the Connecticut General Assembly created the "Collegiate School of Connecticut" at Saybrook, which in 1716 moved to New Haven and became Yale College. An early crisis at Yale occurred when its Congregationalist chief executive shocked the college with his conversion to Episcopalianism. Yale broke the governance pattern of its two predecessor institutions by establishing a single board of control, most of whose members were clergymen, which, with the chief executive, had legal oversight of the college. Yale maintained a relatively strict orthodoxy until the end of the administration of the Reverend Thomas Clap in 1766, although students were not always as docile and compliant as the administration might have wished. Sheldon S. Cohen cites a description of student hijinx, written by a freshman in 1756: "Many of the Students of the College gathered together in the evening, and rung the Bell, and fired Crackers, Ran the Yard, and Hollowed & Screamed in a terrible manner and several of this Riot was catch'd by the Tutors . . . and many others were boxed by the President."[15] One wonders when the last student was boxed by an American college president. Beginning under President Naphtali Daggett, a decade before the Revolution Yale became more secular in both curriculum and social expectations. Science and mathematics were introduced and strengthened, and, as at Harvard, an increasing number of graduates chose secular careers.

A century and a decade after the founding of Harvard, a group of New Light Presbyterian ministers opened the College of New Jersey in Elizabethtown in 1746. Seeking to raise funds for the new college in Britain in 1753, two evangelists, Samuel Davies and Gilbert Tennent, wrote that a core purpose of the colleges was to inculcate "reverence of the Deity" and that its mission was "diffusing the light of Christianity among the ignorant and uncivilized nations of the earth."[16] The school relocated to Princeton in 1756. About half of its pre-Revolutionary graduates entered the clergy. Like Yale, Princeton was from the start governed by a single board of external trustees, most of whom were Presbyterian ministers, although some trustees came from other Protestant churches. After the middle of the eighteenth century, the curriculum at Princeton, too, began to include more secular subjects, although student life regulations remained strict.

In 1754 King's College, later Columbia, opened at Trinity Church in New York City. Initially, its president and only faculty member was Reverend Samuel Johnson (no relation to the lexicographer). It set a different pattern of religious affiliation from its predecessor American colleges. Beginning in the eighteenth century, New York City was home to a variety of Christian sects. At its establishment, it was determined that the institution's president should always be an Episcopalian. However, from the start, Columbia was relatively nonsectarian, proclaiming that "as to religion, there is no intent to impose on the scholars the peculiar tenants of any particular sect of Christians."[17] Unlike its more theologically conceived predecessors, Columbia from the start aspired to teach mathematics, geography, commerce, government, natural sciences, and a range of fields we might see as predecessors of engineering (measuring, surveying, navigation).

Although today Quaker institutions are a distinguished aspect of undergraduate American higher learning, colonial-era Friends were harshly critical of British universities and not eager to establish colleges in the colonies. However, so curious and learned a citizen as Benjamin Franklin became a zealous promoter of education in Quaker Philadelphia and its environs. Franklin was a leader in encouraging the secondary Philadelphia Academy to expand into college-level studies, and in 1755 Franklin and his colleagues created the "College of Philadelphia," today's University of Pennsylvania. Shortly after its founding the College of Philadelphia came under the control of the Episcopalians. This did little to endear it to local Quakers, and the college's enrollment remained quite small throughout the remainder of the colonial period.

Another New England college, the College of Rhode Island, was incorporated in 1764, opened in 1765, and settled in 1770 in Providence and became Brown College. As was universal in this era, its first president was a member of the clergy, Reverend James Manning. Brown describes itself as having been the "Baptist answer to Congregationalist Yale and Harvard, Presbyterian Princeton and Episcopalian Penn and Columbia." The same modern source also notes that "Brown has long since shed its Baptist affiliation."[18] Brown was unusual in its explicit disavowal of sectarian particularity. In the tradition of the founder of Rhode Island, Roger Williams, the college from its inception sought a multidenominational population. Its charter specifies that all Protestants were eligible for faculty positions and that students did not have to submit to any religious test for admission. Similarly, Brown's governing board was, by charter, representative of multiple denominations and included lay representation.

New Jersey's second colonial college, which became today's Rutgers University, was chartered in 1766, just a decade before the end of the colonial period. In the middle of the eighteenth century, the Dutch Reformed Church had grown increasingly concerned about the need to continue to recruit and train its clergy. The college they created was originally called Queen's and was governed by a multidenominational board of trustees, which also included nonclerical representation. But the college was kept firmly in the Dutch Reformed camp by the requirement that its president be a member of that denomination.

The last of the colleges of our colonial era, Dartmouth, grew from a school established for American Indians in Connecticut. Congregationalist minister Eleazar Wheelock had opened the Moor's Charity School in Lebanon. In 1769 the school moved to Hanover, New Hampshire, became a collegiate institution, and began to admit non-Indian students. Although Dartmouth retained its charge to educate Native Americans as part of its mission, it never actually had a very high proportion or number of Indian students. Its collegiate charter established the school as Congregational but included liberal nondenominational provisions.

With its one thousand students and 135 faculty members at the end of the colonial period, American higher education was certainly not a major New World force before the Revolutionary War. But it had already established a pattern in which religious concerns and secular ones were mixed. Early American colleges included some with strict denominational ties, and others that choose to serve a variety of Protestant Christian sects. "Each of the colleges had a church connection . . . [but] church influence was never absolute, and a tradition of lay governance was established early on."[19] Over the years from 1636 to 1776, secular purposes, populations, and curricula gained in relation to religious missions, but at the end of the period it still would not have been possible to imagine an American collegiate institution without a significant religious, Christian character.

From the Revolutionary War to the Civil War, 1776–1865

The first 130 years of American collegiate history produced nine colleges. In less than a century after the War of Independence, literally hundreds more appeared in the young land—and hundreds failed as well. "Higher education would become America's 'cottage industry.'"[20] As was the case in the colonial era, most of the institutions created during this period had both religious and secular missions, although it was during this era that the clear division between these influences took shape. About 175 colleges that came into existence during this ninety-year period continue to exist today; one authority documents 412 that failed.[21] "The colleges tended to be exceedingly weak—underfunded, too small to support a broad curriculum, too poor to pay their staff more than a subsistence wage, and in many cases, too marginal even to survive."[22] Of course, many colleges founded between the Revolutionary War and Civil War have, in fact, not just survived but evolved into strong and distinguished institutions: these begin with places such as Washington College and Washington and Lee (both 1782) and Dickinson (1783), and conclude, just before the Civil War, with Vassar and Seton Hall (1861). Almost half (103) of the 212 institutions identified by David Breneman in *Liberal Arts Colleges* as "true" institutions of liberal learning began before 1865.[23]

As we have seen, the colonial colleges all have followed the same pattern of religious evolution: all initially served religious and secular purposes, and all have evolved into religiously unaffiliated institutions today. But the 175 colleges that were founded in the 1776–1865 era, which are still alive today, have far more diverse religious histories and are today far more religiously varied. This group of institutions includes:

- Smaller liberal arts colleges that initially had a strong religious affiliation but which today would be considered thoroughly nonsectarian, including institutions such as Grinnell College (initially Congregational) and Antioch College (Christian Church)
- Small, church affiliated colleges that evolved into largely nonsectarian universities, such as Duke (Methodist) and Alfred University (Baptist)
- Colleges that today retain a strong religious identity and are members of the Council for Christian Colleges and Universities (CCCU), such as Wheaton and Carson Newman
- America's first Roman Catholic institutions, beginning with Georgetown and Mount St. Mary's
- Wholly nonreligious, state-sponsored universities, created well before the passage of the Morrill Act in 1862, the first being either Georgia (chartered in 1785, first degrees in 1804) or North Carolina (chartered in 1789, first degrees granted in 1798), followed by Vermont, Tennessee, and others[24]
- Pre–Civil War colleges that were, or became, affiliated with municipalities, including the College of Charleston, the University of Louisville, and City College of New York

The majority of these institutions remained Protestant. Of those 175 colleges that survive, 49 began as Presbyterian schools, 34 as Methodist (mostly founded toward the latter end of this time, when the Methodist Church changed dramatically from its prior distrust of higher learning), 25 Baptist, 21 Congregational, and 11 Episcopal. Other denominations founding colleges included Lutherans, Christian (Disciples), the German Reformed, Quakers, Universalists, the Dutch Reformed, Unitarians, and other, smaller, denominations. There were 14 Roman Catholic institutions by the end of this period, and 21 state-sponsored institutions existed before the Civil War.[25]

One of the strongest impulses leading to the creation of colleges in the period between the Revolution and the Civil War was the emphasis on evangelism of the "Second Great Awakening" (roughly from 1800 to 1830), which focused on revival meetings and led to missionary societies designed to evangelize the frontier West. New denominations (e.g., the Christian Church or Disciples of Christ and the Seventh-day Adventists) sprang up, and some of the older ones, especially the Baptists and

Methodists, grew explosively. Unlike the Calvinists of the colonial period, who emphasized humankind's "utter incapacity to overcome this [sinful] nature without the direct action of the grace of God," many mid-nineteenth-century evangelists focused on human deeds and the importance of virtuous actions.[26] Much of the energy and zeal of America's "Second Great Awakening" took place on the developing frontier. As the nation settled its western lands, preachers saw the newly opening territories as opportunities to spread the influence of their denominations in relatively open, fresh regions and populations, and so there was a phenomenal wave of college foundation on the frontier. Although some institutions were established at this time in the relatively settled Northern Atlantic seaboard (e.g., Vassar and Seton Hall), it was during this era that colleges were created in the Carolinas, Alabama, Illinois, Louisiana, Missouri, Wisconsin, Iowa, Minnesota, Kansas, Texas, and California. "The American college was typically a frontier institution," according to Tewksbury, who quotes Absalom Peters's "Discourse before the Society for the Promotion of Collegiate and Theological Education in the West" of 1851: "Our country is to be a land of colleges."[27]

These early Protestant frontier colleges were in a state of constant seething change. As new ones were created, and old ones foundered, many went through a bewildering evolution. Thus, for example, today's Southwestern University in Texas is the result of the coming together of four "root" colleges: Rutersville College (1840); Wesleyan College (1844), which combined with San Augustine University in 1847 as the (private) University of Eastern Texas; McKenzie Institute (1839); and Chappell [sic] Hill Male and Female College, which in 1854 was taken over by the Methodists and renamed Soule University. Although more turbulent than average, this is not an eccentric collegiate history. Often, the exigencies of time and place caused religious colleges to drift back and forth in their sectarian enthusiasm: when times were hard, many decided it was more important to find students able to pay tuition than to enforce strict religious tests.[28]

In addition to bringing colleges to new regions, and with new religious affiliations, the "Second Great Awakening" and the continued development of the new nation also brought higher learning to new constituents. The earliest experiments in coeducation were taking place during the first half of the nineteenth century. In 1837 Oberlin College, founded by the Congregationalists in 1834, admitted four women into the regular collegiate course, and in 1841 three of them became the first females in the

United States to receive the baccalaureate degree. The first of the prestigious "seven sisters" was Vassar College, originally affiliated with the Baptists, founded in 1865 by Matthew Vassar.

Middlebury College, founded in 1800 by the Congregationalists, probably granted the first traditional baccalaureate degree to an African American, Alexander Lucius Twilight, in 1823. Twilight went on to become a teacher in Vermont and a Presbyterian preacher. He was later elected to the state legislature, and there is today a building named for him at the University of Vermont.[29] In 1825 two more African Americans were awarded AB degrees: John Brown Russwurm from Bowdoin and Edward Jones from Amherst. By 1835 Oberlin College, again a leader, described itself as seeking students "irrespective of color." The nation's first "historically black institutions" were also created during this period. They were Cheney College, Lincoln University, Wilberforce College, and Howard University.

One event of profound significance in the history of American religious colleges and universities occurred in 1816, when the legislature of the state of New Hampshire attempted to assert its control over Dartmouth College. The case was initiated by a conflict between the son of Dartmouth's founder, President John Wheelock, and the college's trustees.[30] The state's position was that New Hampshire had chartered a private corporation to oversee the college for the good of the public. The public, in the shape of the state, should therefore have ultimate governance of the institution. The college's case, argued by Daniel Webster, affirmed that once a private entity had been chartered, that charter was inviolable.[31] Thus, once any group, including any church, has legitimately and legally been chartered to operate a college, that group was legally self-governing and autonomous, in perpetuity. In 1819 the Supreme Court sided with the college, moved perhaps by Webster's famous peroration: "It is, Sir, as I have said a small college. And yet there are those who love it." Contemporary historians of higher education take a more nuanced view of the Dartmouth College case than the conventional traditional interpretation. They note, for example, that a state that grants a charter can always revoke it, albeit with some difficulty, if circumstances require. Moreover, because no actual transcript of the case survives, it has perhaps been subject to some mythologizing, as a kind of black-and-white contest between public and private control.[32] Given such salutary skepticism, though, it is still evident that this legal decision had a profound and lasting effect upon the relationship between the state and private colleges and universities, including, importantly, today's private faith-based schools.

In effect, the Dartmouth College case marks the point at which the colonial system of higher education as a kind of joint enterprise of the church and state bifurcates. Henceforth, there were public colleges and universities, and private ones, including religious ones. But they were not to be the same institutions. It is almost impossible to imagine the changed landscape of American higher education, particularly as regards private, religious institutions, had this judicial decision gone the other way.

At the end of the era, a most important step in the growth of public higher education takes place. The Morrill Land Grant Act, finally passed in 1862 (it had been vetoed earlier by President Buchanan), granted to the states land—thirty thousand acres to each state—(thus, "land-grant university") to fund public collegiate instruction.[33] Some of the proceeds of the Morrill Act land were used to create new state universities, and some passed to already existing schools (in some cases, strongly religious institutions), which thus became their states' land-grant universities and were usually significantly strengthened as a result. The latter is the case with North Carolina and Georgia, for example, while the former describes the creation of the Universities of Michigan (1817), Iowa (1847), and Minnesota (1851). The early state universities were considerably more comfortable in affirming a mainstream Christianity as central to their character. Nonetheless, the Morrill Act is of crucial importance in the development of America's religious colleges because it set in motion a vast contrary trend. For better or worse (or both), contemporary higher education in our nation today is dominated (at least in numbers) by large, comprehensive public institutions.

In addition to the creation of the flagship, land-grant state universities, the period between the Revolution and the Civil War also saw the beginnings of American "normal schools." By 1875 there were at least seventy normal schools receiving state support. Many of these institutions developed into teachers colleges, then state colleges, and not infrequently today's regional comprehensive state universities. For example, in February 1857 Governor William Bissell signed a bill to create a teacher training school in Illinois. The attorney for the fledgling normal school was Abraham Lincoln. Illinois State Normal University evolved into today's Illinois

State University, with thirty-four academic departments offering sixty-six majors, thirty-four master's degrees, and eight doctoral programs to a student population of 20,265.[34]

In the period between the Revolution and the Civil War, numerous lasting and many transitory small colleges were founded, often in the frontier West; new student populations, especially women and African Americans, were beginning to be admitted; and the seeds of state-supported public higher education were planted and began to grow rapidly.

From the Civil War to World War II, 1865–1944

After the Civil War, the nation experienced another period of almost explosive collegiate expansion, both in number of institutions and in volume of students and teachers at those institutions. Up to this point, most colleges were small, with fewer than two hundred students, whereas "Harvard, Yale, Virginia and Michigan were the giants of the day with five and six hundred students."[35] In 1870 there were 250 institutions in the nation, with 5,553 professors serving 63,000 students. In 1945, there were 1,768 colleges and universities with more than 1,675,000 students and some 150,000 faculty members.[36] In just two decades, from 1920 to 1940, the population of college students nearly tripled.[37]

Among the new institutions created were colleges designed specifically for populations other than the white males who had dominated higher education in the previous century and who were the only college students of the colonial era. Thus, for example, today's Morehouse College for African American males began as Augusta Institute in the basement of Springfield Baptist Church in Augusta, Georgia (the oldest independent African American church in the United States), in 1867. During the same time, a series of public separate and unequal agricultural and mechanical colleges for students of color were created in the south. Colleges for women as well as coeducation showed strong growth during this period. By 1880 nearly half of U.S. colleges admitted women, led by the public institutions. (It is worth remembering that the country's women were not admitted nationally to the polling place for another forty years.) This period also saw the first attempts to provide more than rudimentary elementary education to American Indians, including the creation of several institutions that are today tribal colleges and several that evolved into colleges and universities that now serve a broad and diverse student population.

Another new development was the creation of the "junior college," beginning, some students of higher education suggest, with the recommendation by the president of Baylor University in 1894 that his institution and some of the smaller Baptist institutions in Texas enter a formal compact whereby the small colleges would provide the first two years of instruction, and Baylor would accept their graduates to complete the final half of their baccalaureate education.[38] In the first decade of the twenty-first century, two-year colleges, including community colleges, technical or vocational, and associate's degree–granting junior colleges, add up to more institutions than BA-, MA-, and PhD-granting institutions combined.[39]

It was also during the time between the Civil War and World War II that the "normal schools" we saw created earlier began to move to "state college" status. Here, too, growth has been dramatic. Today, more institutions offer the master's degree as their highest option (611) than either the baccalaureate (606) or doctoral degree (261).

In spite of these new institutions and new populations, small, traditional, sectarian liberal arts baccalaureate colleges remained at the center of the American higher-education system from the Civil War to World War II. David Breneman estimates that at the turn of the twentieth century fully two-thirds of all American college students were enrolled in such institutions; by 1987, he calculates, that figure had declined radically to 4.4%.[40]

Taken together, the evolutionary developments within American higher education from the 1865 to 1944 can be seen as a key transition from earlier European and colonial models to colleges and universities structured in a way that is recognizable from a contemporary vantage point and which serve most of today's college-going constituencies. But both the colleges and their populations were in significantly different proportions from those in the twenty-first century. At the beginning of this era, sectarian small colleges were ubiquitous. At its end, they still constituted the core of American higher education, but they were becoming less sectarian and less small, and a rival set of collegiate options, mostly in the public sector, was taking hold, growing rapidly, and in the process of becoming dominant.

World War II to the Present, 1945–2009

Tellingly, in terms of the history of religious colleges in America, the ratio between enrollments in public as contrasted to those in private colleges tipped just after the war. In each of the three postwar decades, the percentage of enrollments at public institutions grew by 10%: in 1945 it was 49%, by 1975 it was 79%. At the same time, small liberal arts colleges declined in number. The Carnegie Foundation considered 719 colleges in this category in 1970, and a decade later the number had dropped to 583. David Breneman's study concluded that the number of colleges with a claim to liberal learning fell from roughly six hundred schools to just over two hundred. Douglas Sloan notes, in the two decades after World War II, one major trend was the "nearly complete triumph of the research university in determining the primary ethos and goals of American Higher Education."[41] Still, as late as "the mid 1960s about one third of all colleges and universities in the country were private, and more than half of these . . . were affiliated with religious bodies, 57 percent of these Protestant."[42]

With the return of war veterans in the later 1940s and into the early 1950s, most institutions in the country experienced a rapidly expanding student population, which was particularly welcome and noticeable after the shortages of the war years. Behavior codes that had been universal early in the twentieth century were maintained at some historically Christian colleges but came to be perceived by the educational establishment, and by most students, as outmoded and idiosyncratic. The vestiges of those codes took another beating from the student countercultural activism of the 1960s. The divergence of student behavioral codes and expectations between the Christian colleges and their secular counterparts is a marked feature of postwar collegiate history.

After the war and through the 1950s, the United States also enjoyed a time of economic well-being, and in that era of the GI Bill and Eisenhower aura it seemed that all the nation's institutions of higher education had nowhere to go but up—up in size, up in budget, up in mission expansion. Moreover, the startling launch of the Russian Sputnik space satellite guaranteed a boost, in prestige and in funding, for higher learning in general and especially for the sciences in American colleges and universities. This heightened emphasis on science and engineering is seen by some scholars as entailing a corresponding decrease in interest (and status) in issues of faith, values, and the spirit.[43]

Although contemporary popular culture has sanitized and romanticized the 1960s, it was in reality a difficult time on many of America's college campuses. At mainline Protestant-affiliated campuses, the student activism of the 1960s led to the demise of many of the religious characteristics that had still been vital and important early in the twentieth century—required courses in religion and required chapel, for example, survived the Second World War on most private Protestant campuses but did not survive Vietnam. Douglas Sloan contends that "by the end of 1969, along its entire front, the major twentieth-century engagement of the Protestant church with American higher education had collapsed, and its forces were in rout."[44] Faculty, too, heartened by the activism of the students they instructed, lobbied, often with success, to do away with not only faculty and admissions quotas that had protected founding denominations but also other religious requirements and customs.[45] Finally, college campuses were shocked when students were slain at Kent State University and Jackson State University: student protest and the response to it had collapsed into riot and armed warfare. As more and more institutions reacted by moving toward increased student control over college life, and decreased curricular and social requirements, a contrary development, which sought clear classroom and behavioral expectations, was developing among some students and parents. As a large proportion of public and private institutions moved further away from strong intellectual and personal guidance, the small number of schools that clung to such standards enjoyed renewed popularity among a constituency that sought them. As a general rule, they did not enjoy a similarly high regard within the higher-education community, which tended to dismiss them as intellectually questionable.[46] Many observers have noted, in American culture in general and in colleges and universities in particular, a simultaneous decline of the mainline Protestant churches and rise of evangelical Protestantism. This simplistic image of a mainline-evangelical seesaw is not without justification but needs to be significantly modified by added nuance and complexity. Nonetheless, from the 1970s on, evangelical Christian colleges have emerged as an increasingly successful, popular, and noteworthy segment of the American higher-educational panorama.

Not only did experiments on the political and cultural left flourish during the midcentury period: it was also the time when several new small colleges with deep Christian commitments were launched. This was, perhaps, both a consequence of a revival of interest in evangelical Christianity and a reaction to the perception that many colleges had drifted to the left politically, had simultaneously moved away from a strong program of direct ethical guidance of students, and had weakened or even severed connections with the religious bodies that had created them.

In the final quarter of the twentieth century, the expansion of the college student population began to slow, and for the first time in memory there were more college teachers than there were jobs to be had teaching college. A sense of increased competition for declining resources both strengthened and weakened collegiate religiosity. Some institutions that maintained, or created anew, strongly religious traditions flourished by appealing to a particular market share of the higher-education consumer culture. Others took the opposite tack and lessened their religious emphasis, in order to appeal to a broader clientele.

A crucial development in the history of religious colleges is the movement of "mainstream" institutions that were founded with a religious mission away from that historic mission and toward what many see as secularism. This movement might well be seen to span the entire sweep of our nation's history, from the colonial era to the present, but it could arguably be said that it reached its peak in the century and a half between the Civil War and the end of the twentieth century. Several students of higher education and religion, perhaps most notably James Burtchaell, have written to lament strongly this development; others have taken issue with their grim interpretations.[47] While some contend that most American colleges and universities have lost their religious underpinnings, others assert that those core principles have merely evolved in a fashion that keeps pace with the rest of the world. Regardless of how one interprets the data, however, it is clear that a great many institutions that saw themselves as overtly sectarian in the 1860s had redefined themselves in terms of student population, faculty characteristics, curriculum, and governance by the mid-twentieth century. John Thelin notes that "the secularization of American life in general, rather than academic atheism, altered the place of religion on the American campus."[48] The shift is cultural as much as it is academic.

The theme of "secularization" of religious colleges is a continuing motif throughout this volume. Was there a point (or points) in the history of individual colleges or in the collective history of American colleges when, to cite Burtchaell's dramatic phrase, the light died? I have studied carefully the amply documented history of one college that might be seen as an archetype of a once religious, now secular school, Cornell College in Mount Vernon, Iowa. Cornell began as a rigorously Methodist institution, founded by Elder George Bryant Bowman as Iowa Conference Seminary in 1853.[49] By its sesquicentennial in 2003, the college welcomed students, faculty, trustees, and staff, including senior administrative leadership, of all faiths, or no faith. It required no worship activity of students or faculty, or any test or affirmation of faith. The majority of its governing board was selected without regard to religion. After reaching a high point in the 1970s, direct financial support for the college from the church steadily declined. At the time of its 150th birthday, Cornell still had a chaplain, but she was ordained in the Episcopal Church. And yet that chaplain could vigorously declare, "Methodism is still in the DNA of this college's mission and campus ethos."[50] The previous (Methodist) chaplain reflects: "A powerful wave of secularization characterized the twentieth century and forced considerable hard thinking about the historic partnership [between Cornell and the Methodist Church]. The shape and meaning of affiliation is not a static matter. At the sesquicentennial, both parties of the partnership remained committed to substantive dialogue regarding the nature of future relationships. The faith and church that inspired the college have directly . . . contributed to its sustained development."

To the pessimists, Cornell is a prime example of a religious college that has lost its way, but to many who care about the college and its faith tradition, it remains a deeply religious place. It continues its attention to "spiritual care and compassionate support; opportunities for spiritual inquiry, growth and practice; the use of reason for theological and ethical reflection, spiritual growth and care, scriptural analysis and interfaith conversations; dialogue between people of differing faith traditions; the pursuit of service, justice and reconciliation."[51] As it was in the middle of the 1800s, Cornell's motto in the twenty-first century remains "Deus et Humanitas."

This historical sketch suggests the pattern by which today's panoply of religious higher education has evolved. From origins that were wholly religious in the colonial era, we have created a system that includes public and private nonsectarian colleges and universities and a remarkably diverse range of institutions with religious traditions and connections. There have been dramatic fits and starts, ebbs and flows in the patterns of piety and religious affiliation. Some have seen a steady decline in religious influence, whereas others believe we are now in a period of conspicuous religious renaissance. The remainder of this book is devoted to seeking a balanced and objective picture of the contemporary status of religious colleges, focusing finally upon the particular and noteworthy story of today's evangelical Christian colleges.

Denominational Contexts

If the historical evolution of religious postsecondary education in America is the "warp" of contextualizing today's Christian colleges and universities, the panorama of contemporary collegiate religious affiliations is the "woof." In the sections that follow, we examine first the range of non-Christian colleges and universities in our nation today, by taking a brief look at three representative non-Christian colleges: one Buddhist, one Hindu, and one Jewish. Then we turn briefly to the colleges and universities of the Church of Jesus Christ of Latter-day Saints (Mormons). Then, in the next chapter I survey three Roman Catholic institutions, each quite different from the other two.

A broad range of institutions offers postsecondary instruction in affiliation with non-Christian religions in contemporary American society. Although these include clerical training institutes and continuing-education enterprises, I concentrate primarily on the more traditional colleges and universities: those which offer the BA degree, or some fairly close approximation thereof, in subjects that go beyond straightforward instruction in the doctrines and practices of the particular religious of affiliation. So, for example, the International Museum of Muslin Cultures in Jackson, Mississippi, or Isralight, a nationwide, largely electronic Jewish instruction center, is not considered. These exclusions narrow the field considerably, but a remarkable range of institutions contributing to our complex fabric of religiously based higher learning remains.

Naropa University, Boulder, Colorado

Naropa University (Buddhist), in Boulder, Colorado, describes itself as offering "four-year undergraduate college and graduate programs in the arts, education, environmental leadership, psychology and religious studies. It offers BA, BFA, MA, MFA and MDiv degrees, as well as professional development training and classes for the community."[52] Naropa is accredited by the Higher Learning Commission of the North Central Association of Colleges and Schools.

The university grew out of the Naropa Institute, which was founded by Chögyam Trungpa Rinpoche in 1974. An important and controversial figure in American Buddhism, Trungpa was born in 1939 or 1940 (sources differ) in Tibet but became an exile in 1959, following the Chinese invasion of his homeland. He went first to the United Kingdom, where rock star David Bowie was among his students, and came to the United States and Canada in 1970. In addition to Naropa, he founded scores of other Buddhist institutions around the world. Trungpa died in Nova Scotia in 1987, reputedly at least in part because of a long history of heavy alcohol use.[53] Among the early teachers at Naropa were some important mid-twentieth-century countercultural literary figures, including Allan Ginsburg and William Burroughs.

Naropa describes itself as blending the cultural legacies of the East and the West, of classical India and ancient Greece.[54] It emphasizes, distinctively, what it refers to as "contemplative education":

> The first step to understanding contemplative education is to grasp that it doesn't mean solely self reflection, and it is not the act of contemplation alone that makes it unique. Contemplative education is learning infused with the experience of awareness, insight and compassion for oneself and others, honed through the practice of sitting meditation and other contemplative disciplines. The rigor of these disciplined practices prepares the mind to process information in new and perhaps unexpected ways. Contemplative practice unlocks the power of deep inward observation, enabling the learner to tap into a wellspring of knowledge about the nature of mind, self and other that has been largely overlooked by traditional, Western-oriented liberal education. This approach to learning captures the spark of East and West.

Naropa will strike the conventional American academic, including this writer, as a mix of the exotic and the familiar: there is a vice president for academic affairs but also the Jack Kerouac School of Disembodied Poetics. Courses are offered in unconventional subjects like "somatic intelligence" and in traditional ones such as "physical geography."

As a Buddhist college, Naropa University has a sharply distinctive perspective on higher education. Its curriculum and its instructional philosophy set it apart from conventional Western colleges and universities. At the same time, it has poured new wine into the familiar old bottles of collegiate structures—graduation requirements, majors, core curriculum, and the like. It emerges as a combination of the comfortingly recognizable with the intriguingly exotic.

Maharishi University, Fairfield, Iowa

Maharishi University (which currently refers to itself in some of its publications as Maharishi University of Management or MUM) is located on a 272-acre campus in Fairfield, Iowa.[55] From 1875 until 1973, the campus belonged to Parsons College, a small, fairly typical, unselective midwestern liberal arts college. In 1955 the college appointed Millard G. Roberts its president. Roberts over the next dozen years shepherded the college through a period of incredible boom, followed by a terminal bust. Parsons went out of business in 1972, and the campus was sold to Maharishi Mahesh Yogi. The Maharishi was a well-known Vedic practitioner, who garnered an impressive celebrity following in the countercultural days of the 1960s and 1970s. His numerous followers included the Beatles, the Beach Boys, Andy Kaufman, Clint Eastwood, and David Lynch. *Time* magazine featured him on its cover in October 1975.

In the mid 1990s the campus was thoroughly rebuilt, and today there are few remnants of the Parsons College days.[56] Indeed, a 2008 article notes that forty-three buildings have been demolished since 2000 and seventy new ones built since then, all "according to principles of Maharishi Vedic architecture."[57] Maharishi University of Management is accredited by the Higher Learning Commission of the North Central Association of Colleges and Schools, the major regional accreditation agency, serving most public and private institutions in the Midwest.

The college's meals are all vegetarian, all organic. Some of the food is produced on site at the community's "Vedic organic farm." All students meditate twice daily, and the college encourages students to "hit the hay at 10 p.m."[58]

Most of MUM's nine hundred students live in single rooms, including those in the seven residence halls completed in 2005. Those halls, which are built in accord with the Maharishi's philosophy, are all designed to be ecologically friendly, using natural materials and geothermal heating. (The college was cited by the *Des Moines Register* for its ecological sensitivity.)[59] Maharishi University of Management foregrounds its performance on the National Survey of Student Engagement. It notes that it scores in the top 3% in the area of "active and collaborative learning," the top 4% in "enriching educational experiences," the highest 7% in the area of "student/faculty interaction," the top 8% in "supportive campus environment," and the top 26% in "level of academic challenge." MUM graduates also report much higher than average satisfaction with their college experiences on the nationwide annual ACT alumni survey: 73% indicate they would choose MUM as their undergraduate college again, as compared to 32% nationally.[60]

Maharishi University of Management's signature offering, of course, is "consciousness-based education," which it defines for prospective students: "In Consciousness-Based education, you'll study traditional subjects. But at the same time, you'll systematically cultivate your total potential from within. Day by day, you'll develop your creativity, your learning ability, your ability to see the big picture, your ability to relate to others. You'll cultivate the total potential of your brain."[61] This, MUM affirms, is done through the daily practice of transcendental meditation (TM) by the entire campus community. Twice a day, for twenty minutes, all students and faculty members sit, with eyes closed, and silently meditate. Many supplement this basic TM technique with the practice of yoga and breathing techniques. Students who come to MUM not knowing the technique of TM are enrolled in a course that introduces them to it. The university claims that TM is currently practiced by some six million people worldwide and has been scientifically validated in more than six hundred studies.

Maharishi Mahesh Yogi has been both an individual of significant veneration by a number of influential and regular people and an object of some jocularity. His university in Fairfield, Iowa, has had something of the same dual repute. Many in the mainstream higher-education community did not take the successor to Parson's College seriously when it began more than three decades ago; some still do not. On the other hand, it is clear that the college, like its founder, has persisted cheerfully and gone its own blissful way, for a goodly duration. The results it achieves with its students are incontestably impressive.

Yeshiva University, New York

Several postsecondary institutions in contemporary America are Jewish in affiliation. Many of these are specialized: the multicampus Hebrew Union College–Jewish Institute of Religion is a seminary for clerical training. Gratz College in Philadelphia focuses entirely on Jewish studies. Spertus Institute of Jewish Studies in Chicago is a continuing education and enrichment center, also with an exclusively Judaic focus. Brandeis University, on the other hand, proclaims itself to be a research university and a liberal arts institution that is wholly nonsectarian but "sponsored" by the American Jewish community. It defines itself not as a religious college but as a nonreligious college that was founded by, and continues to be supported by, an American religious community.[62]

Yeshiva University, however, is a comprehensive university that systematically combines study of a wide range of academic subject matters with learning about Jewish tradition and the Torah.[63] Yeshiva is a true "university," with several schools: Yeshiva College, which is the arts and sciences institution for men; Stern College, which is the equivalent for women; a School of Business, a Law School, and the Albert Einstein College of Medicine; a Graduate School of Jewish Studies, and one of Psychology, and the School of Social Work; a Graduate School of Jewish Education and Administration and a Theological Seminary. In addition to the BA and BS degrees, the university offers MA, MS, MD, PhD, JD, LLM, PsyD, MSA, CJCS, and EdD degrees. It is fully accredited by the Middle States Association of Colleges and Schools, a major mainstream regional accreditation association.

The graduate programs at Yeshiva are prestigious and successful. In 2004–5, for example, the university garnered $180 million in sponsored research. Applications to the Einstein College of Medicine are such that the acceptance rate most recently reported was a mere 8.4%—more than nine out of ten applications are rejected.

Yeshiva grew out of the merger, in 1915, of two prior New York institutions: Yeshiva Eitz Chaim (1886) and the Rabbi Isaac Elchanan Theological Seminary (1897). Since 1915, Yeshiva has had only four presidents: Dr. Bernard Revel (1915–40), Dr. Samuel Belkin (1943–76), Dr. Norman Lamm (1976–2002), and currently Richard M. Joel (an Orthodox Jew but, somewhat controversially, neither a rabbi nor a scholar of Judaism). This is a remarkable record of leadership continuity.

Today, Yeshiva has a total of about 7,010 students, which includes 2,875 undergraduates, 3,230 graduate and postgraduate students, and about 1,000 at Yeshiva-affiliated high schools and the theological seminary. The students come from thirty-eight states and fifty-five other countries. The university has a substantial endowment of just over $1 billion and an annual operating budget of about a half-billion dollars a year.

Stern College for women is not co-located with Yeshiva College for men, and the faculties of the two colleges are not the same. Unlike the case in some men's-women's linked campuses (e.g., St. Johns and St. Benedict's in Collegeville, Minnesota, or Hobart and William Smith in Geneva, New York), Stern and Yeshiva colleges remain separate and distinct entities, segregated by gender.

A defining characteristic of Yeshiva University is that all undergraduates, in addition to pursuing a traditional major, complete a rigorous program in the area of Jewish studies. This program differs somewhat from college to college, and within Yeshiva and Stern colleges there are also options. Thus, at Yeshiva College, there are four tracks of Jewish studies offered through various "schools." All require course work in Bible studies, the Hebrew language, and Jewish history. At Stern College, students take thirty-two to fifty credits in Jewish studies, including eight hours of lecture weekly for three years plus fourteen credits in addition in the areas of Bible, Hebrew, Jewish education, and Jewish history. Except for the Jewish studies component, graduation requirements for the BA degree at Yeshiva are traditional. International programs concentrate heavily on work in Israel, which the university supports with a variety of programs.

One way in which Yeshiva honors its Jewish affiliation is through a series of affiliated institutions. These include, for example, the Association of Modern Orthodox Day Schools and Yeshiva High Schools; the Center for the Jewish Future; and the program for Advanced Talmudic Studies for women. The university is home to a Center for Ethics and another for International Affairs. The Yeshiva University Museum opened in 1973 and describes its mission as celebrating three thousand years of Jewish tradition, history, and culture, through exhibitions, programs, and publications. The university is also home to a special library of Hebraica and Judaica.

Yeshiva offers a full program of fitness and competitive recreational opportunities, including swimming, basketball, and fitness training. Yeshiva's interscholastic athletic teams are known as the Maccabees and Lady Maccabees.[64]

Campus residence halls insist that students live up to halachic (the corpus of Jewish law) norms and Torah ideals. Yeshiva also sponsors an "independent housing" option on its Wilf campus, where students live in nearby apartment buildings. In discussing student life, the university stresses the unique and virtually infinite opportunities of living in New York City and simultaneously addresses directly and reassuringly its attentiveness to security issues.

As an Orthodox Jewish affiliated institution (although technically nonsectarian), Yeshiva adheres strictly to Orthodox practice: for example, the school closes down entirely on the Sabbath and on Jewish holidays, and only kosher food is served in the dining halls.

In many ways, but especially in its defining program of Torah Umadda, liberal scholarship combined with Jewish studies, Yeshiva University is an emblem of the experience of the American Jewish community. It strives for excellence as an American research university, using the standards of institutions like Yale and Duke and the University of Michigan. It competes for research dollars, it builds major libraries, it houses centers and institutes, and it recruits prestigious international scholars as faculty and talented young people as undergraduates and graduate students. And, at the same time, it affirms continually and strongly its identity as a Jewish institution, one that stresses the Hebrew language, strong ties to Israel, course work in Jewish law at the Benjamin Cardozo School of Law, and a demanding all-university program requiring study of Jewish history and culture. This dual emphasis (like the similar focus on management and transcendental meditation at Maharishi University or the liberal arts and contemplative practices at Naropa) produces not institutional schizophrenia but a strong sense of identity and a clear mission. Only in America.

Brigham Young University, Provo, Utah

The largest sectarian university in America is Brigham Young University, in Provo, Utah, with about thirty-four thousand students. There are also several other collegiate institutions affiliated with the Church of Jesus Christ of Latter-day Saints or its offshoots. But where do those institutions fit into this study? Mormons see themselves as "Restorationists": they believe that the LDS Church restores the original purity and truth of Christianity. In this framework, Restored Christianity is neither Catholic, Protestant, nor Orthodox, but original. It is the Christian Church before it divided into those branches. From the perspective of the Christian colleges, however, a different perception of the Mormon colleges emerges. The Council for Christian Colleges and Universities (which lists two Friends institutions and one Roman Catholic college among its members and affiliates) has no Mormon members. As one faculty member at a nondenominational evangelical university puts it in conversation, "They don't have the same concept of the Christian faith that most [all?] Catholics and Protestants have." The exclusion of LDS schools from the CCCU is another reminder that, for many within the evangelical community, the word "Christian" does not mean "one who believes in Christ" so much as "an evangelical Protestant believer in Christ." Like the Mormons themselves, their colleges and universities are in some ways comfortably within the fold of Christian academe and in some ways quite distinctive.

Brigham Young University was founded by its namesake, in Provo, Utah, in 1875. It was officially absorbed by the LDS Church in 1896 and remains today administered by the Church Educational System. Roughly 98% of its students are LDS, about a third of them from Utah. It is an academically selective campus, with an average ACT score of 27.9.[65] In 2006 it had eighty-eight National Merit Scholars, ranking twenty-sixth in the United States. The Carnegie Corporation ranks BYU as a "high research" university. The university has eleven colleges and offers 187 undergraduate academic degree programs, sixty-four masters degrees, twenty-four doctorates, and the JD.

Student demographics as reported by the university merit attention. Of 32,964 "daytime" students in 2007, 28,073 are classified as white, 1,339 as Asian/Pacific Islander, 1,145 as Hispanic, 166 as American Indian, 158 as black, and the remainder as other or unknown. About 0.5% of BYU's students are African American. The reported religions of the students are shown as 32,178 LDS, 74 Catholics, 59 Protestants, 46 Muslims, 37 "other Christian," 66 Hindu, 17 Buddhist, and 13 "other religions" (including Jewish, Baha'i, etc.), with 174 indicating no religious preference. Thus, fewer than five hundred students were non-LDS of any sort.

From its founding, BYU has insisted that all learning should be infused with religious content: Brigham Young himself, it is frequently noted, said "you ought not to teach even the alphabet or the multiplication tables without the Spirit of God."[66] The university seeks to be true to this injunction today, saying that its curriculum "flows from a conscious intent to envelop BYU's intellectual aims within a more complete, even eternal perspective that begins with spiritual knowledge."[67] "Spiritual Strengthening" is one of four overarching goals of the university, the other three being intellectual enlarging, character building, and lifelong learning/service.

A 2002 article compares faculty attitudes toward religion at BYU, Baylor, Notre Dame, and Boston College.[68] In every feature compared, the faculty at Brigham Young were significantly more inclined toward a religious perspective than its colleagues at the Baptist and two Catholic schools. (In most categories, the Boston College faculty was the least religiously inclined; Baylor and Notre Dame tended to shift relative places in the middle.) So, for example, at Baylor, 54.5% of the faculty agreed or strongly agreed that the institution should hire faculty who shared the religious commitment of the institution, but at BYU that number was 81.8%. Conversely, when asked if the institution should hire new faculty with the strongest academic promise or performance, regardless of religious persuasion, only 10.2% at BYU agreed, compared to 35.9% at Baylor, 58% at Notre Dame, and 73.6% at BC. On a similarly revealing question, most BYU faculty members (92.5%) said they currently do discuss faith-related questions in class and only a few (1.1%) said they would never do so. At Boston College, less than half have such discussions (48.3%) and nearly a quarter (21.3%) would avoid them. The study did note that almost all BYU's faculty are LDS (98%) and concluded that this probably explains, at least in part, why "Brigham Young faculty are distinctively committed to their school's religious tradition."[69]

The student honor code at Brigham Young is prefaced with the affirmation that the university exists "to provide an education in an atmosphere consistent with the ideals and principles of the Church of Jesus Christ of Latter-day Saints. That atmosphere is created and preserved through commitment to conduct that reflects those ideals and principles."[70] The code, which all must sign, specifies the rules that all students, faculty, and staff at BYU should follow:

Be honest.
Obey the law and all campus policies.
Live a chaste and virtuous life.
Respect others.
Abstain from alcoholic beverages, tobacco, tea, coffee, and substance abuse.
Encourage others in their commitment to comply with the Honor Code.
Observe dress and grooming standards.
Participate regularly in church services.
Use clean language.

The dress and grooming standards are detailed and explicit, with a paragraph devoted to each gender. The men's standards, for example, specify types of clothing, offer advice on hairstyles and facial hair, forbid any sorts of earrings or body piercings, and require shoes.

Recently, the honor code was clarified (not revised) to note that, while homosexual behavior was a violation, ungratified same-sex impulses were not. In other words, homosexuality per se is not against the code, but homosexual acts are.

Students are required, annually, to document that they are active in their churches, in the great majority of cases through submitting an "ecclesiastical endorsement" from their LDS church of choice. In many cases, those "churches" are small "wards" on campus (each with about 175 members).

The emphasis on family within the LDS church leads many BYU students to marry at a younger age than the national average. Slightly more than half the 2005 graduates of the university were married. In a chapter profiling BYU in her *God on the Quad*, Naomi Schaefer Riley devotes considerable attention to the BYU student preoccupation with marriage and beginning a family, noting, at one point, "as the crowd around me nibbles on cookies and punch, I slowly become aware that every conversation in the room is about marriage."[71]

A significant number of BYU students serve as missionaries during their college years, commonly during a two-year, mid-college-career interval. This has led to a particular university emphasis on the study of foreign languages.

BYU has two other campuses, as well as a handful of "centers" (e.g., in Jerusalem; the Missionary Training Center). The two full-fledged colleges are in Idaho and Hawaii.

The campus that is now Brigham Young University at Idaho was earlier one of the nation's largest private two-year colleges, Ricks College, in Rexburg, Idaho. It was originally founded by LDS in 1888. The school underwent several changes of name and leadership and weathered some substantial crises. At one point, it was nearly taken over by the state of Idaho; it went from being a two-year institution to a four-year one, then back to junior college status. In 2000 Ricks College again became a four-year institution, and its name changed to BYU-Idaho. Today, BYU-Idaho has about twelve thousand students, mostly Mormon. About 50% have completed an LDS mission, and about 25% are married.

The Hawaii campus of Brigham Young University is known to literally millions of tourists as the partner of the incredibly popular Polynesian Cultural Center, the top-ranked paid tourist attraction in the state, where about a third of the college's students work.[72] To date, more than thirty million visitors have seen the center. The college and the center are in the community of Laie, on the northern shore of the island of Oahu. The collegiate enrollment today is about twenty-four hundred undergraduate students, nearly half of whom are international students, primarily from the Asian-Pacific region. About 91% of BYU-Hawaii's students are members of the LDS faith. BYU-Hawaii was founded in 1955 as a two-year institution, first called the Church College of Hawaii. BYU-Hawaii students are governed by an honor code essentially similar to that at the Provo campus, although it is expressed somewhat differently. The principles—abstinence, chastity, careful grooming, and the like—are the same.

After the murder of LDS founder Joseph Smith, in Nauvoo, Illinois, in 1844, there was dissension in Mormon ranks regarding the succession of leadership within the church. The larger group, now headquartered in Salt Lake City, Utah, and the controlling denomination at the Brigham Young University campuses in Provo, Idaho, and Hawaii, chose to follow Brigham Young as the church moved west. Another group believed that the founder's son, Joseph Smith III, was the true leader. This second group (today it numbers about two hundred thousand adherents) eventually made its headquarters in Independence, Missouri, where it was called the Reorganized Church of Jesus Christ of Latter-day Saints. Today, its name is the Community of Christ, and it is the sponsor of Graceland University, in Lamoni, Iowa. Graceland has another campus in Independence, Missouri, which is the home of its seminary, school of nursing, and graduate and undergraduate programs in education. Graceland also operates satellite campuses at a handful of community colleges in Iowa and Missouri.

The Community of Christ, and Graceland University, takes a number of positions that would generally be understood to be more liberal than those of the Church of Jesus Christ of Latter-day Saints. For example, it encourages the ordination of female ministers. Not surprisingly, Graceland University is less sectarian than Brigham Young. Its mission, thus, proactively welcomes "persons of all faiths" and affirms that the college "promotes opportunity, justice, and world peace."[73]

The main campus of Graceland has about 2,350 students, with forty-three undergraduate majors. It has a threefold statement of values:

Learning—We believe in the life long process of the open and free pursuit of truth.

Wholeness—We believe that the development of the intellectual, physical, social and spiritual dimensions of all persons is necessary for healthy and fulfilling lives.

Community—We appreciate and welcome diversity and, as an institution sponsored by the Community of Christ, believe in the inherent worth of all persons expressed through relationships built on the foundation of unconditional love and acceptance.

From its founding in 1895 until 1960, Graceland was a two-year institution, and Iowa's first accredited junior college. After adding baccalaureate programs in 1960, the former Graceland College became Graceland University in 2000.

Like BYU, Graceland has a policy prohibiting the use of alcohol, drugs, and tobacco but does not have the extensive dress and grooming code of Brigham Young or the practice of requiring documentation of church activity.

Altogether, some fifty thousand college students are enrolled in American colleges and universities affiliated either with the Church of Jesus Christ of Latter-day Saints or the Community of Christ—not an insignificant number. Mormon higher education ranges from the very large and vigorously LDS Brigham Young University (Provo) to the considerably smaller and far less religiously monolithic Graceland University. In that range of size and breadth of religious rigor, the Mormon institutions mirror, in smaller scale, the diversity of all the nation's schools of faith-based higher learning.

♦♦♦

Buddhist, Hindu, Jewish, and Mormon colleges and universities have had a significant impact on American higher education, past and present. But by far the largest group of non-Protestant institutions has been and continues to be the many and diverse schools linked to Roman Catholicism. The next chapter concludes the discussion of the contextual setting of contemporary Protestant postsecondary education as it focuses on three distinct institutions from that Catholic tradition.

3 | Three Roman Catholic Colleges
and Universities

In the following three discussions we continue to examine the contexts of contemporary evangelical Protestant, Christian colleges, by taking a careful look at three Roman Catholic institutions. Catholic colleges and universities are by far the largest cluster of religiously grounded American higher-educational institutions after the Protestant ones, more than all non-Christian schools combined. Their history is a long and rich one. Today, many Roman Catholic colleges and universities enjoy high academic reputations, selective admissions, and diverse student and faculty populations. This has not, of course, always been the case. Early in the past century, when public higher education was still relatively provincial and unabashedly Protestant, Catholic students (and teachers) tended not to be warmly welcomed there. Thus, the Catholic institutions became, in effect, the quasi-public "open door" schools for members of the faith.[1] Walking through that door were members of working families of relatively recent immigrant communities such as the Irish, Germans, Italians, and Eastern Europeans.[2] Not surprisingly, these colleges and universities did not originally have high stature within the larger academic community.

In many respects the issues, challenges, and victories within American Catholic higher education mirror those in the Protestant realm. For example, the question of whether Catholic schools have lost, or abandoned, their Catholicism parallels exactly the concern that Protestant institutions have gone down the path toward secularization. Indeed, arguably the most vigorous and influential attack on collegiate secularization, James Burtchaell's *The Dying of the Light,* takes aim at both, with particular harshness in its treatment of the Catholic sector, from which Dr. Burtchaell emerged (see Essay on Sources). On the other hand, of course, some of the issues at Catholic colleges and universities are idiosyncratic.

Some of the recent debates about Roman Catholic higher education can be traced to July 1967, when a group of twenty-six Catholic educators gathered at the Land O'Lakes Center in Wisconsin to discuss the implications of the Second Vatican Council (which had ended in 1965) for their institutions. President Theodore Hesburgh of Notre Dame was a major leader of this conclave. From this conference emerged the "Land O' Lakes Statement," which affirmed the independence of Catholic universities from direct church control. Academic freedom and institutional autonomy were seen as "essential conditions of life and growth and indeed of survival for Catholic universities."[3]

To some, this statement was a breath of much-needed fresh air in Catholic education. To others, it was a catastrophic error. The latter claimed that "the signatories of the Land O' Lakes statement, by refusing to be shepherded by the Church's bishops, set the sheep free to roam into whatever error academic freedom might lead them. Nearly forty years later, the shepherds are still trying to gather their scattered flocks."[4]

In 1990 Pope John Paul II issued a document entitled *Ex Corde Ecclesiae* (From the Heart of the Church), which reaffirmed the close link between the church and its colleges that, to some, the Land O' Lakes Statement had brought into question. As prefect of the Congregation for the Doctrine of Faith, the current pope, Benedict XVI, was a key drafter of this document.[5] In 1999 the United States Conference of Catholic Bishops issued "Application of Ex Corde Ecclesiae for the United States." A particularly controversial aspect of this effort is the *mandatum,* the process by which a local American bishop validates that specific professors of theology are teaching as individuals within the full communion of the church and are therefore guided by the church hierarchy or Magisterium. Some Catholic institutions and professors of theology, and some local bishops, have complied with the mandatum, some have not. Those who fear that American Catholic colleges and universities have lost their Catholic identity tend to believe that only those individuals and institutions that subscribe to this process are genuinely committed to a truly Catholic education.[6] There has been considerable writing around this subject: for example, Wilcox and King's *Enhancing Religious Identity* collects essays from a variety of authors and sources about the nature of collegiate Catholic identity and how to promote it with a particular emphasis on the guidance of *Ex Corde Ecclesiae.*[7]

Another (unrelated) issue is the challenge of transforming institutions that had depended upon female clerics as teachers and administrators at a moment when there are dramatically fewer nuns and expanded opportunities for careers and service for those who remain.

The three institutions studied in this chapter can hardly be said to encompass the entire span of American Catholic higher education, but they do represent three widely divergent strands of that tradition. Villanova University grew from the men's college sector into a significant research university, with a variety of graduate, professional, and undergraduate programs. The College of New Rochelle is a historically single-sex women's liberal arts college, located in a major metropolitan area, which today serves a largely non-Catholic, coeducational, interracial student body, with a religiously diverse faculty, in both its traditional liberal arts mission and its professional and continuing education enterprises. Finally, Thomas Aquinas College began as a reaction to the perceived loss of religious clarity and academic rigor elsewhere in the world of Catholic institutions and is today a very small, rural institution with a vigorous universal curriculum and a very strong, uncompromising Catholic culture: a "new Catholic" college.

"Publish or Parish": Villanova University, Villanova, Pennsylvania

At most contemporary American colleges and universities, few students and perhaps not all that many faculty members or staff could describe or explain the institutional seal or crest and, I would guess, fewer still would find in the official collegiate emblem a meaningful and powerful symbol. Villanova University is different. Almost every group or individual with whom I spoke on campus made overt reference to the crest itself, or to one or more of its emblematic elements. The university's crest is based upon the historic symbol of the Augustinian Friars.[8] Like the visual emblem of St. Augustine himself, Villanova's crest depicts a flaming heart, pierced by an arrow, superimposed on a book. In addition, it includes the motto of the school, "Veritas, Unitas, Caritas," and a collection of additional meaningful symbolic objects: a cincture, staff, crosses, and a laurel wreath. In every conversation I had at Villanova, someone spontaneously spoke about the importance of the *heart*. Clearly, at this University, the *book* is important: Villanova aspires to intellectual excellence, had sought resources to promote the life of the mind, and is proud of its growing reputation as an institution that nurtures and stimulates the mind. (St. Augustine's account of his conversion tells of a voice that told him "tolle lege" [take up and read] the Bible.) But the crest of the order, and of the university, shows the heart in front of, and on top of, the book. The quest for "veritas" is vital at Villanova, and it is certainly a place that strives for "unitas" internally and through the world, but "caritas" is the most significant concept.

The Augustinians, of course, see their history going directly back to St. Augustine of Hippo (354–430), who converted to Christianity in 386.[9]

After his conversion in Milan, the saint and some of his friends adopted a monastic life in Hippo, which set the precedent for the order. Nearly a millennium later, in 1243, Pope Innocent IV brought together several monastic groups into a collective Order of Augustinians.[10] Today's Augustinians include several subgroups of men and women, lay and religious. They describe the core of their contemporary spiritual life in collective terms, "seeking and worshipping God together." Although the order's origins are in a sequestered tradition, the Augustinians are now deeply engaged in global society and believe that "we must, if we wish to love Christ, spread charity abroad to the whole world."[11]

Villanova traces its beginnings to 1841 when Augustinians Father Thomas Kyle and Father Patrick Moriarty acquired a substantial tract of land in what is now suburban Philadelphia. Taking as its patron the sixteenth-century Spanish bishop and educator, St. Thomas of Villanova, the college opened its doors in 1843 as a school for boys and a center for the training of new members of the order. As a consequence of anti-Catholic riots in Philadelphia, the campus closed in 1845, reopened in 1846, but had to close again in 1857, remained closed during the Civil War, and reopened finally in 1865. The college, still an all-male institution, added a School of Technology (now the College of Engineering) and a premedical program early in the twentieth century. The School of Business was launched in 1922. The first women came to Villanova (but not to the main campus) in 1918 to take evening classes for nuns preparing to teach. A laywoman received a degree in 1938, and when the College of Nursing opened in 1953, women came to the main campus on a full-time basis. Villanova became fully coed in 1968. The college became Villanova University in 1953, with the addition of the College of Nursing and the School of Law. Today, Villanova sees itself "trying to reconcile the social imperatives of the times with what being a Catholic institution means in an age of diversity, academic freedom and constantly changing civil and moral traditions."[12] It occupies a dignified campus in which older buildings and new ones blend harmoniously, dominated by the gray stone St. Thomas of Villanova Church. The campus is located centrally on Philadelphia's Main Line, an attractive and prestigious string of western suburban towns.

In addition to students and faculty groups, I met with several senior administrators at Villanova, including the president, vice president for academic affairs, vice president for mission effectiveness, executive director of Campus Ministry and dean of freshmen.

Father Peter Donohue, an Augustinian, became Villanova's president in 2006, after chairing the theater department there for more than a dozen years. He stresses the ways in which the university's Augustinian heritage influences everything that is done at the university, and he affirms that all the students have heard about that heritage (an affirmation that my conversations with students confirmed). Like others with whom I spoke, Father Donohue emphasized Villanova's strong efforts to build and sustain community, and he sees this effort as characteristically Augustinian: St. Augustine teaches that we come to know God through knowing other people. The president also emphasized the active service and service learning programs at the university, noting that none are required but that about half of the undergraduates participate. He believes that there is "more heart" in the Augustinian heritage and less of an impulse toward compulsion. While many institutions have struggled with the mandatum provisions of the American bishops, the issue is not contentious at Villanova. The president has not felt significant pressures from the diocese on concerns having to do with the Catholicism of the university, although periodically he is asked to discuss or prepare documents on this subject. He characterizes the Augustinians as "moderates."

The president at Villanova has always been an Augustinian, but that has not been the case at all the Augustinian colleges, and one currently has a lay president. At Villanova, there are about thirty-two full- and part-time teachers who are Augustinian Friars, which strengthens the sense of a continual faith community at the institution. So, too, does the strong Augustinian representation on the board of trustees.[13] Villanova is the home site of the Province of St. Thomas of Villanova. At Villanova are the Institute for the Study of Augustine and the Augustinian Historical Institute. It also houses the Augustinian Endowed Chair in the Thought of St. Augustine. I asked President Donohue if all the deans and department chairs at Villanova were Catholic, and he responded that the former were but that the latter were not.

President Donohue, and several others, mentioned the three Sunday night masses at Villanova, at six, eight, and ten o'clock. These events, which are not required ("'you must' is not very Augustinian") are always packed. This, and the many other ways students serve others, the president believes, indicates that Villanova is successful in its efforts to graduate faith-filled people. "We believe in what we do, and we think we do it well."

Overall, it was my sense from conversations with the president and with other senior leaders that issues having to do with pressures for secularization (or, for that matter, concerns about excessive religiosity), while certainly discussed, were not as intense and constant a preoccupation at Villanova as at some other Catholic colleges and universities, including both the College of New Rochelle and Thomas Aquinas College.

I asked President Donohue what he saw as Villanova's peer institutions. He mentioned Boston College, Holy Cross, Bucknell, Lehigh, and the University of Richmond—all eastern, midsized comprehensive institutions. When I asked Villanova students what other colleges and universities they had considered when making their college choice, their list was similar to the president's. He does not believe that Georgetown or Notre Dame is an actual competitor. He noted, in this context, a relatively small endowment of $360 million. The university has just completed a $300 million capital campaign.

Like several others, including the students themselves, the president characterized Villanova's students as predominantly upper-middle class or wealthy in background—the school is "not cheap at $45,000 per year."

The president concluded our discussion by affirming that everything done at Villanova is done in the context of the Catholic faith.

Like President Donohue, the vice president for academic affairs at the university, Dr. John R. Johannes, possesses impeccable scholarly credentials: he holds the PhD in political science from Harvard University, and his resume includes an impressive list of honors, awards, grants, publications, and professional responsibilities. That made it all the more noteworthy to me that he defines the particularly Augustinian nature of Villanova in terms of "starting from the heart" to go to the mind. Dr. Johannes contrasted the character of Augustinian collegiate enterprises with those of the Jesuits, whom he described as beginning with the mind. (An amusing allegory I heard during my time at Villanova suggested that if one approached a door next to a Jesuit, he would courteously open it; if you came to a door next to an Augustinian, he, too, would open it, and then engage you in a conversation.) Dr. Johannes noted that Villanova is a university, it is a Catholic university, and it is an Augustinian Catholic university. He observed that Villanova aspires to a scholarly ranking in the top four or five Catholic comprehensive universities. At the same time, he also stressed the strength of "community" there, noting the many and wide-ranging social activities built into the life of the institution. Villanova strives to be inclusive, but at the same time it remains important that it retain a "critical mass" of Catholics, especially in the faculty. What, exactly, that "critical mass" should be is a subject of ongoing and lively discussion on campus. The vice president believes it should be somewhere in the 60–65% range, and he would be concerned if fewer than half the faculty identified themselves as Catholics. However, he also noted that Villanova does not make a concerted formal effort to actually tally the religious demographics of the faculty; it does not keep a running count of the proportion of faculty who are Catholic. In this regard, Villanova seems positioned between the College of New Rochelle, which (especially away from the New Rochelle campus) makes no effort explicitly to seek or to tabulate Roman Catholic teachers, and Thomas Aquinas College, which is firm in its commitment to a professorate that is dominated by the faithful.

Villanova does keep track of the proportion of Catholic students: currently it is about 72%, with some 5% unidentified. This is down slightly from about 80% a decade ago. Both the president and the vice president emphasized that, even more important than religious affiliation, members of the Villanova community are all expected to be individuals who take religion seriously and who are respectful of the Augustinian Catholic tradition and character of the university: casual atheism or contemptuous anti-Catholicism would not be welcome. I asked how these characteristics were promulgated or enforced. Dr. Johannes affirmed that he had not seen any particular problems in this area and observed that he often spoke with the deans, and they with department chairs, about recruiting an appropriate faculty.

Villanova offers graduate and professional programs but continues to see itself as a place where undergraduate education is primary. Faith-related curricular requirements at the baccalaureate level are fairly extensive. All students take two theology courses, including a mandatory introductory course; all also take two in philosophy in which they are highly likely to encounter serious consideration of religious issues. In addition, all undergraduates take a course in ethics, which overtly focuses on Jewish and Christian ethical traditions. A distinctive Villanova offering is a two-semester introductory seminar in Augustine and culture. This course is taken by all first-year students and maintains small classes, so there are more than one hundred sections. It seeks to combine the commonality of a shared curriculum with the freedom of professorial choice: thus, each section has to read *something* by St. Augustine, but that reading can and will vary from section to section. Similarly, each has to include something by Shakespeare, but different instructors choose different plays. All sections are introduced to the High Renaissance, but in a myriad of different readings, and so on.[14] Altogether, then, virtually all undergraduates take seven courses that focus in one way or another on the religious core of the university.[15]

At Villanova, it seems to be desired, and is clearly acceptable, that faith issues will sometimes be included within the curricular offerings across the campus. On the other hand, there is no rigorous institutional policy requiring the integration of faith and learning and no formal monitoring takes place. In some areas, such as ethics and theology, this integration is obviously common; in others, such as engineering, less so. I questioned Vice President Johannes regarding the teaching of religiously controversial subjects, such as evolution, stem cell research, and the like at Villanova. He was very clear that he believed it was encouraged to discuss anything appropriate to the subject matter of the course in class. Students are free to take positions on controversial issues; if those positions violate the tenants of the Catholic faith, the university will not officially endorse or sponsor individuals or groups that espouse them.

Two other offices on campus, in particular, are charged with strengthening and clarifying the university's Augustinian Catholic core: the Office of Campus Ministry and the Office of Mission Effectiveness. The latter office is directed by Dr. Barbara Wall, special assistant to the president; the former by Dr. Beth Hassel, PBVM, executive director.

The Office of Mission Effectiveness seeks to enhance Villanova's role as a transmitter of the Catholic intellectual tradition. It focuses upon the social teachings of the church, emphasizing that the "caritas" of the college motto should motivate *justice* more than *charity*. Through programs such as a weeklong retreat each spring, faculty members are encouraged to understand the social teachings of the Catholic Church and are helped to incorporate those teachings into their curricular offerings. The majority of those participating in this program are not Catholics. This office also sponsors an orientation for new members of the faculty early in their first terms at Villanova and conferences in fall and spring on Catholic social teaching. The orientation includes a panel of non-Catholics who talk about the Augustinian tradition, possible connections between faith and reason, and the importance of service across campus; in addition, a blessing of the faculty is performed by the president.

Dr. Wall and the Office of Mission Effectiveness have also worked with others at Villanova on the faculty hiring process. The university has created a "Guide for Faculty Search Committees" on *mission-centered hiring.* This document sets forth some general principles that guide the university and its faculty (e.g., "A Catholic, Augustinian university must be an advocate for the voiceless in God's creation"). It also defines some general principles of faculty hiring and some goals of mission-centered hiring. And it details some specific strategies for informing faculty candidates about the mission of Villanova and suggests interview questions that "encourage discussion of Villanova's mission, its Catholic and Augustinian character."[16] An example of one such question is: "In light of Villanova's mission and its continuing reflection on the life of St. Thomas of Villanova and his commitment to the poor, and the American Bishops' support for the 'preferential option for the poor,' in decision making and social policy in order to bring about social transformation, how might you contribute to this aspect of our mission?" I asked the director of the office about openly homosexual members of the Villanova community. She believes that the school needs to be more proactive in fighting homophobia and noted that there is an institutionally endorsed GLBT student organization, the Gay-Straight Coalition, OASIS (a support group), and some openly gay faculty who have successful careers at Villanova. Dr. Wall stressed that an important aspect of Villanova's religious mission was to stress St. Augustine's teaching that each human person is sacred and inviolable.

The Office of Campus Ministry at Villanova is a large and multifaceted operation. In addition to seven student interns, the office employs seventeen individuals, including an office staff of three. It even has its own coordinator of information systems and Web master (although that person has other responsibilities as well). Campus Ministry at Villanova is divided into three program areas. The first of these is *liturgy,* which oversees a wide variety of liturgical opportunities including Sunday and daily worship, student liturgical leaders, and pastoral music programs. I asked Sister Beth for an estimate of the percentage of Villanova students who participate in a liturgical exercise of one sort or another in any given week: her guess was around 40%. The *service and social justice* programs include service opportunities, both on a daily and weekly basis and at campus breaks, and special events such as hunger/homelessness awareness week, volunteerism, "Bigs and Littles" (a program that links college students and inner-city young people), Best Buddies (to enhance the lives of people with intellectual disabilities), and the like. Villanova is proud that it has one of the largest service programs in the nation. Students meet for discussion before leaving campus on service projects, both domestic and foreign, and also reflect on their experiences afterward (often informally, e.g., on a van ride home). Each of the break service programs has a staff member and two student leaders. For service programs that require travel to foreign or distant domestic destinations, the students raise all the funds to support their experience. Domestic travel programs have frequently involved work with Habitat for Humanity. International programs have gone to places like India, South America, Mexico, and Cambodia. The students with whom I spoke were uniformly enthusiastic about Villanova's service opportunities, even the few who had not yet participated in those programs. The third area of emphasis for Campus Ministry is *spiritual growth and outreach*. This includes retreats, Bible study groups, the Gay-Straight coalition and OASIS, faith-sharing groups, and a freshman "Escape" that gives first-year students a weekend pause to reflect as they adjust to college. An Interfaith Coalition is also sponsored by the ministry as a spiritual growth endeavor. Like others, Beth Hassel characterized most Villanova students as coming from conservative and moneyed backgrounds. Thus, many of these students find themselves doing substantial soul searching during their college years. The programs offered through Campus Ministry stimulate, encourage, and guide that searching. Dr. Hassel also notes that those students do know something about St. Augustine and Augustinian Catholicism and hear about those subjects constantly.

In my meetings with students, that thesis was confirmed. I spoke with two groups of undergraduate students, and in both sessions we discussed Augustinian Catholicism, at the students' initiation. They agreed that everyone at Villanova gains a familiarity with the main themes of St. Augustine's theology. When I asked for an example, one student spoke of a goal of the university being to transform the hearts and minds of the students, and particularly to instill in them "restless hearts." I asked what a "restless heart" was, and the reply, which I found moving and impressive, was, in effect, "my heart is restless when I go to bed at night knowing that all around the world others are living in need and without justice." They stressed the importance of community, as so many others had, and of Villanova's openness to a range of religious and spiritual practice. Another recurrent theme that came up again in these discussions was the distinction between "charity" and "justice." Several students spoke enthusiastically about their experiences on fall, winter, or spring break service programs, noting especially the ways in which they had found themselves involved in religious practices that were unfamiliar to them—for example, African American Baptist worship in the New Orleans region. They said that they believed such experiences were especially valuable in their largely white, largely upper-middle-class student body. Students also told me that many of their classes included serious examination of ethical issues—in the business school, for example. A few of their classes, across the curriculum, begin with a prayer, but that is the exception rather than the rule.

About half the students with whom I spoke had attended public high schools, an accurate representation of the overall proportion within Villanova's student population. Most of the rest had gone to private high schools, many of those Catholic ones. Very few Villanova undergraduates come from home schooling backgrounds. One student, who is not a Catholic, spoke about sometimes feeling a bit like an outsider at Villanova, but also affirmed vigorously that she had made many very close friendships and gained respect for the traditions of the school.

I asked the students to tell me some of the other schools to which they had applied. Among those named were Davidson, Emory, the University of Maryland, Georgetown, Pennsylvania, Boston College, the University of Southern California, Fordham, St. Louis University, Notre Dame, American University, Texas A&M, Lemoyne, the University of Richmond. This seemed to me a quite eclectic list, slight in the realm of smaller liberal arts colleges.

One of the students remarked, and others assented, that while some students are dissatisfied and wish to transfer, it was her impression that students at Villanova are highly motivated and are "happy to be here." It seemed to me that the interactions between the students with whom I spoke, who came from different majors (e.g., accounting, human services, finance, communications, English, economics, journalism), were different class years, hailed from different parts of the country, and had different opinions, conspicuously demonstrated the accuracy of the "unitas" element of Villanova's motto: they seemed to regard each other with genuine respect and affection and were unusually comfortable in each other's presence. They seemed to have learned how to disagree with each other while maintaining an atmosphere of respect and friendship.

I was also able to meet with a group of faculty members, skewed somewhat, their convener told me, in favor of those who are particularly sympathetic to the religious mission of the university (others, he said, were invited, but had not chosen to attend). The group included professors of ethics, theology, business, nursing, philosophy, and writing, among others. One of those attending has been at the university for as long as forty years, another for only two. They noted the ways in which Catholic social thought and faith issues can enter the Villanova classroom not just in predictable areas like ethics, theology, and philosophy, but also in programs such as business and nursing. Some faculty members are more comfortable than others when it comes to the integration of faith and learning, and some departments or schools emphasize this theme more than some others. All agreed that it was generally acceptable to raise faith issues in the classroom, but proselytizing was not acceptable, and the institution itself made no specific demands when it came to curricular and classroom integration of reason and religion. Indeed, this moderate combination of, on the one hand, not being forced into a particular religious position or practice and, on the other hand, not being forbidden to introduce religious themes into teaching struck several of the faculty members as a very important element in their comfort at Villanova. There was some discussion of a recent off-campus gala fund-raising celebration that apparently seemed to some of the faculty who attended uncomfortably devoid of religious content: donors, they worry, are perhaps overly impressed by the university's academic prowess but not particularly interested in its religious emphasis. Others, however, suspected that those donors take for granted Villanova's Catholicism but need to be convinced of its scholarly excellence. The faculty reports that there has been some internal discussion of different models of what constitutes a good "critical mass" of Catholic faculty members—currently they believe it hovers around 70–75% (actually, according to the vice president for academic affairs, it is about 10% lower), and many think that is an appropriate figure, while some find it too high and some too low.

This group reported that there were some serious, thoughtful atheists on the faculty and that some of those individuals had always been open about their lack of faith and had built successful careers at Villanova. They also noted that the university had occasionally turned down the bid of Augustinian friars for tenure: it was within the context of discussing such cases that the quip "publish or parish" was uttered. Faculty members noted a strong pastoral element in their work with Villanova students, and many of them believe that the faith mission of the university has the effect of promoting a humane and caring pedagogy.

Throughout my discussions at Villanova, I was struck by the frequency with which members of the community compared Augustinians to Jesuits: often when asked to define the distinctive character of Augustinian Catholicism, the response began with such a comparison. A senior member of the faculty responded, when I pointed out this observation to him, that if you ask a soda drinker to describe the distinctiveness of the taste of Pepsi, she is likely to begin with a comparison to Coke. It was his belief that, while there are certainly Catholic institutions affiliated with other orders (e.g., Notre Dame), the Augustinians and the Jesuits seem the two best-known traditional teaching orders.

Villanova University has grown in recent decades, in academic repute, in physical plant, and in size. It seems to me to have done so in ways that have not seriously compromised or brought into question its historic character and mission. More than many colleges and universities, Villanova seems comfortable with itself. The university is certainly not complacent, nor is it without disagreement and contention. But its sense of identity and purpose seem clear and consensual. It does not seek to become something or someplace else, it is not ashamed of its past nor afraid of its future.

Villanova stands in revealing and instructive contrast to the other two Roman Catholic institutions examined in this study, Thomas Aquinas College and the College of New Rochelle. CNR has today a very small proportion of Catholic students among its entire student body, and even in the historic core School of Arts and Sciences, there is not a dominant Catholic student demographic. Thomas Aquinas, by contrast, is virtually all Catholic. Villanova is comfortable with about three-fourths of its students professing Catholicism. The faculty at CNR would resist vigorously any effort to recruit a professoriate that maintained a critical mass of Catholics. At Thomas Aquinas, virtually the entire teaching staff is deeply committed to the faith. Villanova follows a middle course, seeking a strong Catholic presence in the faculty, but welcoming individuals from other faith traditions, and even respectful nonbelievers.

Ursuline? Catholic? Christian?: College of New Rochelle, New Rochelle, New York

The College of New Rochelle is a small, traditional, Catholic women's liberal arts college that, it has been argued in various places by various commentators, is not small, not traditional, not for women, not a liberal arts institution, and not Catholic. Beginning in the late 1960s and continuing through the next decade, CNR in suburban New Rochelle, New York, re-invented itself.[17] Some would argue that the reinvention was necessary in order to preserve and nurture the college's core mission and values.[18] Others, most notably James T. Burtchaell, contend that, in order to ensure its institutional survival, CNR has abandoned its historical Christian identity and character: "New Rochelle survives, but it is not the same college."[19]

The College of New Rochelle began in 1904 as the first Catholic college for women in the state of New York, a state where women were not enfranchised until 1920. It was founded by the Order of St. Ursula, led by Mother Irene Gill. Challenged by the changing roles of Catholic colleges, women's colleges, and liberal arts colleges, CNR added graduate programs in 1969, the School of New Resources (primarily a continuing education enterprise for adult learners) in 1972, and a School of Nursing in 1976. The original program of the small, Catholic, women's college is today that of the School of Arts and Sciences. It is still a women's liberal arts college, but the majority of its students are no longer Catholic. Altogether, the CNR now enrolls about seven thousand students on six campuses, including the original New Rochelle site. Fewer than five hundred students are registered in the School of Arts and Sciences in New Rochelle: one could argue that the "main" campus has, in some demographic and fiscal senses, become peripheral. And yet, it still seems to be seen by just about everyone at CNR as the primary carrier of the mission and vision of the entire conglomerate college.

A very large proportion of CNR's students receive some form of financial aid, including about 80% in the School of Arts and Sciences. The comprehensive cost for full-time students in 2008–9 is about $32,400.

New Rochelle is a pleasant suburban city some twenty miles north of Manhattan. The College's New Rochelle campus is located in a residential neighborhood, not far from a small downtown area, which has itself seen some dramatic redevelopment in the past decade. The campus is mostly a cluster of harmonious Gothic structures, built of a rough-finished light gray stone. At the core of the campus is the nineteenth-century Leland Castle, a Gothic revival residential mansion dating from the 1850s. The castle has housed a number of the college's operations over the years and continues to be the home of its senior central administrative offices. The New Rochelle campus of CNR makes the college look considerably smaller than it actually is, since the great majority of students take their classes in the cluster of other facilities scattered in three boroughs of New York

City: Brooklyn, Manhattan, and the Bronx. More than two-thirds of the overall student population, including the School of Arts and Sciences, are students of color; white students are a distinct minority. So, for example, one visible and popular program of the CNR Office of Campus Ministry is the CNR Gospel Choir, which welcomes students of all races and colors but is predominantly African American.

CNR takes pride in its status as the first Catholic women's college in New York, and it is apparent to today's visitor that the School of Arts and Sciences has remained focused on that identity (the other schools are co-educational). It is important to CNR students, faculty, and administration that it began as a women's college and that its liberal arts unit retains that identity. Thus, the "About CNR" section of the college's Web site features a section on the institution as a women's college. Even though the largest three of its four units are open to men, the site notes that women outnumber men significantly in the schools of Nursing, New Resources, and the Graduate School; that faculty, administrators, and fellow students offer important role models for women; and that female students who attend women's colleges have statistically higher earnings than those who do not. Notably, however, when I spoke to a small group of student leaders from the School of Arts and Sciences in February 2007, most of them told me that they had not known CNR was a single-sex institution when they applied for admission there. Although that group was selected by the director of Campus Ministry, Helen Wolf, as excellent students who had been particularly active in religious affairs on campus, none of them was Roman Catholic. The majority were women of color, who described themselves as "Pentecostal" in religious affiliation. All of them, however, were aware that CNR was a Catholic institution and that had figured in their choice of a college. They spoke with passion about the local and international service programs sponsored by the Office of Campus Ministry. They believe that, regardless of their particular religious backgrounds, they all learned something about religion, and specifically about Catholicism, while at CNR. They mentioned that they knew many students who had been drawn, or redrawn, toward Catholicism while at the college.

The College of New Rochelle emphasizes the quality of individualized attention students receive, especially but not exclusively in the School of Arts and Sciences. Also often cited are a strong cooperative spirit, and the development of strong, independent women leaders. Increasingly that theme includes the importance of leadership development in students from traditionally underrepresented groups, especially black women. On the New Rochelle campus, there seems to me to remain a tradition of female students (and faculty and administrators) interacting with each other, and with male peers and leaders, with more assertiveness than in many coeducational settings, especially in academic or governance conversations. Women at New Rochelle, it is my subjective impression, grow more accustomed to diplomacy without excessive delicacy and cultivate a habitual pattern of interacting with others with friendly firmness.

Is today's College of New Rochelle an Ursuline university? Is it distinctively Catholic? Is it, in fact, even Christian? Mr. Burtchaell would emphatically answer all these questions in the negative. In *The Dying of the Light,* he seems to focus with particular harshness on Catholic institutions (his own background is as a Catholic higher educator). The college, on the other hand, would affirm all these affiliations, contending that its Catholicism has evolved to fit the needs of the twenty-first century. Thus, for example, the official mission statement approved by the board of trustees in 1991, begins: "The College of New Rochelle, founded in 1904 by the Ursuline Order, is an independent College which is Catholic in origin and heritage." A few sentences later, it defines the contemporary implications of that Catholic heritage:

> The College is committed to a respect and concern for each individual. . . . It encourages the examination of values through the creative and responsible use of reason. The College strives to articulate its academic tradition and religious heritage in ways that are consonant with the best contemporary understandings of both. It provides opportunities for spiritual growth in a context of freedom and ecumenism. Finally, with justice as its guiding principle, the College tries to respond to the needs of society through its educational programs and service activities."[20]

A faculty member says, "This is a holistic community that is sensitive to the physical, intellectual, social, and spiritual development of its members. . . . The community honors its founding principles and its mission to educate the underserved, particularly women."[21]

Burtchaell is especially contemptuous of such language. He castigates the substitution of words and phrases such as "the examination of values," "religious heritage," and "spiritual growth" for the more demanding and precise teachings of the Magisterium: "Within the degraded rhetoric of American higher education, this ranks with the literary masters."[22] From his perspective, the college began in the 1960s to turn from a past that now embarrassed it: "'Catholic' had come to evoke everything the college was happy to have left behind."[23] However CNR's Web site has, in the section entitled "About CNR" an essay entitled "Ursuline Heritage," excerpted from a history of the college by James T. Schleifer. This essay discusses, at some length, the history of the Ursulines beginning in 1535. It thoroughly traces the work of Mother Irene Gill and her colleagues in establishing the college. But the section of the book selected for inclusion for public consumption on the Web site ends with the founding of CNR in 1904. Mr. Schleifer cites as Ursuline characteristics that still animate CNR "the legacy of resolute action, of confident innovation, of service in the world, and of faithful adaptation to new times."[24]

From the Burtchaellian perspective, the principle leader in the college's move from Catholic to secular is Sister Dorothy Ann Kelly, PhD, herself an Ursuline, who served the college as acting president, then full president, from 1971 until 1997—a remarkable tenure in contemporary American higher education. I had the opportunity to speak at some length with Sister Dorothy about many of these issues.[25] She noted that the college has a wider appeal now than it did a half century ago, both for principled and for pragmatic reasons, looking beyond the eighteen-year-old Catholic girl. Today's CNR student body is more diverse than in the past and more ecumenical—many of CNR's contemporary students, Sister Dorothy noted, are African Americans and many have a Baptist or similar religious heritage, especially in the School of New Resources. In the graduate program, a very large proportion of the faculty is Jewish. A growing contingent of students is of Hispanic heritage, and many of those students practice a Pentecostal Christianity. The faculty maintains a strong tradition of caring for the students and thinking about the role of personal, social, and religious values in undergraduate learning. The college continues to offer opportunities for spiritual contemplation and growth. It sponsors religious services and even maintains space for quiet contemplative prayer on each of its branch campuses. In New Rochelle, CNR offers an optional daily and Sunday mass. Perhaps 10% of the student body participates in these liturgical offerings, as well as a substantial contingent from the surrounding community. She believes that the College of New Rochelle was founded on a basis of respect for religion and for women, and that founding characteristic remains essential to the college today. CNR is qualitatively different from secular institutions in its atmosphere of spirituality and interpersonal caring and in the pervasive importance of religion and spirituality on campus and in the classroom. Part of the blend of faith and reason in class has to do with how the teachers treat their students, as well as an intellectual perspective on the material covered in a course. The college offers a value-centered education, and one of its strongest values is empowering women—giving them the tools to succeed in life. This is part of the college's religious stance, although it is not specifically Catholic.

At the same time, Dr. Kelly says, the institution affirms freedom in its intellectual offerings and does not see itself as moving backward toward either a subservient role for women or an older image of the church-related college. The college helps to promote a local interreligious group of clergy, but its former chief executive notes that not all of the nearby congregations participate. She characterizes the current population of the college as not a church-going crowd, except on the occasion of big events, or during significant crises. The college has created a niche for itself, in the middle of contemporary Catholic colleges. It needs not only to attract new populations, including new immigrant groups who may not be Catholic, but at the same time to affirm its Catholic heritage and its belief in the doctrine of Aquinas that faith and reason reinforce each other. She noted that only a relatively small proportion of the college's entire student body lives on campus, and those students, she feels, do not find themselves living under very strict behavioral regulations. The college does not, however, tolerate alcohol or drug use by students on campus.

As at other colleges I visited, I asked Sister Dorothy what would happen if a student came to the administration seeking to found a campus student organization to advocate for abortion rights. Her response was unequivocal: the college would tell the student why such a cause violated the core values of CNR, and if the student remained unpersuaded, she would be told she could not publicly advocate for this cause. A second standard query concerning the status of gay students on campus, however, produced the answer that they would be regarded more favorably and not expelled. Students with whom I spoke described the campus residence life as "restrained." They felt that there are some fairly traditional rules but that the students generally accept them as appropriate to a religious college.

Sister Dorothy believes that CNR's primary competition comes from coeducational Catholic colleges and universities, institutions such as Fordham and nearby (formerly male, now coeducational) Iona. Some of CNR's students have also considered attending two-year institutions such as Westchester Community College. The college does not compete for students with the top tier of prestigious women's colleges. (A recent college guide cites the SAT math/verbal scores of new students in the School of Arts and Sciences and the School of Nursing as 480/460, and the ACT as 18.)

I asked this former president what she saw in the coming years for Ursuline higher education. She believes that there is, in fact, a future for collegiate work for her order, but there will be fewer and fewer sisters in the short term. Ursuline education will have to become even less exclusive, even more inclusive. She envisions a world where perhaps 10% of the students at urban colleges like CNR would be Caucasian. This is a different world from that of the past or the present, and one with different expectations for a college education. And she envisions a continuing sharp rise in the requirements on the college to provide scholarship aid for more and more of its students.

In a subsequent interview, I asked Joan Bristol, the current vice president for student services, about many of these issues. Bristol has been at CNR, like former President Kelly, more than three decades. During that time, the core of the college, she believes, has remained constant. She affirmed that the college's mission as an Ursuline institution is the "essence of who we are, how we act, and what we do." Student service policies and services stress inclusiveness and at the same time honor the specific theology of the Catholic faith. The college seeks to honor the value of every human being. She estimated that 90% of the students were religious (not just "spiritual"), and most of the college's population believes in God. For some of the faculty, Vice President Bristol believes, faith and reason still are linked in the classroom; for others, this link has been severed. She concludes that the college is now seeking to refine its understanding of this linkage. Many of the core values that define the true essence of being Catholic are widely shared across the college, including among non-Catholic members of the community.

Student behavior at CNR is allowed tremendous freedom, within the bonds of security and safety. The college does not cling to antiquated rules. Like Sister Dorothy, she does not believe that advocacy for abortion rights would have a place in an institution as respectful of its Catholic tradition as this one. Nor does she believe that an overt GLBT group would be officially sanctioned on campus, but that such a group that functioned off campus would be acceptable. On this issue, she felt (and I agree), CNR was considerably different from the "new Catholic" colleges such as Thomas

Aquinas. Ms. Bristol mentioned Pace and the College of Mount Saint Vincent as competing colleges. (Students with whom I spoke mentioned some of the CUNY campuses, Albertus Magnus, D'Youville, and Mount Saint Vincent also.) She felt that the largest challenge the college now faces is one of resources.

I also had an opportunity to speak with Helen Wolf, the director of Campus Ministry at CNR. She, too, believes that its Catholic identity defines the College of New Rochelle and that the institution is guided by its social mission to advocate and practice values such as peace and justice and service to others. The college has a strong program of peer ministers, most of whom are not Catholic. She estimated, as did Vice President Bristol, that 90% of CNR's students were, in some respect, religious, perhaps 40% Catholic. While she could not speak of the relationship between faith and reason in the classroom, she does see that relationship as a strong one in the college's co-curricular life. She noted that there is a straight and gay alliance on campus. And she believes that some members of the faculty would prefer that the school be "less Catholic." She also believes that the college's current president, Dr. Stephen Sweeny (who came to CNR in the late 1970s and has served in several capacities since that time) has reaffirmed its Catholic identity. Ms. Wolf estimates that perhaps 125 CNR students attend mass on a fairly regular basis. She notes that a large percentage of CNR's students, including non-Catholics, attended Catholic high schools. Her belief is that the college supports the Office of Campus Ministry strongly, with a relatively large professional staff. Her office has a range of community service outreach programs, such as a soup kitchen, a program for English as a second language, a meal delivery program, and an after-school music program. It also takes an active role in promoting peace and justice offerings such as the "peace builders" program that both prays about and takes action on issues of peace and justice both locally and internationally. "The Plunge" is a program wherein students and staff use their breaks to travel to Mexico and to depressed areas of the United States to participate in service activities. Campus Ministry has also been involved in Habitat for Humanity. And the Office of Campus Ministry offers spiritual development programs including instruction in receiving the sacraments and joining the Catholic Church. It sponsors the peer ministry and oversees worship at CNR. It is also the home of both the CNR Chapel Choir (which has a liturgical mission) and the (apparently more widely known and popular) CNR Gospel Choir mentioned earlier.

Is this an Ursuline college? Is it Catholic? Is it Christian? It is glib to say that the College of New Rochelle is not your mother's Catholic women's college—but that is a true statement. There are fewer and fewer Ursuline nuns on campus, and those are no longer visually distinguishable from their secular colleagues. The college does not impose a religious test, of any sort, on its faculty, or require a student behavioral pledge. There is no institutional mandate to link faith and learning in every course. The students, too, do not "look" like yesterday's pupils in a suburban Catholic women's college. And most of those students, and many of their faculty, are not members of the Catholic Church. But most of CNR's people see themselves as working at or attending a Catholic institution. They characterize that affiliation as one that honors the school's long Ursuline tradition, ministers to the spiritual needs and development of its students, promotes thoughtful and active social engagement in personal and political spheres, and fosters an atmosphere of affection and attentive caring in personal interactions. The Order of St. Ursula was founded in the early 1500s by Angela Merica. St. Angela and her Company of Women did not withdraw from the world or shirk from change. She urged her followers to "Act, bestir yourselves," and encouraged a flexible and future-directed stance: "If, with change of times and circumstances, it becomes necessary to make fresh rules, or to alter anything, then do it with prudence, after taking good advice."[26] The College of New Rochelle today, nearly a half millennium later, remains true to these admonitions to take action, and to change with the times. St. Angela would be pleased.

Everything Old Is New Again: Thomas Aquinas College, Santa Paula, California

Thomas Aquinas College is a "new" Roman Catholic college. It is new in several senses: the college offers a curriculum and a college life program that are radically different from those of virtually all other American institutions of higher education, Catholic or not. Thomas Aquinas is physically new, occupying a recently constructed campus in Santa Paula, California. And it is new as an incorporated entity, having come into existence less than a half century ago. But Thomas Aquinas College is perhaps most radically "new" in its overt passion for the old. The college describes the vision of its founders who sought to return to an earlier philosophy of higher learning: "They wanted not to return to some earlier form of education in America, but to something that resonated with the kind of academic excellence that flourished in ancient Greece or in the great medieval universities in Europe. Simply put, they wanted to return not to the 1950's, but to the 1350's."[27]

How did a college that overtly aspired to return to a six-hundred-year-old ideal and model of learning come into existence, and what does it look like today, about four decades after its founding?

The history of Thomas Aquinas College is deeply revealing. It tells the story not just of this small, fascinating place, but also of much of the discussion of the nature and direction of Catholic higher education in America since World War II.

In the 1960s a group of lay and clerical Catholic faculty was teaching at St. Mary's College in Moraga, California, across the bay from San Francisco and not too far from the University of California at Berkeley, where other memorable events were also taking place at the same time. These professors were linked to a program called the "Integrated Liberal Arts" that was offered, as an option, to some of the (all male) students at St. Mary's.[28] It was overtly modeled upon, and had several links to, the Great Books curriculum at St. John's College in Annapolis, which had, in turn, grown out of curricular engagement with primary texts of primary importance in Western civilization at Columbia University and the University of Chicago. This small group of faculty members combined a keen interest in the Great Books approach with an equally sharp sense that Catholic education in America was increasingly secularized, and losing its devotion to a valued and unique Catholic tradition of higher learning. The group began a series of discussions that took the form of seeking to define an ideal Catholic and liberal arts college.

St. Mary's College, perhaps not coincidentally, is one of three Catholic colleges excoriated in James Burtchaell's *The Dying of the Light: The Disengagement of Colleges and Universities from Their Christian Churches.* Noting the foundation of Thomas Aquinas College by disenchanted faculty from St. Mary's, Burtchaell says of St. Mary's that its "definition of [academic] excellence denied any essential place to the Catholic Church or its faith."[29]

From these conversations came a draft of a statement of educational principles entitled "A Proposal for the Fulfillment of Catholic Liberal Education," which came to be known as the "Blue Book." In this document, the case is made for the link between faith and reason, between Catholic collegiate instruction and liberal education. It proposed a curriculum based on the St. John's model and the Great Books. Classes would all be small tutorials conducted in the Socratic discussion mode. All students would cover the same materials, all primary texts, in the same order: there were to be no electives, no majors, no minors. Thus, each class could presume an identical set of predecessors and successors, and the instructional program could be seen as an integrated whole. Faculty members would teach across the curriculum: they would not be affiliated with specialized academic departments such as English, philosophy, physics, and psychology.

This program, however, differed from the St. John's model (still, of course, practiced in both Annapolis, Maryland, and Santa Fe, New Mexico) in an important way: it was overtly linked to Roman Catholicism. The Great Books were to be selected from a Catholic perspective—both great Catholic writers, such as St. Thomas and St. Augustine, and authors who overtly challenged the Catholic tradition, and whose arguments, therefore, needed to be understood in order to be rebutted—for example, Machiavelli. It is assumed that students will discover for themselves the falseness of these authors.[30] Theological and philosophical works would be central to the curriculum. Moreover, a Catholic style of living would prevail: Catholic worship would take place on campus and a strong code of Catholic morality would be firmly enforced. The proposal in the "Blue Book" is startling in its willingness to envision moving in a radically different direction from other American colleges and universities. It is extraordinarily shocking in that its creators were willing to hazard their professional lives to actually put it in place. The result of that powerful commitment is today's Thomas Aquinas College.

It did not happen overnight. In 1968 the group that would become the college was incorporated as the Institute for Christian Education, and a relatively small but important major gift came for the start up of the incipient college from a conservative businessman and philanthropist. (With its firm code of conduct, classical curriculum, and vigorous religious life, Thomas Aquinas has always had a strong appeal to individuals on the political right: in spring of 2007, for example, the college was selected as one of the "Top 10" institutions by the Young America's Foundation, a conservative group headquartered at the Ronald Reagan Ranch.) A gala founding dinner was held in San Francisco in 1970 at the Fairmont Hotel, at which the keynote speaker was Archbishop Fulton J. Sheen. The college was offered use of the campus of Dominican College of San Rafael, but before Thomas Aquinas actually began operations, Dominican College retracted its offer. The cardinal archbishop of Los Angeles was persuaded to help the institution relocate in Southern California, and facilitated the leasing of facilities at the former novitiate and seminary of the Claretian order. In September 1971 thirty-three pioneering students registered, with four faculty members, and in 1975 the first class graduated.

By then, Thomas Aquinas was seeking a campus of its own and, among other options, came to investigate a property in an isolated and lovely canyon outside the town of Santa Paula. Complex negotiations followed, given greater urgency by the sale of the Claretian property in 1977. Major funding was needed, and seemingly miraculously, substantial gifts were forthcoming. Ground was broken in January 1978. The campus operated from temporary, modular buildings during the 1978 and 1979 academic years, but construction moved forward, and a campus took shape. The college incurred substantial financial obligations in making this move and in building a whole new campus from scratch. During the 1980s, the college matured, winning full accreditation in 1981. A campaign to recruit more students was given a boost by the appearance of Mother Teresa as graduation speaker in 1982. The college began a pattern of steady growth that took it from about 120 students in the early 1980s to about 350 today—the maximum the physical campus and the character of the academic program seem to permit. In the early 1990s the founding president, Dr. Ronald McArthur was succeeded by his former student from St. Mary's College, Dr. Thomas Dillon, who remained chief executive until his death in 2009.

The campus of Thomas Aquinas College today is harmonious and integrated. Buildings are generally of modest dimensions, in the California mission style. Currently, construction is moving forward on a campus chapel, which will serve both as a physical and spiritual anchor for the college and as a faculty building. One particularly stunning feature of the physical plant is the seventeenth-century Spanish ceiling of the St. Bernadine of Siena Library, which was donated by William P. Clark Jr., former secretary of the interior and national security advisor under President Reagan, and whose father was the real estate agent for the sellers of the property on which the college is now sited.

Students and faculty at Thomas Aquinas College are as distinctive in their personal style as in their academic program. Unlike, for example, nearby Westmont College, where students appear indistinguishable from middle-of-the-road collegiate peers at other Southern California institutions, Thomas Aquinas students look different. Not all the men wear neckties to class, but I noticed some with ties in every class I visited. All were extremely neat and conservative in personal appearance. T-Shirts are not permitted in class, nor are sandals without socks. Women students wore skirts, of a more-than-demure length. Male faculty members tended to teach in coats and ties and females in equally traditional garb. When I asked students about the dress code (e.g., skirts, collared shirts), they affirmed that they understood, and endorsed, the notion that respectful dress was a way of indicating their respect for their teachers and the classroom work of the college. Similarly, in class, students refer to each other as "Mr." or "Miss," as in "Miss Jones, do you think Shakespeare might have meant something else by that line?" The students with whom I spoke affirmed that the college's seminar methodology taught them to carry the classroom discussion and to grill each other rigorously.

I attended several classes at Thomas Aquinas. Indeed, more than any other college I have visited, Thomas Aquinas is eager to put guests into the classroom to watch students interact with each other and with their instructors. The Socratic method remains pervasive: faculty tutors ask questions, sometimes clarify the implications of answers, but do not lecture or adopt an authoritarian stance. When asked a direct question by students, some faculty will respond with an answer, others will frame a question in return that will move the class toward an answer. It is clear to a campus visitor that not every faculty member at the college is always a perfect Socratic tutor, nor is every student equally prepared and articulate. The standard, however, is remarkably high. Clearly, expectations that students will have done the reading thoroughly and carefully and will have grappled seriously with it, are extremely high. Of course, not every student is equally comfortable with, for example, Archimedes and Aristophanes, or with Dalton and Dante. The classroom atmosphere is challenging but always respectful, usually fairly formal. I noted that in many classes, there are often fairly long, contemplative periods of silence following questions: students (and faculty) are comfortable giving each other time to think through responses.

Of thirty-seven individuals listed as members of the faculty in 2006, fifteen hold the BA degree from Thomas Aquinas College and five from St. Mary's College. In addition, six hold the PhD (or are candidates for that degree) from the University of Notre Dame, six from the Université

Laval (Quebec), and five from the Catholic University of America. Catholic members of the faculty take an "Oath of Fidelity" upon beginning their service to the college. They affirm that they shall always maintain communion with the Catholic Church in word and action; preserve the faith, hand it on, and make it shine forth; look after the observance of all ecclesiastical laws; and act with Christian obedience to that which is expressed by the Church's rulers. Prospective faculty members are asked to provide a thoughtful essay detailing their philosophy of collegiate education. All faculty members are called "tutors": there is no additional rank or formal tenure.

Because the curriculum at Thomas Aquinas is universal and nonelective, the entire curricular program of the college can be listed in a very few pages: the complete list of four years of readings fills six pages of the college bulletin. Schematically, it consists of two years of language tutorial (Latin), logic (one year), four years of mathematics, a year of music, three years of philosophy and four of theology, four years of laboratory science, and four years of seminar (literature, history, philosophy, more philosophy, and theology). As a sample, here are the authors read in the sophomore year by all Thomas Aquinas College students:

> *Seminar*—Vergil, Lucretius, Cicero, Livy, Plutarch, Tacitus, Epictetus, St. Augustine, Boethius, Dante, Chaucer, Spencer, St. Thomas Aquinas
>
> *Language*—Wheelock (*Latin: An Introductory Course Based on Ancient Authors*), Martin of Denmark, Horace, Cicero, St. Thomas Aquinas
>
> *Mathematics*—Plato, Ptolemy, Copernicus, Apollonius, Kepler, Archimedes
>
> *Laboratory*—Aristotle, St. Thomas Aquinas, Lavoisier, Avogadro, Dalton, Gay-Lussac, Pascal, miscellaneous scientific papers by various authors
>
> *Philosophy*—Pre-Socratic philosophers, Aristotle
>
> *Theology*—St. Augustine, St. Athanasius, Gaunilo, St. Anselm, St. John Damascene

This is not a curriculum for either teachers or students who are faint of heart. The college, moreover, makes an unremitting effort to approach these authors and their most important works from a Christian, Catholic perspective. Theology is acknowledged as chief among the academic disciplines. The truth, the college teaches, is discovered, not invented. It is illuminated always by faith. Thus, the catalog affirms, "Christ is the truth, revelation tells us, and it is in the wisdom of His words that men are made truly free. The truth we glean from nature is truth seen through a mirror darkly compared the Light from above. The Christian orders his mind and soul to supernatural truth. Christian liberal education has divine wisdom as its ultimate objective."[31]

President Dillon, Dean Michael McLean, as well as other student, faculty, and staff members of the Thomas Aquinas community, are thoughtful and articulate about their belief in the compatibility of reason and faith. Faith leads one to truth; scholarship leads one to truth. If faith and scholarship seem incompatible, a seeker is misunderstanding one or both of them. The dean stressed that the college's confidence in the unity of the truths derived from faith and from learning is the inheritance of its namesake, St. Thomas Aquinas. He affirmed his belief that that which is true is also that which is beautiful and good. The *College Bulletin* (2007) begins with a portrait of "St. Thomas, Our Patron," noting that "in him is the consummate union of sanctity and intellect."

Not all Thomas Aquinas College students are Catholic, nor is there any regulation that all faculty be. As the Bulletin notes, "Faith is a gift. We rejoice with those who have it and we welcome those without it."[32] Non-Catholic faculty members cannot teach theology at the college. Both the president and the faculty with whom I spoke estimate that perhaps three current faculty members and ten to fifteen students are not Catholic. There is some emphasis and pride across campus constituencies on the frequency with which students who come to Thomas Aquinas College as non-Catholics embrace the faith during their undergraduate careers. There is a firm belief that this happens with far greater frequency than the opposite. Similarly, the college takes great pride in the number of its graduates who choose a religious career—as of 2006, 11% of its graduates. In the grand commemorative volume published in 2006 to commemorate the thirty-fifth anniversary of the college's founding, a section profiles selected individuals who have entered fields such as law, education, medicine, journalism, or business. But it lists each graduate who has entered a religious profession.

Thomas Aquinas College offers mass three times daily, as well as other liturgies, devotions, confessions, and spiritual exercises. None of these is required, but all seem well attended. Social regulations are unambiguous, rigorous, and enforced. As the *Bulletin* notes, "Time-honored Christian values, not contemporary permissiveness, are the basis for these rules."[33] Thus, men's and women's residence halls are always off limits to the opposite gender, and alcohol and drugs are strictly forbidden on campus. Students who violate such proscriptions are expelled. I asked a group of students with whom I met what they thought would happen to a student who openly advocated for abortion rights. They were quite clear that such advocacy would not be tolerated: such a student would be counseled regarding the church's position on this issue, urged to adhere to that position, and, if intransigent, told she or he must leave the college community. President Dillon gave exactly the same answer to a similar query. In both cases, it was clear that the understanding was that the college was in a position of moral instruction, not one of eagerly policing student life. President Dillon and the students with whom I met agree that moral standards are high and share the perception that happiness is to be found in living the virtuous life.

Campus life at Thomas Aquinas College is certainly not dour, although the prevailing tone is surely serious. The arts, especially music, are encouraged and cultivated both on campus and through occasional field trips. A recent issue of the *Alumni News* focused on music and included a discussion of the four to six annual "Schubertiades" at which members of the college community, as individuals or in ensembles, perform.[34] There is a lively and apparently near universal program of informal, intramural sports, although there is no interscholastic athletic program. The college's setting encourages hiking and other outdoor recreational options. There are dances, picnics, movies, drama and poetry readings, and the like.

The comprehensive cost of a year at Thomas Aquinas College in 2007 is $25,300, and 72% of the students receive some form of financial aid. The current student body of 359 is evenly divided between men and women, with 129 students from California, and a very even spread of students from forty additional states (Virginia, with 14 students, has the second greatest number). Students come from several foreign nations, with Canada sending 23. The ACT average of Thomas Aquinas students is 27; the SAT is 1293, with the middle 50% running from 1220 to 1390. The college sponsors a thriving summer program for high school students, giving them an introduction to the methods and materials of the collegiate curriculum. When asked about comparable institutions, the faculty noted some of the other smaller, "new" Catholic institutions such as Christendom College. Faculty and President Dillon cited St. Johns, and the latter added the University of Dallas as an institution that sometimes competes with Thomas Aquinas College for students.

In the context of our discussion of Roman Catholic colleges and universities, Thomas Aquinas is, perhaps, at a polar opposite of the College of New Rochelle. The latter institution has expanded into several areas overtly outside the liberal arts, has sought to manifest its Catholic heritage by embracing a diverse faculty and student body and championing social justice, and imposes few personal behavioral standards beyond those of safety and civility on its constituents. Thomas Aquinas, on the distinct other hand, has chosen to remain very small, has a rigorously unitary liberal arts curriculum, and is unabashed in promulgating a strict, and strictly Catholic, style of living.

Thomas Aquinas College faces an admissions challenge that many colleges, large and small, would love to have. It believes it should be able to offer its unique program to any and all students who seek it and who have the intellect and the character to complete it with success. But in recent years there have been two such applicants for every spot available in the entering class if the college is to remain at 350 students, which all agree is the desirable size. This paradox has led to some initial and very preliminary contemplation of the possibility of creating another campus or campuses. This option seems more desirable than any serious additional growth at the Santa Paula site. Thomas Aquinas College is a "new" Catholic college, but soon it may find itself generating even newer offshoots.

PART II

Baptist Schools

There are more Baptist colleges and universities in contemporary America than are affiliated with any other Protestant denomination. We begin by looking at two schools with strong Baptist links that are revealing to compare—both the schools and the links. In many ways, Anderson University and Baylor University are a study in contrasts, although they share deeply some commitments and goals. Both are Baptist universities in the South, but they are not both Southern Baptist colleges: Anderson remains closely linked to its state of South Carolina and the national Southern Baptist Convention; Baylor has, while remaining deeply Baptist, moved away dramatically from those linkages. Baylor prides itself on being a "moderate" Baptist university, but at Anderson such a description would be anathema. The Texas university is large and aspires to status as a premier doctoral research university; Anderson, which within the not-too-distant past was a two-year college, is much smaller and has only recently moved to create a few master's-level options. Baylor lives within a city; Anderson's setting is considerably more bucolic. But both, it turns out, are deeply committed to the simultaneous strengthening of religious roots and academic achievement. Baylor's route to this goal has been very public and often seriously contentious; Anderson has made a virtue of civility and is far less visible.

4 | Pro Ecclesia, Pro Texana

Baylor University, Waco, Texas

With more than fourteen thousand students, Baylor is the largest Baptist university in the world. Arguably, it is also the only research-intensive evangelical Christian institution in contemporary America. Behind the seemingly innocuous phrase " research-intensive evangelical Christian" is a story of considerable intensity and substantial interest to any student of contemporary religious colleges and universities.

Baylor is a fascinating, appropriate, and instructive institution with which to begin our in-depth look at evangelical Christian colleges and universities. In part because of its size, and also partially because of its historical development, Baylor provides a broad introduction to many of the issues that surface throughout contemporary American religious higher education. These include such themes as the integration of faith and learning in the curriculum; the tension and the synergy between the impulse toward wide recognition for conventional academic excellence and the desire to remain deeply rooted in a religious heritage; the issue of theological or faith tests in the matter of faculty hiring and student recruiting; relations with external constituencies, especially denominational groups; dealing with scandals and embarrassing public relations challenges; and the problems and values of growth, of graduate education, and of heightened funding expectations. Baylor has explored and often wrestled with all these issues, generally in a very public way, over the past few years. It is, in that respect, something of a microcosm of the larger universe of twenty-first-century American Christian collegiate education.

The university traces its origins to 1841, when the Union Baptist Association decided to found a Baptist university in Texas. One of the proponents of this proposal was Judge R. E. B. Baylor, who gave the institution its name. The then Republic of Texas granted a charter in 1845: Baylor is the oldest institution of higher learning in Texas. Originally located in Independence, the young institution moved to Waco, a railroad town, in 1885. Its women's branch moved to Belton, and later changed its name to the University of Mary Hardin-Baylor, its present identity and now a wholly separate institution. Back in Waco, Baylor University itself shortly began to admit women, becoming coeducational in 1887. One early president at Baylor was George Washington Baines, a great-grandfather of Lyndon Baines Johnson. A college of medicine has been affiliated with Baylor since the beginning of the twentieth century, an affiliation that remains today, although the Baylor College of Medicine is now legally independent and located in Houston. Baylor's athletic teams are the "Bears," and two of the school's mascot American brown bears live in an on-campus habitat.[1] Baylor is home to the Armstrong Browning Library, a dignified on-campus facility, which has an extensive collection of materials and artifacts related to the Victorian poets Robert and Elizabeth Barrett Browning. The collection of Browning materials is reputed to be the world's largest, and there are as well sixty-two stained glass windows illuminating aspects of their works.[2]

Early in the 1990s, Texas Baptists were riven by a split between the fundamentalist branch of the church and its more moderate followers. In 1991 Baylor altered the terms of its charter, through the Texas legislature, seeking a moderate bulwark against the apparent threat of a fundamentalist takeover. In that same year, Texas Baptists as a whole split into two large groups, the Southern Baptists of Texas Convention, which is affiliated with the Southern Baptist Convention (the conservative wing of the church) and the Baptist General Convention of Texas, the more moderate branch, with which Baylor is linked. The latter group by statute continues to elect 25% of the members of the university's all Baptist Board. At this same vexed time in Texas Baptist history, Baylor sought and received a charter to launch its own theological seminary, named the George W. Truett Theological Seminary. The first class came to the seminary three years later, in autumn 1994. The seminary is in some part also an effort to maintain Baylor in the moderate Baptist camp, in the face of fundamentalist challenges.

In 1995 Robert Sloan became president at Baylor, succeeding Herbert Reynolds, who served from 1981to 1995 (and, thus, managed Baylor's distancing itself from the Southern Baptist Convention). Five years into his term of office, at the dawn of the new millennium, President Sloan moved Baylor into a comprehensive planning and institutional reenvisioning process. About two years later, the outcome of this effort was a new "vision" for Baylor, entitled "Baylor 2012" designed to guide the university through the decade. This plan aroused strong emotions from its launching and continues to be controversial today. I visited Baylor in 2008, at roughly the midpoint of this ten-year-long endeavor. The university had at that point a new president and a new provost, and clearly the controversy surrounding Baylor 2012 played a significant part in the departure of the senior administration that led the planning effort.

Baylor 2012 consists of twelve "imperatives," each of which contains a handful of explicit measurable outcomes.[3] At its core, though, the plan is both simple and daring. It basically affirms two goals. First, Baylor University aims to move into the "top tier" of American research universities—"the upper echelons of higher education." At BU, unequivocally, this has meant the top tier of PhD-granting research institutions. Second, BU vowed to maintain and even strengthen its Baptist, Christian character: "retaining and remaining grounded in our strong Christian commitment."

Thus, for example, one imperative is "Develop a World-Class Faculty." The description of this item states: "Baylor will continue to recruit faculty from a variety of backgrounds capable of achieving the best of scholarship, both in teaching and research. We will recruit high-potential junior faculty as well as highly esteemed senior faculty who embrace the Christian faith and are knowledgeable of the Christian intellectual tradition. Many of these faculty will especially exemplify the integration of faith and learning in their disciplines and in interdisciplinary or collaborative activities. A significant number of Baylor faculty will continue to be recognized as leaders in their respective disciplines and in productive, cutting-edge research."

Of the five "steps being taken" to achieve this imperative, the first is "recruit and retain faculty members who combine strong teaching abilities with a commitment to scholarship and to the Christian mission of Baylor."[4] In spring 2008 a significant controversy erupted at Baylor, when the president and provost rejected the tenure bids of twelve out of thirty candidates, nine of whom had been approved by their academic departments and the university tenure committee. President John Lilley and Provost J. Randall O'Brien rejected the twelve faculty members because they judged that their research records were insufficient to meet the goals of Baylor 2012. In reaction, in May 2008 the faculty senate passed by a margin of 29–0 a resolution strongly critical of the university's administration and decrying a "failure of shared governance."[5] This controversy, too, led shortly to a leadership turnover.

Similarly, under the imperative concerning student life is a call to "expand the chapel program and create generation-specific spiritual activities." In this dual set of aspirations—strengthening both scholarly repute and faith commitment simultaneously—Baylor sees itself as swimming against the current. I believe they are, more or less, correct in that perception. Institutions that have risen to the upper echelon of national research universities have tended to lose or weaken significantly their religious ties. Those which have maintained a pervasive and powerful faith commitment have either remained in the ranks of smaller, liberal arts colleges or not ascended to the top tier in scholarly repute. Perhaps the most conspicuous exception to this pattern is the University of Notre Dame, which is, of course, hardly in the evangelical camp. And even at Catholic Notre Dame, some constituents have expressed fear that the university has lost its spiritual bona fides in its quest for national research recognition.[6] Baylor has, in fact, prospered in the academic market place—for example, qualitative profiles of entering students have risen steadily to an impressive SAT cumulative score of 1220, up 50 points since 1999.[7] Baylor also has increased its minority enrollment simultaneously to 29% for entering first-year students in 2007. It has nearly three thousand graduate students and offers seventy-six MA and twenty-two PhD programs and the JD degree. At the same time, BU is unquestionably Baptist and Christian in character. All first-year students are required to attend chapel twice weekly, and there is a six-credit-hour religion requirement (one course in the Christian scriptures, one in the Christian heritage).

Baylor has an explicit faculty hiring religious hierarchy: "Our policy mandates that we look (and this is an ordinal listing) for Baptists, other evangelicals, mainline Protestants, Catholics, Greek-Orthodox, and Jews," writes Baylor's former president Robert B. Sloan Jr.[8] Candidates of any and all other religious traditions (e.g., Muslims, Hindus, Buddhists) and nonbelievers are excluded from consideration. In the interview process, candidates for faculty positions are questioned about their faith, both by their prospective departments and by the provost's office. Later, tenure is accompanied by a reaffirmation by both the candidate and the institution of the centrality and importance of religious beliefs and behavior.[9]

A plan such as Baylor 2012 to strengthen two areas simultaneously offers a daunting and enhanced range of permutations of support or disagreement. Thus, one person may endorse increased strength in scholarship and in religion. Another may be enthusiastic about raising research repute but dubious about strengthening faith commitments. A third may be all for reinforcing Christian ties within the university but leery of the research agenda. And, inevitably, some will be opposed to both. All these reactions, in quite a range of strengths, were aroused by Baylor 2012. Some feared that by its heightened scholarly aspirations, BU would lose its Christian character, whereas others worried that by reaffirming its Baptist heritage, it would sacrifice its claims to serious scholarship. It can be a challenge for the visitor to Baylor to grasp these complexities, and the interpersonal ties and tensions to which they have led, and perhaps an even greater challenge to see through them to the realities of the university today. Many of these perspectives appear in a volume edited by former provost Donald D. Schmeltekopf and Dianna Vitanza, *The Baptist and Christian Character of Baylor.*[10]

Here is what I think I found: bright and enthusiastic students from many backgrounds and with diverse academic interests, many of whom were deeply faithful and most of whom seemed to respect BU's religious tradition; hardworking and ambitious faculty, working to balance a strong teaching commitment with vigorous scholarly aspirations; an administration seeking to create and maintain a series of delicate balances—between past and present, baccalaureate and graduate programs, religious devotion (specifically to Baptist principles and practices) and nonsectarian openness.

I attended Baylor's required chapel during my visit. Chapel is held every Monday and Wednesday morning. Because chapel attendance is required of all first-year students, and the space assigned to this event (a large multipurpose auditorium) is too small to hold all attendees, there are two chapel services back-to-back at ten and eleven o'clock. On the day I was present, there were few nonstudents in evidence, and I was subsequently told by the university chaplain that the great majority of attenders were, in fact, usually freshmen. Even in two groups, the Waco Hall auditorium is crowded, and two large-screen TVs amplified the image of the speakers and displayed the words of the songs performed. Worship began with singing, led by two students and the liturgical director. I observed that most students did join the singing, but rather quietly (students later told me that occasionally the singing becomes passionate and demonstrative). When requested to stand for the opening hymns, some 90–95% of the audience complied. There were several small groups who did not rise. I thought this curious and asked a group of students with whom I met later how they interpreted that behavior. They suggested that most of these nonrisers may have been students who are devout but dislike public demonstrative affirmations of devotion. Others, including the chaplain, were more inclined to believe that the nonparticipants were individuals who were in chapel because it was required but did not wish to worship at all. After the opening songs, the chaplain spoke briefly, followed by the morning's main speaker, the pastor of a local Baptist church. Most students seemed attentive, although there was some reading, quiet talking, doing of homework, and text messaging going on in the hall during the talk. It is clear that required chapel is a strong link to Baylor's Baptist roots. The loss of a chapel requirement is seen by many who are concerned about secularization in religious higher education as a common first step down a slippery slope and has thus been carefully avoided here.[11] At the same time, inevitably some who are required to attend do so only because it is mandatory. This has been a conundrum for institutions—and for chaplains—for generations. There seems no clear pathway to creating the enthusiasm of voluntary attendance and maintaining the community commitment of complete, or nearly complete, participation.

I was able to meet with a small group of Baylor faculty, in a range of disciplines. We spoke primarily about the relation of faith and learning at Baylor, from the professorial perspective. All were in agreement that in their work as counselors and mentors of students, issues of faith arose regularly—helping students to find their calling in life, for example. When the discussion focused more particularly on the relation of faith and learning in the more formal classroom setting, however, greater variety was evident. Some faculty members who teach in the university's "great texts" course see that as an excellent opportunity to raise issues overtly religious (many of the texts themselves, are, of course, religious writings—that of Augustine, for example). Generally, the faculty with whom I spoke felt there was a wide spectrum across BU's courses when it came to the integration of faith and learning. They told me that they looked first for colleagues who would be excellent in their discipline. One faculty member, who had previously taught at Westmont, stated her belief that at Baylor there is a considerably wider range of pedagogical behaviors in this area than at Westmont (discussed in chapter 10). Individuals stressed that they saw each other as, for example, biologists who are Christian, not Christian biologists. (There has been some controversy at BU over the issue of evolution versus intelligent design, but the three proponents of the latter approach at BU were two philosophers and an electrical engineer, not biologists.)[12] In general, the faculty seemed to feel that discussions of the spiritual dimensions of their subject matters tended to emerge more often in small group discussions than in the formal context of in-class work. Faculty members with whom I spoke do not themselves often offer personal religious testimonies in class, and they discourage such demonstrations by their students. They are, they reiterated, first of all scholars. Indeed, they noted that some students are disturbed by what they perceive as the wide variety of religious belief and practice among the faculty. And sometimes parents get exercised over the shifts in their students' religious perspectives while at BU (e.g., one student recently decided to become a Roman Catholic, to the great and vigorous distress of parents). Similarly upsetting to some in the communities around Baylor are teachings that seem to touch on public issues, such as evolution, especially in the sciences. But these faculty members were solidly convinced that Baylor was a place for asking questions, not offering dogmatic answers. They felt safe in that position, and they believe that helps make Baylor a transformative institution for its students.

I did have a chance to meet with some of those students, and they were a very impressive group. Many were from Texas, but others came from distant U.S. cities, and one from Canada. Their majors ranged from biology to great texts, international studies, and philosophy. As always, I asked them where else they had applied to go to college. There was a considerably wider range than I expected: Wheaton; the University of Texas, Austin; Washington University; Air Force Academy; Vanderbilt; McGill; Princeton; Gettysburg. Clearly, neither large nor small, secular nor religious, public nor private institutions dominated this list. The students said they were particularly attracted to the opportunities at BU for interdisciplinary studies: within the Honors College, the Honors Program, the Great Texts Program, and the like. They affirmed their belief that Baylor's undergraduate program was teaching them how to think, and in a way that included both intellectual and spiritual growth. In this group, some came to Baylor because it was a religious university, and some came in spite of that affiliation. It is their sense that many Baylor students grow and change in their religious beliefs during their undergraduate careers here. In general, they felt, students move toward a more intellectual faith and toward becoming engaged in service work.

These students feel that Baylor does have behavioral expectations and that most students, most of the time, behave in accord with them. They particularly mentioned a distaste for drinking alcohol and the "party scene," although they acknowledged that some students did indulge in sexual experimentation, drugs, and drinking, but that was not the dominant campus culture, as they believed it was at some other schools they knew of. They did not know of any dress code but suspected there might be one; in any event, they affirmed, almost everyone dressed reasonably modestly (I would agree).[13] Baylor's first on-campus dance was held in 1996, although there had never apparently been an explicit written prohibition against dancing during the prior century and a half.

Greek life is important at Baylor. The current Greek life Web site lists twenty-one fraternities and eighteen sororities active on campus.[14] Seven of these organizations are affiliated with the National Pan-Hellenic council, a collection of historically African American fraternities and sororities. Greek organizations on the Baylor campus do not have separate residential facilities. About 25% of Baylor's male students are affiliated with fraternities, slightly fewer females.

Baylor currently has eleven residence halls, housing about 35% of the students. The university also maintains four apartment units on campus for students. The goals of Baylor 2012 call for a higher percentage of residential students, but as the population of the university overall has grown dramatically during recent years, residence hall construction has struggled just to keep pace.

The students affirmed that they believed their experiences at Baylor had prepared them to enter the (secular) world. They are not worried about graduate school, jobs, the more challenging and diverse environment of a non-Baptist setting. It is their perception that Baylor represents a kind of middle course between what they termed extreme fundamentalism and extreme secularism. Baylor's aim is to examine everything, including religion, from an intellectual perspective: its Baptist character is not antirational.

These students were very fond and respectful of their teachers. They found them attentive and caring. Several mentioned that their teachers would take them out to coffee. This "personable" attitude they compared to their perception of the University of Texas at Austin, which they believed was far less humane and individualized. It is noteworthy that the students at Baylor speak of larger universities in virtually identical words that students at places such as Westmont, Wheaton, or Calvin speak of institutions the size of Baylor—or students at New Saint Andrews or

Thomas Aquinas use to describe institutions of 1,000–3,500 enrollment. Some of these students were concerned about the way the Baylor administration had treated "dissenters from evolutionary theory" (presumable in the context of the evolution–intelligent design controversy noted earlier). But, they believed, Baylor was a place where individuals and groups who had made mistakes were encouraged to realize their errors and given opportunities to correct them.

Burt Burleson is the university chaplain at Baylor. He came to that position from a ministry in Waco, at a Baptist church attended by many BU students and faculty. He was relatively new on the job when I spoke with him, having served less than one full academic year. He is himself a 1980 graduate of Baylor. Dr. Burleson spends some part of each day in pastoral care functions, meeting with individual students once or twice a day. He serves something of the same function, on an informal basis, with faculty and staff members who want to chat about spiritual matters in their lives. Much spiritual counseling of students, he noted, is done by resident chaplains, from the Baylor Seminary, who serve in each campus residence hall. He also schedules the twice-weekly chapel programs and often appears in them. Chapel services tend to offer a more general Christian program on Mondays and to be more liturgically oriented on Wednesdays. Among the other responsibilities of the chaplain's office are international ministry, dorm groups, missions, retreats, and other ceremonial functions of the university.

The chaplain is enthusiastic about Baylor's program of discipline-specific mission trips—that is, engineering students building something, liberal arts students teaching in their major, and the like. He believes there is great value in the guided reflection that follows such trips: they become educational as well as service ventures.

Dr. Burleson reports that a recent survey found that about 50% of Baylor's students report doing something they describe as "spiritual" at least once a month on average. They choose from a large palette of Baylor and regional opportunities for worship and service. This proportion seemed a bit low to me—certainly it is lower than at institutions that require chapel for all students, not just those in the first year (if we assume, of course, that most students find chapel "spiritual"). He does believe that Baylor self-consciously pays attention to spiritual development issues for its students. Many students and faculty regularly attend Christian churches in

Waco and vicinity—indeed, he mentioned some concern that some students might be being captured by some of the more fiery, emotional, and demonstrative congregations in the region.

Dr. Marc H. Ellis holds the honored title of "University Professor" at Baylor, where he has served for a decade, coming to the university in 1998 at the invitation of President Sloan. Dr. Ellis is director of the Center for Jewish Studies at Baylor and the senior Jewish faculty member at the university. His scholarly record is impressive and focuses upon such areas as the "Jewish theology of liberation," Holocaust studies, and Israeli-Palestinian relations. My own background and faith as a Jew made me curious about Dr. Ellis's role at Baylor and his perceptions regarding the role of religion there.

Professor Ellis, as he would be the first to proclaim, is in some ways an outsider at Baylor because he is not a Christian, and he is equally an outsider in much of the Jewish community because of some of his work at Baylor and the plain fact that he works there. His championing of Palestinian social justice issues and his opening of the Center for Jewish Studies for programs on Islam and to groups of local Muslim students and community members have not been universally well received by the central Texas Jewish community. Not surprisingly, Dr. Ellis has an outsider's analytic perspective on some of the religious issues that have surfaced at Baylor over recent years—for example, the conflicts between fundamentalist and moderate Baptist views—and how those issues have been embodied in various individuals and offices. Ellis respected President Sloan highly, felt he "stood for something," and, while a strong evangelical, was also committed to diversity at Baylor. Dr. Ellis, like many of his colleagues throughout the university, expressed some regret that the internal battles of the past decade had broken the Baylor family into contending groups. From his non-Christian perspective, Professor Ellis fears that much of the behavior he has witnessed at Baylor has not been true to the best of the Christian tradition.

We discussed some of the programs of the Center for Jewish Studies, such as a recent conference on global liberation movements. In addition to hosting students of non-Judeo-Christian backgrounds, the center has also tried to be hospitable to other underrepresented groups within the Baylor community including African Americans and gay students, for example. Dr. Ellis clearly believes he is accepted at BU and that he is doing important, sometimes countercultural work there. He also noted his conviction that to be accepted at Baylor, a Jew probably has to exhibit some brilliance.

Dr. John Lilley began serving as president at Baylor on 1 January 2006.[15] He holds three degrees, all in music, from Baylor and his doctorate, also in music, is from University of Southern California. Baylor is his third presidency. (William Underwood served as interim president between Robert Sloan and John Lilley.) We spoke about Baylor's history and the vision of its founders as a growing Baptist presence in Texas. Dr. Lilley stressed repeatedly BU's stance as a "moderate" within the Baptist higher-educational spectrum. In his view, the university has steered a middle course between ardent fundamentalism and liberal secularism. It is a place where faith, the Bible, and science are seen as coexisting. He noted that Baylor has and continues to hire non-Christian faculty members, citing especially the dean of music and the director of the Center for Jewish Studies (Dr. Ellis), and reiterated the hierarchy of hiring: Baptist, evangelical Protestant, Christian, Jewish. Baylor seeks people of faith for all its positions. Some at BU believe in integrating faith and learning in classroom work, whereas others are content with a more generalized sense that the Christian environment of the institution permeates all its endeavors, including instruction.

I asked President Lilley about some behavioral expectations for Baylor faculty and staff. Baylor believes that the only sanctified sexual relations are those between a man and a woman in marriage. Faculty members can be (and apparently some are) homosexual by inclination but celibate in practice. The university would not sanction an abortion rights group as a campus organization, but students would not be penalized for joining such an organization off campus. I asked what his reaction would be if a faculty member revealed to him that she had lost her faith. His response was that, thankfully, he had not had to confront that situation yet. He also remarked that he had had to deal with some parental anger when students shifted their religious beliefs.

Today, the university's board of regents is composed of individuals selected by the board itself (75%) and others nominated by the Baptist General Convention of Texas (25%).

In discussing Baylor's efforts to achieve the status of a major research university, the president was clear that a series of balances needed to be struck. He is proud of the rising SAT scores of undergraduates, the increasing applicant pool of the university, and the growing number of PhD programs in areas where Baylor is strong.[16] Thinking about orchestrating Baylor's constituencies to achieve those balances, Dr. Lilley observed that his training in music has served him in good stead: being the president of the university is rather like the task of an orchestra conductor.

As with the presidency, the history of Baylor's provostship has been somewhat turbulent in recent years. Dr. Donald Schmeltekopf held the post from 1991 to 2003, through the early years of the Sloan presidency.[17] He was succeeded by Dr. David Lyle Jeffrey. In 2005, according to *Christianity Today*, "On his first day as Interim President at Baylor University, William Underwood fired the Texas Baptist school's highly visible symbol of Vision 2012: provost David Jeffrey."[18] Dr. Jeffrey was immediately followed, first as interim then continuing provost, by J. Randall O'Brien. On the occasion of that abrupt transition, Dr. O'Brien observed "We're an army shooting at each other. When will this madness end?"[19] When Dr. Underwood was followed by President Lilley, Provost O'Brien remained in office. I had the opportunity to speak to all three of these past and present provosts while I was visiting in Waco.[20]

Provost O'Brien noted that, when we spoke, BU was about halfway through the Vision 2012 time span and that the university had made dramatic progress in almost every area.[21] He described the 2012 plan as a grand experiment, one that sought to move Baylor from a collegiate culture to that of a leading university. Today, he believes, it is no longer in the experimental stage: it is succeeding.

He observed that the university has tried to remain vigilant in hiring, without making the interview process some sort of inquisition. Hiring committees do ask candidates about their faith commitments, and each is asked about church membership. Applicants are also asked to submit a statement of faith, and these are reviewed in the provost's office. There is not a set list of queries put to all candidates. I asked Provost O'Brien what would happen if a faculty member came to him and confessed that she had experienced a loss of faith. He responded that he would commend that person's integrity in bringing the issue to him and try to listen with sensitivity to her story. He remarked that "leadership is an acoustical art." Doubt, he would remind the faculty member, can be the cutting edge of faith. If the loss seemed irreversible, he would probably say to the faculty member, with sadness, that she had left Baylor, not the other way around. Provost O'Brien's style seemed to me gentle and pastoral (he is a professor of religion and holds three graduate divinity and theology degrees). It was clear that this hypothetical conversation would not be an abrupt or brutal one. Dr. O'Brien was quick to stress that there is room for considerable variety of faith positions among Baylor's faculty, noting that the university did embrace Jewish faculty members. He also told me that people of other, and no, religious traditions are frequently invited to campus as guest speakers, program participants, and the like.

I asked the provost what institutions he saw as Baylor's peers. He mentioned the university's athletic conference, the Big 12, which are also seen sometimes as BU's academic comparison group. He also cited Rice, Southern Methodist University, Texas Christian University, and, as aspirational peers, Notre Dame and Boston College.

I met as well with former provosts Schmeltekopf and Jeffrey, both of whom had been deeply involved in the early period of devising, promulgating, and seeking to implement Baylor 2012. They reiterated the university's ambitious goal of striving to be simultaneously a top research institution and a profoundly Christian college. We discussed the possibilities, and the actualities, of combinations of support and discomfort with those dual goals. Dr. Jeffrey noted that some thought it would be difficult to hire top scholars while seeking to maintain a clear and pervasive and universal faith orientation within the faculty. But, he said, it actually was easier to find those prestigious and productive scholars while affirming Baylor's Baptist and Christian character. For scholars of strong religious principles, seeking a major research university post at an avowedly Christian institution, there are very few choices, and Baylor is one of the best. Where else, the former provosts rhetorically asked, can such scholars go?

5 | A Civil College

Anderson University, Anderson, South Carolina

Baptists believe strongly in the priesthood of all individual believers and the autonomy of each church congregation.[1] This spirit of individualism and rejection of centralized pervasive uniform control characterizes not just Baptist persons and churches but colleges and universities as well. Including all of the various denominational subgroups (e.g., American Baptist, Southern Baptist), there are far more Baptist institutions in the Council for Christian Colleges and Universities than any other denomination, and many more schools are affiliated with this branch of Protestantism but are not members of the consortium (e.g., Baylor, which is an "affiliate" member). The Southern Baptist Convention, with which Anderson is affiliated, is the largest Baptist organization in the world and (with more than 16 million members) the largest Protestant denomination in the United States. It illuminates the principle of intradenominational variation to look briefly at Anderson University after our study of Baylor. Both are Baptist and seek to combine religious conviction with academic excellence, but they are anything but clones.

Anderson University finds its roots in the Johnson Female Seminary, founded on the eve of the Civil War by the Reverend William B. Johnson, the first president of the Southern Baptist Convention.[2] Anderson, South Carolina, was then a relatively isolated village; today, it is located within the busy and booming I-85 corridor, running through nearby Greenville and Spartanburg, South Carolina, from Charlotte to Atlanta. Like so many nineteenth-century colleges, Reverend Johnson's seminary for girls was short-lived. In this case, as in many others, the ravages of the Civil War forced the school to close. A half century later, a group of local citizens made a gift of land in Anderson and a grant of $100,000 to the South Carolina Baptist Convention, and in 1912 Anderson College admitted its first class. It was, at that point and for the next two decades, a four-year women's college.

In 1929 Anderson College became a junior college, and the following year it became coeducational. Then, in 1989, the school's board of trustees and the South Carolina Baptist Convention decided to return to baccalaureate status, and the first four-year class graduated in 1993.[3] More recently, in 2006, Anderson College reconfigured its internal structure and became Anderson University, with colleges of business, education, visual and performing arts, arts and sciences, adult and professional studies, and a school of interior design. It has recently added an MBA program. Currently, teacher education and business are, by a significant margin, the two most popular majors on campus. With its College of Visual and Performing Arts, the university has a full and diverse schedule of performances and exhibits.

Today, Anderson University has about 1,650 full-time, continuing students, closer to 1,900 if one includes adult and special students. Enrollment has grown modestly but steadily over the past few years. The entering classes of 2005, 2006, and 2007 were each, successively, the largest in institutional history. The university has an enrollment goal of 2,200 students. About half the traditional undergraduates live on campus. There are some seventy-two faculty members. The college has a six-year graduation rate of about 40%. Tuition for the 2007–8 academic year was $16,600 per year; room, board, and fees brought the annual cost to $24,600. Its endowment is modest: $17.1 million in 2007. Anderson University occupies an attractive, leafy campus, with three of its original buildings now housing administrative offices and student residences, and a number of new structures in a harmonious red brick style. Several older facilities have recently been renovated, and new ones (a library, residence hall, fine arts center) built. The physical campus has an aura of well-being. Anderson has a formal set of "aspirant" institutions, as well as a published set of "peers." Neither list includes any public institutions, although some publics are among Anderson's competitors for new students (especially Clemson and the University of South Carolina). Both lists include Baptist and non-Baptist affiliated schools. Included on the list that Anderson aspires to join are Bellarmine, Belmont, Converse, Meredith, Samford, Mary Baldwin, and Ouachita Baptist. The peers include Mary Hardin-Baylor, Presbyterian, Gardner-Webb, and Lynchburg. All are smaller master's degree–granting institutions. From the perspective of an outsider, there does not appear to be much of a gap between the aspirant list and the peers. In student academic qualifications, for example, Carson-Newman College in Tennessee is on the aspirant list and has student ACT scores of 19–25, while Union University, also in Tennessee, is a peer, and has ACT scores in the 21–27 range.

I had the opportunity to learn about religious life at Anderson, especially for students, from the vice president for Christian life, Dr. Bob Cline, and from Dr. Bob Hanley, the vice president for student affairs. They noted that Anderson retained its strong link to the Southern Baptist Convention and the South Carolina Baptist Convention, relationships that have been important and supportive for the school. Unlike some state groups within the Southern Baptist Convention, the South Carolina Convention has not suffered from deeply traumatic conflicts between conservative and moderate wings.[4] Anderson's trustees are appointed by the state convention.

In the views of these two vice presidents, the university's Christianity influences every aspect of collegiate life. Faculty development activities, for example, encourage professors to find ways to think about integrating faith and learning within the confines of their disciplinary areas. That curricular integration, while encouraged, is neither monitored nor mandated: some faculty members demonstrate their Christian commitment in their pedagogical behaviors, their relationships, and their out-of-class life, but not within their course syllabi; others do bring faith issues into their curricular work. For students, the values of a Christian college should be manifested in their relationships and their service work, as well as their intellectual growth. Drs. Cline and Hanley estimate that slightly more than half of Anderson's students are Baptists, another 30% or so affiliated with another Protestant denomination, and the remainder are Catholic or some other religion, or see themselves as unchurched. About a third of the students complete some sort of mission work during their time at the institution. All students take two religion courses: an "Introduction to the Bible" course in the first year, and "The Teachings of Jesus and Their Contemporary Application" in the third year.

Chapel at Anderson is called "The Journey." All full-time students are required to attend Journey programs at least eight times per semester for every semester of attendance. Some programs beyond traditional chapel worship opportunities can be counted toward meeting this requirement. Students are also required to participate in at least four service activities during at least six of eight semesters of attendance. In spite of these requirements, Anderson seeks to present its program of religious life as a desirable opportunity for students, not an unpleasant or enforced obligation. Many of those with whom I spoke at the university stressed that they did not feel compelled by a kind of theological or behavioral legalism, and that if individuals slipped, the reaction was conversation and counseling, not immediate or strict punishment. So, for example, students are expected to dress "modestly," but if and when they do not, the effort is made gently to suggest alterations.

As I did elsewhere, I asked about attitudes toward gay students at Anderson. It would not be likely that such students would be able to form any sort of official campus club or organization, and it is clear that homosexual behaviors violate the college's norms; but so does unmarried heterosexual activity. Both vice presidents declared that a student who was a celibate homosexual would be welcome on campus. Similarly, while the institution would not sanction an on-campus abortion advocacy group, a student who wished to affiliate with such a group off-campus, if that affiliation was not "high profile," would be free to do so. Again, the emphasis seems to be on guidance and counseling, not on strict codes and punishment.

I spoke with a small group of students at Anderson, and we covered many of the same issues. The students with whom I met came from both nearby (e.g., Greenville) and far away (e.g., St. Louis). All were graduates of public high schools, as are some 90% of Anderson's pupils. The students had sought a Christian college environment, although some secular and public institutions had been included in their college applications (e.g., Clemson, which is nearby). Other popular cross-application institutions also include some non-Christian and some non-private institutions, such as Winthrop College and the University of South Carolina.

Students find at Anderson a religious common denominator, which they believe unites the college community; they feel a unity with fellow students, faculty, and staff. The students suggested that perhaps 10% of their professors will sometimes offer prayer during class. They reiterated that education and management were the most popular areas of study. Occasionally, professors will introduce religious matters into the classroom curriculum, but these students felt that this happened infrequently. They did speak of a close in- and out-of-class mentoring relationship with their faculty.

The students have a clear idea of behavioral standards at the university and believe they are "held to a higher standard" at Anderson than are students at other, secular, institutions. It is "assumed" their behavior will be better. Anderson does have a behavior code, which forbids smoking and drinking on campus and at college events. It does not explicitly forbid legal-age students from drinking in moderation off-campus. As noted earlier, heterosexual marriage is seen as the only legitimate venue for sexual activity. Although Anderson does have a dress code (according to the vice president for student affairs), the students did not know much about it, but assumed they were supposed to dress modestly. I asked about the consequences if a student were to appear demonstrably drunk on campus. The college, and perhaps fellow students, would try to help that individual. He or she would be invited to write a letter of apology. If the offense was repeated frequently, the student would, they felt, be expelled.

There are many service opportunities on campus and off for students, including some foreign missions (e.g., Italy, Guatemala, and Costa Rica in 2007–8) and service trips to places like hurricane-struck New Orleans. The students knew other students from around the world, including Brazil, India, Cambodia, Jamaica, China, and several African countries. They noted that some of the international students, such as those from Brazil, had been recruited as student athletes. Most Anderson students, they believed, came from the university's region.

Faculty members at Anderson University are required, by contract, to be professing Christians. This is defined, formally, as being active members of a Christian church, including the Roman Catholic Church. Dr. Danny Parker, senior vice president for academic affairs, spoke to me about the faculty recruitment process. He interviews every finalist for a faculty post, even those being considered for temporary or part-time positions. Tenure-track faculty searches are conducted by cross-disciplinary faculty search committees, which make a recommendation to the chief academic officer and, ultimately, to the board. The university has a standard faculty employment application, and it asks the prospective professor to write an essay on issues of faith and teaching. Dr. Parker stressed that different teachers, in different disciplines, have different ways of expressing their Christianity. In many cases, he believes, out-of-class interactions are as important as curricular incorporations of religious content. I asked Dr. Parker how he would react if a well-regarded, senior faculty member told him she remained active in her church, for social and service reasons, but had lost her faith. He responded that he would certainly not make a snap judgment in such a case, but that if that loss seemed to be more than a temporary development, he would probably ask the faculty member if she believed she was teaching at the right place.

In areas of potential curricular controversy, Anderson has some clear practices and policies. Thus, for example, all biology classes state, in the syllabus, that Anderson's philosophy is to make sure biology students understand Darwinian evolution but that no particular set of beliefs about creation is going to be either punished or rewarded at the school. Evolution will be taught, but students are free to believe what their convictions lead them to espouse. Dr. Parker noted that Anderson students go on to medical school and need to know well secular, mainstream science. Like many others, the vice president stressed his conviction that Anderson could, and does, link a strong base in faith with academic excellence.

In response to my query, the vice president said that he thinks the most dramatic changes at Anderson in recent years have to do with the planning and evaluation process for regional accreditation and with the president's oversight of an effective strategic planning process. He believes that, as the affiliation of (nearby) Furman University with the Southern Baptist Convention has waned, Anderson is moving to become a regional leader in the integration of academic ambition and religious conviction. (The other two Southern Baptist schools in South Carolina are North Greenville University and Charleston Southern University.) He, like others, suggested that the institution's strategic plan was an important, and living, document.

That plan, entitled Vision 2014, is not only found on the university's Web site but also, unusually, at the front of the college catalog. It consists of fourteen "strategies," each of which is followed by a list of specific "priorities" and "initiatives." The "strategies" are sweeping; for example, the first is:

> Create an exceptional, future-driven Christian learning environment that emphasizes values, high standards of scholarship, mutual respect, and nurturing support for all members of the Anderson University Community.

This is followed by five priorities of greater specificity, for example:

> Keeping excellent teaching as our primary focus, embrace a broad view of scholarship that includes teaching, discovery, application, and integration; develop discipline-specific standards for quality scholarly and creative faculty contributions."

And these, in turn, lead to some very specific initiatives, for example:

> Maintain an overall student to faculty ratio between 13:1 and 17:1.

> Increase percentage of full-time faculty with terminal degrees from 65% to 80–85%.

About half the "strategies" explicitly address Anderson's Christianity. Some are devoted to it wholly, for example, Strategy Eight:

> Guide all AU students in academic and student life programs to understand the Christian perspective of life, embody the attitudes of leadership and stewardship, and view work as vocation.

The first "priority" subsumed under this head is:

> Affirm the teachings of Jesus Christ with special emphasis on the Great Commandment, the Great Commission, Christian civility and the Golden rule.

This, in turn, leads to initiatives such as enhancing the budget of the chapel and extending chapel to evening students.

Much of the credit for Anderson's fully developed strategic plan is given to (relatively) new president, Dr. Evans Whitaker. An especially important point for President Whitaker is the notion that "Christian civility" is central to the university's well-being and mission.

In his opening convocation address to the Anderson University community in the fall of 2007, Dr. Whitaker focused on "civility" as one of three important qualities that he hopes characterize the university and its people.[5] He begins by noting that he often describes Anderson as "a place of uncommon civility." He defines "civility" as, in part, the cultivation of habits of personal living that are important to the success of a community and stresses that Anderson is a Christian community, small and close. He notes that students who go out into the workplace will be competing against often-uncivil graduates; they may be young people with bad personal manners and deportment, or who are not good communicators. Anderson graduates, in contrast, should be "respectful, graceful, considerate." This theme is echoed in a South Carolina magazine, *Sandlapper*, which included an article about Anderson in its winter 2007–8 issue entitled "A Place of Uncommon Civility."[6] The article discusses the close relationship between Anderson students and faculty, beginning with the story of a biology faculty member whose students researched treatment options for her breast cancer. It also stresses the university's community service emphasis and reiterates President Whitaker's conviction: "It's a loving Christian environment rather than a legalistic one." He notes the school's high behavioral standards but also observes that violators are treated with a "graceful and redemptive approach."[7] While recruiting view books are hardly an unbiased source of information, it is telling that, in addition to touting the close student-faculty relationship and the wide-spread community involvement at Anderson (as most small college admissions materials do), this university's admissions materials describe it as "a warm place, a kind place."[8]

President Whitaker sees Anderson as fully embracing its Christian mission choosing to be intentionally religious, as it was founded to be. He rejects the notion that striving for high academic standards is in any way contradictory to maintaining equally high Christian values: Anderson wants both, and not just for purposes of convenience or marketing. He sees as key to this endeavor the influence of faculty members who come to the university with a faithful mind-set, who seek to help students grow in their faith and recognize that it is impossible to ignore the spiritual dimension of being human. He says Anderson wishes to demonstrate a "welcoming spirit" and to employ people who will be an inspiring and loving influence on students.

Dr. Whitaker believes that students and parents see important differences between faith-based and secular higher education. On one hand, they look for an integration of faith and learning and have confidence that Christian colleges will not tear down the beliefs of students who come there. The college welcomes non-Christian students and is proud that some of those who have chosen to attend have become enthusiastic converts. For example, a recent tennis player from India converted from Hinduism to Christianity—a story the university was happy to feature in its publications.[9] The president sees Anderson growing by some three hundred or four hundred students in the coming years. He stresses that Anderson is rooted in the liberal arts, but not exclusively so, with strong programs in teacher education and business.

Repeatedly, Dr. Whitaker emphasizes the campus's gentle culture, its loving, respectful spirit of mutual support and sense of civility. He attempts to encourage those aspects of campus culture which most effectively cultivate those virtues. And he notes that it is important at Anderson that you cannot have an opinion without having the facts.

In contemplating the range and diversity of faith-based higher education in contemporary America, it is illuminating, as I suggested in the opening paragraph of this chapter, to compare two such different Baptist universities as Anderson and Baylor. Baylor is a research university, proud of its size and of its status as a PhD degree–granting institution. Anderson is basically an undergraduate institution, which has recently added some MA-level programs. Like Baylor, Anderson is proud of its size, but in Anderson's case, it is its small size that it brags about: "Because our campus is intentionally smaller, there are all kinds of opportunities to meet and get to know others. Ours is a friendly, caring campus, and it's evidenced everywhere—from our students, to our faculty, to our President, to our dining staff."[10] Baylor University has moved to distance itself from the Texas Baptist Convention; Anderson has worked to maintain its strong attachment to the equivalent South Carolina group. Anderson's governing board is appointed by the state convention; Baylor's is not. At Baylor, there is a strong sentiment that the university is "moderate," in comparison to the "fundamentalist" leaning of Texas Baptists. But at Anderson, there is a strong self-identification as "conservative," as opposed to "moderate." While Baylor has undergone successive waves of campus (and community and even national) controversy, Anderson makes a conspicuous virtue of civility, caring, and kindness. Where the two Baptist institutions seem identical, though, is in their insistence that it is possible to strive simultaneously for greater academic quality and for deeper religious commitment.

Denominational Colleges

The three schools examined in part III remain deeply tied to their founding Protestant denominations. New Saint Andrews College in Moscow, Idaho, is a very small, curricularly and structurally innovative institution that was founded by a particular church (Christ Church, also in Moscow) affiliated with a small, focused denomination (Confederation of Reformed Evangelical Churches, a traditionalist offspring of the Presbyterian Church).

Calvin College is often considered, along with Wheaton, one of the premier Christian liberal arts colleges in the nation. It is strongly linked to its founding denomination, the Christian Reformed Church. The CRC is originally ethnically Dutch, and that national link is far from invisible today, but the church is more distinctive now for its intellectual and theological rigor than for its nationalistic origins. For a college with its national reputation, Calvin is remarkably pure in its denominationalism: for example, all full-time continuing members of the faculty are required to be practicing members of a Christian Reformed Church or of one affiliated with it.

Also linked to a particular national version of Protestantism, North Park University in Chicago, was founded by the Swedish Covenant Church, today known as the Evangelical Covenant Church. While North Park retains strong links to its founding denomination, it has been aggressive in reaching out to the very diverse city in which it makes its home. Quite differently from either New Saint Andrews or Calvin, it prides itself on the range of theological and affiliational Protestantism of its faculty and administration, as well as its student body. Of all the institutions I visited in the course of researching *Seeing the Light,* North Park seemed to me to most fervently embrace the diversity of its urban setting.

6 | "At the Front Lines of the Culture Wars"

New Saint Andrews College, Moscow, Idaho

Moscow, Idaho, is the home of the University of Idaho. Less than ten miles away is Washington State University in Pullman. Both of these public research universities are moderately large, comprehensive in program, explicitly secular, and devoted, in the spirit of the Morrill Act, to collegiate education that serves a utilitarian as well as an intrinsically developmental purpose. Also in Moscow is relatively tiny New Saint Andrews College, small by design, with fewer than two hundred students, and about fifteen faculty members. Its curriculum consists of courses not in agricultural resource economics or electrical engineering, but ones with names like Tradition Occidentis, Natural Philosophy, Principia Theologiae, and "Classical Rhetoric." In many respects New Saint Andrews College (NSA) is so different from any conventional paradigm that it is daunting to describe it. Not only are its courses given unusual names, but its academic terms, its grades, its classrooms, and its faculty ranks sound equally unfamiliar. Its history is unique, its funding counterintuitive, its governance idiosyncratic, and its student life program startlingly different. Not everyone is attracted to New Saint Andrews, but for those who are, the attraction is powerful. On my first evening visiting NSA, college president Roy Atwood and Mrs. Atwood took me to a sophisticated French restaurant, located in part of the first floor of the nineteenth-century building the college occupies in the center of downtown Moscow. The restaurant is owned by a chef who came to Idaho from urban France and who specializes in such culinary treats as lavender crème brulee and duck breast in orange and anise sauce. He came to keep his family close together; his son wanted to attend New Saint Andrews College, and his family wanted him to. The college reports that this is not an idiosyncratic case. I suspect that such a family relocation would be very rare for Washington State University or the University of Idaho.

Perhaps the best way to begin to understand the ethos and individuality of New Saint Andrews is to look at its history. New Saint Andrews College began as a reading list compiled by members of Christ Church in Moscow in the early 1980s.[1] (Christ Church in Moscow is a member of the Confederation of Reformed Evangelical Churches, a late twentieth-century offshoot of the Presbyterian Church, which rejects both modernism and fundamentalism.) The bibliography of classical and theological readings was meant for "survivors of the government education system." From the list evolved a program of evening enrichment courses, especially in classical languages, for adults. About a decade later, the church asked a three-person committee to study the possibility of beginning a baccalaureate college with a classical and Christian core. The college defines "Classical Christian higher education" as that which "tutored men and women in the Christian worldview and immersed them thoroughly in the Scriptures and the great works of Western civilization, which had been radically transformed by the Gospel."[2] Those three individuals, Douglas Jones, Douglas Wilson, and Roy Atwood remain at the college as of this writing.[3] Dr. Atwood is now president. The group looked particularly at the curricula of (old) St. Andrews University, Scotland, in the 1500s and at seventeenth-century Harvard. Jones, Wilson, and Atwood became the college's first faculty members, serving on a voluntary basis, and in 1994 the college enrolled its first class of four students, who met in Dr. Atwood's kitchen. Two years later the first paid faculty member was hired. After moving to a number of temporary quarters, NSA bought a historic building, the 25,000-square-foot Skattaboe Block (1893) in the center of Moscow and has renovated it to house its academic program, offices, library, and meeting rooms. Today, New Saint Andrews has a student population of about 150 and eleven full-time equivalent (FTE) faculty. College leaders feel that this growth has come slowly and organically, and are not at all eager to grow significantly larger; on the other hand, they know it would be fiscally dangerous to shrink. The students have come from thirty states and five foreign nations, and the Pacific Northwest does not dominate student origin demographics.

"Learning how to live, love, and think as a Christian" is how one of the college founders describes the mission of New Saint Andrews.[4] I asked if a professed unbeliever would be admitted as a student to NSA, and the response was that she or he would not. But if a continuing student came to nonbelief, that student would receive pastoral counseling.

NSA has no majors: all undergraduates "major" in "Liberal Arts and Culture," and the college offers both the BA and AA degrees. Its accreditation is from the Transnational Association of Christian Colleges and Schools, which is recognized, in turn, by the Council for Higher Education Accreditation (CHEA). NSA's annual budget is about $1.25 million. The college has just launched a small (beginning with five students) master's program in Trinitarian theology and culture. It is also closely connected with Logos School, a private classical Christian school (preschool through high school) also in Moscow, of which one of the founders of New Saint Andrews was one of three principle creators in 1981.

NSA is clearly proud of its individuality. Some of the college's unusual features are reflected in a unique lexicon. Thus, for example, a student might well say, "My grade in Traditio was SCH (Summo Cum Honore) for the Chalcedon Term." These locutions are not merely an affectation, though. By calling a course "Tradition Occidentis" instead of, say, "Western Civilization," the college aims to call attention to an integrated view of Western culture that is classical in its origins and profoundly shaped by Christianity. The Latinate grading system (in which SCH is the equivalent of a 3.30 on a 4.00 scale—that is, a B+), NSA feels, returns the focus of class evaluation to a measure of actual knowledge acquired, frees the students from anxiety if they do not make an A, and is seen as combating the grade inflation that plagues other institutions. And the college year is divided into four eight-week terms, with some classes lasting one, some two, and some four terms—that is, translated, courses are year-long, one semester, or half semester. The terms have all been given the names of historical councils of the Christian Church—Jerusalem, Nicaea, Chalcedon, and Westminster. So, while the hypothetical student quoted above could have said "I got a B+ in 'Western Civ' first term spring semester," that would not be saying exactly the same thing.

The curriculum at New Saint Andrews bears some resemblance to that of St. John's Colleges, and perhaps an even stronger similarity to the instructional program at Thomas Aquinas College, described in chapter 3. It is focused on the great books, which are defined largely, but not wholly, as the masterpieces of classical antiquity. There is a very heavy emphasis on theological learning and rhetoric; music and languages also receive unusually significant attention. It is reported that some Protestant, reformed, colleges have expressed surprise at what they perceive as a Roman Catholic aspect of the NSA great books reading list. Except for four, eight-week electives in the third and fourth year, all students take the same courses, in the same order. NSA does not, however, seek to have all faculty teaching all courses, as is the case at St. John's and Thomas Aquinas, although there is a strong emphasis on faculty flexibility and clearly the fellows (as professors are termed) are all generalists. Students all study classical languages for all four years, beginning with a year and a half of Latin and then an equivalent period of Greek. Students who have already studied one (or both) classical languages begin at a higher level but are still required to study a classical language (Hebrew is also taught). First-year students all participate in a yearlong "Lordship Colloquium" that studies the historical Protestant Christian worldview. They also have mathematics and a rhetoric colloquium. Second-year students, in addition to continuing language classes, have music for one semester (including history and theory, and also sight singing) and "natural philosophy" (science) for another, and yearlong courses in theology and in classical culture and history. In the third year, students continue music and science, each for a semester, and begin work on their thesis for a semester. They also begin work on a two-year course, "Traditio Occidentis," discussed above, and can select electives. The final year includes the thesis, language, additional electives, and the Traditio course.

Most course work consists of a weekly lecture to a fairly large group—for example, the entire third-year class—followed later in the week by small "Oxford-style" recitations in groups of about five students. Unlike St. John's and Thomas Aquinas colleges, with their strict seminar format, faculty at NSA are expected to be more than discussion leaders: they give lectures that provide information, and they provide answers. Recitations are frequently held in faculty homes. Courses conclude with an oral examination at the end of each term, in which all the student's instructors assess the progress of the student's knowledge for the past eight weeks. The thesis, too, involves a public oral examination.

Two additional aspects of the New Saint Andrews program also stress oral communication. Weekly, there is a "Disputatio," in which a guest speaker, usually from outside the community, gives a presentation to the entire student and faculty body of the college, followed by a question period. And, also weekly, NSA holds "Declamations," in which students are responsible for oral presentations to their peers and to the faculty.

Few textbooks are used at New Saint Andrews, although they do not seem to be held there in the same complete abhorrence as at the other "Great Books" schools. The reading of primary texts is daunting. The catalog, for example, lists the following texts, in what it specifies is not a comprehensive list, for the Traditio course (the categories are those assigned by NSA):

THEOLOGY
Anselm, *Proslogion and Monologion*
Aquinas, Selections from the *Summa*

SOCIAL AND POLITICAL SCIENCE
Adam Smith, *Wealth of Nations*
Aristotle, *Ethics* and *Politics*
Federalist and *Anti-Federalist Papers*
Hobbes, *Leviathan*
John of Salisbury, *Policraticus*
Locke, *On Civil Government*
Machiavelli, *Prince*
Marsiglius de Padua, Selections, *Defensor Pacis*
Marx, *Das Capital* or *Communist Manifesto*
Plato, *Republic*
Rousseau, *Social Contract*
U.S. Constitution and Declaration of Independence
Weber, *Protestant Ethic*

EPICS
Beowulf
Chaucer, *Canterbury Tales*
Dante, *Divine Comedy*
Homer, *Iliad* and *Odyssey*
Milton, *Paradise Lost*
Ovid, *Metamorphoses*
Spenser, *Fairie Queene*
Vergil, *Aeneid*

DRAMA
Aeschylus, *Oresteia*
Aristophanes, Selections
Euripides, Selections
Shakespeare, Selections
Sophocles, Theban Plays

NOVELS
Austen, Selections
Bunyan, *Pilgrims Progress*
Cervantes, *Don Quixote*

Conrad, *Heart of Darkness*
Defoe, *Robinson Crusoe*
Dickens, Selections
Dostoevsky, *Brothers Karamazov*
Faulkner, *The Sound and the Fury*
Goethe, *Faust*
Melville, *Moby Dick*

LETTERS
Aristotle, *Poetics*
Montaigne, Selections
Plutarch, Selections from *Moralia*

ART AND ARCHITECTURE
Palladio, *The Four Books of Architecture*
Ruskin, *The Seven Lamps of Architecture*
Suger, Abbot of St. Denis, *On the Abbey of the Church of St. Denis and Its Art Treasures*
Vitruvius, *On Architecture*

PHILOSOPHY
Berkeley, Selections
Boethius, *Consolation of Philosophy*
Duns Scotus, Selections
Derrida, Selections
Descartes, *Meditations*
Hume, Selections
Kant, Selections
Leibniz, Selections
Locke, Selections,
Nietzsche, *Beyond Good and Evil*
Plato, Selections
Plotinus, Selections
Russell, Selections,
William of Ockham, Selections
Wittgenstein, Selections.

Even for a full two-year course, this is a daunting syllabus.

Extracurricular student life at New Saint Andrews College is as idiosyncratic as the curricular program. All students live in the community of Moscow, either renting an apartment, living at home, or boarding. The college takes a sharply negative view of student residence halls:

> We reject, in principle, the very idea of dormitory living. Dormitories dominate Christian and non-Christian student housing on virtually every campus. But dorms, by their very nature, breed immaturity, immorality, and irresponsibility. Despite claims to the contrary, no one can provide adequate supervision or accountability for dozens, sometimes hundreds of 18 to 21 year-olds living in the same space with other 20-somethings (typically) acting as "residence advisors." That setup follows the historical origins of dormitories, dating from when the Bauhaus style swept the Western architectural community and extended its modernist-socialist vision particularly to apartment complexes and dormitories. In fact, Walter Gropius, founder of the Bauhaus movement, invented the modern undergraduate dormitory at Bauhaus as a way of creating communal living and reinforcing the Bauhaus socialist way of life in a university setting.[5]

There are, as well, very few "student activities" of a conventional sort: for example, there are no college-sponsored sports, although the college handbook notes, "We are also prepared to recognize that active or passive participation in sport, drama, music, etc., will contribute much to the quality of your life; but we urge moderation."[6] Students do organize such activities for themselves: during my visit, for example, they were producing an Oscar Wilde play. Each class beyond the freshman selects one female and one male "class whip," whose task is to help with organizing service events and to "pray for the student body and discuss the spiritual climate of the school" with the director of student affairs.[7]

Student behavior is regulated by a "student code of conduct."[8] Unlike most such codes, especially at institutions with a conservative approach to student behavior, that at NSA is deliberately nonspecific. Students are enjoined to pledge their commitment in four areas: personal holiness, sound doctrine, cultural reformation, and academic integrity. Thus, for example, in the first of those categories, students are told to "exercise their Christian liberties not as an occasion to indulge the flesh, but to serve others out of love through the wise and moderate exercise of their liberty. By God's grace and through the church's instruction and discipline, students should abstain from works of the flesh, such as sexual immorality, idolatry, hatred, discord, jealousy, wrath, selfish ambition, drunkenness, or debauchery, and to flee all temptations to those sins." That is the NSA "alcohol policy," an item that in many student handbooks can run to pages of particulars. Students understand that, if of legal age, they may drink in appropriate ways in appropriate situations (and they seem to agree without further regulation about what those ways and situations in fact are), and they are not to drink to the point of drunkenness. The three college founders noted that students would be disciplined firmly for action that violated the college's code but that no one would ever be punished for his or her temptations.

Similarly, the "dress code" simply states that students must dress "appropriately," but overtly refuses to go beyond saying that this means "neat, clean, modest, not casual and not outlandish." Unlike, say, the code at Thomas Aquinas that specifies male shirt collars, no pants for females, and socks with sandals, NSA students are expected to understand what "appropriate" dress is without amplification. There are provisions for remedying inappropriate dress. The students with whom I met (on a Saturday afternoon) were, in fact, neat, not outlandish, informal (no ties), but not "casual" in the sense of, say, shorts and T-shirts.

The students with whom I met were also very clear that seriously inappropriate behavior—"fornication," continued excessive drinking, and similarly disruptive behavior would result in dismissal. And they noted that when students were dismissed, they very commonly attempted to come back to NSA, a point that was also made by faculty and administrators. The students agreed that the college's expectation was that they would live like Christians, and they understood what that meant.

The college founders noted that about half the students were home schooled before coming to college and that fewer than 5% had any significant experience in public schools. This was confirmed when I spoke to students, all of whom had been either home schooled or educated in private Christian schools. Many had some experience with both, but none had spent any significant amount of time in public elementary or secondary institutions. Several, however, had taken some course work at community colleges or at the University of Idaho, and none reported serious problems with those ventures. Many had older siblings or other relatives, or close friends, who had previously attended NSA.

All of the students cited the college's challenging curriculum as one of the major factors in their choice of New Saint Andrews. One, for example, was taken with the fact that the NSA curriculum is similar to that of Harvard University in the seventeenth century. They are also acutely conscious of the academic demands placed upon them: they remarked that some weeks they cannot see how they will be able to do all that is asked of them. Indeed, as the college itself notes in its handbook, "daunted by their workload, some students lose all sense of judgment. They sacrifice food and drink and sleep and Sabbath-rest at the altar of schoolwork."[9] Their plans for postgraduate education and work were not at all unusual—one planned to seek an MBA, another aims to attend law school, others mentioned business and teaching. President Roy Atwood estimates that 25–30% go to graduate or professional school, about a third become teachers, usually at Christian institutions, and the remainder go into business or devote themselves to family life.

New Saint Andrews students do not feel themselves to be sheltered or protected from the rigors and diversity of the world outside of Christian education. They noted that the college frequently brought to campus guest speakers of very wide-ranging, often non-Christian viewpoints, usually for the Disputatio series. The founding trio noted that the reading list includes both those friendly to the Protestant, Reformed tradition and its most persuasive enemies. Their rationale is that at NSA, students should encounter the best arguments unbelief has to offer. Students read and study Montaigne and Darwin, for example. I also spoke about Darwin with the faculty member teaching the natural philosophy science course, who stressed that NSA students actually read Darwin in the original, which he believes is rarely the case for those college students who are Darwinists. He, himself, is a believer in intelligent design and a creationist, but when he teaches the course focusing upon the diversity of life, he makes sure that students understand *Origin of Species* and have a more than superficial grasp of Darwin's arguments. That faculty member, Gordon Wilson, affirms that he would not find Darwinian evolution intellectually satisfactory, even if he lost his faith. The students graphically described a range of opinions and beliefs to which they were exposed: NSA is "not a germ-free environment."

The interim director of student affairs described his work with students in strongly religious terms. He said that, when difficult issues in student behavior arise, he reminds students of the authority of scripture. He appeals to them "as a Christian brother," reminding them that the Bible enjoins them to be quick to forgive and quick to confess. He tells them, "You're a Christian, act like it!" He finds it hard to imagine how someone in his position in a secular institution can function, with no higher authority to which to appeal. He feels such student affairs work is adrift on a relativistic sea, with no ultimate anchor. Like the students, he believes that the lack of codified behavioral rules is a positive aspect of student life at NSA.

New Saint Andrews faculty members have two ranks—fellows and senior fellows. They are initially hired on one-year contracts as fellows, become senior fellows after about six years, at which point they are offered two five-year contracts, and thereafter ten-year ones. Because the college is only in its early teens, few have actually followed very much of this career path. In the 2006–7 academic year, according to President Atwood, there were eleven FTE faculty, of whom seven or eight are actually full time, and about fifteen head-count fellows, counting volunteers and part-timers. The college catalog notes, "Because a student becomes like his teacher, our professors must be well qualified, with personal integrity, spiritual maturity, good standing in the church, a love of students, and excellent academic and professional credentials and experience."[10] There is a statement of faith to which the entire faculty subscribes. Following a preamble ("Authority and Witness") that puts the statement in context (e.g., with historic creedal statements), this document has ten headings: The Triune Majesty, Revelation, Creation, Sin, The Incarnate Christ, Salvation, Law, Covenant, Witness, and Eschatology. Many of its points are explicit and have clear pedagogical implications. For example, under Creation, the statement affirms, "In the beginning, God created the material universe from nothing in six ordinary days."[11]

The NSA faculty is a closely knit group. Of those fifteen individuals, three are related. Some are graduates of New Saint Andrews. Most, however, have had significant experience outside the world of Christian higher education—PhD degrees are from such institutions as the University of Iowa, Cambridge University, and George Mason University. Most of the faculty members do not hold the doctorate, and President Atwood was quite open in expressing his conviction that the PhD is not particularly relevant to the quality and the sort of teaching New Saint Andrews seeks. The NSA faculty is almost all male. When I asked a group of gender-mixed students how they reacted to this, the males responded that they had not noticed; the females said they had and that it would be good to have a few more women teachers. Nobody, though, was very upset about this unbalance.

The faculty does publish, usually at Christian presses, for Christian audiences. It is not dour. For example, one faculty member has published parodies of the popular evangelical "Left Behind" literary series. Like the students, they are not discouraged from alcohol consumption, just drunkenness: one faculty member met me at a local pub late in the afternoon and enjoyed a beer while I drank a coffee; at a dinner with the president, wine was served. Many of the faculty have worked at other jobs or other institutions, and several of them are pastors or have done pastoral work. Faculty members describe themselves as very different from each other, with different beliefs on some important issues (e.g., the war in Iraq), but in concord on the really important issues of Christian faith and conduct. Given the smallness of the college and its newness, NSA has not yet had to confront most of the difficult faculty personnel issues other institutions have faced—the faculty has prodded itself along and grown with the school. One member of the community described it as a "school of thought."

New Saint Andrews tends to find faculty members by seeking them out, not by broadcasting openings in publications like the *Chronicle of Higher Education*. It was mentioned that some colleges, including some in the reformed tradition, hire faculty members on the basis of their academic credentials primarily, to fill slots in the curriculum, and that this tends to dilute the Christian emphasis of such institutions. While there is no expectation that every faculty member would teach every subject, it is clear that most teach several—I spoke to one, for example, who was teaching Shakespeare and math concurrently. The NSA faculty finds it difficult to imagine a separation of learning and faith, because they see learning as the servant of faith. When I questioned the faculty member cited above about the nature of "Christian math," he responded that many issues in his teaching of mathematics touched religious issues: Can there be numbers independent of God? What does the triune nature of God teach about universality or divisiveness of numbers? He noted that in his experience in graduate school, math was about calculation, not thinking. He wants his students to ask, "What is math?" In a NSA publication, he adds, "There are many amazing things about mathematics—things that are simply inexplicable without attributing them ultimately to God."[12]

Not surprisingly, New Saint Andrews College manages itself in ways that are distinct from ordinary collegiate administration. Indeed, President Atwood remarks that when other Christian colleges learn how NSA operates, their first reaction is, "You are kidding," but the more they learn, the more seriously they take the college. The college catalog affirms, "Our primary objective for our administration is to provide academic leadership for the faculty, students and the College as a whole, and to nurture Godly personal relationships characterized by mutual submission, respect, and honor with and between the faculty and students."[13] Of NSA's annual budget of about $1.25 million, about 80% is devoted to salaries. The faculty salaries paid at NSA are actually above the competitive rates at the University of Idaho and Washington State University. A new ABD faculty member would, in 2007, start around $40,000 per year, a new PhD at about $45,000. The college is about 85% tuition dependent, according to President Atwell but would like to be 100% tuition dependent—exactly the opposite aspiration of most institutions. Moreover, its tuition is set deliberately low: $7,200 for 2006–7, $7,800 for 2007–8, with the option of "locking in" the tuition rate for four years with a $750 payment at the beginning of the collegiate career, which is applied to the final year's tuition. There is, of course, no room or board. Tuition is set low to avoid significant financial aid costs: the college accepts no federal or public financial aid. It tries to calculate what most parents in its target population would be expected to pay, before financial aid, and just charge that (noting that, among its constituents, many families choose not to have two working parents). There are significant volunteer contributions to the college, and several of its "administrators" are also faculty members or are the relatives of faculty members.

Perhaps more surprising than the nonacceptance of federal financial aid money is the fact that the college has also chosen not to become a 501(c)3 not-for-profit entity. Their thinking is that such status would put them under the control of public agencies, who might insist on policies or actions contrary to NSA principles in order to maintain nonprofit status. NSA does not have a significant endowment and is not actively trying to build one, although it does not oppose endowing, say, scholarships. NSA's leaders note that they tend to have a deep suspicion of things going well and are skeptical about acquiring significant fiscal resources. They note that most colleges have "more money than gravitas" and are determined to avoid that pitfall. They seem to be succeeding with that goal.

The college is now governed by a board of trustees of seven members. It includes two of the three founders, and the third, President Atwell, serves on the executive committee but is not a voting member of the board. The two founders, and the principal of Logos School are permanent members, and the remaining four, elected by the board for four-year terms, are all local pastors: no board members are selected for their material well-being. There are no financial philanthropic expectations for the board. The board has the final voice on all collegiate hirings. In terms of curricular decisions, there is a faculty curriculum committee, which makes recommendations to the academic dean, who, in turn goes to the board for a final determination.

One of the first things I heard from one of New Saint Andrews College's founders was that he had wanted to found a college because he discovered there were no collegiate institutions in the United States to which he would send his daughter or son. He felt that other Christian colleges had allowed their missions to drift toward secularism. At both Christian and non-Christian colleges and universities, academic and behavioral standards have sunk catastrophically, it seems to him. The NSA college catalog observes, "Academic standards have fallen so far that most graduates . . . of our best universities today could not meet the admissions requirements of the classical Christian colleges of the 18th and 19th centuries."[14] The college, thus, was explicitly created to stand apart from and, in some overt senses, "against" the rest of American higher education, public and private, secular and religious. To this visitor at least, there appears to be something of a besieged stance about this college. Certainly, I was hospitably received when I visited Moscow, and faculty, students, and staff were open and eager to respond to my (sometimes surely irritating) queries. I was always treated with a friendly respect. But I encountered more than once the perspective that the American academic establishment, including some "formerly" Christian colleges, seeks to be "inclusive" and to honor the perspectives of virtually everyone—*except* serious Christians. The first issue of the college's magazine speaks of "colleges at war spiritually with the Western tradition and the Christian church that nourished it."[15] Many members of the NSA community believe that places like New Saint Andrews College, and people like those who work and study there, are dramatically misunderstood and unappreciated by the dominant and overwhelming majority of the American higher-education community, including many institutions that traditionally or currently describe themselves as "Christian." President Atwood writes, "It is a commonplace that public and private colleges are dominated by radically liberal professors, multiculturalism, immorality, relativism, and declining academic standards."[16] I found, thus, a kind of split between amiable good humor and militant Calvinism. The college recognizes this duality by noting in one of its admissions brochures, "Play is labor" and "Laughter is warfare."[17]

Perhaps what I am seeking to describe here is a consequence of taking Calvinism with the utmost sincerity: there is belief and there is unbelief; there are the saved and unsaved. The lines are clear, and the usual academic love of ambiguity can only serve to mask these stark contrasts. Perhaps, too, New Saint Andrews College cannot help but react to its physical place nestled in a region dominated by two institutions that dwarf it in population, wealth, and facilities, but not in spirit. The college directory has stopped publishing address information for students, faculty, and staff, noting that "it seems there are people in the community who make a hobby of causing trouble for local Christian families who extend hospitality to NSA students. So as a courtesy to these families, and as a hedge against whatever else the 'Intoleristas' have up their sleeve, we're making it a tad bit harder for them."[18] New Saint Andrews people have fun, they enjoy life, and they are amiable, but they see themselves as wholehearted fighters in the culture war, using "culture" in the largest, anthropological sense: the contest between Augustine's City of Man and City of God. The college's 2006–8 catalog, which is subtitled *A Better Paradigm, a Higher Education*, begins on exactly this martial note: "In the spiritual battle for the hearts and minds of the next generation raging in higher education today, New Saint Andrews College stands firmly committed to the classical Christian tradition."[19]

7 | "To Clear Some Part of the Human Jungle"

Calvin College, Grand Rapids, Michigan

Late in the spring of 2005, Karl Rove, the White House political adviser and conservative guru, was seeking a hospitable college graduation venue for an appearance by President George W. Bush.[1] Mr. Rove was perhaps influenced in his choice of Calvin College in Grand Rapids, Michigan, by theological reasons: the college adheres firmly to the conservative religious doctrines of the Christian Reformed Church. Or, political considerations may have played a part: Dick DeVos Jr., whose family possesses the Amway fortune and who lives in Grand Rapids and has played an important role in Calvin's support, was running for governor.[2] In any event, Calvin must surely have seemed a careful and safe choice for a presidential commencement event: this was no liberal haven, no Antioch or Grinnell nor even the University of Michigan. But Mr. Rove made a mistake. In late May, nearly eight hundred students (out of about forty-two hundred) and some alumni took out a full page advertisement in the *Grand Rapids Press* accusing the president of "neglecting the needy to coddle the rich, desecrating the environment and misleading the country into war." And, if the students' objections were not enough, the next day about a third of Calvin's three hundred faculty members sent another letter to the newspaper reiterating opposition to policies that "favor the wealthy of our society and burden the poor" and to "an unjust and unjustified war."[3] One Calvin professor of religion was quoted in the *Chronicle of Higher Education* as affirming that the one hundred faculty signers "wanted to object to some specific policies but also to object to the way that the language of orthodox evangelical Christianity has been hijacked by the religious right."[4] President Bush and Karl Rove were not the first, nor the last, to think they had a handle on Calvin College, only to discover that the college, its people and its vision, is complex, nuanced, and exceptionally difficult to pin down.

Calvin College remains an educational institution of the Christian Reformed Church: it is not "affiliated" with the CRC or "traditionally related"; it and the Calvin Seminary are institutions *of* the church. Other colleges have associations with the CRC (e.g., Dordt, Kuyper College, and Trinity

Christian College), but Calvin is the church's college. To grasp Calvin as an institution of higher education, it is necessary to understand the CRC as a denomination.

The CRC traces its denominational history to the Protestant Reformation of the sixteenth century, in particular, its Dutch manifestation.[5] It considers itself theologically distinctive in its tenacious embracing of the teachings of John Calvin. Particularly important are the beliefs in predestination and election, the teaching that salvation is a divine gift unearned by inevitably broken humans: "Reformed Christians take seriously the corrupting force of sin, and therefore lay heavy emphasis upon the need to reform our lives and our view of life according to the incorruptible Word of God. But Reformed Christians also take seriously the renewing power of God's grace, released in human hearts and human societies by the Spirit of God, and they spot signs of this grace wherever they live."[6] The church asserts that these beliefs are a source of comfort, because they assure the believers that "no one and nothing, not even our own bad choices, can snatch us out of God's hand." This core theology seems (at least to an outsider) part of the elusive nature of the CRC and Calvin College, which perhaps proved problematic to President Bush: it is a kind of somber optimism which celebrates divine grace and human salvation even as it proclaims the inevitability and universality of mankind's fall ("'the world' is lost in sin and evil").[7]

A key figure in the development of Dutch Reformed culture is Abraham Kuyper (1837–1920), an important political figure in the Netherlands and a theologian who advocated an outward-looking social awareness and responsibility.[8] While there is a strand within the CRC that embraces an inward, pietistic, and thus anti-Kuyperian philosophy, Calvin College overtly embraces the view that it is the work of the Christian to "be busy doing the Father's work in this world."[9] Conversely, it equally overtly rejects the pietistic stance: "By its [the Reformed Church's] lights, the Christian life cannot be an inward piety cut off from all worldly involvement. . . . Reformed spirituality insists on the wedding of personal piety and cultural engagement." Calvin has always seen as part of its mission to prepare students to go into the larger world, "as agents of transformation."

Like many other Protestant denominations, the CRC places a heavy emphasis on the authority of the Bible: "Reformed Christianity holds the Bible to be the prime authority for faith and life, inspired by God and infallible with respect to its purpose."[10]

The convolutions of various branches of the Dutch Reformed Christians are many and complex. In this country, one key moment was the schism between the Christian Reformed Church and the Reformed Church in America in 1857. Although this is an American development, it was sparked in part because of a theological dispute in the Netherlands. (It also gave rise to the long-standing athletic rivalry between Calvin College in Grand Rapids and Hope College in Holland, which is affiliated with the RCA.) In the twentieth century, the Dutch Reformed churches had a dramatic growth in Canada, especially after World War II. Today, both the CRC and the RCA have about three hundred thousand members each. The Christian Reformed Church, while still recognizably Dutch in its ethnic ancestry, has had success in reaching out to other ethnic groups, including recent immigrant communities and African Americans. It has wrestled, hotly at times, with gender-related issues such as the ordination of women as elders and as ministers.

Calvin College began its life in 1876 when the CRC created a curriculum for ministerial training consisting of four years of "literary" training and two years of theology.[11] Calvin's first faculty member, Reverend Gerrit E. Boer, set a standard for hard work that still can be found at the college: he taught all seventeen subjects the new school offered, served as pastor of a very large congregation, and edited the denomination's magazine.[12] In 1894 nonministerial students were admitted, and the institution became, thus, a kind of preparatory academy. After a substantial expansion of the curriculum in 1900, in 1906 the former "Literary Department" became John Calvin Junior College, granting a two-year degree, which, by the 1920s evolved into a four-year, baccalaureate institution. In 1917 the college moved to a campus near the center of Grand Rapids. With the usual ups and downs, enrollment grew to more than twelve hundred by 1950, and the college outgrew its downtown campus. It acquired a farm (Knollcrest) in the southeastern section of the city, an area of nearly four hundred acres, including a hundred-acre nature center (now called an ecosystem preserve and featuring a state-of-the-art "green" building as its interpretative center). Its "new" campus consists of sprawling, low-rise brick buildings, spread across a very handsome landscape. A large and busy highway divides the main academic campus from a new conference center, the DeVos Communication Center, and the ecosystem preserve. The highway is spanned by an impressive enclosed pedestrian overpass.

In the autumn of 2007, Calvin launched the public phase of a $150 million campaign, with $64 million to build endowment for student financial aid, faculty support, and campus maintenance and renovation and $86 million for facilities improvement, including a field house complex, campus commons, fine arts center, ecosystem interpretive center, and equipment and technology. Calvin's endowment was valued at just over $90 million in June 2006; in 2007–8 tuition, room, and board charges were about $29,000.

A threefold statement of purpose animates the college:

1. Engage in vigorous liberal arts education that promotes lifelong Christian service.
2. Produce substantial and challenging art and scholarship.
3. Perform all our tasks as a caring and diverse educational community.

Calvin has grown to include a number of preprofessional programs, such as engineering but still asserts vigorously its core educational mission as a liberal arts institution. A large range of traditional liberal arts and preprofessional majors is offered. The college's core requirements are not eccentric for liberal arts institutions and include, for example, written rhetoric, information technology, foreign language, health and fitness, history, and cross-cultural engagement. Students are required to take two courses in biblical or theological foundations; a "First Year Prelude"; and, in the first year, a course entitled "Developing the Christian Mind," which "introduces students to the central intellectual project of Calvin College, the development of a Christian worldview and a broad, faith-based engagement with the ambient culture. A set of common readings sketches out basic biblical themes and helps students begin to formulate a Christian frame of reference as they pursue their academic vocation. In addition to these common readings and themes, each section of the course defines a particular academic issue to explore from the perspective of Christian faith and praxis." The Bible course is a survey of biblical literature and themes, and the theology course is similarly broad ("a study of Christian theology in light of its historical development and ongoing significance, this course surveys the central teachings of the Christian church"). A faculty member notes that Calvin's philosophy of education sees all courses within the curriculum as manifesting a religious nature.

Remarkably, Calvin's long and careful description of its core curriculum includes a chapter on "Core Virtues."[13] The college affirms its goals for moral formation for its students, noting that "in the course of the education it offers, to lift them above the tyranny of personal problems, beyond the clutches of the imperial self, into an expansive world that invites their best efforts on behalf of God's kingdom of truth, justice, and peace." Moreover, it attempts "to name and describe traits that mark such a life." In some detail, the document goes on to discuss fourteen virtues: diligence, patience, honesty, courage, charity, creativity, empathy, humility, stewardship, compassion, justice, faith, hope, and wisdom. In each case, in addition to defining the virtue (e.g., diligence is "the acquired habit of expending considerable energy in the steady pursuit of some goal"), each section notes how the curriculum and/or pedagogy of the college cultivates that virtue. Thus, again for "diligence" it is suggested that the academic workload of Calvin courses should be such that "it is impossible for students to do well without exercising a great deal of this particular virtue." The chapter ends with the virtue of wisdom, and with the statement that students at Calvin, as a Christian college, "should find much evidence of the kind of wisdom that is more precious than silver, and learn to look for it as if it were gold."

Calvin offers a wide range of campus-based and college-endorsed off-campus programs. These include semester-long offerings in Britain, China, France, Ghana, Honduras, Hungary, Spain, New Mexico, and Washington, D.C. There are a variety of shorter domestic and international programs during the January term. In addition, the college maintains a careful list of "endorsed off-campus programs," such as that of Central College in Vienna, and "approved off-campus programs," such as the Creation Care Stewardship Program in Belize or New Zealand. It participates, of course, in the range of CCCU off-campus options. An annual presentation entitled "Rangeela" is an international student pageant with music, drama, costumes, and dances.

Student life at Calvin reflects the traditions both of liberal arts colleges and of Christian institutions. Thus, for example, the college offers more than seven hundred planned worship activities each academic year, such as participating in the national initiative "40 Days of Prayer."[14] There are daily chapel services, foreign-language chapels, Bible studies, hymn sings, Bible study groups, a faith Web site, and a student-led program called LOFT (living our faith together). At the same time, there is an energetic NCAA Division III athletic program, which has produced a number of national championships, including an exceptionally strong record in men's and women's cross country and track and field in recent years. And Calvin sponsors a number of events that its own Web site calls "fun and wacky," including Chaos Day, the Mud Bowl, the Cold Knight Plunge, and a cardboard canoe contest.[15]

About half Calvin's students come from Michigan, and close to 10% from other countries. In an unusual profile for strong contemporary Christian colleges, 58% attended private schools, 41% public institutions, and only 1% were home schooled. The college has a higher retention and five-year graduation rate than national averages: 88% of first-year students returned for the second year in 2006–7 and 75% graduated in five years or less. The middle 50% of Calvin students scored 23–29 on the ACT composite test and 1100–1330 on the SAT.

I met with a small group of students. About half were local. When I asked them what other institutions they had considered attending, they generally cited both Christian and secular institutions. Fairly typically, one mentioned the University of Michigan and Hope. Other options included Northwestern University, Lawrence, the University of Minnesota, and Wheaton College. These students felt that issues of faith were very important at the college but not in a specifically CRC fashion. They did feel that they learned about the Christian Reformed Church during their college years. In terms of student behavior, they characterized Calvin as having strong rules (e.g., forbidding drinking on campus) but humane enforcement. Students are required to live on campus for their first two years. It was their impression that, overall, students arrived at Calvin more conservative in their theological and political beliefs than they departed—for example, one student estimated that 70% of the students entered college not believing in Darwinian evolution, but few graduated as creationists. Issues like stem cell research and same-sex marriage are openly discussed and often vigorously debated. The students agreed that there were a number of openly homosexual students on campus. They speculated that the college would not allow a campus chapter of a pro-abortion group to achieve official status but would encourage discussion of such issues and do nothing to stop a Calvin student from joining such an organization, openly, off-campus. Their shared guess was that the student body was split perhaps 60–40 Republicans versus Democrats and that the faculty was more liberal than the students. They were also in accord that campus student government was "a joke," with no particular power, and little broad-based student interest. The students felt intellectually comfortable at Calvin, believed they could discuss anything in and out of class, and that nobody tried to enforce any particular belief system on them. There is no student dress code, and the group seemed surprised to imagine other colleges that had such regulations. The range of student political opinion and action is illustrated by a recent (2003) incident in which the editor of the college's student newspaper sent a fiery e-mail to an antiabortion speaker scheduled to visit the campus, whom he called "a hate-mongering homophobic bigot."[16] While, on the one hand, a conservative group called the Intercollegiate Studies Institute gave Calvin an award in 2000 as a school opposing political correctness, on the other, at least one prominent conservative (Gary Bauer, president of the Campaign for Working Families) found that "leftwing ideology had gained a foothold" there.

Calvin students seemed relaxed, informal, and clean-cut. The students with whom I met, all of whom are Honors Program students, were remarkably serious in their reported extracurricular activities. When I asked them what they did for "fun," their rather remarkable replies were: tutoring (multiple students), discussing popular culture in the college's cultural discerners group, serving on the campus security staff or as a resident adviser, and working with the dorm-community partnership group or an inner-city church. While I would not say this group of students seemed "dour," this certainly did not seem like a list of wild and crazy activities. (It has been suggested by members of the Calvin family that I might have been able to find some students whose extracurricular activities were a bit shadier than these.)

All the students with whom I spoke were contemplating graduate or professional school, in areas such as law, biotechnology, and education. More than one of them planned to do missionary work between their BA and further schooling.

As part of a wide-ranging effort to enhance the racial and ethnic diversity of the student body, Calvin sponsors a number of programs to bring precollege students of color to the campus: a "Pathways to Possibilities" program, campus visitations, the Discovery Club Fellowship, an annual "Striving towards Educational Possibilities (STEP)" conference, the Entrada Scholars Program of summer school courses open to minority eleventh and twelfth graders, and the MLK Young Leaders Weekend. A new summer program aimed at Latino middle school and high school students is called Aspirando Alto. In the most recent available report of the college's Multicultural Affairs Committee, 6.9% of the entering students were identified as students of color and another 3.2% were international students. In 2004 the Calvin College faculty formally adopted a report entitled "From Every Nation: A Revised Comprehensive Plan for Racial Justice, Reconciliation and Cross-Cultural Engagement at Calvin College" known by the acronym FEN. This plan spans the entire population and program of the college, and empowers the Multicultural Affairs Committee to serve as "the principal agent of policy and accountability for the college in the development and maintenance of a genuinely multicultural educational community that discerns and counters the sin of racism and embodies the reconciling power of the gospel."[17] The college sponsors a wide range of multicultural events beyond those for recruiting students or as activities for current students. These include, for example, an annual "Consultation of Afro-Christian Scholars in Higher Education," an annual Institute for Healing Racism, and a black alumni chapter. Racial reconciliation and understanding seem to be endeavors about which Calvin College is very serious. In 2006 the college's biennial Festival of Faith and Writing included presentations by two major literary figures, Marilynne Robinson, author of the Pulitzer Prize–winning novel *Gilead,* and Salman Rushdie. The schedule for 2008 included Gail Godwin and Yann Martel (*Life of Pi*).

A section of the Multicultural Affairs Committee annual report deals with the diversity of the faculty in the context of the goals of the FEN document. Over the past few years, the percentage of faculty of color has hovered at around 7%, without either dramatic increases or declines. Academic departments are strongly encouraged to seek faculty of color to fill vacancies, and the report indicates that some, but perhaps not all, have embraced that mandate. Most minority faculty members are of Asian background. Sometimes Calvin's efforts to diversify its faculty have encountered obstacles: in October 2007 an African American faculty member, Denise Isom, sought an exemption to the college's requirement that all faculty members join either a CRC church or one in ecclesiastical fellowship with the CRC. Dr. Isom asked to be allowed to substitute membership in a local black Baptist church. The board of trustees denied Professor Isom's request. Provost Claudia Beversluis, noting the difficulty of the issue and affirming Calvin's respect for the Baptist institution involved, commented on the importance of the membership requirement: "Nearly all Christian colleges and universities that distanced themselves from their founding denominations and theological traditions eventually also drifted away from being Christian in any meaningful way." Dr. Isom's options were either to affiliate with the CRC or to have her tenure-track position converted to a terminal term contract for the 2007–8 academic year.[18] In May 2008 Dr. Isom and two of her colleagues in the Education Department resigned from Calvin as a consequence of this decision.[19]

Calvin's faculty numbers about three hundred individuals. As might be expected, a number of them are graduates of Calvin itself or of other similar Reformed or Christian undergraduate institutions. So, for example, in a recent tribute to a retiring faculty member in biology, it is noted that "nearly all his colleagues in the department had taken at least one course from him as undergrad students."[20] Indeed, of eleven retiring members of the faculty profiled in the summer 2007 college magazine for alumni and friends, seven are Calvin graduates. However, most have also had significant educational experience outside the realm of Christian schools, commonly at the graduate level. When I spoke to a group of five faculty members, their terminal degrees were from Michigan State University, the University of Minnesota, Ohio University, Duquesne University, and Purdue University.

The college's religious expectations for faculty members are high and are stated unambiguously. The faculty handbook states the general principle:

> Foundational to the College's mission is its identity as a confessional Christian institution. . . . Membership in the Calvin College teaching faculty therefore requires adherence to these standards of faith and engagement in the ministry of God's people who gather under them.[21]

This injunction is rendered more explicit in a later section:

> Calvin College faculty members are required to sign a synodically approved Form of Subscription in which they affirm three forms of unity—the Belgic Confession, the Heidelberg Catechism, and the Canons of Dort—and pledge to teach, speak, and write in harmony with the confessions.

This, in turn, leads to requirements of church membership. All faculty members

> are required to be professing members in good standing and active participants in the life, worship, and activities of a Christian Reformed Church (CRC) or of any church which is a member of a denomination in ecclesiastical fellowship with the CRC as defined by its Synod. A current list of such denominations is kept in the Provost's Office.[22]

Although 40% of Calvin's students are the products of public precollege education, Calvin faculty themselves are "required to provide their children with Christian schooling." This applies to grades K through 12, and schools that are members of "Christian Schools International" are cited as the most desirable. On approval, home schooling or "other schools that base their education on the Christian faith" are acceptable.

At the same time, the same handbook strongly affirms Calvin's adherence to principles of academic freedom:

> Every faculty member, whether tenured or untenured, shall be entitled to the right of academic freedom in the performance of his or her duties. The faculty member shall be judged only by the confessional standards of Calvin College, and by the professional standards appropriate to his or her role and discipline. ... [Academic freedom] extends to the discipline in the classroom, to research, writings, and other public utterances in the field of professional competence.

A final document in the handbook in this area is the very short but clear and explicit "Procedures for Handling Allegations of Confessional Unorthodoxy." Such allegations will ultimately be handled by the board of trustees, although the academic administration and institutional committee structure participate.

An important feature of faculty work life at Calvin is the Professional Status Committee (PSC). This is a joint faculty-administration group, with five tenured faculty members (one as secretary and with a goal that one be a person of color), the provost, the dean for multicultural affairs (if none of the selected faculty members is, in fact, an individual of color), and the president, who serves as chair. This major committee is charged "as the principal agent of the college faculty in matters pertaining to the status of the professional staff of the college." As such, it oversees appointment, reappointment, tenure and promotion guidelines, procedures, and actual reviews, including all new appointments to the faculty; recommends new faculty positions; advises the president and provost in regards to faculty reviews and appointments; recommends leaves and policies governing workload; and reviews cases involving punitive actions. But the PSC is also charged to "insure that the college professional staff possesses a firm Christian commitment." In this last capacity, the PSC is the campus body with the duty of making sure that faculty members affirm their subscription to the principles of the CRC upon appointment and at each subsequent important step of the academic career, such as the granting of tenure.[23]

When I spoke with Dr. Beversluis shortly after her appointment as provost at Calvin, she described the very deliberate relationship between faith and learning at the college. She noted that faculty members were expected to emphasize that relationship but were free to build those curricular connections in ways that were appropriate to their disciplines and personal leanings. So, for example, students studying the laws of physics might be asked to mull how those principles had been turned to ethical or evil ends. She noted that Calvin believes that God gave humans minds to use and that, therefore, to study the book of nature is a worshipful activity. Thus, Calvin teaches evolutionary biology from the perspective of a firm faith. She also told me (and this was also noted by students) that the college offers chapel worship each weekday morning but does not require attendance. Most days, the participation is relatively slight (perhaps one or two hundred worshipers), but each Friday the service involves a more celebratory praise and singing event and is always packed with participants.

Provost Beversluis also narrated to me the campus's official reaction when the gay rights Soulforce Equity Ride visited Calvin: the visitors were welcomed to the campus and even invited to use the college's facilities, but it was also clearly reiterated that Calvin's position was that homosexual activities were not accepted, although the college took no stance on homosexual orientation per se. This sequence of events was featured in a full-page story in the college's alumni magazine.[24]

The provost believes that the campus has become more evangelical in recent years, and the students more faithful. She described the mainstream of the CRC as "not quite evangelical" and told the story of how theologian Martin Marty described the Christian Reformed Church as "the Jewish denomination of Protestantism." (I subsequently heard the same story from several other sources on campus.) She also noted that the college has a strong president and a history of thoughtful participation by the board of trustees in key personnel decisions. Dr. Beversluis responded to my query about peer institutions by citing St. Olaf, Pepperdine, Valparaiso, Baylor, Wheaton, and Gordon—all small to midsized Christian institutions.

I met with a group of faculty from the areas of political science, engineering, philosophy (represented by the most recent winner of Calvin's top teaching award), biology, and English. They noted that the CRC was a small but diverse denomination, with, for example, pietist, Kuyperian, and fundamentalist wings. Nonetheless, they affirmed that religious values were the glue that holds divisions and departments at Calvin together. It is their sense that students tend to be more nondenominational and to know less about the specifics of the CRC, but that Calvin communicates the Reformed tradition to them.

These teachers spoke convincingly about their efforts to integrate faith and learning in their classrooms. The engineer, for example, spoke of her consideration in class of the effect on the environment of various chemicals used in manufacturing processes and of efforts to find appropriate technologies. The political scientist described seeking Christian perspectives on political and cultural assumptions. The faculty member in literature and language cited his belief that language is a great gift from God and that literature can illuminate a broken world. From the biological perspective, the teacher can raise issues such as genetic engineering and ask Reformed questions such as, "Are all genes fallen into sin?" The biologist also mentioned that it seemed to him about half of his students were initially open to Darwinism but that most of them were willing to learn about evolution once they got over their shock. He also noted that he was frequently asked by parents, "What is Calvin College's official position on evolution?"

This group of professors believed that there was a strong bond of trust between the various constituencies at Calvin and the faculty and that, accordingly, the faculty more or less ran the educational program of the institution. They noted that the institutional deans were drawn from the faculty for rotating terms. Like others, they cited the central role of the Professional Status Committee but noted that that group has very rarely had to overrule departmental recommendations on personnel actions.

When I asked these professors to list Calvin's peer institutions, the responses were varied: Wheaton, St. Olaf, Grand Valley State (a local institution), Michigan State, Hope, Dordt, Trinity, Westmont, and Gordon. I specifically asked if they considered midwestern liberal arts institutions like Grinnell, Carleton, and Oberlin as "peers," and they responded that they did not; those institutions had a more "elite" repute. They were unanimous in stressing Calvin's welcoming their diverse intellectual perspectives and in affirming the college's enormous strength.

A powerful and poetic statement of Calvin's mission has been written by 1967 graduate Cornelius Plantinga Jr., now president of the Calvin Theological Seminary and entitled "Educating for Shalom: Our Calling as a Christian College."[25] Plantinga defines the Hebrew *Shalom* as "the webbing together of God, humans and all creation in justice, fulfillment, and delight." He notes that humans are fallen creatures in a fallen world: "The Christian gospel tells us that all hell has broken loose in this sorry world but also that, in Christ, all heaven has come to do battle," and that battle for shalom is what Christian higher education is for. In a Christ-centered college, Plantinga argues, "we learn what we can about creation itself," and he cites Lewis Thomas's description of the wonderment we should feel at the joining of sperm and egg into a cell that becomes a human brain. We should learn at such places, he says, to distrust simple accounts of complex events. Christian colleges teach skills: how to read and to read critically, how to compute and do it precisely, how to experiment scrupulously, and how to write better so as to spread the truth. In art and music, he says, we learn "to delight in sheer beauty." Christian colleges prepare students for jobs, Plantinga says, but they also teach us to ask "what those jobs themselves are for. How will the job I'm preparing for serve God by serving other people?" We should ask, he concludes how the things learned in a Christian college will "be used to clear some part of the human jungle, or restore some part of the lost loveliness of God's world, or introduce some novel beauty into it?"

Plantinga catches the nuanced Reformed Calvinism of this college. His view of fallen humankind in a fallen world could be seen as grim; his faith in the restorative power of a God who can put things right is ecstatic. The people of Calvin College seem intellectually serious—joyful practitioners of a sometimes dour faith.

8 | Swedes and the City

North Park University, Chicago, Illinois

North Park University defines itself through a triad of "distinctives." It is Christian, it is urban, and it is multicultural. Of course, none of these characteristics is unique in itself—there are many Christian colleges, many institutions in urban settings, and many that strive for and achieve a multicultural student body. But North Park is distinct in the degree to which it integrates all three of these elements and in the ways in which it sees each element as reinforcing and, indeed, necessary to the others. Thus, for example, North Parkers believe that their Christian character is shaped by their setting in the heart of the city of Chicago and that a contemporary Christian culture must be diverse. As a visitor to the university, I was impressed and surprised by the way in which NPU has combined a vigorous and unapologetic Christian mission and identity with an openness to a student population that is widely eclectic in terms of race, ethnicity, economic background and, yes, religion. One of North Park's six defining values is "affirmation of racial and ethnic diversity as reflective of the vision of the Kingdom of God."[1] When I asked North Park's relatively new president, David Parkyn, about his aspirations for the university, he responded that he hoped it would become a case study within its genre of institutions for engagement with its home city and for paying more than lip service to multiculturalism.

North Park was founded by what was then the Swedish Covenant Church in 1891. In the late nineteenth century, large concentrations of recent Swedish immigrants settled in the Midwest, especially in Minneapolis and Chicago, where they organized themselves into the Covenant Church.[2] The first educational enterprise for these new Americans was a school begun by E. August Skogsbergh in Minneapolis in 1884. At first, a college met at Skogsbergh's school in Minnesota, but in 1894 it moved from Minneapolis to Chicago, settling at its present location at Foster Ave. and Kedzie. Not surprisingly, the move upset some of the Minneapolis members. Old Main Hall was dedicated in June of 1894.[3] One important and intriguing early supporter of the school was a Covenant missionary, P. H. Anderson, who struck it rich during the Alaska gold rush. Disputes surrounding his claim were a source of financial tension at the new, sometimes struggling, college. In its early years, North Park was a two-year institution, but in 1958 it began offering baccalaureate-degree programs and became known as North Park College. It became North Park University in 1997, recognizing the theological seminary, and, over time, schools of business, education, and nursing. NPU is fully accredited by the North Central Association of Colleges and Schools, as well as a number of specific program accreditation agencies.

Today, North Park University remains deeply and clearly tied to what is now called the Evangelical Covenant Church. It is located in a richly mixed ethnic neighborhood about six miles northwest of the Loop, the center of downtown Chicago. Adjacent to North Park is Von Steuben High School, an old core-city institution, where today's students speak fifty-five primary languages.[4] Impressively, this is a fact about which the university brags in its admissions publications. Near the university are Swedish Covenant Hospital and the Covenant Home, a retirement community that has been at the same location since the 1880s. Across Foster Avenue, at the Tre Kroner restaurant, one can order pickled herring and hear Swedish spoken. But North Park's admissions office also recommends neighborhood restaurants that serve Italian, Mexican, Thai, Japanese, Cuban, and Mediterranean cuisine. Of course, there is also a McDonald's on the corner. The university still celebrates the Santa Lucia Festival each December. According to President Parkyn, the Evangelical Covenant Church now has some 20% of its membership in "ethnic congregations" and, especially in the South, has also created some megachurches.

The core campus is divided into two different zones by the North Branch of the Chicago River. On one side, NPU looks like a typical, rather idyllic little liberal arts college. Its landmark Old Main Hall, which today houses much of the administration and the admissions offices, is surrounded by grassy fields that, on a warm day, are filled with students tossing Frisbees, sunbathing, trying to do homework, and hanging out. (I noted during my visit, on such a spring day, that the students were dressed in a manner indistinguishable from secular college students hanging out and sunbathing.) The seminary building, a new library, a classroom tower, gymnasium, and similar facilities are scattered among spacious and well-kept lawns. On the other side of the creek, a few fairly new, purpose-built college buildings, including a fitness center and residence halls, are nestled among older apartment buildings and private residences. Many of these structures have been purchased by the university, but others have not. Much of the neighborhood looks and feels like a pleasant urban neighborhood, not a private liberal arts college. A few blocks away, separated by commercial and residential areas, are NPU's athletic fields for football, baseball, track, and soccer. Impressively, the university has completed more than $50 million in new construction since 2000. It successfully concluded a $26 million capital campaign in the spring of 2006.

Of course, the current site of North Park University was not so urban when the Swedish Covenanters moved there at the end of the nineteenth century. Old Main Hall was built in the midst of a farm field: over the course of a century, the City expanded out to the college. In his inaugural speech, President Parkyn cites a description of North Park's neighborhood by a university historian: "Foster Avenue . . . was a muddy wagon road, well-nigh impassable after a heavy rain. . . . Old Main stood like a lone sentinel surveying the surrounding territory of onion fields, cabbage patches and cornfields. . . . There were no water mains or sewers, no sidewalks or parking lots, no schools or cafes . . . and hardly any people."[5] For a time, the top of Old Main Hall was such a landmark in northwest Chicago that pilots used it as a navigation point when flying into Orly Field, today's O'Hare Airport. When, in the 1970s, North Park had the opportunity to move to a less urban setting, it did not do so. In 1979, it was offered free land outside the city, in Wisconsin; after debating the move, the trustees decided to remain in the city. This is an emblematic moment in the history of the school, one that affirms its commitment to its urban site and mission. A similar emblematic moment occurred earlier in North Park's history, when another opportunity for change was embraced, and the college changed the language of instruction from Swedish to English.

Many Christian colleges are, in effect, nondenominational evangelical institutions: Westmont College, for example. Others have a historical or fiscal affiliation with a particular church or denomination but perceive themselves as serving members of congenial denominations: New Saint Andrews College, for example, was founded by the Reformed Evangelical Church but defines itself as within the "reformed" tradition. North Park is both more and less denominational than such schools.

It is more denominational in that it is still clearly identified as the sole college of the Evangelical Covenant Church. The executive vice president, for example, describes the relationship with its founding denomination as "tighter" than at most Christian colleges. That abiding link is featured explicitly in virtually everything the college says about itself—it is mentioned on the first page of the admissions view book and on the first page of the printed version of the president's inaugural remarks; an editorial in the student newspaper notes, "In my youth, I learned a catechism of the Covenant Church which stated . . .";[6] the "Facts at a Glance" section of the College's Web site refers to the college's "founding in 1891 by the Evangelical Covenant Church."[7] And the University is the home of the North Park Theological Seminary, which prepares students "to serve the Evangelical Covenant Church" and offers a number of pastoral graduate degrees. One of the six "values" affirmed in the mission, vision, and values statement is "fidelity to the Christian faith and to our particular heritage in the Evangelical Covenant Church."[8] North Park University's athletic teams are "the Vikings." Many of the university's thirty-five-member board of trustees are members of the church, and, by statute, several trustees are Evangelical Covenant pastors. The university describes "a Covenant Education" as "distinctively Christian." This is defined as:

- Rooted in the Christian tradition, with the Bible valued and explored
- Profound and practical, with classroom learning and "enduring wisdom" linked to real-world applications
- Formative and transformative—students grow and develop as women and men of integrity whose living reflects core values
- Balancing freedom with disciplined responsibility. Students move confidently into life in a complex world
- Focused on the important, shared concerns and values that unite the Christian community and the entire human family

All religious activities at the college are voluntary, assuming that "young adults are best served when given the opportunity to make constructive" life choices and exercise their freedom within a supportive and value-rich environment. On its Web site, North Park says, "We are a Christian university, committed to relating faith in Jesus Christ to the aims of higher education."

On the other hand, North Park University seems less focused upon theological conformity than most strongly Christian Colleges.

Full-time faculty members, by board decision, must be Christians by faith and by action. This, obviously, includes members of the Evangelical Covenant Church, but those are a minority of the teaching cadre. Faculty members may also be members of other Protestant denominations, both evangelical and nonevangelical, including "mainstream" churches such as Methodist, Episcopalian, or Lutheran. Some are Mennonite and others are Baptist. Roman Catholics and Eastern Orthodox believers are also welcome on the North Park University faculty. I asked if Unitarians or members of the LDS church would be accepted by the board as Christians by faith and action, and it appeared that would be doubtful. Obviously, Muslims, Jews, Hindus, and atheists would not be full-time teachers at NPU. All prospective full-time faculty members have a "missional interview" with the president of the theological seminary. On the other hand, some individuals who are not Christians in faith and action have been accepted as part-time, adjunct members of the faculty, although not in religiously sensitive areas (e.g., teaching theology or philosophy), but in professional areas such as accounting or business law. Vice presidents Carl Balsam (executive vice president and CFO) and Dan Tepke (senior vice president) were clear in my interview that the university would not welcome any faculty member, full or part time, who overtly contradicted the basic religious tenets of the college in any sort of official capacity.[9] Faculty members are expected to be actively practicing their Christianity, not merely affirming nominal membership within a faith tradition.

Even the broad definition of Christian affiliation that is applied to faculty members at North Park is eschewed when it comes to students. Everyone with whom I spoke at North Park, including the president, two vice presidents, the academic dean, the director of campus ministries, and a student who was majoring in youth ministries, resoundingly affirmed the university's openness to students of any, or no, religious persuasion. Currently, about 27% of the undergraduate students are members of the Evangelical Covenant Church. Some 30% belong to other Protestant churches, and 14% are Roman Catholic. Students choosing not to identify themselves as members of any faith total 18%, and about 11% are members of a non-Christian church.

The university's "Application for Undergraduate Admission" has a fascinating and, in my experience, unique section entitled "Religious Background." It asks if students are members of a Christian tradition and offers several choices (including "unknown," "other," and "non-denominational Christian," as well as Roman Catholic and Orthodox). For students who describe themselves in this category, it also asks church name, address, and pastor information. It also offers a section to check "Other Religious

Tradition," which includes options for Jewish, Muslin, Hindu, Buddhist, Native Religion, or other; a final option is "No Religious Tradition." The entire section is headed by this paragraph:

> Please tell us about your religious or spiritual background. North Park is an intentionally Christian institution that welcomes and enrolls students from all religious traditions or students without any faith perspective. North Park students engage in a pursuit of truth by exploring the great questions of life that have challenged the human family for centuries. While the viewpoints of all students are respected and welcomed, a North Park education is rooted in the historic values and teaching of the Christian tradition and its sacred book, the Bible.

I met with Rich Johnson, the director of campus ministries. Johnson has a background in academic religion, with an MA in Christian thought, faith and culture, and is currently progressing toward ordination in the Evangelical Covenant Church. He supervises a staff of eight professionals, who work with twelve to fifteen student interns from the theological seminary. The campus pastor reports to the director of campus ministries. North Park University offers twice-weekly chapel services, on Wednesday mornings and Sunday nights. These worship opportunities are, like all co-curricular religious activities at North Park, purely voluntary. Everyone with whom I spoke at North Park felt that the attendance at chapel, which is estimated to be about 300–350 students on Sunday, was satisfactory, even gratifying.

The campus ministries office also offers a variety of nonliturgical programs:

- Urban Outreach provides student and other volunteer opportunities in areas such as tutoring, working with AIDS patients, and helping the homeless.
- Global Partnerships, set in eight locations, including three that are domestic, focuses on issues of oppression and justice. Some of these settings are religiously intense, others are more secular.
- "Sankofa" is a program of racial reconciliation in which African American and white students are paired, meet for intensive discussion, and then visit important civil rights landmark sites in the South.
- Small Groups, about twelve to fifteen students, meet together for "spiritual formation," including, for example, Bible study or prayer.

- *Hands On* is an online social justice magazine that appears three times per year, each issue focusing on a particular topic, such as urban youth.

Mr. Johnson estimated that about 60–70% of the residential undergraduates participate in at least one of these programs. The Office of Campus Ministries does not provide formal counseling, although it frequently does refer students who come with problems to the university counseling staff. It is Mr. Johnson's sense, which I have found widely shared at colleges around the nation, that the percentage of students who seek and need support is growing. The office does not provide much programming in the area of interfaith learning, but it does pay attention to the opportunities and issues involved in spiritual formation of students who are not Christians. Mr. Johnson felt that some of the faculty at North Park University fervently embrace the concept of linking faith and learning, although all are aware that any given classroom may include students from a variety of faith traditions, and some without any religion. Other faculty members are more focused on academic concerns exclusive of spiritual issues. And, of course, those dedicated to bridging faith and learning do so in different ways, appropriate to their beliefs, student populations, and pedagogical opportunities.

North Park University's curriculum is, on the whole, like that of many liberal arts colleges, with a few more distinctive elements. According to Charles Peterson, academic dean, the university has been restructuring its general education program since about 2000. Fairly typically, the college requires work in mathematics, natural sciences, foreign languages, fine arts, "culture and society" (which includes humanities and social science courses), and personal health. It also requires eight semester hours (two courses) in biblical studies, half of which is a required course, Introduction to Biblical Studies, and three courses, one in each of the first three years, that are called The North Park Dialogue.

The Bible and Theological Studies (BTS 1850) is described in the college catalog as "History and theology of Biblical narrative as it informs Christian faith today. Particular emphasis on the theological unity of the Bible's message."

The three Dialogue courses (the third is not required for students in preprofessional programs) were explained to me by Dr. Peterson. All focus on "the big questions." The first, "NPD 1000" addresses the question "Who am I?" Originally, all sections of the class shared a common reading list, consisting largely of autobiographical writings. Now, each faculty member devises her or his own syllabus, but one reading common to all is St. Augustine's *Confessions*. In some cases, multiple sections share all or part of the course. This is also a writing-intensive offering. "NPD 2000," which is taken in the second year, focuses on the question "Why be ethical?" Generally, the emphasis of this course has been on the issue of slavery, both in contemporary times and historically. Some attention is now being given to options investigating environmental ethics. The third course, "NPD 3000," is discipline specific and focuses on major questions raised within particular areas of academe, with a component of experiential learning. Thus, one section with a sociological emphasis might focus on "intentional communities," with students visiting several such communities and interacting with their members.

The North Park Dialogue sequence is related to another program, called the Campus Theme. This is an annual, noncredit offering, which rotates subject matter and brings to the university a series of guest lecturers each year, offering a range of presentations and perspectives. Topics have included "Who is my neighbor?" "What is community?" "Who is God?" "What is a life of significance?" and, for 2007–8, "What is truth?"

These special offerings seem to me to guarantee that all North Park University students will have a significant encounter with major issues of theology and faith and some collegiate study of the Bible. At the same time, these religious curricular offerings will not dominate the academic programs of most students: an English major might, in special courses and surveys, spend more time at North Park studying Shakespeare than the Bible.

I queried the academic dean specifically about the issue of teaching Darwinian evolution. He responded that it was North Park's conviction that a scientific approach to the theory of evolution as presented by Darwin was consistent with biblical faith—that evolution was good science. He noted that creationism or intelligent design would not be included in a NPU science course. He also mentioned that occasionally this stand has resulted in some ire on the part of religiously conservative parents.

NPU offers about twenty-nine majors, some of which are traditional (e.g., history, English, psychology, chemistry) and others of which are more idiosyncratic (e.g., Africana studies, clinical laboratory science, global studies, Scandinavian studies). A few are specifically related to the university's religious identity—biblical and theological studies, youth ministry. There is a wide range of preprofessional programs—for example, law, medicine, and veterinary medicine. It also offers a certificate program in nonprofit leadership and one in conflict transformation.

The university faculty consists of about 115 full-time members, with an additional 15–20 working at the Theological Seminary. Nearly two hundred part-timers come to NPU each year, usually in an adjunct role, to teach specialized courses. Among the regular faculty, members of the Covenant Church make up about 15%. Most (86%) have the appropriate terminal degree in their field, and many have done graduate work at prestigious universities, including Northwestern, Stanford, Harvard, and the University of Chicago. According to President Parkyn, with a 10.5–1 student-faculty ratio, the university has some room to grow without increasing faculty significantly.

North Park has a significant commitment to internationalism within the curriculum. Several languages are taught, including Swedish, as well as the classical languages (through the seminary's instructional program). The university offers an array of international programs, with students in recent years studying in at least twenty-four locales, ranging from Argentina to Sweden. A recent edition of the college alumni magazine was devoted to "North Park University around the World."[10] Prefaced by President Parkyn's reflections on growing up in Guatemala, the issue features an article about a faculty member living and working in Jonkoping, Sweden, a survey of various global offerings available to NPU students, a foldout section with a map of places that NPU students study abroad, and the home countries of international students now studying at NPU, as well as a series of profiles of both "incoming and outgoing" students. There is an article celebrating thirty years of the university's Swedish exchange program, and a reflection by the supervisor of North Park's study abroad program in Australia. The article noted that it is "hard to deny that North Park has become an institution significantly impacted by, and existing in, the global community."[11]

Beginning with the fall term of 2004, North Park University undertook a significant and unusual restructuring of its tuition policy. It *reduced* tuition by 30% and reduced institutional financial aid scholarship funding by an equivalent amount. It explains this tactic in an admissions office publication as follows:

> The fact is that private college tuition usually far exceeds the cost of providing a quality undergraduate educational experience. And while a few students *unwit-*

tingly pay "full fare" at high priced schools, the vast majority of students pay far less. So widespread and entrenched is the disparity between published charges and actual costs that higher education professionals have given this practice a name: tuition discounting. . . . How does tuition discounting work? . . . First, in the form of remarkably large but unfunded or partially funded scholarships. For 2006–07, the average private tuition will be more than $22,000. The typical top academic scholarship will be $10,000. . . . This so-called scholarship is made up of two parts. The first part is a *genuine* scholarship with a real value of perhaps $3000. The balance, which in this example is $7,000, is simply a built-in price discount, a marketing gimmick to make students and parents think the school really values and wants them. . . . We have heard countless students or parents say, "College X gave us $10,000." We know the truth is, in fact, they did not. They really gave you $3000. . . . The rest (7,000) is simply hot air, a discount to adjust for the inflated tuition. . . . At North Park you will find a no-haggle price with straightforward and honest information. . . . we are not playing games with you. What you see is what you get.[12]

For 2008–9, tuition for new students will be $17,600; room, board, and activity fee is $7,580. In the first year of this new program, the university increased the size of its first-year class from 530 to 676. Overall, the institution's enrollment has seen a healthy pattern of growth in recent years. Total graduate and undergraduate enrollment tripled since 1990, reaching 3,160 in September 2006, with goal of 3,500 by 2008. Undergraduate enrollment went from 775 in the early 1990s to 1,620 in the fall of 2006. At the same time, ACT and SAT scores and high school class rank rose: in fall 2007, the average ACT score was 22.5, and the SAT was 1100, while the average high school grade point average was 3.2 and class rank was 65%. And the college actually increased revenues because of savings on financial aid. The university's chief financial officer, Mr. Carl Balsam, notes that tuition strategy needs to account for the fact that family assessment of cost versus value is largely a matter of perception.

North Park's current endowment is valued at $48 million (30 June 2006), and its annual operating budget for the 2006–7 academic year was $41 million. By all accounts, the university is considerably more stable today than it was in 1990.

Student life at North Park is rich and fairly typical of a small, residential liberal arts college. There is a Student Association that sponsors many of the student activities on campus, including the newspaper, yearbook, literary magazine, and coffeehouse. It also oversees a number of academic clubs—for example, Philosophy Club, History Club, Model UN, Student

Nursing Association, Society of Physics Students. There are a number of ethnic cultural groups on campus, including organizations for black, Korean, Latin American, Scandinavian, and Middle Eastern students.

According to the president, about 10% of NPU's students were home schooled or attended private schools for most of their precollege education. This contrasts markedly with, say, New Saint Andrews College, where only about 5% of the students had received most of their prior learning in public settings.

North Park's intercollegiate athletic teams, the Vikings, play in NCAA Division III. At one point, NPU was a major Division III basketball power, winning five national championships between 1979 and 1987. Their football team, on the other hand, had an impressively long losing streak.

In terms of student ethnic diversity, at the undergraduate level, the university lists the following:[13]

Black	9.0%
Nonresident alien	4.2%
Native American	0.4%
Asian	7.2%
Hispanic	8.4%
White	64.3%
Other/unknown	6.5%

The spring 2007 issue of NPU's alumni magazine has a lengthy article on the campus's celebration of Black History Month. Students come from thirty-nine states and forty foreign countries. The university also notes that a quite high 34% of its students come from families with annual incomes less than $40,000 per year.

Of NPU's first-year students, 79% lived on campus, and overall 61% of its undergraduates were residents. This figure seems very high for a campus in as urban a setting as North Park's. In keeping with its urban locale, the college offers three residence options: traditional dorms, condo-type facilities, and apartments.

The North Park Press, the Student Association publication, contains articles that reflect the university's religious heritage (e.g., "Clarifying our Mission," which begins "North Park University is labeled as a Christian liberal arts college") and articles about events of current campus interest (in the case of one typical edition, several articles about an incident of racial harassment in the neighborhood, sports, and complaints about the administration, including "Don't Dump Dibley," an opinion piece regarding the denial of contract renewal to a popular professor).

North Park's "alcohol and drug policy" affirms that students are expected to comply with public laws concerning substance use and abuse. It adds that the university does not condone the public display of alcohol containers or advertising on campus.

When I asked about the issue of abortion, several members of the North Park community I interviewed said that it would not be possible for a student to found an abortion rights advocacy group as an official campus organization, but that if a student openly belonged to such a group off campus, that would not be seen as an issue with which the university would be involved, one way or another. In response to my query on another often-controversial sexual issue, the senior vice president noted that the university has accepted openly gay students for first-year admission.

I asked several of the individuals I interviewed what they saw as North Park's "peer" schools. Some mentioned other Chicago urban institutions, including publics such as the University of Illinois at Chicago and private universities, including the University of Chicago. Others cited local religious institutions such as DePaul and Loyola. Others mentioned small, nonlocal Christian colleges—Calvin, Hope, Northwestern College (Minnesota), Bethel, Wheaton, the University of Seattle, and Azusa Pacific. There was little consensus, and, indeed, this seemed a question that was new to most of those to whom it was put (I did not have a chance to interview anyone other than a student tour guide from the admissions office, where, I am sure, it would not be a new question).

Indeed, I can understand why North Parkers have some difficulty defining peer institutions: they have created a university that is quite distinctive and difficult to compare to others. It is, on the one hand, vigorously religious and strongly denominational with a continuing tie to a particular immigrant population, and yet equally strongly and vigorously open to students from the widest diversity of backgrounds. It occupies a pleasant, green, and historical campus, in the very middle of a bustling major American city. Perhaps most impressive and surprising, not only is North Park University Christian, urban, and multicultural, but it has managed to be all those things and also to be coherent.

Nondenominational Christian Colleges and Universities

Most of the faith-based colleges and universities in America today are, in name or in fact, nondenominational. Some have evolved into that status (e.g., George Fox) while others have taken that stance since their creation (e.g., Wheaton). In part IV, we look at this largest group of institutions.

George Fox University in Oregon (like the College of New Rochelle, examined in chapter 3) has expanded, in both curriculum and locale, beyond the traditional liberal arts college, which was, and remains, at its core. Although named for the founder of the Society of Friends, George Fox presents itself more as a nondenominational evangelical institution than a Quaker college. Very few of its students, and less than a majority of its faculty and staff are Friends. Straddling the sectarian-nondenominational border, then, it makes a good transitional study to introduce this section of our investigation.

Westmont College, also on the West Coast, is located in the dramatically affluent Southern California Santa Barbara region and is often mentioned in the same breath as Wheaton and Calvin as a leading Christian liberal arts institution.

A few Christian institutions are linked strongly to a particular important religious leader. Oral Roberts University is one such. It was founded and continues to be much influenced by the prominent televangelist for whom it is named. Recently, Oral Roberts University has been troubled by revelations not about its founder but about his family, which has played an important role at the university. ORU occupies a unique campus in Tulsa, Oklahoma and, because of the prominence of its creator, is one of the nation's more visible Christian institutions.

Northwestern College in Minnesota (there is another Northwestern College in Iowa, and, of course, Northwestern University in Evanston, Illinois), like Westmont, has several features in common with Wheaton, which is, pretty clearly, in its aspirational group. But it also has several quite unique characteristics, including the record of its football team, the fact that it occupies a campus constructed originally as a Roman Catholic seminary, and its ownership of a network of Christian radio stations.

Finally Wheaton College is universally cited as one of the nation's premier Christian liberal arts institutions. Without giving an appearance of smugness, Wheaton seems secure in its standing as a standard-bearer of faith-based liberal learning. It assumes, and many others assume as well, that it will play a leading role in defining and developing religious higher learning in the twenty-first century.

9 | Friends and/or Friendly?

George Fox University, Newberg, Oregon

George Fox University, in the pleasant town of Newberg, Oregon, about an hour's drive west from Portland, seems, to paraphrase Hamlet, both to be and not to be a Quaker college. In many respects, George Fox is comfortable with, and even seeking to expand, its historic identity as a Friends college. In many other ways, it seems to have much more in common with nondenominational evangelical Christian colleges, including those visited for this book, such as Wheaton or Northwestern, than with other institutions with a strong denominational character, such as Calvin or North Park. GFU belies some of the expectations one might have of a Friends college. A careful and multifaceted look at GFU raises a number of significant issues regarding denominationalism in contemporary higher education. I suspect our examination of this university raises those issues with considerably more clarity than it resolves them.

Named for the founder of the Society of Friends, and a deeply religious institution, George Fox is nonetheless quite removed from the Earlham, Guilford, Swarthmore orb of eastern, theologically conservative, and politically liberal Quakerism.[1] George Fox positions itself strongly in the midst of evangelical Christian colleges. It describes itself in admissions literature and elsewhere as "the only evangelical Christian university in the Pacific Northwest classified as a *national university* by *U.S. News & World Report*." Its threefold admissions brochure describes the institution twice as "Christ-centered" but does not mention the Society of Friends or Quakerism. Similarly, the current view book describes GFU as "a Christ-centered liberal-arts-and-sciences university," but mentions only on the very last page of "facts" that its affiliation is "Northwest Yearly Meeting of Friends (Quaker)."[2] The college is, however, affiliated with the Friends Association of Higher Education and with the Northwest Yearly Meeting, both major "mainstream" Friends' organizations. (The Northwest Yearly Meeting is, in turn, affiliated with the most evangelical of the three Quaker associations, the Evangelical Friends International.)[3]

The university began as Pacific College in 1891. Future president Herbert Hoover spent three years at its predecessor institution, Friends Pacific Academy. It became George Fox College in 1949 and achieved regional accreditation in 1959.[4]

George Fox is guided by a series of "statements" of values, beliefs, faith, and community lifestyles. A brief survey of those statements helps to illuminate the ways in which the university is, and is not, Quakerly in its approach to higher learning.

In 2000 the trustees approved a ten-point statement of faith. This document is certainly not inconsistent with theologically conservative belief within the Society of Friends, but neither does it make reference to Quakerism or any of the more idiosyncratic Quaker beliefs, such as pacificism or unprogrammed worship. The Statement of Faith is very similar to that of other nondenominational evangelical colleges and universities. It speaks of the Trinity, Salvation, the Bible ("We believe God inspired the Bible and has given it to us as the uniquely authoritative, written guide for Christian living and thinking. As illumined by the Holy Spirit, the Scriptures are true and reliable"), the Christian Life and Worship, the Church and the Future ("the resurrection of the dead, in God's judgment of all persons with perfect justice and mercy, and in eternal reward and punishment").[5]

The university's mission statement affirms the university's goal: "To demonstrate the meaning of Jesus Christ by offering a caring educational community in which each individual may achieve the highest intellectual and personal growth and by participating responsibly in our world's concerns." This is followed by a series of brief paragraphs detailing institutional objectives. These include, on the one hand, providing "a center for Quaker leadership where faculty and students learn the history and Christian doctrines of the Friends movement" and, on the other, giving "leadership to evangelical Christianity generally, through scholarship, publication, lecturing and by evangelistic and prophetic proclamation and service."[6]

Like many other Christian colleges, George Fox University has promulgated a statement of behavioral expectations, here called the George Fox University Community Lifestyle Statement. In many ways, this statement, too, is very similar to that of, say, Wheaton College or Northwestern College but very different from the lifestyle expectations of, for example, Earlham. It affirms community values such as kindness, gentleness, academic integrity, faithfulness, and self-control. It excludes immoral practices and affirms heterosexual marriage as the only sexual behavior consistent with God's teaching. Participation in a local church is encouraged but not strictly required (and, as several members of the community made clear, not policed). Gambling is to be avoided. The use of alcohol by traditional undergraduate students is not allowed, but employees and nontraditional students are "given the freedom of Spirit-led conscience in deciding whether to consume alcoholic beverages in moderation." Tobacco is forbidden in university buildings and "by employees or traditional undergraduate students." In Quaker style, the statement ends with a set of queries, for example, "Am I a faithful steward of the resources which God has entrusted to me?" The statement was formally adopted in the spring of 2007.[7]

The community values statement is brief:

Following Christ, the Center of Truth
Honoring the worth, dignity, and potential of the individual
Developing the whole person—spirit, mind, and body
Living and learning in a Christ-centered community
Pursuing integrity over image
Achieving academic excellence in the liberal arts
Preparing every person to serve Christ in the world
Preserving our Friends (Quaker) heritage[8]

The university does not have a dress code, and while most students are fairly modest in appearance, one does occasionally spot gaudy hair color, conspicuous tattooing, and visible body piercing. No one seems to pay very much attention to these vagaries of individual style.

George Fox University's position on some controversial social issues seems to conform closely to that of other evangelical Christian colleges: students would not be permitted to organize an abortion-rights group on campus, but neither would they be punished for discretely participating in such a group off campus. Homosexual behavior is frowned upon, as is any sexual activity outside heterosexual marriage, but same-sex leanings would not be punished (although a student or employee with such leanings might be energetically counseled about them), and a gay person who practiced celibacy would not be unwelcome on campus. (In contrast, Earlham, Guilford, and Swarthmore have formally recognized student organizations for gay students and their allies. And other resources, such as Guilford's Queer and Allied Resource Center, are institutional offices on campus designed to support such students.) When the Soulforce Equity

Ride gay rights group came to Newberg, they were welcomed cordially on campus and debated vigorously.[9]

When I spoke to a group of students, all had searched for a small, Christian college when making their higher-education choices; none had examined any other Quaker schools. At the same time, faculty and administration, if not students, are quite clear that George Fox University's Christianity is filtered through the historical lens of the Society of Friends: concerns such as social justice and peace occupy a more prominent place in the campus consciousness, they affirm, than they likely would at a non-Quaker Christian college. Not surprisingly, it seemed on my two visits to GFU that there are (at least) two perspectives on the part of the faculty regarding the university's Friends affiliation. Some faculty members, including some Quakers, do not find today's institution distinctively Quaker: they point to some widespread beliefs, particularly among students, which seem to run contrary to traditional Friends testimonies, such as pacificism and gender equality. Others, however, see GFU as a bastion of Quakerism, one of the main centers of living Friends higher education still flourishing in America today. Those with this second perspective also point to the college's focus on peace and social justice and its concern with fairness between men and women. (The issue of gender equity is a particularly nuanced one in this situation, since the historical Quaker belief in sexual equality can easily come into conflict with the traditional evangelical affirmation that the primary role of women is linked to home and family. Obviously, this is a matter of more-than-casual interest to female faculty members at George Fox.) One faculty member I had the opportunity to interview is Professor Arthur O. Roberts, who is, in the language of Friends, a "Weighty Quaker." Dr. Roberts (who graduated from George Fox in the 1940s and served a term as the institution's academic dean) has written extensively on Quakerism and Quaker higher education. From his perspective, George Fox has always been a deeply Quaker school, begun by pioneer Quakers in Newberg, although that link to the Friends has evolved over time. He sees a number of challenges to Quaker colleges in general. These are not unfamiliar to students of any religious institutions in contemporary American higher learning—for example, the move from "single community to segmented collegiality" or "from religious to academic priorities in admissions and hiring priorities."[10] He believes GFU is still sustained by a sense of servanthood and that it is important that institutions, including religious ones, retain the right to be true to themselves and their particular missions. He, too, believes that sometimes (e.g., during the Vietnam War) traditional Quaker testimonies have been jarring to non-Friends evangelical Christian students at George Fox.

There is general agreement that the university pays more than lip service to the integration of faith and learning in the classroom. Prospective faculty members are asked about such integration during their candidacy for positions at GFU and need to think carefully about this issue when they undergo various reviews, such as for tenure. One faculty member with whom I spoke, who teaches composition, described her understanding of writing as a gift from God. She also noted that she tries to help her students understand that a lot of contemporary "Christian" writing is just bad writing (a point made by several other professors of language and literature at a variety of Christian colleges I visited). Several individuals mentioned that the integration of faith and learning is a particular interest of the current president. New faculty members at GFU have a course release while they take three orientation classes that promote faith and learning in the classroom: Christian theology, Friends traditions, and faith as it relates to the individual faculty member's discipline. Students take ten credit hours of required religion courses, including courses in the Bible, Christian foundations, and one elective upper-division course. The majority of religion courses are taught by Friends.

George Fox has moved beyond its traditional liberal arts programs at the eighty-five-acre Newberg campus, and offers graduate programs, degree completion programs, and seminary degrees in four other locations—in Portland, Salem, and Redmond, Oregon, and in Boise, Idaho. Consequently, the school has grown from 549 students as recently as 1986 to 3,253 in 2007. Of that number, just over half (1,739) are traditional undergraduates, slightly over one thousand of whom live on the Newberg campus. The Newberg campus retains most of the programs and atmosphere of a traditional, residential, liberal arts Christian college; the majority of the graduate and seminary offerings are at the other venues. This expansion was, in some part, motivated by resource considerations. By all accounts, it was successful in enhancing the finances of the university, while simultaneously expanding its population, name recognition, and service area.

The Newberg campus is, as one might expect in the rural Pacific Northwest, very green and beautifully, carefully landscaped. It is eclectic in architecture with some stunning modern buildings as well as some handsome older structures, including Minthorn Hall, a wooden two-story academic unit that is one of the original college buildings.[11] Many of its older facilities have been renewed in the recent past.

If George Fox is debatably a Friendly college, it is for sure a very friendly one. On my two visits to this campus, the students and staff seemed remarkably open and genuinely eager to be helpful and welcoming. GFU is one of the Christian colleges where if a stranger stands with a baffled look on his face for fifteen seconds, someone is bound to come up to him and offer assistance. It is also one of the more homogeneous campuses I visited: 67% of the students are from Oregon; 80% are white. At the same time, GFU has made a strong and ongoing effort to achieve more diversity: the percentage of white students has dropped from 90% in less than a decade, while the numbers of African American, Asian, and Hispanic students has slowly risen. The college has launched (in 2007) an ambitious program to recruit undergraduate students from China. Most of GFU's students come from public high schools; a lesser number attended private, usually Christian schools, and the smallest fraction were home schooled.[12] About 70% of the traditional undergraduates live in campus residences. As at other Christian colleges, many GFU students go on missions during breaks in the annual academic calendar, they have prayer and study groups within the residence halls, and there are many local service projects and opportunities available. There is a chapel attendance requirement, but it can be met by attending less than half the available opportunities. Some students exceed the required attendance, but not very many, according to Brad Lau, the vice president for student life. Some faculty attend chapel, but there, too, the numbers are not large.

Mirroring national trends, the proportion of students who identify themselves as "nondenominational" has grown from 18.9% in 2002 to 27.4% in 2007. The next largest contingent of students self-identifies as Baptist (including several branches) and has held steadily around 14%. Quakers, during that same five-year period, have fallen slightly from 7.5% to 5.1%. About 10% of the university's students do not state a religious affiliation or preference. A recent survey, however, found that 97% of the university's traditional undergraduates believe that their faith is an important aspect of their lives.

Although exact figures are not kept, there is general agreement that about 25–30% of the faculty is self-identified as Quaker. Some members of the senior administrative staff are Friends, others are not. The president, however, is required to be an attender at a Friends meeting. The current chief executive comes from a Southern Baptist heritage and began attending a local Quaker church regularly upon his appointment. He argues that there are surprising resemblances between the two denominations. Both groups, for example, see the individual as responsible directly to God without the intervention of a priest or pastor.[13] A majority of the board of trustees remains Friends.

On an earlier trip to Newberg, I met with the president, David Brandt, and with the vice presidents for academic affairs and for marketing and advancement, the chief finance officer, a group of students (mostly majoring in business-related areas), and some faculty members. Subsequently, the chief academic officer I had initially met, Dr. Robin Baker, has succeeded President Brandt, and I was able to speak to Dr. Baker in his new role on a recent visit. On that second visit, I was also able to speak to some additional faculty members (two of whom are graduates of GFU but separated by several decades) and the chief student affairs officer. All the conversations were open and, in every case, students, faculty, and administration were eager to talk about the college's religious emphasis, as well as its attention to academic and scholarly concerns. The relationship between the liberal arts emphasis and the newer, nonbaccalaureate programs came up frequently, although faculty members seem to be growing more comfortable with these links in recent years. President Baker spoke at some length about the university's current planning efforts and, particularly, its sharpened attempts to define itself, to ascertain which of its programs most closely fit its mission, and to understand how to present its Quaker heritage.

I asked several of those with whom I spoke about challenges the university is facing early in the twenty-first century. Several mentioned fiscal challenges (GFU does not have a spectacularly large endowment, tuition discounting is a growing fact of life, there remain some facilities in need of renovation), and the difficulty of recruiting a community that is both more diverse and more highly qualified, especially in the student body. Some cultural challenges—for example, contemporary attitudes toward traditional marriage, the Internet, students seeking non-classroom-based learning—were cited.

I also asked those with whom I met to list peer or aspirational institutions. Peers frequently mentioned were Whitworth, Seattle Pacific, Willamette, Westmont, Spring Arbor, and Linfield. Wheaton was most often cited as an aspirational choice. Earlham was also cited in that category, but commonly with a caveat noting that GFU aspires to a higher degree of faith than that midwestern Quaker college.

George Fox University gives the impression of an institution that knows it is operating in a very challenging and competitive marketplace and that it does not have enormous resources to throw into the fray. What it does have, which seems to be serving it very well, is a strong sense of niche and of mission. A pervasive belief that the college is devoted to serving a higher cause generates optimism, enthusiasm, and loyalty.

10 | An Island of Piety . . . in a Sea of Riches

Westmont College, Santa Barbara, California

The first-time visitor to Westmont College should be prepared for an impressive and startling introduction. Westmont is nestled in the verdant hills of Santa Barbara, California, in as opulent a setting for a college as it is possible to imagine. Although today's Westmont includes many buildings of a fairly typical small-college architectural style, including residence halls, classrooms, and gyms, the 111-acre campus is centered around Kerrwood Hall, a 1929 estate built as a luxurious private residence in the California Mediterranean style. The campus is located in a neighborhood of impressive wealth—indeed, few of the nearby estates are actually visible from public roads. The site is heavily wooded and includes some of the gardens of the original mansion. Given Westmont's strong Christian mission, it would not be inappropriate to describe its physical plant as "Edenic."[1]

Westmont began its life in 1937 in Los Angeles as the Bible Missionary Institute. Its primary founder was Ruth Kerr, who was at that time the owner of the Kerr Mason Jar company. (In 1937 Kerr jars were not a cute decorative feature of chain restaurants with a "country" theme but an essential staple of most American kitchens.) It later changed its name to Western Bible College. In 1940, under the leadership of its first chief executive, Dr. Wallace Emerson, the college moved toward its current mission as a Christian liberal arts college and changed its name to "Westmont College." Four years later, the college was outgrowing its Los Angeles site and purchased its current property in Montecito in the Santa Barbara hills. The largest portion of today's campus had been the estate of Dwight Murphy and the Deane School for Boys. Westmont won regional accreditation in 1958. Over the course of two visits to Westmont, I had the opportunity to speak to Dr. David Winter and Dr. Stan Gaede, both now past presidents of the college, as well as a wide range of administrators, faculty, and students.

Westmont's attractive and lush setting influences some of the college's character and some of its choices. For example, it poses both attractions and challenges when it comes to recruiting students and faculty (teachers at Westmont cannot, by and large, afford to live very near campus). Given land values in Santa Barbara, it also means that there is little realistic opportunity for the college to expand its geographical footprint dramatically. This, in turn, seems to lead to less pressure than at many institutions to try to increase sharply the size of the student body.

At first glance, the people of the college fit its setting. There is a pleasant, West Coast informality around campus; the style of dress is neat but casual. In warm weather, shorts seem ubiquitous for students, ties very rare except for those heading off campus. Students are friendly and, when the weather is good, as it usually is in Santa Barbara, frolicsome: Frisbees are in evidence, and the campus's outdoor swimming pool is well used.

But it would be an error to think that Westmont's California locale and style detract or distract from the pervasiveness and seriousness of its mission. Westmont College is deeply Christian and ambitiously academic. Indeed, Westmont goes out of its way to make overt the links between its scholarly aspirations and its spiritual ones. Both in its printed materials and in many of my conversations with students, faculty, and staff, the college moves to the foreground the issues of religious faith and academic freedom. It is a commonly held belief, outside the religious academic establishment, that to the extent a college or institution advances a religious perspective, it veers toward dogma and away from the spirit of free inquiry. Even more than most faith-based colleges, Westmont seems almost obsessed with challenging this stereotype. For example, one student recruitment publication is entitled "Five Great Reasons to Choose a Christian College." At the top of the list is "academic freedom":

> Professors and administrators at the world's top colleges and universities hold one concept dear beyond almost any other: the idea of academic freedom. In order to understand the truth and to allow the best ideas to have dominance in society, they say, we must have the freedom to discuss all ideas. To let them rise and fall on their merits. But just try adding a Christian perspective to the discussion in classrooms on secular campuses around the world, and you may find out where the limits to academic freedom lie. Most public institutions in this country are less than warmly receptive to faith-based perspectives and contributions in the classroom. Why limit yourself? . . . Westmont's commitment to academic freedom is obvious, not only in courses that demand your best critical thinking, but also through a wide range of opportunities and organizations that explore the world of ideas.[2]

Westmont defines itself as devoted to the complimentary dual goals of promoting the liberal arts and Christianity. A former trustee observed that the college's mission was to graduate students well prepared to live out a Christian worldview in their work and lives. Academically, it offers majors in a variety of typical liberal arts areas—for example, biochemistry, cellular and molecular biology, art history, French language and literature, sociology and anthropology, political science, and mathematics. Like many contemporary liberal arts colleges, a variety of preprofessional majors—such as economics and business, communication studies, and kinesiology and physical education—are also offered. Westmont offers minors in gender studies and ethnic studies, disciplines sometimes shunned by conservative religious institutions. One can graduate with a BA in theater arts with a dance emphasis—some of the colleges we discuss in these pages have only recently allowed social dancing to be part of campus life. There is a department of religious studies, which includes a number of areas of concentration that would not be found at a secular liberal arts college—biblical studies, Christian mission, Christian mission with urban concentration. A student can choose a preseminary emphasis within the philosophy major, but she could also select a prelaw or pre-MBA option, a standard undergraduate academic track, or one focusing on Social Issues and the Human Condition. Along with Wheaton College, Westmont is listed in the *U.S. News* top-tier of national liberal arts colleges.

While the college is firm about its mission in liberal learning, Westmont's liberal arts education remains pervasively Christian. All of Westmont's faculty members "are professing Christians who welcome opportunities to contribute to the spiritual life of their students and the campus."[3] This is not a vague or diffuse stipulation. Specifically, all faculty and staff must come from the "evangelical, Protestant heritage." The college has created and published a document entitled *Staffing Westmont,* which includes statements of faith and of community life. The staffing brochure notes that "because we are a residential community of learners, all faculty and staff have an impact on the college's ability to help students grow intellectually, socially, and spiritually. Therefore, all regular employees are required to support Westmont's mission as a liberal arts college rooted in Christ and to demonstrate this support by affirming the Statement of Faith and agreeing to abide by the Community Life Statement."[4] In addition, prospective faculty members are asked to submit a personal statement of their philosophy of the relationship between faith, teaching, and scholarship.

The college's firm staffing requirements exclude, of course, those who adhere to other religious traditions, such as Jews or Muslims, and atheists or agnostics. It also excludes Catholics, although there has been some discussion in recent years about the possibility of including Roman Catholics, especially those who espouse a faith of a more evangelical character, within the faculty.[5] There is an effort made, on the other hand, to bring to campus, as visitors, individuals with a wide variety of different perspectives. In several conversations I had at Westmont, this effort to bring to campus guests of significantly varied backgrounds, beliefs, and perspectives was stressed as an important aspect of preparing well-informed students to function as effective Christians in the "real world."

The statement of faith, to which all subscribe, notes that the college's trustees, administrators, and faculty participate in many different churches, within the worldwide evangelical Protestant tradition. It specifies nine articles of faith, which are, in abbreviated form:

1. One must profess belief in one God and in Jesus Christ.
2. God is infinite, beyond imagination, faithful, and steadfast.
3. God is Triune and redeems the world from its fallenness.
4. God is the source of all that is good and Father to Jesus Christ.
5. God the Son became incarnate in Jesus Christ, one person both human and divine and born of the Virgin Mary, whose death paid the penalty for human sin.
6. The spirit of God inspired the authors of Scripture, which is without error, and guides the church.
7. Apart from God's grace we are lost and dead.
8. Faith in Christ brings humankind into the body and church of Christ.
9. Jesus Christ will return to judge the living and dead; those who do not believe in him will suffer forever a just punishment, those who believe in him will live and reign with him forever in heaven.

The community life statement consists of two parts: living in community and behavioral expectations. The first of these sections addresses the "other-centered" attitudes the colleges seeks to cultivate—integrity, responsibility, trust, compassion, forbearance, respect, and the like. It notes an inevitable tension: "We are committed to inquiry as well as pronouncement, rigorous study as well as kindred friendship, challenging teaching as well as reflective learning. Sometimes these tensions will lead to conflict. To live in unity, we must set ourselves to the practical task of discerning daily how to love well, how to inflesh the Biblical call to justice and mercy."

The behavioral expectations are explicit. They make it clear the college "will not condone practices which Scripture forbids." These include sexual relations outside of marriage, homosexual practice, drunkenness, theft, profanity and dishonesty, as well as "sins of the spirit" such as covetousness, jealousy, pride, and lust. Harassment is forbidden, integrity upheld. It condemns the abuse of tobacco and alcohol, and questions, but does not overtly prohibit their use. Alcohol and tobacco products are not allowed on campus or at college-related student activities.

Westmont requires three courses in religion of all its students: Old Testament, New Testament, and Christian Doctrine.

Mission opportunities abound. Domestically, Westmont students can work in Santa Barbara's juvenile justice system, with people with AIDS/HIV, teaching English as a second language in the Hispanic community, and with the homeless, for example. There are also an impressively large range of options for on-campus ministries, including Bible study, groups advocating sexual purity, and prayer groups. And, of course, there is the usual range of nonreligious clubs and organizations, including a full range of National Association of Intercollegiate Athletics sports. Internationally, student opportunities include service in Guatemala, Honduras, Mexico, China, and Tanzania.

In a conversation with Christian Hoeckley, director of the Gaede Institute of Liberal Arts (which sponsors on- and off-campus programs focusing on liberal learning, including a high-profile, prestigious summer conference on the liberal arts), and another with a group of three faculty members from the Spanish, mathematics, and teacher education disciplines, there was a clear and oft-reiterated theme of the college's duty to lead students away from simplistic views. Dean Hoeckley stressed that a major challenge of the college was to engage students with intellectual issues in a nuanced manner. He cited as specific issues in which this was a challenge biological evolution and stem cell research and stated strongly that the college has a duty not to let students walk away from such subjects with an unsophisticated understanding. And, he noted, often students come to Westmont without having contemplated issues such as these in a complex and thoughtful way. The college seeks to explain to the families of students that such subjects will be part of the curriculum and that unthinking, doctrinaire responses to them will not be satisfactory. The college's mission is to challenge students academically, not to offer them intellectual safety. Faculty members, without prompting from me, stressed the same themes. Students, their teachers agreed, sometimes come from backgrounds that can be intellectually narrow. Our job, they affirmed, is "not to give 'em simple answers!"[6] Interim Provost Warren Rogers noted that Westmont's mission was a rigorous academic program coupled with one of spiritual development. Students should leave the college, he affirmed, as thoughtful individuals, not shaken by tough questions—questions, he noted, that might come from advocates of extreme positions both on the side of naturalistic scientific perspectives and that of religion. No one at Westmont should be afraid to ask any question. He noted the college's steadfast support of science as one avenue to truth.

One theme that emerged from several constituencies at Westmont, including the dean of admissions, was the challenge of recruiting a more diverse student body. Obviously, Westmont is seeking students with a serious Christian faith. But issues of racial, ethnic, national, and economic diversity are a concern, although the general belief was that the college had been making progress in this area. There is a suspicion that Westmont's elite locale does not present an immediately welcoming image to prospective students who might be visiting from less affluent neighborhoods: the last portion of the drive to the Westmont campus is a veritable tour of the residential options open only to the very highest echelons of America's families of wealth. Westmont is trying a program of sending liberal arts "ambassadors" to high schools with a large minority population. I also heard some expressions of concern that the college needed, too, to diversify its faculty, although the students (speaking more of intellectual than racial or ethnic issues) were convinced that the faculty was considerably more diverse than they were.

The integration of the collegiate experience is a recurring theme in conversations with Westmont faculty and administrators. Director Hoeckley, for example, stressed the importance of linking academic work with civic, social, and faith issues. He noted how he had originally been nervous about teaching philosophy within the context of a generally conservative Christian institution but how that concern had very quickly evaporated. The ties between faith and knowledge were often stressed: I asked Provost Rogers, a physicist, how a physics course might be different in a Christian college and a secular institution. He noted how, in a physics course at Westmont, he might invite students not just to learn the facts of nature but to marvel at them. He also mentioned that at a Christian college, a different cast of historical figures from science might be emphasized. And some questions are raised that would not come up in a secular science course: for example, does the Resurrection violate Newton's laws? When asked the same questions about integrating faith and learning, students mentioned as illustrations an emphasis on ethics in business classes or being asked to think about the philosophy of science from a theological perspective. Students also mentioned a concern about diversity issues as one area in which faith and learning were connected. Faculty members noted that they often asked themselves, and their students, questions such as, "How is this class going to make you a better person?"

On my visits to Westmont, I asked a number of constituents, most especially students, about their sense of behavioral restrictions. Students said that they did not feel themselves to be constrained by Westmont's social regulations. When I asked them if it would be acceptable for a Westmont student to advocate in favor of abortion rights, they unanimously concluded that it would not. When I asked them what would be the institution's policy in regards to a homosexual student, they said that the college would tolerate a student who was open about having such sexual inclinations but that it would not accept homosexual behavior. Dr. David Cole, a Westmont trustee emeritus and a former faculty member at the University of California at Berkeley, believes that student behavior at Westmont is more defined than at most collegiate institutions but that the college is not at all heavy-handed in the enforcement of student behavior codes. Students, too, agreed, that for the most part, the college was more interested in development than disciplinary action. They do not feel constrained by the college's behavioral standards. Students also noted that while they felt the majority of their peers at Westmont were probably politically conservative, there was not any great political uniformity, and there was considerable difference of opinion on some issues, such as the war in Iraq. Dr. Cole, the former trustee, believed that the college was very careful to avoid an institutional position on purely political issues, although sometimes moral matters in the political arena did lead Westmont to take a collective stance.

When I asked students why they choose Westmont, most mentioned both religious and academic reasons. Some students with whom I spoke had transferred from public colleges and junior colleges and had been seeking an institution in which issues of faith were more directly addressed. At the same time, a wide variety of additional factors were also relevant: students wanted a school on the West Coast; they wanted a small college; they wanted to play soccer.

When I asked about changes in the institution over the past decade or two, there was accord across faculty, staff, and board members as well as students that there had been little shift in the college's core mission of academic excellence and faith formation. Several individuals with long histories at Westmont felt that the students were more cosmopolitan and perhaps more diverse than in the past.

In terms of collegiate governance, the former trustee cited the happy relationship and great rapport between board, administration, and faculty. He felt they were like a family and that many close personal bonds formed across those groups. The faculty members believed that the faculty dominated academic decision making and noted, a bit ruefully, that faculty decisions sometimes took a while to become final, hardly a distinctive trait in academe.

I asked everyone with whom I spoke at Westmont which institutions they considered "the competition." The answers included Pepperdine, Gordon, Occidental, Wheaton, Calvin, University of California at San Diego, UCLA, and Claremont. The college today has about twelve hundred students on campus and about ninety faculty members. Tuition at Westmont was just under $30,000 in 2006–7. The college endowment is $66 million and its annual operating budget $43.7 million.

Westmont College seems to me to exemplify a spirit of cheerful, uplifting, happy evangelicalism, coupled with a very serious emphasis on a rigorous program of liberal learning. Its home in the lush hills of Southern California must reinforce its sense of optimism and discourage any impulses toward a dour or grim view of life or learning. To a degree that seems to me unusual in American higher education, the college and all its constituencies have a kind of lasting clarity about the college's direction, mission, and character: it is buoyantly uncompromising in its dedication to vigorous liberal education and its firm commitment to pervasive evangelical Protestant Christianity.

11 | "Expect a Miracle"

Oral Roberts University, Tulsa, Oklahoma

Most college campuses I have visited over the past several decades have displayed an architectural style that mixes a few iconic structures or features, combined with a multitude of fairly generic buildings.[1] A signature fountain or dome or Old Main Hall mixes, usually pleasantly, with dorms, classrooms, and office areas that, while often attractive, could be transposed without great shock to most any other campus. Some are red brick, some tan, some concrete; some are architecturally noteworthy, others are pedestrian.

But no one would ever describe the campus of Oral Roberts University (ORU) on some 263 acres in southern Tulsa as "generic" or "pedestrian." Most of the campus was constructed in the 1960s and 1970s in a style that has been described as "modernistic" and as "Disneyesque."[2] At the main entrance to the university is a giant (sixty-foot) statue of praying hands. Behind it is the Prayer Tower, a brightly colored glass and steel structure, shaped like an umbrella or a cross, with a superstructure suggesting Christ's crown of thorns and topped by a perpetually burning torch. Other campus buildings feature multistory concrete pylons, geodesic-style domes, gold-tinted glass, and similar dramatic features. Across the southern boundary of the campus is the former City of Faith Medical Center, the second highest building in the state of Oklahoma, now an office complex, and flanked by two smaller skyscrapers, all of which have today substantial unoccupied space. Across the western border of the campus are a Hilton Hotel and the Victory Christian Center, an archetypical contemporary "megachurch," the pastor of which is Billy Joe Daugherty, who served as interim president of ORU during 2008 (with the title "executive regent"). I had read about the architecture of this charismatic Christian university before visiting and had seen photos of some of its more dramatic buildings. I expected to find the campus less than tasteful, perhaps amusingly idiosyncratic. In fact, I had not reckoned with three factors that do not show up in photographs: the campus is attractively landscaped, bringing the buildings together with abundant and attractive greenery; the overall effect of all this futuristic architecture, albeit to some a bit reminiscent of the Jetsons, is surprisingly harmonious with itself, if not with traditional campus construction; and peopling this dramatic venue, strolling its sidewalks, sitting on its benches, and occupying its offices and classrooms are warm, attractive, and bright students, faculty, and staff. I would suggest that the campus architectural style of ORU is a good emblem of the institution as a whole: certainly not to everyone's taste, but internally consistent, strikingly one-of-a-kind, and inhabited by impressive, dedicated, and sincere people. It combines the most dramatic aspirations with some serious worldly woes.

Granville Oral Roberts was born in 1918 in Oklahoma. His father was a clergyman and his mother had an American Indian grandparent, making Oral one-eighth Native American. The story of Roberts's rise as a prominent and influential American evangelist in the mid-twentieth century is an intriguing one but has only a tangential relationship with the university he founded early in the 1960s. The story of ORU's founding is well known to students, faculty, and staff at the university: several members of each constituency cited to me, word for word, by memory, the exact commission Oral Roberts affirmed he received from God to "build Me a University": "Raise up your students to hear My voice, to go where My light is dim, where My voice is heard small, and My healing power is not known, even to the uttermost bounds of the earth. Their work will exceed yours, and in this I am well pleased."[3] These two sentences have achieved an iconic stature at ORU over the past five decades. The university accepted its first students in 1965 and was accredited by the Higher Learning Commission of the North Central Association of Colleges and Schools a half-dozen years later. Its early history was one of dramatically rapid progress, justifying the claim that "never since the late nineteenth century has a Christian college been so well funded at its inception and so quickly become a leading Christian college in this country."[4]

Oral Roberts also founded the City of Faith Medical Center and medical school in 1981. A school of law, dental school, and graduate nursing school were also created. In the late 1980s, these branches of ORU closed. The school of law's assets, primarily a law library, were transferred to Pat Robertson's Regent University in Virginia Beach, Virginia, where they contributed to the creation of the Regent University School of Law. The medical school and hospital were dismantled. In the case of both professional programs, the primary motivation for closure was fiscal.

In 1993, Oral Roberts's son Richard became president of ORU, with the founder assuming the title chancellor.

"Charismatic" Christianity is not a term the definition of which is universally agreed upon. But it is also a concept without which it is impossible to understand Oral Roberts and ORU. At the simplest, charismatic Christians are those who believe they have been touched by the Holy Spirit. Those who call themselves charismatic believe that this experience is different from either plain belief or the experience of being "born again." The particular gifts of the Holy Spirit can include speaking in tongues, healing, and prophecy. "Charismatic" is an adjective, not a noun: there is no particular denomination that can lay claim to ownership of this subset of the Christian religion: there are charismatic Baptists, Lutherans, Presbyterians, and Episcopalians. Among the ORU faculty who profess a charismatic faith are also Quakers and Catholics, and, in fact, there is a strong contemporary charismatic movement within the Roman Catholic Church. Charismatic beliefs and practices are easily confused with those called "Pentecostal."[5] In both cases, there are various subgroups and theological divisions. Pentecostals also emphasize a personal relationship with the Holy Spirit, and many of them also practice glossolalia. I spoke with both students and faculty-staff groups at ORU, and it was my impression that, while everyone used the phrase "charismatic Christian," the student use of this expression was less theological and perhaps more practice-oriented than that of their elders. It seemed to me that, to many of the students I spoke with, "charismatic" meant primarily an exuberant style of worship, with enthusiastic and joyful praise, and a conviction of a personal connection with the divine.

Possibly as an aspect of charismatic faith, although I do not identify any particular theological justification undergirding this practice, is a community belief that I felt strongly at ORU, in the value of very frank (to an outsider, sometimes embarrassingly frank) self-revelation, in terms of personal crises, temptations, doubts, confusions, trials, and the like, accompanied by caring support and affirmation by friends and colleagues.

My host at ORU was a professor of biology (PhD, University of Michigan). He invited me to start my visit by joining him and some colleagues for an early morning prayer meeting, followed by breakfast in the student cafeteria. The prayer meeting was attended by about ten individuals, mostly faculty members, but including some staff, volunteers, and one

ORU graduate. This group has been gathering weekly for more than a decade. The meeting began with song, led by a professor of geography, with the group moving comfortably and with obvious familiarity from one song to another. Singing recurred throughout the hour-long session. Prayers were offered by individuals in no particular order, on a variety of subjects. In some ways, this session reminded me of a Quaker meeting: individuals spoke when they were moved to do so without any set program or order. There were prayers for missions and for specific students doing missionary work. Some participants asked for comfort for others who had suffered losses. It was clear that most of the participants knew by name a large number of the individuals for whom prayers were offered. There were also more generic statements expressing hope for a large group of prospective students who were visiting the campus that day, speakers at recent chapel gatherings, some prayers for increased academic rigor and scholarship at the college, and some for overturning some pressing institutional problems. Toward the end of the session, a prayer was offered that my visit would be a good one, with positive results for the university. There was a little bit of quiet speaking in tongues interspersed with praying in English.

I had several meetings with faculty members and academic administrators at ORU. All agreed that the intertwining of faith and learning was crucial at the university. One faculty member noted that he thought it improper to preach in class, but he also believed that religion permeated everything he did and was not just for celebration on the Sabbath. There was, for this scientist, no disconnect between his respect for the principles of open scientific investigation and his appreciation of the beauty of God's creation. One academic administrator described the university's mission, and the charismatic vision of Oral Roberts, as being alive to the gifts of the Holy Spirit, gifts such as prophecy, tongues, and healing. God is active at ORU, he affirmed, working to transform the body, mind, and spirit of students.

That triad—mental, physical, and spiritual health and growth—is a consistent focus at ORU. It is often called the philosophy of "whole-person education."[6] Thus, the mission statement of the university reads:

> The mission of Oral Roberts University—in its commitment to the Christian faith—is to educate the whole person in spirit, mind, and body, thereby preparing its graduates to be *professionally competent* servant-leaders who are

spiritually alive, intellectually alert, physically disciplined, and *socially adept.* The University seeks to synthesize the best practices of liberal arts, professional, and graduate education with a charismatic emphasis to enable students to go into every person's world with God's message of salvation and healing for the totality of human need.

I have italicized the five "university learning outcomes."[7] The mission statement goes on to indicate that the goal of its instructional program—the "mind" leg of the triad—is "critical thinking; information literacy; global and historical perspectives; aesthetic appreciation; intellectual creativity."

Undergraduate general education requirements are carefully coordinated with the threefold growth mission of the university. For the *spirit*, students are required to take three three-credit courses in religion, one each in Old Testament, New Testament, and charismatic life and healing ministry. Students (as well as faculty) are also required to attend chapel twice weekly. There are also a variety of optional religious experiences, of course, such as retreats and dorm devotions. For the *body*, students must complete two introductory fitness courses, pass a swimming test, and participate in one aerobic activity course every semester of attendance. (Until 1988 faculty members were also required to maintain and document a regular program of fitness activities.) ORU must be one of a very few institutions left that has a "gym requirement." For the *mind*, all undergraduates must complete nine credit hours of English communication; the equivalent of six hours in foreign languages; eleven hours in natural science, including eight in a laboratory science and three in math; twelve hours in humanities, literature, and fine arts; and nine credit hours in the social sciences including courses in American government and American history. To the observer familiar with other faith-based colleges and universities, and with American higher education generally, these requirements seem unusually rigorous in the physical fitness area, typical in the range of required general education coursework, and slight in the area of religious studies.

ORU is determined to assess student progress in mind, body, and sprit and has initiated an ambitious electronic portfolio program (ePortfolio) that is required of all students. It is organized according to the five learning outcomes noted earlier (intellectual, spiritual, physical, social, and professional). Students complete specific exercises and submit "artifacts," some of which are linked to course work, that result in a "Personal Growth

Assessment (PGA)" on a 0–4 scale (not unlike a conventional grade point average or GPA).[8] One senior administrator described the electronic portfolio as a tool to help students find God's plan for their lives, to discover what they *can* do, and what they *want* to do. (I also encountered some concern that ePortfolio, while valuable, was perhaps excessively time consuming.)

ORU students are, in one sense, homogeneous: as one of them said, "We are all charismatic Christians." But in many other ways, they are strikingly diverse. About 27% of them are members of minority groups, primarily African American. During my time on campus, I saw a more significant mixing of minority and majority students than one finds on most college campuses today. There did not seem to me to be the kind of informal voluntary segregation in the social realm that is unfortunately not uncommon: groups of students walking about campus or sitting in the dining hall appeared to be pretty randomly mixed when it came to race and ethnicity. There is no rule that students need to be charismatic or Protestant or even Christian at ORU. In the 2006 CIRP Freshman Survey, the largest proportion of students, by far (84.7%), described themselves as "other Christian Protestant" rather than identifying with a denomination.[9] Of those who did so identify, 4.3% were Baptist, 2.8% were Methodist, 2.8% indicated "none," and 3.2% indicated "other religion." There was a sprinkling of most Protestant denominations (e.g., Congregational, Episcopal, Lutheran, Presbyterian). Roman Catholic students are welcome on campus.

Of particular interest to me was the manner in which Jewish students were singled out as explicitly welcomed at ORU.[10] In the student code brochure, several paragraphs are directed specifically to Jewish students. This section begins with the note that "since we of the Christian faith have our roots in the Hebrew faith, maintain the deepest love and respect for the Jewish people, and are ardent believers in the State of Israel, Jewish students have also been enrolled." It goes on to state that Jewish students are expected to attend chapel services and to abide by the university's student lifestyle requirements. It asks Jewish students to adopt an "integrity of openness" to Christianity but overtly states that this does not mean that "by virtue of your enrollment that you have necessarily believed on Jesus Christ. But it does mean that you are sincerely open to God's dealings in your life." The document says "We are honored to admit such students."[11]

About 60% of the students at ORU attended public high school, 27% a private Christian school (4% some other private high school), and 9% were home schooled. According to the vice president for academic administration, about 91% of the students at ORU are Republicans in political affiliation. The college has many opportunities for student civic engagement and service learning, and there is no particular political stance required. According to this administrator, "Oral likes freedom." So, for example, there would be a variety of opinions on campus about the ethics of stem cell research; students would be allowed a wide range of off-campus political and social affiliations; and students whose sexual orientation was gay but who maintained a chaste lifestyle would not be excluded from attendance.

Each ORU student signs an honor code pledge that is kept in her or his file.[12] This pledge includes general affirmations (e.g., to grow in my spirit by developing my own relationship with God; to apply myself wholeheartedly to my intellectual pursuits) as well as specific affirmations and injunctions: students promise not to lie, steal, curse, or cheat. They pledge to abstain from drugs, alcohol, and tobacco, on and off campus. They are not to "engage in any illicit, unscriptural sexual acts, which include any homosexual activity and sexual intercourse with one who is not my spouse through traditional marriage of one man and one woman." There is a student dress code, which has been significantly modified and loosened in recent years, which suggests appropriate attire for different activities and venues on campus. So, for example, male students should wear collared shirts to class but can wear T-shirts or sweatshirts for informal activities.

I met with a group of students, many of whom were in an English class, but with several other majors as well, including biomedical chemistry. They had applied to a wide variety of institutions as well as ORU when making their college decision: The schools they mentioned included the University of Texas at Austin, Boston University, Wheaton, Washington University (St. Louis), Northwestern, Indiana University, Nyack College (in New York), North Dakota State University, Vanderbilt, Macalester, the University of Minnesota, the University of North Dakota, and Penn. This list is of interest in that it is certainly weighted toward non-Christian institutions, but the sampling was not large enough to draw a reasoned conclusion.

I asked the students why they choose ORU. Some were following a relative, friend, or pastor. Several said that, when they came to visit campus, the atmosphere they found convinced them that ORU was where they belonged.

The students believed that the interaction of faith and learning in their education gave them a "broader view" of the world than they would have received at a secular institution and that, at such a nonreligious institution, many of them would feel that religion was an intellectual "compromise." They noted that much of what they studied in humanities classes—Shakespeare's plays, for example—was written in a culture where religion was pervasive; thus, they understood such material better than those with a wholly secular perspective. They observed that on issues such as evolution and creation, teachers presented multiple theories and said it was up to students to make up their own minds.

I asked, as I always do, if they felt they were well prepared to enter a secular world after leaving college. They believed they were, in fact, well equipped to participate in that world and that their years of questioning at ORU gave them a solid belief structure on which to build their postcollege lives. Some students came to ORU from religiously sheltered families; some challenged that past, and others tried to maintain it. They did note that some students they knew tried to hide after graduation, to stay within the "Christian bubble."[13] They characterized ORU as a harmonious environment, a family, all the members of which shared one powerful belief (this at a time of considerable institutional strife and trauma).

The students observed that they believed that the strongest conversational taboo at ORU was the subject of religious differences—that where such differences did surface, the prevailing student culture avoided facing them directly. (It was not my sense that this was a taboo topic for faculty or administrators at ORU.) If another student came to doubt the truth of Christianity, they said, they would pray for him but not argue him into a change of heart or mind. If they encountered a fellow student who was violating the conduct expectations of ORU, they might intervene, but they might also look the other way.

Some of the students raised (without prompting) some skepticism about the notion of "seed faith" and the prosperity gospel—the notion that giving, especially financial gifts, is planting the seeds for later material rewards. This philosophy is discussed at some length in the student honor code handbook, which notes that "God has promised to meet not one or two but all your needs." Seed faith is defined as the cheerful "giving of money, time, talent, care and total self" in the expectation of "a miracle return."[14] They were also amused at their own propensity to seek marriage partners while in college and noted with laughter that many outside the college, and some within it, believed that the motivation for early weddings at Christian schools was the strict injunction to remain abstinent before marriage.

At the same time, the students were unanimous and enthusiastic in describing themselves as charismatic; they said they found the chapel worship "awesome" and delighted in "the joy of the Lord." I thought this group of students was bright, open, not at all afraid to disagree with each other, and happily committed to their growth in scholarship and belief at ORU.

Unlike students, faculty members at Oral Roberts University are expected to be Christians, although non-Christians are occasionally invited into the classroom to make presentations that are a part of a course. Faculty members are expected to be regular participants in a local church of their choice. There is an expectation that faculty members will be "open to the Holy Spirit." About 35% of the faculty responded to a religious preference survey in spring 2007 by describing themselves as nondenominational or interdenominational charismatic Christians. About 14% said they were Methodists, and 13% members of an Assemblies of God congregation. The remainder came from a variety of denominational traditions. Two were Episcopalian, three were Catholic, and one was Quaker.[15]

I had the opportunity to discuss pedagogical issues with a faculty member who, like me, professes English literature. He noted how contemporary literature often embodies a "hidden movement of grace," and he described how part of his job was to reach students who arrive in college with the notion that Christian literature is what is found at a Christian bookstore. He also noted that some students from the charismatic tradition tend to separate religious celebration from the exigencies of daily life and that some of the parents of those students send their young people to colleges, including ORU, to acquire the skill to make money, in a collegiate atmosphere that they believe will not destroy their Christian faith. Mature spiritual formation is a goal in this professor's classes. A requirement for the English major, thus, is an upper-division course focusing on Christian aesthetic encounters. Students at ORU, he finds, are eager to learn but not particularly eager to talk about religious doctrine because they tend toward following nondenominational and experiential religious pathways. This faculty member, and others with whom I spoke at ORU, were firm in their conviction that they had greater academic freedom there than in a secular institution, where they would "have to watch what they said." He was particularly attracted by the absence of strict denominational require-ments. English literature majors at ORU, he noted, learn a variety of criti-cal theories and approaches, including some such as Marxist approach-es or feminist ones, which challenge their perspectives. I asked where some English majors from ORU had gone on to graduate school, and he mentioned the University of Virginia, Miami University, the University of Wisconsin, Johns Hopkins University, Yale, the University of Tulsa, and William and Mary. He also noted that in the past fifteen years or so, the majority of students at ORU had moved from traditional denomina-tional affiliations to the nondenominational megachurches, a move that is both local and widespread nationally. Another change he mentioned was that the university's board of trustees has migrated from one domi-nated by business leaders to one predominantly composed of evangelists. Given some of the university's fiscal challenges, he noted, this might be problematic.

I asked several faculty members and academic administrators about the faculty role in institutional governance. This is an area in which there has been some tension in recent years. One administrator, for example, noted that the faculty does not "own" the curriculum. Clearly, there is an explicit process for faculty decision making in academic decisions such as faculty hiring, reviews, and curricular development. At the same time, there have been administrative pressures, for example, to add new majors. By and large, it seems, faculty members have only rarely been overruled on academic matters, but at times they have felt themselves the objects of fairly energetic persuasive efforts, particularly by the recent president, Richard Roberts. And, some members of the ORU family have raised con-cerns about the role of the faculty in recent actions concerning the man-agement of the university, especially the recent "no confidence" vote in President Roberts.

At the time of my visit, Oral Roberts was about ninety years old, lived in California, and had the title chancellor. His son, Richard, had served as president for about a decade and a half, but had recently taken a leave of absence. The senior Roberts had just returned to campus and resumed a more visible role at the institution. I had not been to an institution such as ORU that was named for a still-living founder and made an effort to un-derstand how students, faculty, and staff related to Oral Roberts, the man, and what they thought would be the course of the university he created in the next century. What I found was a great deal of respect, bordering in some cases on veneration. Many faculty and staff, especially those with a long connection to ORU, referred to the evangelist as "Oral." One noted that Oral Roberts had had a "charismatic (lower case) influence on the Charismatic (upper case) movement," an observation echoed by several reference works that discuss charismatic Christianity. Just before my arrival on campus, Mr. Roberts had spoken at chapel, expressing his hopes that the university would not lose its spiritual purpose, would not drift into the secular camp as so many other schools (he cited the colonial colleges) have. I heard nothing during my visit to suggest that ORU's founder was not regarded with fondness and some reverence by the students, faculty, and staff at the college that bears his name.

I asked faculty members what they thought were peer institutions. They mentioned, among others, Abilene Christian, Baylor, Calvin, Wheaton, and Seattle Pacific. They noted, though, that there were many student cross-applications with the University of Oklahoma, the University of Tulsa, and Oklahoma State University.

If a faculty member lost her faith, I asked, what would happen? Such an individual, it was agreed, would be counseled and encouraged, but if the loss appeared permanent, it would be unlikely that individual could stay at ORU (or, there was general agreement, would want to). The faculty agreed, though, that some students were explicitly atheist. The campus ethos at ORU encourages faculty to disagree with each other and with their students, but within an overarching context of a shared sense of mission that encourages civility and pleasant relations. Faculty members believe they get to know the students in an intense and personal way, and the students tend to agree. They discuss personal as well as classroom issues, and students are often in faculty homes; "they like each other and we like them." Because the college is devoted to education of the whole person, faculty said, it is easier to discuss serious personal issues with them.

Faculty members reported their perception that today's ORU students are less denominational than their predecessors were; more are coming from nondenominational, often charismatic, megachurches. They believe that some of the university's students are atheists and that some become Christians while at ORU. They pray with their students, frequently at the start of class, but also in their offices, or in the midst of a discussion that seems vexed. They find most of the students pleasant and are proud of their close relationships with them, which they characterize as support-ive, even when there are disagreements or when students need reminders about academic rigor.

I also had the opportunity to meet with Dr. Clarence Boyd, the dean for student development and campus ministry. He has been at ORU nearly thirty-five years, in various capacities, and among his assignments now is planning the twice-weekly chapel services. He noted that chapel could feature music, outreach, or celebration of a particular event or individu-al such as Martin Luther King Jr. day, the athletics program, or student athletes. Many of the chapel services are led by students, and about half feature an outside speaker. Students are encouraged to attend a nearby church of their choice on Sundays, and there is a Sunday evening church service on campus as well, which began in August 2007. Most of the fac-ulty attends most of the chapel sessions, sitting in a designated section. I asked what an "athletics chapel" would consist of and a recent one was described: it began with words of worship and praise, some comments from an associate athletic director, three student testimonies, one student speaker, a brief talk by the athletics director about the vision for athlet-ics at ORU, words from the faculty athletics representative, and a closing prayer for the student athletes. Dr. Boyd believes that most students look forward to chapel.

He described his philosophy of student development at ORU in a nauti-cal metaphor. As ships are built in a harbor but meant when done to sail out of it, so too ORU students are shaped by their education at this Chris-tian college, but they leave its safe harbor when they sail out into the larger world upon graduation, when their mission is to take God to the ends of the earth. The dean noted that ORU's students and staff represent God's kingdom, and so they need a biblical foundation to carry the vision of that kingdom beyond the campus. The university needs to focus upon biblical and Christian teachings, as students are not coming to college well rooted in the Bible. The university, he believes, encourages students to talk about virtually anything, in a safe atmosphere, but asks that they maintain a biblical base.

We discussed the honor code and its prohibitions against smoking and drinking. The dean noted that the university was trying to move from prohibitions to affirming the benefits of the lifestyle it advances. He noted that the dress code has been relaxed but that there still remained stric-tures against certain styles in certain situations—for example, just about anything goes in the student cafeteria, but for class a more formal code applies.

Finally, I asked the dean if he had seen changes in the ORU student body over his three and a half decades there. He noted that fiscal pressures caused by university indebtedness posed challenges: there have been cuts of faculty and staff positions and of programs, and it was his belief that the university was in a hiring freeze during the fall when we spoke.

My visit to Oral Roberts University came at what was, perhaps, the best of times and the worst of times to learn about the school. The day before my arrival, the visiting team of the Higher Learning Commission, the accreditation arm of the North Central Association, had left campus. And, in the days just before and just after my visit to campus, ORU was in the midst of a very public, multifaceted crisis, one that put the institution into a situation of genuine peril and would certainly change it forever.[16]

Early in October 2007, three former professors at ORU sued the institution and four of its administrators, basing their suit on charges of wrongful termination and unlawful pressures to resign. The administrators named in the suit were President Richard Roberts, the provost, a vice president, and a dean. The professors affirmed that the cause of their terminations was the fact that they gave to officials there a document reporting that the family of President Richard Roberts had made inappropriate expenditures of college funds for personal expenses. This information came from an internal report, prepared by the sister-in-law of President Roberts, which apparently came to light when a computer was being repaired. The suit alleged that the president had sought to use a political science class to campaign for a mayoral candidate in Tulsa; that one of President Robert's children misused equipment from the athletics department; that university employees did the homework of the Roberts's children; that ORU was billed for nearly $30,000 for a vacation trip for one of Roberts's daughters; that Lindsey Roberts, Richard's wife, awarded scholarships to children of her friends who should not have otherwise been eligible for such aid; and that she used university security personnel inappropriately when doing personal travel. Subsequently, additional charges emerged, of a personal, moral nature, namely that Lindsay Roberts had nine times spent the night with an underage male guest at a university facility, been photographed in the company of many such young men, and had relocated a sixteen-year-old boy to their home. A further charge subsequently emerged, that the Roberts family had hired as a student "mentor" a young man with a known record of sexual transgressions. President and Mrs. Roberts denied the charges and sought to reassure the campus at a highly publicized chapel appearance. Oral Roberts returned to Tulsa from California.

About two weeks after the initial charges surfaced, it was also widely reported that ORU had an accumulated debt of approximately $50 million, which had grown over a period of many years, during which the Roberts family had lived an extravagant life style.

On 17 October 2007, Richard Roberts announced that he would take an indefinite leave of absence from ORU. The regents appointed Billy Joe Daugherty, senior pastor of the Victory Christian Center across the highway from ORU's campus, to serve as "executive regent" while President Roberts was on leave, sharing the administration of the university with Oral Roberts.

On 12 November, the tenured faculty members of the university voted "no confidence" in the academic leadership of President Richard Roberts. They carefully noted that the vote did not apply to President Roberts's leadership of the Oral Roberts evangelical ministries. Simultaneously, they voted positively in their confidence in the work of Provost Mark Lewandowski, who had called for greater transparency in university funding and an increased governance role for the faculty. Just a few days later, an additional lawsuit was filed by a former ORU senior accountant who claimed that "he was directed against his will and over his objections" to defraud the IRS, the Oklahoma Tax oversight body, and the public by not interfering with university funds being spent on personal luxuries for Richard and Lindsay Roberts.[17] Two students also filed suits that allege the university devalued their academic degrees. The day after Thanksgiving, the university announced the immediate resignation of Richard Roberts as president. Just hours later, an Oklahoma businessman, Mart Green, whose family owns the "Hobby Lobby" chain of craft stores, as well as "Mardel," a chain of Christian educational supply stores and a film production company, announced a huge gift to ORU. He donated $8 million at once and promised an additional $62 million after a three-month period in which he asked the university to demonstrate "good governance" and increased transparency in its financial management. Green is not a graduate of the university and has no prior connection to it. Green said at a news conference: "Let's get integrity. Let's get trust built back, and the financial issues will go away."[18] Simultaneously, the Associated Press reported that representatives from Pat Robertson's Regent University had contacted Oral Roberts University to explore options for future relationships between the two institutions. One year later, in winter 2008–9, some of these issues remain unresolved, although the crisis atmosphere of the fall of 2007 has abated considerably. Mart Green chairs the board of trustees, and a longtime faculty member, Dr. Ralph Fagan, is serving as interim president. A presidential search process is in place and moving forward, with the goal of selecting a new president by summer 2009.

Oral Roberts University stands today at a crossroads. On the one hand, it demonstrates a vigorous consistency in its drive to educate the minds, bodies, and spirits of its fifty-three hundred students. Simultaneously, it embodies and seeks to cope with the dangers and temptations of a powerfully dynastic model of collegiate leadership. One hopes that the former virtues will overcome the threats of the latter. One faculty member said of these events, "God is cleansing us, which is good."

12 | A Christian Walk Up North

Northwestern College, St. Paul, Minnesota

As one might expect in Garrison Keillor's Minnesota, Northwestern College, in Roseville, a near north suburb of St. Paul, is generally a quiet and unassuming kind of place. Where Baylor's efforts to raise academic standards and religious commitment drew national attention, with full-throated expressions of endorsement and of condemnation from press and pulpit, Northwestern College is probably known only slightly, and perhaps sometimes not at all, by many who live even within the greater Twin Cities region. But on closer examination Northwestern is, in many ways, not only noteworthy but idiosyncratic and unique. For example, it is the only NCAA institution to have played *two* football games on the same day. In October 2005, NWC first crushed Trinity Bible College by a score of 59–0. Later that afternoon, the team traveled to Macalester College, where it scored another decisive 47–14 victory. Not many college football teams score 106 points in one afternoon, much less in two complete, regulation contests. (In Northwestern's admissions view book, an entire page is devoted to describing how all of Northwestern's teams "don't leave their faith behind when they take the field.")

Nor do many evangelical Protestant colleges occupy proudly, and publicize the fact widely, a former Roman Catholic seminary. Although NWC now has several major new buildings and facilities on its attractive, lakeside campus, the centerpiece of the college's facilities is Nazareth Hall. This large and impressive structure, centered on the lovely Annunciation Chapel, was built in the early 1920s, on land the Catholic Church began acquiring as early as 1866. Annunciation Hall served as a seminary until 1970 when the training of priests in St. Paul was consolidated at the University of St. Thomas. It contained offices, classrooms, and living accommodations for the seminarians. Northwestern purchased the property at that time and reopened it in 1972. It remains the core of today's campus. Through the work of its Preservation of Campus Heritage Committee, NWC has prepared a handsome, glossy, colored brochure describing Nazareth Hall depicting, for example, the Stations of the Cross and the Old and New Testament stained glass windows. The brochure includes a substantial amount of information and several photos of the building in its initial Catholic uses. Today, Nazareth Hall houses faculty and administrative offices, classrooms, laboratories, the chapel, and the campus dining facility.

Although Northwestern is well within the greater Twin Cities urban area, the campus has a distinctly rural feel: it is set well back from roadways, has only one (guarded) entrance, and is beautifully sited on the shores of a small lake. In contrast to, say, North Park University in Chicago, Northwestern's physical space has an inward focus (this may be a partial heritage from its seminary days). College materials, while acknowledging a location "just a few miles from the Minneapolis–St. Paul metropolitan area," speak of the "peace and comfort of a secluded Christian academic community."[1]

Another distinctive feature of Northwestern College is that it owns and operates a network of fifteen Christian radio stations. Operating in eight locations, in Minnesota, North and South Dakota, Wisconsin, Iowa, and Florida, the stations are wholly professional media operations; they are not "college radio" enterprises. In some of these venues, both AM and FM broadcasts are involved. Each station does independent programming. The "home" enterprise is KTIS radio, which occupies a modern building adjacent to the St. Paul campus. Additionally, the SkyLight Network offers twenty-four-hours-a-day Christian programming via satellite to some three hundred other Christian radio outlets, and LifeNet.FM is an Internet Christian Contemporary Music Station. The NWC radio network evolved as a parallel means of promulgating the Christian message of the college. Today, it is a major income producer for the collegiate enterprise. The president of Northwestern, Dr. Alan Cureton, refers to the radio network as "our endowment." While this aspect of Northwestern's operations has been financially beneficial, it has also sometimes caused problems: traditional accrediting agencies do not equate an income-producing Christian broadcasting network with an income-producing endowment, invested in more conventional ways.

Northwestern College, although now a nondenominational evangelical Christian college, began as a Baptist institution. That affiliation has not been entirely lost, as a significant percentage of today's students and faculty have a Baptist affiliation. The college began in 1902 at the First Baptist Church in Minneapolis, with seven students. It was called "Northwestern Bible and Missionary School." Its first graduate, Anna Gooch, became a missionary in Burma, and many NWC students continue to think of mission work as an important part of their life goals. Indeed, a historian of Christian higher education describes the early Northwestern as "perhaps the most aggressive of the fundamentalist Bible schools."[2] The young college moved to a purchased property outside the church in 1905 and moved again in 1920. In the mid-1930s, the Bible college added a theological seminary. At the start of the Second World War, in 1941, Northwestern had an enrollment of just over five hundred students and a faculty of seventeen. For four postwar years, from 1948 to 1952, Evangelist and Wheaton College graduate Billy Graham served as president of Northwestern. At the beginning of his term, the campus moved to the Loring Park neighborhood in Minneapolis and began to acquire a range of facilities, including a gymnasium, fine arts building, and dormitories there. The seminary and the Bible school closed in the mid 1950s because of fiscal constraints, leaving a liberal arts college, which took the name of Northwestern College. But by 1966, the North Central Association delayed accreditation of Northwestern, primarily for financial concerns. The college was closed by new president William Berntsen, formerly a member of the music faculty. In 1970 the Loring Park campus was sold to the State of Minnesota two-year college system, and Nazareth Hall was purchased. Two years later, in 1972, the college reopened at the new location with 186 students and eleven faculty members. In 1977 Rev. Billy Graham helped celebrate NWC's seventy-fifth anniversary, and in 1978 the school was finally accredited by the North Central Association. Throughout the 1980s and 1990s, the college continued to grow, and its current president arrived just in time for the centennial celebration in 2002. One of the more dramatic new buildings on campus is the Totino Fine Arts Center, which the college view book notes is *not* named for a frozen pizza—sort of. It is named for Rose Totino, who invented the frozen pizza with her husband Jim at a Minneapolis restaurant, and who became a Christian while listening to KTIS radio in her car in 1965 and was thereafter a generous benefactor to the college.[3] The contemporary campus includes 107 acres and a mile of shoreline on Lake Johanna, as well as facilities nearby for student residences and KTIS radio. Admissions materials cite as the top reason for prospective students to choose Northwestern College: "You gave God your heart—now you want to do something important with your life."

Today, Northwestern enrolls about eighteen hundred undergraduates, and has close to three thousand students in all its programs, including a degree completion program for adults, a distance education enterprise, the Center for Graduate Studies, and a Christian Center for Communications in Ecuador.[4] Undergraduate tuition, room, and board at Northwestern totaled $27,740 in the 2007–8 academic year, with virtually all students receiving financial aid of some sort. The college offers a 10% discount to the children of Christian workers, and the same program for families with more than one student on campus at the same time and for children of Northwestern alumni. There are slightly more than one hundred full-time continuing members of the faculty and about the same number of part-time and/or temporary instructors.

Northwestern offers a large array of majors, mostly bachelor's degrees, but with a few associate degrees, certificate programs, and graduate offerings. Majors include many traditional liberal arts areas (e.g., art, biology, English literature, mathematics, and psychology), as well as some more vocationally oriented fields (e.g., accounting, general business, kinesiology, management information systems, marketing, and public relations). There are also several majors in religious areas: adult and family ministry, biblical studies, children and family ministry, ministry, pastoral ministry, urban ministry, and youth ministry. The catalog divides the college's academic offerings into thirteen departments (e.g., art and graphic design, biblical and theological studies, science, and mathematics) and the Division of Graduate and Continuing Education.

In a meeting with the senior academic administration (Provost Alford H. Ottley, Associate Provost Barbara Lindman, and Dean of the Faculty Mark Baden), we discussed the connections between faith and learning at NWC. These leaders (all of whom hold the PhD from mainstream research universities) affirmed, and students and faculty subsequently reiterated, that all courses at Northwestern are taught from a biblical worldview, and with a biblical foundation. So, for example, in science courses, it is emphasized that the world is ordered by a God of order who created the laws of nature. Moreover, recalling the institution's origins as a Bible college, all students take thirty credits in biblical subjects, earning, in effect, a minor in Bible. There is daily, required chapel. The combination of these requirements—daily chapel and thirty credits in biblical studies—is unusually high, even for vigorously Christian liberal arts colleges.

I asked, in this meeting and elsewhere, about the teaching of evolution, creationism, and intelligent design in science courses. There is a range of beliefs in this area within the biology faculty at Northwestern, and it is clear that students of science would be exposed to a range of theories of plant and animal development, including human origins. A member of the Biology Department with whom I also spoke was clearly and vigorously a non-Darwinian. There is, though, some pride that Northwestern students tend to know more about evolutionary biology that many students from secular colleges and universities, even if they do not believe in it. Students at NWC do have opportunities to learn about other religions in elective course work, but there are no non-Christian instructors for any courses, and guest speakers on campus present a Christian perspective.

Faculty members at Northwestern are clear and eloquent about the connections between faith and learning in their work.[5] In fact, each prospective faculty member is asked to submit a thoughtful piece of writing on this subject, and a similar essay is required for promotion once one is at the college. There is, though, considerable variation within the faculty about how the connections between faith and learning are forged. To some, it has to do with an interpersonal-pedagogical stance: teachers letting their students always know that "I care about you." In other cases, personally modeling a life of Christian virtue is central. For most, curricular connections are evident and important. For example, most in the physical sciences have opportunities to discuss human, natural, and universal origins and, in that context, to include the first books of Genesis in that discussion. One professor affirmed how, to him, the study of the universe showed how all created things fit each other perfectly, and how even the slightest differences might have made all plant, animal, and human life impossible. Another noted principles of mathematical regularity in the Bible. (The dean of students also cited math as evidence of a God of order and sequence.) And yet another spoke about how the study of chemistry led to pondering the philosophy of science, which, in turn, opens the door to theology. Most Northwestern College teachers begin class with a prayer, or a prayerful meditation, and it is not uncommon for students to ask a class to pray for a specific individual or for a positive outcome for a particular action or event.

I asked both the academic leadership and administrators in the Office of Student Affairs if a student pro-choice group would be tolerated. Clearly, this was not an issue that had arisen. Abortion is seen as contrary to biblical teaching, but key administrators were reluctant to completely deny the possibility of such a group, if it promoted open discussion and a range of viewpoints. All were in agreement that a NWC student could openly join such a group off campus.

Academic administrators there believe that NWC's academic standards are rising and that the institution is becoming less a Bible college and more a strong liberal arts institution. The school is growing, in programs and population, with a controlled admissions growth of fifty students per year. With increasing applications, this goal has been easily met recently, while simultaneously raising criteria such as the ACT scores of entering students. Retention rates are rising, and about 60% of the entering first-year students graduate within five years. The college takes pride in a greater diversity of students and faculty, and the creation of a more intentional community. Northwestern students younger than twenty years of age, and with fewer than sixty credits are required to live on campus, unless they are married, part-time students, or living at their parents' home.

Meeting with leaders in student affairs (the dean and associate dean of students), I learned more about the required daily chapel program. Each weekday morning from 10:30 to 11:00, the students (and some but not all of the faculty) gather for chapel. While still technically a universal requirement, students can be excused from chapel for a variety of reasons (e.g., not having classes on campus that day). Chapel can include different styles of worship, such as different ethnic groups' liturgy, teaching, outside speakers, serious and comical presentations, and formal and informal styles. With a chapel program five days a week, programming this event is a significant task. There are also many other official and unofficial faith gatherings on campus continually.

Northwestern sponsors each year some fourteen short-term noncredit mission experiences for students, usually consisting of twelve to twenty students and a faculty or staff leader. Most, but not all of these are international, and often involve service projects. Most students participate in at least one of these endeavors, but they are not required to do so. They are seen as good preparation for mission and ministerial careers, which attract a very significant proportion of NWC students (about half the students with whom I spoke had some serious interest in such pursuits).

Students and student affairs professionals spoke frequently about the dangers of isolationist tendencies, what they called the "holy huddle." Students are encouraged to learn about other religious traditions and the beliefs of individuals from a wide range of backgrounds. They also stressed that Northwestern's style of dealing with faith issues tends more toward interpersonal communication and support rather than legalistic codes. The goal, the dean of students believes, is to look at what is beneath student behavior, not to overregulate it: student affairs professionals seem to define their job as asking students *how* they are doing, not policing *what* they are doing.

There is, however, a significant and lengthy pledge that all students, faculty, and staff are required to affirm and sign. Although there are sections of this document that are specifically focused on leaders, faculty members, employees, and students, everyone signs the same pledge. This document is entitled "A Declaration of Christian Community." It was significantly revised through a process that began with the board of trustees in 2005 and went into effect in the summer of 2007. It is supplemented by a "Statement of Philosophy" and a "Doctrinal Statement."[6] In many cases, biblical citations are presented in support of the declaration's statements. The declaration consists of ten sections, which include very broad theological affirmations and very specific behavioral injunctions. The former include, for example, under the heading "We will honor Christ," "We believe that it is our duty, honor and delight to live under the Lordship of Christ, to study His Holy Scriptures, to reach all nations with the Gospel of Salvation through faith in Christ and teach them how to be disciples, to participate in the relentless and joyous pursuit of His Truth." Some of the behavioral injunctions are deliberately vague: for example, under the heading "As employees, we will seek Christ-centered community" is found "We voluntarily abstain from certain activities that might draw us or others away from God (I Cor. 8–9, Gal. 5:19–21), particularly on behalf of those students and listeners who are new to their freedom and have placed themselves in our environment or in our care." Others, however, are explicit. These include the condemnation of "greed and materialism, dishonesty (plagiarism included), prejudice, social injustice, impurity and debauchery, casual and disrespectful use of the name of the Lord, drunkenness, violent behavior, occult practices, hatred, jealousy, pride and discord, immodesty in dress or behavior, sexual immorality (including the use of pornography), premarital sex, homosexual behavior and all other sexual relations outside the bounds of marriage between one man and one woman, murder/homicide (including abortion), slander, gossip, gluttony, vulgar or obscene language and any activities that are illegal [seven biblical citations]." Gambling is forbidden. Traditional undergraduates are not to use tobacco or alcohol anywhere, and the campus itself is alcohol and tobacco free.

The current declaration differs from its predecessors. The board of trustees is no longer excluded from some of its restrictions. The earlier injunction against dancing now applies to "certain contemporary dances that are terribly inappropriate."[7] Rules governing alcohol are more nuanced (e.g., communion wine is acceptable). It is widely understood that there is a "dress code" at Northwestern, but it is simply that immodest dress is not to be worn: there are no legalistic requirements regarding such issues as sandals, bare feet, and shirt styles.[8] By and large, NWC students are visually indistinguishable from those at other, non-Christian institutions, with the exceptions of flamboyant visual idiosyncrasies (on campus one does not see, e.g., wild colored hair, T-shirts with obscene or sexually explicit messages, and bare midriffs).

Northwestern's code of conduct seeks to be uncompromisingly biblical, but not simply to put forth a list of forbidden actions; it is communitarian in language and spirit ("we will . . ."). It makes an effort to suggest what people should be and do, rather than what they should not. In this, it seems to reflect a thoughtful and humane approach to conservative Christian values, an approach that NWC's president, Dr. Alan Cureton, describes as his. He says he has sought to help the college move further away from rigid legalism to a more grace-oriented approach. Dr. Cureton works with a board of trustees that meets quarterly and includes at any given time about twenty members. That group is in the process of making the transition from a daily management function to that of a policy advisory group, and Dr. Cureton is candid that some of the board do not feel that the new declaration is sufficiently explicitly conservatively Christian and are concerned as well that other campus constituencies, including the faculty, are playing too central a role in defining key college policies. There now exists, for example, a new faculty campus assembly.

In addition to the declaration, and the two statements of philosophy and doctrine, Northwestern has widely promulgated three other self-defining proclamations: in a vision statement, NWC proclaims, "Because of God's compelling love, we will teach wisdom and understanding to reach all nations for Christ"; in a mission statement, "Northwestern College exists to provide Christ-centered higher education equipping students to grow intellectually and spiritually, to serve effectively in their professions, and to give God-honoring leadership in the home, church, community, and world"; and in a statement of core values, "Scripturally Grounded, Intellectually Challenging, People Centered, Culturally Engaging, and Contagiously Christian."

Dr. Cureton discussed the last reaccreditation process for NWC, close to a decade ago, which raised issues concerning the absence of a tenure policy, no institutional statement of philosophy of education, and fiscal concerns. Today, the college has a detailed statement of philosophy, which includes sections on foundational beliefs, on educational values (community, life-long learning, ministry, integrity, pursuit of excellence, and wisdom and leadership in the culture), and on educational framework (including curriculum, methodology, and outcomes). At NWC, faculty members do not receive tenure and are offered four-year contracts that are renewed on a two-year basis. Although the president remains involved in faculty personnel decisions, they are increasingly the responsibility of department chairs, the dean, and the Provost. He interviews the top candidate for each faculty opening, for example, but not all candidates.

Faculty members with whom I spoke reinforced the sense that there is a wide acceptance of community standards on issues such as smoking, drinking, and dress, rather than a strict legalism. They noted, for example, that there would probably be no problem with a faculty member who was explicitly gay, assuming that the individual practiced abstinence. At the same time, they believe that students or faculty who had no Christian faith would not fit at Northwestern and would not want to be there.

On specific issues of student behavioral expectations, the president, like others at NWC, emphasizes a pastoral rather than a policing function. For example, a gay student, he believes, especially one who abstained from sexual activity, would be counseled, not punished. When the Soulforce Equity Ride gay rights group came to the upper Midwest, it was not excluded from the Northwestern campus, and NWC students listened to its position with polite disagreement. Christ, Dr. Cureton reminds his listeners, would not have turned away anyone: the church should not be separatist.

I asked Dr. Cureton what percentage of his time he spends overseeing the broadcasting enterprises of Northwestern College, and he estimated it was 25% of his time. He believes that NWC's peer institutions are the other members of the CCCU and the Council of Independent Colleges–affiliated institutions.

Northwestern College students, like most of those I have met at Christian colleges, are serious about their studies and about their faith. They tend to manifest that seriousness in a slightly different manner from many of their peers. I met with about a dozen students over lunch. Half of them were male and half were female, and they came from a wide diversity of academic majors, including biology, music education, psychology, theater, intercultural studies, and adult ministries. Most were from the upper Midwest, and I spoke to students at all stages of the undergraduate experience. About half the students in this group (which may or may not have been a representative sample, of course) were planning on pursuing a religious career (e.g., music education at a Christian school). It was their sense of their peers that there were some, but not very many, who had been home schooled, and that the majority had attended either public high school or private Christian schools. Though serious, Northwestern and its students are not without a sense of humor. For example, the admissions view book has a list of "frequently unanswered questions" including "Exactly what is Northwestern northwest of?" and "Is it true that the men's synchronized swim team is going to nationals?" (the answer to the latter is "no").

I asked the students what other colleges they had contemplated attending when they first applied to college. Many had applied to Bethel (located just next door to Northwestern and not too dissimilar in mission, size, or reputation). Others included Wheaton, the University of Chicago, Cornell University, Luther, DePaul, and Georgetown College in Kentucky. In the course of this discussion, it was repeatedly affirmed that the Lord had taken a personal and active role in determining these students' college choice. Some said that God led them to Northwestern, some believed that the Lord had closed other options: "God shut the door at all the other schools where I applied." In some cases, this was a reference to applications that had been turned down. In other situations, students had been accepted elsewhere but (from their current perspectives) had been personally led by the Lord away from other choices or toward Northwestern College. One student noted the differences between a campus with Christian students and Christian campuses: NWC is clearly the latter. Many of the students said that, while they had visited other Christian college campuses, Northwestern was much more pervasively in tune with their faith: for example, one said "faith took a back seat at 'x' College." They also saw the non-Christian colleges, such as the nearby huge University of Minnesota in the Twin Cities, not as neutral but as actively espousing "naturalism" and trying to impose a view of the universe in which there was no room for God.

Northwestern students are not worried that they have been protected from the outside, non-Christian world and express their eagerness to move into that world as Christian witnesses. They believe that faith should not be blind and that they need to learn to defend their faith. They worry about spending too much time in the "Christian bubble." And they are not naive about student life at Northwestern: they recognize that there are opportunities for illicit sex, drinking, and drugs available to them and that some of their colleagues at the college will not always be able to resist these temptations. We humans are all sinners, they say. Too, they affirm that they could be, and in several cases, are, good friends with young people of different religious backgrounds or with no faith at all.

To an outside observer, Northwestern College students seem to spend a lot of time in profoundly intense conversation with each other—even more than most college students. It is very common to see two or more students in what is obviously a deep interaction: more than once in my time on campus, tears were part of such conversations. Often, it seemed to me, these intense interactions ended with an embrace. Students say that they seek to love and guide and help each other.

Northwestern College students report that they are fond and respectful of their professors, who they see as mature in their faith. They recognize that, on issues such as evolution, their teachers do not all believe exactly the same things. One of the students in the group with which I was speaking took this occasion, however, to give an impassioned and lengthy lecture on the flaws of Darwinian theories of human origins. This young man echoed the argument I heard from a biology faculty member as well, namely that there is no fossil record of slow, evolutionary, biological change. The students recognize that, in their words, "ideology plays a huge role in the advancement of science."

As with their decisions concerning college entrance, Northwestern College students believe that God is guiding them in their choice of academic major and vocation. One said, for example, that "God was speaking to me to go into youth ministry" when describing the change of a major field. Another said of her music major that she was "doing this for the glory of

God." They all agreed that, with a degree in any subject, one could have a ministry.

Although there is a desire of Northwestern College students, faculty, and administrators to avoid isolation and separatism, there is also still a contradictory tendency to define themselves and their institution as "countercultural"—the "culture" being contemporary secularism. One of the students remarked, "As Christians, we are in opposition to the world." And the longest section of the college's "Declaration of Christian Community" is the one entitled "Northwestern will be set apart." The vision of the committed Christian as deeply *in* the world, but not *of* it, remains viable here.

Most of the longer-term constituents at Northwestern believe that the college has modestly changed within the past decade. They believe it has become more academically rigorous, that its physical plant has been well developed, and that there has been a sharp increase in the professionalism of all the staff. Students are better qualified, and there are progressively more of them. As the campus has grown, personal relationships have inevitably become more diffuse, and the college now needs to work harder to function as a united community. Faculty members believe that they are moving toward a more important voice in campus governance. Some express concern about what they perceive as an inclination on the part of the board of trustees to retain a "top down" business model of decision making. Like students, faculty members believe that they came to Northwestern through the workings of God.

I asked each group with which I spoke in Roseville about what colleges they see as the peers of Northwestern. Most often, nearby Bethel was cited. Others included Taylor, Wheaton, Westmont, Freed-Hardeman, Biola, Calvin, and Cedarville.

Most colleges, in fact, probably most institutions of any sort, tend to develop their own vocabulary, a kind of internal, community shortcut for articulating common and shared concepts. At Northwestern, almost every individual with whom I spoke—students, faculty, and administrators alike—used the phrase "walk" or "the walk." The "Christian walk" is certainly an expression with wide currency in the evangelical culture, but at Northwestern, in contrast to the other colleges and universities I visited, it has become almost a verbal reflex. By this phrase, NWC people clearly meant something like "walking in the way of the Lord," "acting consistently as God wishes." Thus, individuals would say things such as "We don't want students just obeying what they see as arbitrary rules; we want them really to be doing their walk." Or, "When I came here, I was just a casual Christian, but at Northwestern I met Jesus, and truly started my walk." This locution is certainly linked to the fairly common "walking the walk, talking the talk" dichotomy, with the latter part of the phrase indicating mere show, but the former expressing committed sincerity. "Sincere" and "committed" seem to me accurate and fair descriptions of the people of Northwestern College: they are, in fact, deeply and daily engaged in their walk.

13 | "For Christ and His Kingdom"

Wheaton College, Wheaton, Illinois

In C. S. Lewis's *The Chronicles of Narnia* (and in Disney Studio's popular recent *The Lion, The Witch and the Wardrobe*), young people staying at a professor's house discover a magical land, where an evil white witch does battle with a Christly lion, Aslan. The portal through which they enter enchanted kingdom is a humble wardrobe. It is commonly believed that the original of that piece of furniture was one actually owned by C. S. Lewis. Today, that very wardrobe, along with Lewis's writing desk, 2,363 volumes from his personal library, and the original map of Narnia drawn by illustrator Pauline Baynes reside at the Marion E. Wade Center at Wheaton College. The Wade center holds, as well, similarly impressive bibliographic and personal collections for British writers Owen Barfield, G. K. Chesterton, George MacDonald, Dorothy L. Sayers, J. R. R. Tolkien, and Charles Williams.[1] The visitor to Wheaton College may well be subject to the impression of having entered just such a wardrobe and, through it, having crossed the portal not to a Narnia-like land of Christian allegory but certainly to a Christian college the programs and achievements of which seem sometimes equally fantastic. Here, too, young people live in a house of kindly professors, and here, too, they are introduced to a world in which they see themselves as active participants in an eternal battle between the forces of evil and the armies of Christ. Wheaton's motto, which is unambiguous and ubiquitous, is "For Christ and His Kingdom."

Wheaton College dates its founding to 1860, when Jonathan Blanchard came to the Illinois Institute, a preparatory school that had been created a half-dozen years earlier by Wesleyan Methodists, and changed it into a college.[2] Blanchard had previously served as the chief executive at Knox College in Galesburg, Illinois. The college and the town are both named for Warren L. Wheaton, who donated farmland to the nascent institution. Jonathan Blanchard led his new college until 1882. He began a tradition at the college of holding strong nondenominational Christian positions on important social issues. In Blanchard's particular case, during the Civil War years, this included a vigorous and uncompromising abolitionism.[3] A historian of the college listing Blanchard's great passions describes him as "abolitionist, anti-Mason, and temperance advocate."[4] At its founding, Wheaton was the first institution in Illinois to offer college-level instruction to women as well as men.

Jonathan Blanchard was followed as Wheaton's president by his son, Charles Albert Blanchard, who remained in that post a remarkable forty-three years, until 1925. Thus, for the first sixty-five years of its existence, Wheaton had only two presidents, both Blanchards. It is not surprising that the old main college building, which now houses offices of the administration as well as academic facilities, is Blanchard Hall. To this day, Wheaton has had only seven chief executives.

Its third president, the Reverend James Oliver Buswell Jr., was a strong conservative leader, who did much to enhance the college's academic stature, while at the same time guarding vigorously its orthodox Christian character. Buswell was only thirty-one years old when he became Wheaton's chief executive. During his term (1925–40), Wheaton was accredited, became a respected collegiate athletic force, and celebrated community chapel every morning. Reverend Buswell was a Presbyterian minister, who "took his stand fearlessly for the Word of God in opposition to the forces of modernism in the Presbyterian church U.S.A.,"[5] from which he, and others, broke. As a consequence, Buswell became a controversial figure within Presbyterianism, leading to his dismissal by the Wheaton College board of trustees in 1940. Buswell is described by a historian of Christian higher education as an "unequivocal fundamentalist," and Wheaton as ""the best known fundamentalist college in the 1920's."[6] The more conservative wing of the church to which Buswell was drawn has evolved into today's Presbyterian Church in America (PCA); the more liberal branch of contemporary Presbyterianism is the Presbyterian Church U.S.A. (PCUSA). Wheaton College had been, from its first days, nondenominational evangelical Christian, and the board of trustees found the publicity surrounding Buswell's confrontations with liberal Presbyterianism institutionally embarrassing. He died in 1977.[7]

When Buswell was dismissed, V. Raymond Edman, a teacher of political science, was appointed acting, then continuing president. According to his biographer, "Dr. Edman was at home playing ping pong with his son David when the chairman of the board telephoned, asking him to come to the meeting of the board on that Saturday evening. Not knowing what had gone on in the meeting up to this point, he was surprised to learn they had voted that he become president."[8] Nonetheless, like his predecessors, his tenure proved a long one, from 1940 to 1965. As its fourth head, he led the college through its centennial celebration. The current main college chapel, which seats twenty-four hundred, is named for President Edman. He, too, was succeeded by an "insider," Hudson T. Armeding, a Wheaton College graduate (and University of Chicago PhD) who had been Edman's assistant and whose term of office lasted from 1962 to 1982. Richard Chase, who had been president at Biola University in Los Angeles for a dozen years before, came to Wheaton in 1982, served until 1993, and was, in turn, followed by the current (2009) president, Dr. Duane Litfin.

Dr. Litfin has dual doctoral degrees, one in communications from Purdue University and one in New Testament from Oxford. His career has been in leadership posts in both the church and the college. Among his writings is the influential *Conceiving the Christian College*, which, while not primarily about Wheaton College, certainly sheds considerable light on the educational and theological underpinnings of its current leader.[9] In addition to reading his book, I had the opportunity to converse with Dr. Litfin while I was visiting Wheaton. By the overall standards of the contemporary American scene, Dr. Litfin would certainly be described as a conservative, orthodox Protestant Christian in his administrative stance and expressed philosophy. However, he is surely seen by some within the Wheaton orb as less conservative than they would like, having, for example, played a key role in promulgating a new community covenant that relaxed some traditional college rules.

Often, in our conversation, Dr. Litfin stressed his belief that it is essential to the continued well-being of Wheaton College that it not let itself be unthinkingly swayed by current trends in politics, ethics, and higher education: the college needs to "stay the course," hold to its core commitments as a nondenominational evangelical Protestant institution. In his book, Dr. Litfin defines two types of religious-affiliated institutions (not including the "historically religious" colleges that are now largely secular). First is the "umbrella" institution, which welcomes a variety of voices and perspectives, while perhaps privileging one particular tradition. The University of Notre Dame might be an example of such a school. The other is the "systemic" college or university, which engages all ideas from one particular religious perspective. To Dr. Litfin, Wheaton is squarely in the camp of the "systemic" colleges and therefore has promulgated both the community covenant and the statement of faith, which prescribe an evangelical Protestant belief system for all members of the community.

In his book, Dr. Litfin describes a situation in which, early in his career at Wheaton, a faculty member came to him and stated that he felt himself drifting away from wholehearted endorsement of their institution's faith affirmation. The president encouraged him to remain on the faculty and to work to change the statement, but the faculty member responded that he believed the affirmation was essential to the college's character, and it would be wrong for him to work to reshape it. The faculty member left, and today Dr. Litfin says that the faculty member was correct, and he was wrong. Indeed, in one of the more controversial decisions of his administration, a popular faculty member who had converted to Roman Catholicism was dismissed from the college because of his conversion.[10] The president affirms that he both liked and respected that teacher but that holding true to the College's core mission and identity means unanimous and wholehearted affirmation of the statement of faith.

That statement is a relatively brief list of twelve beliefs, and it is annually subscribed to by the board, faculty, and staff of the college. It is "a summary of biblical doctrine that is consonant with evangelical Christianity."[11] It identifies the college "not only with the Scriptures but also with the reformers and the evangelical movement of recent years." In abbreviated form, the statement affirms belief:

in one sovereign God, eternally existing in three persons;

that God revealed himself in creation, the Scriptures, and in Jesus Christ, and that the Bible is "verbally inspired by God and inerrant in the original writing";

that Christ was conceived of the Holy Spirit and born of the Virgin Mary, and is true God and true man;

that "God directly created Adam and Eve, the historical parents of the entire human race . . . in His own image, distinct from all other living creatures . . .";

that Adam and Eve sinned;

in the existence of Satan;

that Christ died for our sins;

that those who receive Jesus Christ are by faith born again into the Holy Spirit;

that the Holy Spirit indwells and gives life, power, and understanding to believers;

that the universal Church is the body of Christ and the community of
His people;

that Christ will soon return to earth, personally, visibly and
unexpectedly, in glory, to raise the dead, judge the nations, and bring
His Kingdom to fulfillment; and

in the bodily resurrection of the just and unjust, with eternal
punishment for the lost and blessedness for the saved.

I also spoke with President Litfin about the college and its relation to the
external world. He noted that there are good town-gown relations between
Wheaton College and Wheaton, but that the college is a national institution and not really dependent upon strictly local support, although it en-
joys and seeks that support.

We also discussed how Wheaton's national stature has subjected it to
widespread and closer scrutiny than most—perhaps any—of its fellow
Christian colleges. So, for example, when Northwestern College in Minnesota changed its campus "Declaration of Christian Community" a few
years ago in such a way as to permit some student dancing, of a modest
nature, which had previously been wholly forbidden, that move received
virtually no publicity outside its immediate proximity. When Wheaton revised the covenant and eliminated the long-standing prohibition on student dancing, it was very widely reported around the country; for example,
CNN reported on the air and on its Web site, "Wheaton College Lifts 143-
Year Dance Ban."[12] At Westmont College, to the occasional quiet, local,
disgruntlement of some parents, students learn the facts of Darwinian
evolution. When they learn those facts at Wheaton, they become part of a
PBS series on evolution and are lambasted on fundamentalist Web sites
such as that of *Answers in Genesis* in which Dr. Jonathan Sarfati waxes
indignant that a Wheaton College professor proclaimed an earthly land
form "33 million years old" that, along with similar statements by members of the college community, he brands as "vacuous tripe."[13] Wheaton
has been criticized in national media for being too liberal about stem cell
research and too conservative on gay rights. The college has also received
negative national publicity in the case of the dismissal in 2000 of an an-
thropologist, Alex Bolyanatz. Dr. Bolyanatz received a letter critical of his
efforts to integrate faith and learning from the provost, but he and his
supporters generally believe that the actual cause of his dismissal was his
straightforward advocacy of Darwinian evolution and his failure to treat

creationist theories with respect.[14] So, not infrequently, as on the issues of human origins and student dancing, it is criticized sharply for being both too liberal and too conservative. The college is, in short, a highly visible institution and one that has had to come to grips with a level of ongoing national scrutiny on almost every aspect of its institutional life, especially whenever it seeks to make any sort of substantive change. To President Litfin and other supporters of the college, such attention is simply a consequence of the college's stature and an irrelevance when it comes to remaining true to its historical mission.

Wheaton graduates span the career range, and a large range it is, from former Speaker of the House Dennis Hastert, Wake Forest University president Nathan Hatch, horror film director Was Craven to probably the most famous alumnus, the Reverend Billy Graham. A major building on the campus is named for Reverend Graham and houses a very professional museum of evangelism as well as an equally impressive display about the evangelist himself. (It also contains academic facilities for the Graduate School, broadcasting facilities, and the college's archives.) Another facility named for a graduate is the 2004 Todd M. Beamer Student Center. Beamer was one of the passengers who, on September 11, 2001, resisted the hijackers of United Airlines flight 93, causing it to crash in rural Pennsylvania, rather than reach its projected target. The Beamer Center contains numerous student facilities, including Wheaton's main dining area, which has consistently been ranked as one of the best collegiate food service operations in the country.[15]

The college has a current endowment of well over $300 million, which is substantial, but certainly not record-breaking for an institution of its size, quality, and aspirations. (By comparison, Calvin's at the same period was $90 million; Westmont $66 million, and George Fox $20 million. Baylor's was $870 million. Grinnell's, with about half as many students, was $1.4 *billion*.) Tuition, room, and board costs are about $30,000 per year. The campus appears unified architecturally and in excellent physical condition, with several impressive new facilities, broad sweeps of lawn and sidewalk, and no internal roadways disrupting the central core. The town of Wheaton itself is a comfortable, affluent suburb, approximately thirty miles west of Chicago.

While there are many impressive aspects of this college, perhaps its strongest claim to elite status among America's Christian colleges lies in its student body. In the entering class of 2005, for example, there were

578 first-year students. Their average high school grade point average was 3.7, and there were thirty National Merit Scholarship finalists among them. On quantified entrance exams, the middle 50% for the SAT was 1260–1420, and for the ACT 27–31. Such numbers clearly put Wheaton in the top tier of nationally selective liberal arts colleges. About 78% of its students come from outside the state, and international students come from thirty-three countries. The college identifies 12% of its student body of approximately twenty-four hundred undergraduates as "Multicultural Students."

The college's widely respected conservatory of music enrolls about 220 students. Music majors can focus on performance, education, composition, or history/literature or can major in music with elective studies or an emphasis in an outside field (e.g., a music major with an elective in English). On my visit to Wheaton, I was able to hear the student orchestra perform during a weekly chapel service, and its level of musical professionalism was high. The college is also home to more than five hundred graduate students, enrolled in master's and doctoral programs in biblical and theological studies and in clinical psychology.

Wheaton offers a traditional variety of liberal arts majors (e.g., history, biology, psychology, English, French, political science). In a few areas, its offerings are perhaps deeper than average, either for liberal arts colleges or for Christian institutions: thus, for example, there is an anthropology major and another one in biblical archaeology. In addition to Spanish, German, and French majors, there is one in ancient languages, and the college has recently begun teaching Mandarin. There are relatively few "vocational" majors, and those have a distinct liberal arts emphasis (e.g., there are majors entitled "liberal arts–engineering" and "liberal arts–nursing"). There are also majors offered in biblical and theological studies, Christian education and ministry. The college's admissions materials identify the most enrolled majors as English, business/economics, music, communications, and psychology. Writing about Wheaton, Michael Hamilton and James Mathisen observe that its combination of liberal learning and a fundamentalist evangelicalism make it "a true hybrid, a two-culture institution."[16]

General education graduation requirements are full and somewhat complex. Requirements are divided into "competency" requirements, including biblical competency, foreign language, quantitative skills, oral communication, writing, and applied health science / wellness, and "learning clusters." Most of the "competency" requirements can be met either by successfully passing appropriate course work or through examination. The "learning clusters," in which forty-two to forty-eight semester hours are mandated include:

Faith and Reason—14–18 credit hours
    10–14 in biblical and theological studies
    4 in philosophy
Studies in Society—12 hours
    4 in history
    8 in two other social sciences
Studies in Nature—8 hours
    Including at least one four-credit laboratory course
Studies in Literature and the Arts—8 hours
    4 in literature
    4 in fine arts
Senior Capstone course—2–4 hours

The courses in Faith and Reason, both in the competency area and as a learning cluster are:

An introductory two-credit-hour course, Gospel, Church and Culture, which is described as "an introduction to the Christian faith and the Evangelical Protestant" tradition, with emphasis on the church's engagement in culture and society and the integration of faith and learning within the liberal arts context
A course in Old Testament (usually a four-credit-hour course)
A course in New Testament (also usually four credits)
A concluding course in Christian thought, usually a course in the Biblical and Theological Studies Department described as "an investigation into the basic beliefs of the Christian faith."

In addition to participation in several off-campus opportunities offered by consortia and other organizations, Wheaton itself maintains Honey Rock Camp, a Northwoods wilderness site in Three Lakes, Wisconsin, and a science field station in the Black Hills of South Dakota. The college also offers a program entitled "Human Needs and Global Resources" that focuses upon developing regions of the world.

Student life outside the classroom at Wheaton College is, characteristically, distinctive. There is, of course, the usual panoply of opportunities—clubs that range from recreational (a jazz club, for example, and a rugby organization) to educational (German club) to religious (the Council on Faith and International Affairs). There are College Republicans and College Democrats, a chapter of Amnesty International, Student Global AIDS Campaign, Students for Free Enterprise, a prelaw club, and the like. There is a student newspaper (the *Wheaton Record*, in 2007 at volume 133), yearbook, and radio station. Students serve on a wide range of committees for special events such as homecoming and orientation. Wheaton is a strong member of NCAA Division III, affiliated with the College Conference of Illinois and Wisconsin (CCIW) with a record of several team and individual national NCAA champions (the college's teams are "the Thunder"; earlier they were known as the "Crusaders," but this mascot was recently deemed potentially offensive). The college also offers club sports and intramural activities. There is a large new sports and recreation complex. The college itself brings to campus a full range of outside cultural attractions, with a strong emphasis on musical events. It also stresses its nearness to downtown Chicago and the convenience of a commuter passenger rail line that stops just outside the college and provides easy access to Chicago's vast range of recreational and cultural resources. There is, of course, a full range of religious study, worship, and service groups and events on campus.

Wheaton College is a residential institution. All undergraduates are expected to live on campus, although exceptions are made for married students, students living with their families, and other special circumstances. As with most other aspects of Wheaton, this requirement is expressed in overt Christian terms. The residential policy states that "Wheaton college exists to develop Christian students into whole and effective servants of Jesus Christ," and some of this development occurs in interpersonal living situations because of the "Holy Spirit's work in students' lives through relationships with other people." "We believe it is necessary for students to be immersed in community living for key life-to-life encounters to be possible. In community, students give and receive, are shaped by and contribute to campus life, and are challenged to integrate their classroom learning with their life experiences."[17] (It is interesting to compare this policy to that described in chapter 6 at New Saint Andrews College, which is exactly the opposite.) Visitation policies are clear and firm. There are residence halls with women's floors alternating with men's, but there are no room-by-room coed dorms. The college also maintains as student residences some homes and apartments, where students have increased autonomy, and, it is stressed, correspondingly increased responsibility.

In all of their activities, curricular and extracurricular, students and other members of the Wheaton College community are expected to abide by the Wheaton College Community Covenant. That document has evolved and changed over time, most recently in a new version inaugurated, after widespread discussion among multiple constituencies, in February 2003. Both internally and in the outside world, the new covenant drew significant attention and provoked significant controversy. Even with abbreviated scriptural references, the covenant is several pages long. It begins with an explanatory preface and continues with a statement of the college's mission as the "development of whole and effective Christians who will impact the church and society worldwide 'For Christ and His Kingdom.'" The following section of the Covenant is entitled "Affirming Biblical Standards" and acknowledges community callings such as the calls to love God, pursue holiness, and participate in the worship and activities of the local church. Next, the covenant addresses "Living the Christian Life," stating first what followers of Jesus Christ are expected to do. These expectations include showing evidence of the Holy Spirit through such virtues as love, patience, and kindness. Of greater topical intensity are the expectations to "uphold the God-given worth of human beings, from conception to death" and to "uphold chastity among the unmarried and the sanctity of marriage between a man and a woman." Then, by contrast, are detailed those things which Scripture condemns, including pride, dishonesty, injustice, immodesty in dress or behavior, vulgar or obscene language, hypocrisy, legalism, sinful attitudes and behaviors, and "sexual immorality such as the use of pornography, premarital sex, adultery, homosexual behavior and all other sexual relations outside the bounds of marriage between a man and a woman." The next section focuses upon "Exercising Responsible Freedom" and deals with alcohol, drugs, and tobacco. It notes that the Bible requires moderation in the use of alcohol, not abstinence, but also notes the widespread problems caused by its consumption. Thus, "the question of alcohol consumption represents a prime opportunity for Christians to exercise their freedom responsibly, carefully and in Christ-like love." A similar call for thoughtful moderation in other matters of entertainment follows. The final section is "Embracing College Standards." These include the standard of a tobacco- and alcohol-free campus, and a similar prohibition at all college programs on and off-campus and the stipulation that all undergraduates will refrain from all consumption of alcohol or use of tobacco "in all settings." A second "standard" involves dancing: "On-campus dances will take place only with official College sponsorship. All members of the Wheaton community will take care to avoid any entertainment or behavior, on or off campus, which may be immodest, sinfully erotic, or harmfully violent."[18] Students (and others), thus, are to affirm the sacredness of life from conception onward, to eschew drinking and smoking, and to dance only modestly. Other than the call for modesty and moderation, there is no student dress code at Wheaton, and standards seem to permit a pretty wide range of styles: a few students sport a few visible pierced body parts, and a couple have flamboyantly dyed hair, but most were dressed in a very conventionally casual collegiate style.

No person with whom I spoke at the college stated a belief that all students, at all times and all places, complied fully with all the provisions of the community covenant. On the other hand, there was no equivocation on the part of students, faculty, or the administration that the document was a serious and binding one: its standards are expectational, not aspirational.

Periodically, Wheaton College, especially the students of Wheaton College, has experienced the phenomenon known as "revival." In general usage, this term has come to signify a planned, emotion-laden event, often led by a fiery professional evangelist such as Sinclair Lewis's fictional Elmer Gantry. This is not what "revival" means at Wheaton College today or, I believe, at other evangelical colleges. Rather, it signifies a more spontaneous outpouring of heightened religious feelings, often coupled with intense personal declarations and confessions of sinful behavior, in an atmosphere that the participants feel to be unusually infused with the Holy Spirit.[19] Wheaton College has recorded such periods of special spiritual intensity in 1936, 1943, 1950, 1970, and 1995. The events of the 1995 campus revival have been carefully and thoroughly documented and offer an important insight into the faith and the psychology of the college's students.

On 19 March 1995, a Sunday night, the weekly meeting of the World Christian Fellowship began at 7:30. It was expected to conclude around ninety minutes later. Two students from a college in Texas were speaking, and each testified to the impact and power of a recent spiritual revival on their campus. Then, first a few Wheaton College students came forward to confess their sins, then several, then an outpouring. More students came into the Chapel from around campus. Sometime around midnight, a group of faculty and staff leaders were alerted to the unusual events taking place and decided that the night's meeting needed to end early the next morning (6:00) but could reconvene the following evening at 9:30. It did, and more than a thousand students gathered, first for singing and prayer, then intense individual testimony. That night, it was decided to stop at 2:00 a.m. and continue on Tuesday night, again at 9:30. On Tuesday night more than thirteen hundred students gathered and again continued until the early morning hours. On Wednesday, even more students gathered, and that night the last confession took place at 2:45 in the morning. The final session began again at 9:30 on Thursday evening, again with singing, followed by a message from the chaplain. Several speakers praised the events of the past days, and some noted the importance of international missionary and ministerial work. More than two hundred students came forward to the stage to indicate their intention to pursue full-time Christian vocations. Late that night, weary but exuberant students returned to their residences. Those who were present and participated in these events believe "it is clear that the college community experienced an unusual blessing and visitation from the Holy Spirit."[20] Following the events in Wheaton that spring, students from the college visited other campus to describe and inspire revivals. Among those visited were Northwestern College, Asbury College, Trinity International University, Gordon College, Eastern Nazarene College, Cornerstone College, Taylor University, Judson College, Hope College, Iowa State University, George Fox College, Multnomah School of the Bible, Moody Bible Institute, Messiah College, Trinity Christian College, Columbia University, Yale University, the University of Wisconsin at Stevens Point, and Greenville College. High schools and churches were also visited.

It is difficult, perhaps impossible, for individuals like me, who come from a religious and cultural tradition in which such events simply do not take place, to explain or assess this and similar campus revivals. I am content simply to narrate the sequence of acts and reactions and to note that, to those who did take part, the Wheaton College revival of 1995 was a profound and transformative moment.

Wheaton College has always stressed the importance of missions, missionaries, and mission work. In the hallway just outside the president's office in Blanchard Hall is a series of panels listing the names of every

Wheaton College graduate who has served as a missionary.[21] The display announces "the names on this wall represent those Wheaton graduates who have taken the good news of Jesus Christ to a culture not their own." Missionaries who were martyred in service are indicated with a small black cross after their names. The list begins with two members of the class of 1873, Henry Martyn Bissell and Anastasios D. Zaraphonithes and continues to the present. An entire small book has been devoted to chronicling the mission work of Wheaton students and graduates: *From Wheaton to the Nations* by David M. Howard, a Wheaton College graduate and former missions director for InterVarsity Christian Fellowship.[22]

Some of the spiritual needs of Wheaton students are served by an Office of Christian Outreach, a branch of the Student Development office, with a director and assistant director. The OCO oversees seven enterprises:

1. Youth Hostel Ministries, in which students spend the summer ministering to student travelers in Europe
2. Breakaway Ministry, spring break work at both U.S. and international sites
3. World Christian Fellowship, a weekly gathering hosting students from all around the world
4. Christian Service Council, which focuses on service in the Chicagoland area
5. Global Urban Perspectives, dedicated to study and service in worldwide urban centers
6. Missions in Focus, which hosts a campuswide annual missions conference
7. Student Missionary Project, a summer program offering short-term mission opportunities

I was able to meet with a small group of Wheaton College student leaders. They were articulate, thoughtful, charming, and careful.[23] They weighed what they had to say before they said it but certainly seemed sincere and forthcoming. The students expressed understanding and enthusiasm for the college's mission of integrating faith and learning, which one of them described as balancing curricular subjects with orthodox Christian belief. They were clear that such integration was not simply a matter of beginning classes with prayer. The students stressed the philosophical and theological diversity on campus: not all students or professors had the same worldview. They are convinced that their Wheaton College education prepares them well for the remainder of their lives in the more secular world.

When I asked the students about behavioral issues, they responded, cheerfully, that at Wheaton "boy-girl relations are quite peculiar." Several of them assented that they "laughed at" the way students interact across gender lines. This confirmed an earlier impression I had gained during a video that was shown at that morning's mandatory chapel. In preparation for discussions of "friendship" and gender issues, the video had portrayed a small group of male and female students debating the question, "Can college men and women just be friends?" The males in the video doubted it, asserting that some sexual overtones were never able to be completely removed from male-female relations. At that point in the video, there was widespread laughter from the audience. The students spoke of the fact that Wheaton College students marry younger than many of their contemporaries: they believe this is because their relationships are more "real" than those of others of their age.

I asked these students what they thought would happen if one of their fellows was obviously behaving in a manner that ran contrary to the ethos of the college—for example, was exhibiting behaviors that indicated serious and continuing substance abuse. Their response was that fellow students would confront such a peer; they would not be inclined to "report" him or her until they had taken an opportunity to speak to the individual. They stressed that such confrontations would be pastoral, not judgmental.

These students spoke of their fondness for college chapel, a fondness that they said grew stronger the longer they were at Wheaton. For them, it strengthened their sense of being a bonded community. I also asked them about the nature and effectiveness of student government. They believe its effectiveness ebbs and flows but that, when at a high point, it has a positive and measurable effect on issues such as educational policies and requirements. They believe that the faculty and administration listen to them carefully. The faculty is "tremendous," and, again, they "come from all these different perspectives." They stressed that the faculty fulfill a strong pastoral function; students feel that their teachers are caring mentors and friends.

Some of the other institutions to which these Wheaton College students had applied when seniors in high school include Hope College, Illinois Wesleyan, Biola, Taylor, Westmar, Lee, Western Oregon, and George Fox. Given the quality of Wheaton College students in general, and these student leaders in particular, this seemed a surprising list—it included no Ivy League schools, no prestigious private non-Christian liberal arts colleges, and no flagship state universities. It did include several Christian colleges and universities that most would rank significantly below Wheaton in intellectual challenge. Their career aspirations, though, were high: one wanted to work in Third World development, one in international law, one in area studies, with a focus on research in Asia, and one plans graduate study in English. At the conclusion of our conversation, one of the students said, with passion, and to the accord of her fellows, "Students really *love* this campus."

Wheaton College currently has just under two hundred full-time faculty members and about one hundred part-time. Its Web site describes the average class size as twenty-two and the student/faculty ratio as 12.2 to 1. More than 90% of the faculty members hold the PhD. A perusal of the faculty pages of the college catalog suggest that a significant proportion— less than half, more than a quarter—of the faculty hold undergraduate degrees from Wheaton itself. Their PhDs are from a very wide range of the nation's top graduate schools, including Tulane, the University of North Carolina at Chapel Hill, Harvard, the University of Chicago, American University, Emory, Northwestern, Vanderbilt, Fordham, Eastman, Ohio State, and Duke. A significant number hold degrees from foreign universities, including Cambridge, Edinburgh, Aberdeen, Louvain, and St. Andrews. Relatively few graduate credentials are from theological seminaries or strongly religious institutions. If Wheaton's faculty members do have those pastoral skills their students uniformly praise, they did not develop them in graduate school. They perhaps recall them from their undergraduate days. More likely, they developed them as part of a thorough faculty orientation process and, perhaps, in part through osmosis of an institutional culture. That faculty orientation most dramatically takes the form of a seminar during new professors' second year on campus, which focuses primarily on issues of faith and learning. The seminar involves readings and discussions of works that raise relevant issues (e.g., Marilynn Robinson's fine novel *Gilead*) and serious writing. Faculty members also write a paper on issues of faith and learning at the time of their tenure review.

I spoke with a diverse group of faculty members at Wheaton College, and it was clear that they had thought often and deeply about these issues, both generally and in terms of their own teaching and disciplines.

They noted, for example, that in many areas, especially scientific course areas, the actual "facts" of their disciplines are exactly the same at secular and religious colleges: mathematical equations will produce the same results; the measurements of plants and animals and their parts will be the same; great literary texts use the same words; observed human behavior in controlled circumstances will not change. But at Wheaton, and schools like it, these faculty members believe, they are free to encourage students to understand these facts from the perspective of a Christian worldview. They often use the same texts used in secular colleges, but their students expect them to do more with those materials than would be the case at secular colleges and universities. Indeed, they believed that students at Wheaton were most interested in coming to a Christian understanding of the materials they find in their textbooks and integrating those materials into their spiritual worldview. These faculty members felt they could talk about important issues openly and freely but also understood that they needed to share the basic belief structure of the institution as a whole. They also were clear that these questions of faith and learning differ from discipline to discipline and individual to individual, and they felt that the college understood this diversity well. And they believe that it is more common to encounter theological thinking, as well as pastoral reflection, in many subject matter areas, at Wheaton than elsewhere.

Wheaton College faculty teach, on average, three four-credit courses per semester, a load fairly typical of better private liberal arts colleges.

Quite by accident, one of the Wheaton College faculty members with whom I spoke had also served as a faculty member at a small public liberal arts college where I had worked as well (although not at the same time), so I was able to ask this professor of biology some questions that compared the two institutions. She noted that she used the same introductory biology textbooks at both schools and that she covered, briefly, Darwinian evolutional biology at both, but that at Wheaton, evolution was set within a context of other views of human origins. She stressed the difference between teaching "about" such a subject and teaching that it was the sole and unquestioned truth. At the same time, she reaffirmed the belief that "all truth is God's truth" and that her goal, and that of her colleagues in her own and sister disciplines, was to be driven in her teaching by good, careful science. Another goal was to help students move away from the sometimes-unnuanced formulations of some who came from church backgrounds that offered simplistic views of the natural world. Such students, she hoped, would move toward a more "aware faith."

The faculty members stressed that they understood their job as helping students to live in a contemporary world, not that of thousands of years ago.

They reiterated the college policy that faculty members belong to Protestant denominations and are expected to affiliate with local church congregations, though nobody "policed" that membership. It is understood and accepted that this embraces a wide range of denominations: Episcopalians to Pentecostals. I asked about the thinking on campus in regards to the possibility of "evangelical Catholics" joining the faculty, and they said that this was a subject that they thought needed to be faced and discussed, but they did not believe that discussion would happen in the short-term future. On politics, as well as religion, there is significant variation: some, for example, are strongly opposed to U.S actions in Iraq. On other issues, such as abortion and gay rights that are directly addressed by the statement of faith, however, there is unanimity.

When I asked this group of teachers how they thought Wheaton College had changed in the past decade or so, a variety of opinions emerged, and there was some gentle disagreement about some of the responses. Some believed that the faculty had become more research active and had more outside, often disciplinary, affiliations. They worried, as do most faculty members everywhere, that student prowess was less than it once was, especially in scientific literacy and writing ability, and yet students were more competitive on national quantitative benchmarks. They agreed that the general level of biblical literacy among students was down. Some of them found the current pace of faculty life more hectic than the past and worried about what they were modeling for students in terms of living a balanced lifestyle.

Wheaton's faculty plays a significant role in institutional governance, through a faculty council that meets monthly, and through its standing committees, which deal with important faculty issues such as promotion, reappointment, and tenure; curriculum; and hiring. At the same time, there is a clear chain of command on major decisions running through the college administration to the board of trustees.

When I asked faculty members what they saw as Wheaton's peer group, they were reluctant to note *any* peers. When pressed, they mentioned Calvin, Westmont, Seattle Pacific, Baylor, Grinnell, Carleton, and St. Olaf. Obviously, those in the first group are peers in terms of religious emphasis, those in the second a group of highly selective midwestern private liberal arts colleges.

Finally, Wheaton's faculty members expressed their consciousness of some of the "great people" who had preceded them there: Mark Noll, leading evangelical historian, and Clyde Kilby, the English professor who brought the C. S. Lewis/Inklings collection to Wheaton, were mentioned.

I had as well two opportunities to interact with Dr. Steve Kellough, Wheaton's chaplain. I attended a chapel session where Reverend Kellough spoke on the subject of "unanswered prayers," and I later had a chance to chat with him in his office.

Wheaton's chapel is required for all undergraduates, and meets three times a week, on Monday, Wednesday, and Friday mornings from 10:35 to 11:15. The chaplain organizes the chapel schedule, which includes a wide variety of events. On some occasions, the chaplain himself speaks, on others Wheaton's president is featured. There are student chaplains, and sometimes they are responsible for making presentations. Campus visitors often speak, including visitors from abroad. There are special series—for example, a "relationship" series, in which there are chapels separated by gender and by college class year, topical emphasis gatherings (e.g., "Global Aids Crisis" or "Creation Care"). In addition to the chaplain's message, on the day I attended chapel included two short, professionally performed musical pieces by the college symphony, and a series of prayers for specific members of the community (e.g., the family of a recently deceased former professor) led by a student. Dr. Kellough's talk was scholarly, thoughtful, and fairly formal without being stiff (he read prepared remarks). Although I spotted a very few students surreptitiously doing last-minute homework, most were attentive and responsive to the program: it certainly did not give any impression of being an onerous required duty.

In my conversation with Dr. Kellough, we spoke about faith and learning at Wheaton and his sense that the uniqueness of the institution is in the intersection of these qualities. He has found that the Wheaton community takes the integration of scholarship and spirituality very seriously. He noted, as did the faculty, the ways in which senior members of the faculty mentor junior colleagues into the culture of the college and remarked on how most of the younger teachers were, of course, recent arrivals from graduate school in secular academe. At Wheaton, the chaplain is *not* seen as an officer housed within the Student Development Office but reports directly to the president. He has deep and steady access to faculty and staff members and often their families, as well as students.

Dr. Kellough is assisted by four student chaplains, two men and two women. These undergraduates help with counseling as well as liturgical responsibilities. They are sometimes, but by no means always, heading for a ministerial career.

I asked the chaplain if other religious traditions were ever presented or discussed in chapel. He said that they were not, as chapel is seen as a worship opportunity and therefore conducted within the evangelical Protestant belief structure of the college. It adheres to the college's statement of faith. However, he continued, students have ample opportunities to learn about other religious traditions in the classroom and through co-curricular activities.

Dr. Kellough said that he finds Wheaton College students are enthusiastic about the new revision of the community covenant, which, he believes, shows a transition from a rule-oriented document to one focusing on freedom, responsibility, privilege, and voluntarism. What happens, I asked the chaplain, when students "fall" from the demanding standards of the college. He noted the importance of the student chaplains in counseling in such situations, and the similar role of the residence hall advisers. At Wheaton, he said, students will "challenge" each other on behavioral and moral issues, and such peer interactions can be most effective. When behavioral issues go beyond peer assistance, the student affairs administration seeks to treat them on a case-by-case basis, with "redemption in mind," not punishment. This discussion corroborated the comments of the students on the same issue.

Across from Wheaton College is a large institution named the College Church. At my request, Dr. Kellough clarified the relationship between the college and the College Church. The latter was established by the college's founders but now has no official connection with the college. There is no expectation, for example, that either the president or the chaplain would worship there. Indeed, Dr. Kellough himself is a member of a local Presbyterian Church U.S.A. congregation. When I asked Dr. Kellough what he saw as peer colleges, he mentioned the CCCU consortium institutions, especially Westmont, Gordon, Messiah, and Bethel.

Wheaton College has a long history and a continuous tradition of conservative evangelical Protestant Christianity. It has a splendid campus, influential alumni, distinguished faculty, and exceptional students. Wheaton has a national stature that makes it a leader among contemporary American Christian colleges. The college sees itself, as others see it, as an exemplar of its type. Its stance is one of neither unseemly pride nor false modesty. It does a lot; it knows what it is doing; and what it does, it does very well.

PART V

Conclusions

What have we learned about faith-based colleges and universities in America today? And, even more important, what can we learn from them?

14 | What Can We Learn?

Religious colleges and universities in twenty-first-century America merit study for reasons both intrinsic and extrinsic. I hope the preceding pages have demonstrated the intrinsic attraction of such an examination: these are intriguing places, and those of us who are engaged in the world of higher education should find pleasure and profit in learning more about them.

At the same time, there are perhaps even more important extrinsic reasons to learn about this significant and growing segment of our collegiate community. Religious institutions are, as we have seen, doing well. They are attracting increasing numbers of students, of increasing quality. They are providing an experience that those students rate highly (e.g., Kuh and Gonyea find a high correlation between students who engage in spirituality-enhancing activities in college and overall satisfaction with the college experience and with the out-of-class environment).[1] Capable faculty and administrators and generous donors of substantial means are also drawn to these schools. It would be foolish and closed-minded for those of us outside these institutions not to ask what we can learn from religious colleges and universities that could improve and make more attractive the rest of the American postsecondary establishment yet would not deflect us from our very different nonsectarian missions. And, I believe, it could also be helpful for these colleges and universities to continue to look at themselves and at each other and to continue to grapple with their place within the larger context of American higher learning. I have visited and viewed and mulled over these colleges as an outsider, and as an outsider I want to know how to understand their successes and to make some of them my own.

Stepping back, then, from the examination of specific institutions, what have we learned?

Infinite Variety

Like human beings, Christian colleges all may seem to look alike, until one really looks at them. Then, suddenly, each seems startlingly unique. In order to understand these institutions collectively, we need to reflect on their variety. Indeed, one of the strengths of American higher education, and of religious colleges and universities in the United States, is heterogeneity.

♦♦♦

The first way in which Christian colleges and universities differ from each other is that some are colleges and some are universities. In this regard, the Christian institutions cover nearly as full a range as the larger universe of American postsecondary schools altogether. Thus, in terms of size, I visited New Saint Andrews College in Idaho with fewer than two hundred students, fifteen faculty members, and one building. It has one undergraduate major and, like Thomas Aquinas College, a unitary curriculum wherein all the students take essentially the same courses in the same order. Baylor University occupies a 735-acre campus in Waco and has a 14,000-student population, with 850 faculty. Baylor offers 150 baccalaureate majors in comparison to New Saint Andrews's one, and it has as well 76 master's programs and 22 doctoral degrees, awards the JD, and offers several advanced ministerial programs. Baylor is, in every respect, a full-fledged university; New Saint Andrews is a tightly focused college community.

Something of the same range of institutional type can be found within American Catholic institutions as well. Thomas Aquinas College offers a single curriculum to 351 undergraduate students with 37 tutors; Notre Dame has more than eleven thousand students and includes 46 MA programs and 23 doctorates. Its campus comprises 137 buildings on 1,250 acres, including the fourteen-story library.

Of course, the majority of religious institutions fall between these extremes. There are larger, more traditionally sized colleges and universities, such as Calvin, Westmont, and North Park and smaller universities, such as Oral Roberts (5,723 students), Biola University (5,752) or Azusa Pacific (8,084). Villanova University has about 6,350 undergraduates.

For the prospective student (or faculty member) the panoply of institutional types within the religious collegiate spectrum runs from very small, intensely focused undergraduate colleges to large, diverse, research universities.

♦♦♦

One very important way in which Christian colleges are different one from another has to do with their ties to specific denominational affiliations. Here, again, there is a range, conveniently illustrated by two of the premier Christian liberal arts colleges, Calvin and Wheaton.

Wheaton College, as we have seen, was aggressively nondenominational from its inception. Founder and first president Jonathan Blanchard, his son and successor Charles, and the college's third leader, James O. Buswell, all overtly declared Wheaton a conservative Christian institution, without any link to a specific denomination (although, of course, these leaders were themselves members of denominations: both Blanchards were Congregationalist and Buswell a Presbyterian). Today, Wheaton describes itself (accurately, in my opinion) as an "interdenominational Christian college that takes the pursuit of faith and learning very seriously."[2] Wheaton asks its students and its faculty to participate in the worship and society of a local Protestant church but does not specify which one, and in my conversations with several of the senior administrators at the college it became apparent that they were affiliated with different church homes.

Calvin College, on the other hand, is very strongly tied to the Christian Reformed Church. While it serves students from a variety of denominational backgrounds, it is explicitly denominational. Its Web site, in contrast to that of Wheaton College, observes that "we affirm the confessions and respect the rich traditions of reformed believers worldwide, and, in particular, those of the Christian Reformed Church."[3] There is a link to the CRC Web site on that of the college. Calvin faculty members are required to affiliate with a congregation within the Christian Reformed Church or linked to it. The faculty handbook states, "Calvin College faculty members are required to be professing members in good standing and active participants in the life, worship, and activities of a Christian Reformed Church (CRC) or of any church which is a member of a denomination in ecclesiastical fellowship with the CRC."[4] As noted earlier, a serious issue during the 2007–8 academic year involved an African American faculty member who sought, unsuccessfully, to win permission to join a historically black Baptist institution rather than a CRC church.

Again, other institutions fall between the extremes of the denominational-nondenominational spectrum. North Park University, for example, is clearly and unequivocally affiliated with the Evangelical Covenant Church (originally the Swedish Covenant Church) but welcomes students of any or no religious conviction and background. Faculty members are expected to be affiliated with churches of an evangelical character, but only a few faculty members belong to congregations specifically affiliated with the Evangelical Covenant Church.

◆◆◆

Another significant variability among religious institutions, especially Protestant evangelical ones, has to do with the extent to which they focus internally and externally. What makes this an important distinction is that it mirrors a larger division within conservative Protestant Christians.

On the one hand, denominations and groups of a pietistic persuasion tend to be inwardly focused, seeking to detach themselves from a world that they see as inevitably corrupt and corrupting and to focus on the personal salvation of individual Christian believers or particular congregations or sects. Over against this impulse to withdraw is an equally strong tradition within conservative evangelicals to engage the world, to bring the message of salvation to those who have not had a personal conversion experience and to be deeply involved in public, social issues. Where the first group sees disengagement from a broken world as the route to personal salvation, the second sees enthusiastic engagement in that world and seeks to improve or mend it as doing the work of God.

Christian colleges, too, sometimes turn inward and sometimes diligently seek outward involvement. Most, of course, do some of both. So, for example, Westmont College, steering a middle course, has many events that turn inward—worship occasions for the campus community; a certain tendency to seek for faculty, administrators, and trustees individuals with some prior connection with the institution or very similar ones; and a physically self-contained campus. But it also sends students to worship at churches outside the college, involves them in social service work in the nearby and distant communities, and hosts events (such as an annual conference on liberal learning) to which are invited participants from a variety of backgrounds. Of the institutions I visited in the course of doing the research for *Seeing the Light,* I think perhaps North Park University in Chicago was the most assertively outward looking in its philosophy. North Park overtly, and in multiple ways, sees itself as part of its Northside neighborhood—indeed, as we noted earlier, its physical campus now includes several blocks in which houses are alternately owned and used by the university and by private homeowners. So, for example, the fall 2007 issue of the *North Parker* magazine for alumni and friends features on the cover three university students pictured not on campus but at the downtown Chicago Millennium Park, with the cover story focusing on "Our Place in Chicago." The president's column focuses upon Chicago's neighborhoods and the "love affair" between the school and the city. The same issue also features articles on a professor's work in the Ukraine, a partnership between the university and a large midwestern Hispanic non-profit, and North Park's significant role in a Chicagoland women's football team that plays its games on campus.

In contrast, New Saint Andrews College in Moscow, Idaho, while it certainly does not neglect the world outside its campus, seems largely inward looking. It remains closely tied to its founding church, Christ Church of Moscow. The three men initially appointed by Christ Church to study the feasibility of the church's establishing a Christian college went on to become the founding board of governors of the college and its first faculty members. A decade and a half later, one of those three is the school's president and one the acting director of student affairs, and two of the three are senior (teaching) fellows. They are three of the four members of the college's executive council. The two senior fellows are also members of the seven-person board of trustees. The small faculty and staff include some New Saint Andrews graduates, relatives of other members of the college family, and several with strong connections to Christ Church (e.g., the conductor of the college choir also conducts the church choir). At New Saint Andrews College, a view of life as a battleground is often heard. The catalog begins with the words "In the spiritual battle for the hearts and minds of the next generation raging in higher education today." Just a few pages later, that same document focuses upon "this cultural war—between what Augustine described as the City of God and the City of Man—continues down to our own day," and it speaks of the importance of "discerning the antithesis between truth and falsehood, between the City of God and the City of Man."[5] The students, faculty, staff, and leaders of New Saint Andrews College are certainly not hermits, nor are they some sort of antisocial survivalists. But it is clear the college's vision is one in which much of contemporary culture is understood to be contaminated and contaminating. This contrasts dramatically with the posture of places like North Park, which work vigorously to push students out into the complexity of a modern urban environment and to pull into the orb of the university the multifaceted neighborhood around it.

♦♦♦

Many Christian colleges have a faculty or student pledge, which can range from specific behavioral and belief affirmations to very general statements.

Thus, for example, the Northwestern College Declaration of Christian Community (discussed in chapter 16) has recently been revised but maintains explicit injunctions against such behaviors as gambling, smoking, and (carefully defined) sexual immorality. The declaration has separate sections for students, faculty, staff, administration, and trustees, as well as large sections that apply to everyone at the college. Citing scripture, it includes some explicit affirmations of Christian belief.

In contrast, at North Park University, faculty are assumed to "articulate, embrace and model Christian faith and commitment" but are not asked to sign a particular statement to that effect. Students are expected to respect the Christian faith, but the university goes out of its way to state that students from other faith traditions are welcome, and its most recent (2008) statistics indicate that a significant 29% of the students self-identify either as coming from a non-Christian faith tradition or as having no faith tradition at all.[6]

At New Saint Andrews, members of the college community are required to pledge in writing their affirmation of a statement of faith, and there is a signed student code of conduct. The former includes very explicit theological statements, for example: "Because all sons of Adam are spiritually dead, they are consequently incapable of saving themselves. But out of his sovereign mercy, God the father elected a countless number to eternal salvation, leaving the remainder to their sinful desires." The student code avoids explicit nonbiblical behavioral rules but is quite directive nonetheless, affirming, for example: "Students should embrace and encourage the development of distinctively Christian music, art, literature, poetry, drama and crafts."[7]

Some of the institutions I visited have very strict behavioral expectations for students. A few have dress codes—some (e.g., Thomas Aquinas College) are formal, others (e.g., Oral Roberts University) are only modestly directive. At some of these institutions, student behavior expectations fall into a "conservative" social mode, at others more "liberal" standards prevail. At each institution I visited, I asked, as a kind of template on this issue, questions about institutional stands on the matter of homosexual students. At one institution, it was clear that a homosexual student would not be allowed to remain at the college under any circumstances. At several the policy was that homosexual behavior was forbidden, though students who found in themselves impulses toward same-sex physical attraction but who maintained a celibate lifestyle could remain at the school. And, at one institution, there were gay and lesbian student support groups officially sanctioned by the institution.[8] I also asked what would happen if an academically successful, serious female student sought to establish an abortion rights club as an official campus organization. Almost universally, the answer was that because such a club would probably violate the principles that undergirded the institution, formal collegiate recognition would be impossible. No place I visited believed, however, that such a student would be prohibited from or punished for joining such an organization based off-campus.

The matter of pledges, signed statements, declarations, and the like is clearly related to the issues of denominationalism and pietism discussed earlier, but it seems to me a separate subject nonetheless.

• • •

All evangelical colleges affirm the central importance of the Bible, and most explicitly announce their belief in its lack of error. But biblical inerrancy can mean different things at different institutions, especially when it comes to areas in which literalist interpretations of the Bible might be seen as conflicting with contemporary science. At each institution I visited, I tried to ascertain the degree of biblical literalism by asking how issues concerning "creation studies" were handled. Here, again, there was a considerable range.

At Calvin College, the provost reported that all members of the Biology Department were Darwinists and that Darwinian evolution was the standard curricular approach. In conversation with faculty members, it became clear that some students arrive at Calvin with backgrounds and beliefs that are not consistent with a Darwinian interpretation of human origins. The faculty notes that challenging familial or community assumptions that students have not themselves seriously considered is an important part of their job, and the institution's. At the same time, they are concerned that their approach to such controversial issues needs to be attentive to student and family traditions, pastoral, and understanding.

Several of the schools I visited (e.g., Oral Roberts University) said that they offered students both evolutionary and creationist versions of human and animal origins. Generally, in these schools, faculty members said that thcy tried to give students the arguments for and against each approach, and let them make up their own minds. Some faculty members said that they told students which they believed, whereas others did not reveal their personal convictions.

At some institutions, a biblical-based creationist approach was the standard, although students might well learn Darwinian evolution so that they were prepared to make the case against it. At New Saint Andrews College, for example, the faculty member who teaches the natural philosophy science course stated that he found the case for Darwinian evolution an unconvincing one and that it was his conviction that even if he lost his religious faith, he would not be able to believe in Darwinism. At the same time, the college has students read substantially in Darwin's writing, in the original texts, not in secondary biology textbooks, so as to understand, and be able to refute, his arguments.

As a general rule, faculty and administrators (and usually students) believed that the role of Christian colleges was not to indoctrinate students in an unthinking biblical literalism but to help them to learn to think for themselves about important questions. I encountered frequently concerns about students who came to college accepting uncritically the beliefs of their parents, churches, and home communities. Only very rarely did I see any indication of an opposite concern—students who came to Christian colleges with a secular, materialist view of the universe, or who moved toward such a position of biblical skepticism during their college years.

♦♦♦

Like their colleague institutions across the entire spectrum of contemporary American higher learning, religious colleges manifest a range of fiscal health. Several of the religious institutions cited earlier in *Seeing the Light* have impressive, or at least comfortable, endowments. Boston College, for example, ranks 39th on the National Association of College and University Business Officers' (NACUBO) ranking of endowments, at more than $1.4 billion.[9] Baylor's endowment is more than $870 million and its separate medical school endowment is even larger at more than $1 billion. Yeshiva (more than $1.2 billion) is also ranked very high. Among the Christian colleges, Wheaton's endowment is more than $303 million and Calvin's rather modest $82.5 million ranks it 373rd, pretty close to the exact middle of the list. Also at the midrange are schools like Westmont, ranked 442 with a $66 million endowment and Northwestern College, ranked 553 at

$38 million (but note that Northwestern's extensive and profitable broadcasting network is not included in these figures). Of the NACUBO's 765 institutions, some religious schools are at the very bottom of the list of endowment value: Multinomah Bible College is ranked 745, Cornerstone College is 751, Caldwell College is 756, and Vanguard is at 762.

Considerably more dramatic is the case of Sheldon Jackson College in Sitka, Alaska, profiled earlier. In the summer of 2007 Sheldon Jackson ceased operations, dismissed its faculty and staff, and canceled course work for students because of overwhelming debt. Also discussed earlier was the approximately $50 million in accumulated indebtedness at Oral Roberts University, potentially erased by a last-minute philanthropic miracle (see chapter 11).

I doubt that any Christian college or university, even the University of Notre Dame, which is ranked seventeenth at an endowment of nearly $4.5 billion, considers itself wholly free from financial stresses. I have yet to find any American postsecondary school in that enviable position. But it is clear that the range from a Notre Dame, Baylor, or Wheaton to Sheldon Jackson, Vanguard, or Oral Roberts mirrors the very wide gulf in the fiscal resources across the entire collegiate spectrum.

Institutional heterogeneity, like biological diversity, is a valuable trait, with a strong link to survival predictions. Compared to higher learning in most countries around the world, American colleges and universities are remarkably varied, and that has been a source of strength and pride. Too commonly, it is assumed by too many casual observers that the religious college segment of that larger community is more homogeneous than the whole. Such a hasty assumption obviously undergirds the comment cited in the opening sentences of this study regarding "two-bit Bible colleges" and how they are all the same. Clearly, a careful examination of contemporary religious colleges and universities reveals a remarkable range, across a wide spectrum of institutional characteristics (intellectual, spiritual, material). This is good news for the supporters of these schools, and it is an important finding for all students of our educational system.

Introspection

Contemporary American religious colleges are not only different from each other but also quite self-aware, both individually and collectively. One of the most impressive discoveries I made while researching these institutions for *Seeing the Light* was the extent to which this group of colleges has collaborated with each other and, even more impressively, the degree to which they have studied themselves.

•••

As the essay on sources should make robustly clear, there has been a daunting productivity on the subject of religion and the American collegiate experience in recent years. In that discussion, we examine writings about religious colleges from the perspective of subject matter areas—for example, works on faith and learning, works on student spirituality, and studies of secularization trends.[10] It is also worthwhile to note the different kinds of writing these schools have inspired.

Some works have focused on one particular institution. There is a collection of essays on the University of Notre Dame as a Catholic university, and two on Baylor as a Baptist institution. Most colleges and universities, religious and nonreligious, have published their own histories. Some of these are splendidly objective, thoughtful, and readable volumes (the history of Cornell College cited earlier is a good illustration), while others tend toward the parochial and pedestrian. Perhaps because their very religious nature gives their histories a consistent theme, my subjective impression is that such works at religious colleges tend to be slightly more coherent and readable than the average institutional history produced by nonreligious peers. Wheaton College, while perhaps more productive than usual, is not eccentric in the range and quantity of works it has generated that focus on itself. In addition to a general collegiate history, there are biographies of several of its presidents and even studies of particular programs (e.g., international missionary outreach and internal campus revivals).

Books have been written that focus, also, on particular institutions but consider several specific colleges and universities in a comparative context. These include works such as Robert Benne's study of six Christian colleges that have maintained their religious ties or Cherry, Deberg, and Porterfield's study of four institutions.

In addition to studies of individual institutions, there are also a great many volumes devoted to particular issues at multiple institutions—for example, secularization, faith and learning, college presidents as moral leaders, and teaching at Christian schools. Some of these works, such as Burtchaell's and Marsden's books on secularization are single-author studies. Many others are collections of essays by multiple authors, from multiple institutions, such as Carpenter and Shipps's volume on *Making*

Higher Education Christian or Paul Dovre's collection on *The Future of Religious Colleges.*

As noted in the essay on sources, there have been scores of articles on particular issues, generally or at specific institutions—for example, legal issues and contests surrounding Christian institutions or some action or program at religious schools.

Some of this scholarship is good, some is weak, pretty much in the same proportions as other scholarship that I have encountered on higher education issues. What was surprising to me, and impressive as well, was its sheer volume. Educator-scholars at religious colleges and universities have looked often at their home institutions and at their kinds of institutions, and often they have looked deeply and thoughtfully. There seems to be a strong need at these colleges and universities to understand and articulate their nature and mission. Some of this desire may be defensive ("nobody understands us"), some may be evangelical ("we have a message for the world"), some may well be both, and some may simply reflect a recognition that these schools have a worthwhile and unique story to be told.

•••

Not surprisingly, two occasionally troublesome notes are sounded in some of the writing (and speaking and thinking) about religious colleges. The first is a kind of triumphalism that can be irritating, even offensive, to those beyond the pale. It is to be expected that religious institutions believe they are seeking the truth in the best way possible and that the cultures they have created to do so are optimal. Sometimes, however, this secure spiritual grounding can drift into a tone that suggests that specific institutions, at this present moment, have arrived at the perfect and final answers and have promulgated behavioral expectations that are the only ones that promote lives of genuine virtue. Obviously, this is a question of balance. No religious institution is inclined to cultivate an attitude that prizes ambivalence and ambiguity when it comes to core theological beliefs or to suggest that a wide range of lifestyles, in matters deemed important, is appropriate. On the other hand, there is always the danger that conviction will lapse into self-important smugness, and such lapses, while rare, do occur. For example: "A college education was meant to be about pursuit: the pursuit of knowledge, of truth and of character. But how many people passionately seek these things today? Information masquerades as knowledge, truth is considered a moving target, and character, well, it's often left to chance. We live in a world that has given up on the pursuit. 'X' College has not. At 'X,' we're committed to be a community that fearlessly pursues Truth, upholds an academically rigorous curriculum and promotes virtue."[11]

The other infrequently but occasionally encountered lapse involves the drift into a siege mentality. As many commentators (e.g., Randall Balmer) have pointed out, evangelical Protestant Christianity has become a potent, sometimes dominant force on the contemporary American scene. Several recent presidents of the United States have embraced evangelicalism (recall, for example, President George W. Bush's 2005 call to teach creationism alongside evolution).[12] Yet, there is an impulse within this powerful community to perceive itself as a persecuted minority within contemporary culture, and this impulse sometimes can be seen in the writings of evangelical colleges. So, for example, one institution, as noted earlier, does not reveal where students live within the community housing the college because "it seems there are people in the community who make a hobby of causing trouble for local Christian families who extend hospitality to . . . [our] students. So as a courtesy to these families, and as a hedge against whatever else the 'Intoleristas' have up their sleeve, we're making it a tad bit harder for them."

The Pew Forum on Religion and Public Life studied the religious affiliations of Americans in 2008. Evangelical Protestants were the largest segment of the population, at 26.3%. A category called "Historically Black," which is closely linked with evangelical Protestantism (both include Pentecostals and Baptists) accounts for an additional 6.9%. The next largest group is Roman Catholic (23.9%), followed by Mainline Protestant (18.1) and Unaffiliated (16.1). Only about a quarter of those Unaffiliated describe themselves as Atheist or Agnostic, with the remainder "Nothing in Particular." No other groups accounted for as much as 2% of contemporary Americans. There can be little doubt that self-described evangelical Protestants are hardly a besieged minority on the current scene.[13]

◆◆◆

Religious colleges and collegians communicate with and about each other in a wide variety of venues, often in impressive depth.

They have sometimes formed subgroups within larger academic organizations. Thus, as one illustration, within the National Collegiate Honors Council, there is a group of Christian colleges that sponsors a few discussions and sections as part of the regular program of the NCHC annual conference, as well as an annual informal social event at that meeting. At the 2007 annual meeting, there was a session on the relationship between honors work and the particular missions of Christian colleges. Occasionally, this group has additional gatherings and events—for example, a two-day summer seminar at Calvin College focusing on special issues in honors programs at Christian institutions, such as the integration of faith and learning within honors courses.

Several academic disciplines have organizations of Christian scholars within them. Many but not all of those scholars are, logically, from Christian institutions. Thus, for example, there is a "Conference on Faith and History" within the history discipline. This organization has a biennial conference (in recent years at Hope and at Houghton colleges) that brings together more than two hundred professional historians. It also publishes the journal *Fides et Historia* as well as a regular newsletter. The Conference on Faith and History is an affiliate member of the American Historical Association. A similar group is the Society of Christian Philosophers, a group that includes philosophers interested in Christian philosophical studies, both within the Protestant and the Catholic traditions. It publishes *Faith and Philosophy*, a scholarly journal, and meets regularly in conjunction with regional meetings of the American Philosophical Association. Begun in 1950, the Conference on Christianity and Literature is an organization of Christian scholars in literary studies. It publishes the well-regarded journal *Christianity and Literature.*

Similar professional organizations exist for Roman Catholic scholars within their academic disciplines. For example, the American Catholic Philosophical Association has been meeting annually since its founding in 1926 and publishes the *American Catholic Philosophical Quarterly*. There is an *American Catholic Sociology Review*, published by the Association for the Sociology of Religion, which grew out of the American Catholic Sociology Society (1936) and multiple similar publications and organizations.

Evangelical Christian colleges are banded together in the Council for Christian Colleges and Universities (CCCU).[14] This group is little recognized outside the realm of the Christian colleges but is impressively active within it. The CCCU was founded in 1976 with 32 members. Today, it claims 105 members in North America and 75 affiliates worldwide in twenty-four additional nations. It has an annual budget of more than $11 million and sixty-five professional employees plus leadership from dozens of volunteers. It sponsors a variety of publications, including a monthly electronic newsletter, "CCCU eAdvance." It maintains a multifaceted Web site.[15]

CCCU describes its mission as: "To advance the cause of Christ-centered higher education and to help our institutions transform lives by faithfully relating scholarship and service to biblical truth." Among other requirements for membership (full regional accreditation, fiscal soundness, and the like) is the rule that all full-time faculty and administrators at CCCU institutions be Christians. The institutions themselves represent some twenty-eight denominations. There are currently more than 319,000 students and 15,600 faculty members at CCCU institutions and another 100,000 students at the affiliate international campuses. The CCCU headquarters occupies a row of townhouses and a new facility in the Capitol Hill neighborhood of Washington, D.C.

Each year, more than seven hundred students from CCCU colleges participate in one of its eleven off-campus programs, plus a summer program in Oxford, England. Those programs are in Australia, China, Uganda, Egypt (Middle East Studies), Russia, England, and Costa Rica (Latin American Studies); and in the United States, they include a program of film studies in Los Angeles, two programs in Washington, D.C. (one in American studies and one in journalism), and a program in contemporary music at Martha's Vineyard.[16]

For faculty and administrators, CCCU sponsors a variety of professional development activities. These include, for example, work in the area of "advancing intercultural competencies" with workshops, exchanges, awards, resource materials, and research services such as surveys.[17] For a third of a century, CCCU has held an annual college president's conference. In addition to its multiple building headquarters in Washington, CCCU also owns facilities in Oxford, Costa Rica, and Russia.[18] In recent years attention has been paid to increasing intercultural competencies (especially through the expanding international programs) and political efforts on behalf of religious education in the nation's capitol.

In sum, it is clear that there exists within the American higher education community a fully developed, complex network or matrix of Christian organizations that focus on the advancement and development of religious collegiate education and communication among Christian scholars, students, and institutions.

♦♦♦

In the survey of religious colleges and universities that constitutes the majority of this study, it is clear that one way in which these institutions are distinctive is in their strong sense of a focused mission. This is, I contend, a significant strength, especially in an era when many colleges and universities have responded to various pressures (e.g., market, political) in a manner that has diffused their central identity. So, for example, the American postsecondary community abounds in examples of institutions that in the middle of the twentieth century were small, unified regional teacher-training colleges that have subsequently grown into larger and larger, more and more diverse comprehensive universities, first expanding the range of undergraduate offerings, then adding master's degrees and often doctorates. These institutions serve important and valued functions today, but no thoughtful observer would describe them as "focused." This has not been the case with many religious institutions, although some have also grown and expanded.

Even the major institutions—the Notre Dames, Villanovas, and Baylors—hold tightly to a central religious core that sharpens their identity, internally and to the external world. Certainly this is even truer of smaller places like Calvin, Oral Roberts, Wheaton, and New Saint Andrews. Thus, George Fox University offers the following mission statement:

> To demonstrate the meaning of Jesus Christ by offering a caring educational community in which each individual may achieve the highest intellectual and personal growth and by participating responsibly in our world's concerns.
>
> The following institutional objectives further explain the mission of George Fox University:
>
> Teach all truth as God's truth, integrating all fields of learning around the person and work of Jesus Christ, bringing the divine revelations through sense, reason, and intuition to the confirming test of Scripture.
>
> Support academic programs that liberate the student for a life of purpose and fulfillment through an awareness of the resources of knowledge and culture available; maximize career-oriented education through counseling, curriculum, field experience, and placement.
>
> Maintain a program of varied activities that directs the student to a commitment to Christ as Lord and Savior, encourages attitudes of reverence and devotion toward God, leads to recognition that the revealed commandments of God are the supreme criteria of the good life, enables the student to mirror the example of Christ in human relationships, and develops a greater desire to serve humanity in a spirit of Christian love.

Provide a center for Quaker leadership where faculty and students learn the history and Christian doctrines of the Friends movement and make contemporary applications of these insights.

Give leadership to evangelical Christianity generally, through scholarship publication, lecturing, and by evangelistic and prophetic proclamation and service.

Promote cocurricular activities that will emphasize the development of leadership, initiative, and teamwork by giving opportunity to make practical use of the skills and ideas acquired through academic courses.

Make itself a community in which studies and activities are made relevant to life, develop insight into social and political issues confronting humanity, and learn to participate democratically in decision making and policy implementing as responsible citizens.

Serve as a cultural center for all publics of the University and sponsor programs that are informative and culturally stimulating to the larger college community.

Provide distinctive learning opportunities through continuing education programs and through curriculum enhancements such as off-campus centers, study abroad, honors programs, and other special programs and events.

Cultivate awareness, respect, understanding, and appreciation of cultural diversity throughout the college community to provide members of diverse races and cultures an affirming environment that encourages cross-cultural sharing in the context of Christian lifestyle expectations.[19]

Here is Wheaton College's statement:

Wheaton's mission statement expresses the stable and enduring identity of the College—our reason for existence and our role in society and the church. All the purposes, goals, and activities of the College are guided by this mission.

Wheaton College exists to help build the church and improve society worldwide by promoting the development of whole and effective Christians through excellence in programs of Christian higher education.

This mission expresses our commitment to do all things—"For Christ and His Kingdom."[20]

Here, by contrast, is the mission statement, in its entirety, of a large, comprehensive state university, the largest constituent member of its state's state college and university system:

"X" University is committed to excellence in teaching, learning, and service, fostering scholarship and enhancing collaborative relationships in a global community.[21]

There is probably not much point or much likelihood of success in trying to be all things to all people, but there is no doubt something to be said for trying to be many things for many different people, and comprehensive universities have an important role to play in our complex and multifaceted contemporary culture. But even in such a cultural context, there is also a real strength to be found in institutions that can more sharply define themselves; can state in unequivocal terms their central guiding reason for existing; and can organize themselves, in everything from curricular decisions to hiring to campus architecture, around that guiding premise.

Safe Havens or Challenging Environments?

One common preconception of religious colleges and universities is that they are safe havens, protected and protective environments, where students will not be tempted by either immoral lures or intellectual challenges. Students, it is sometimes assumed, pick Christian colleges because they do not want their lifestyles or religious and academic beliefs put to the test and because faculty will promulgate a kind of docile acceptance of unitary institutional dogma. And parents, in particular, want for their sons and daughters an environment where the (presumed secular) collegiate temptations of sex, drugs, and even rock and roll will be excluded, and where religious conformity will be uniformly and consistently enforced. There is some truth, and a lot of falsehood, in this image of contemporary religious institutions.

♦♦♦

It is certainly true that many Christian colleges and universities promulgate standards for student behavior that are both clearer and more conservative than average. As we have noted earlier, there has been some stir when some of those institutions have budged even a bit in loosening such rules: for example, when Wheaton College in 2003 decided to permit dancing, there were strong objections raised by some who saw this relaxation of student conduct regulation as the beginning of the end. But, by the student cultures that prevail across most public and nonreligious private institutions, Wheaton, and similar schools, remain a very long way from the end, indeed. Thus, the Wheaton College Community Covenant, which all members of the community are required to understand and embrace (and sign), endorses a number of specific virtues (e.g., kindness, faithfulness, gentleness, self-control, compassion, humility, mercy) and explicitly prohibits unchastity among the unmarried, dishonesty including plagiarism, homosexual behavior, rage, drunkenness, smoking, drug use, pornography, immodest dressing, and alcohol use by students and permits only "careful and loving discretion in any use of alcohol" by others.[22]

Wheaton's standards for student behavior are fairly typical of those of Christian colleges and universities in general. Thus, for example, Westmont prohibits the possession and consumption of alcohol on campus and at any college-sponsored event, "holds to the conviction that premarital intercourse conflicts with Biblical teaching," and forbids use or possession of tobacco.[23] Northwestern College prohibits alcohol and tobacco, premarital sex, and gambling. In general, my survey of Christian colleges and universities demonstrates that most of those schools have firm policies in place regarding sexual behavior, substance use and abuse, cheating, and modesty in dress. It is also true that, in recent years, many of those institutions state those expectations and injunctions more in a counseling mode and less in the form of outright prohibitions: they take pains to explain why some behaviors are to be avoided and provide some mechanisms for those who may slip from community expectations.

Similarly, it is true that most religious colleges have certain expectations in regard to personal theology of students and, even more, of faculty. So, for example, all the institutions in the CCCU (those discussed at length here are Wheaton, Calvin, Oral Roberts, North Park, Westmont, George Fox, and Northwestern; the former Sheldon Jackson; and Baylor as an affiliate member) hire only Christians for all full-time faculty and administrative positions. These colleges are not reluctant to advertise this feature to prospective students and their families. So, for example, Calvin notes that "100% of Calvin's faculty are committed Christians" and Northwestern reminds prospective students that "you'll learn from Christian professors."[24]

In sum, Christian colleges do tend to provide a climate in which behavioral expectations for students (and faculty and staff) are explicit and more socially conservative than elsewhere in contemporary American higher education. And they guarantee a certain theological unanimity within their bounds, especially among faculty and senior administrators, which would comfort those who seek to avoid temptations to question core issues of Christian faith within the collegiate environment.

♦♦♦

Faculty members at religious colleges speak often about the image of their institutions as intellectual or behavioral safe havens for shy or overprotected students. They resoundingly reject this notion. Frequently, in my conversations with professors, they have chosen to emphasize that they do not see their role as providing students with simplistic answers to important questions. Indeed, in several cases, they do see their work as challenging students and forcing them to think through, in complex ways, matters that they may have come to college thinking they already understood but grasped simplistically.

Precisely this point was made by the director of the liberal arts program at Westmont, who observes that students need a "nuanced" understanding of complex issues; they should "not leave with an unsophisticated understanding" on matters such as stem cell research. In college, and at his college specifically, he finds, students can tend to move away from the religious perspectives of their family and parents. The college does not exist to provide intellectual safety. I asked how family members react to this movement, and he responded that he thinks Westmont does a good job of explaining this process of independence and maturation to the parents.

Similarly, on controversial topics such as evolution, says a faculty member at New Saint Andrews, "we make sure they hear all the arguments, on all sides."

A faculty member at North Park described an experience teaching Darwin in a science class, causing a student to complain to his or her family that the college was promoting evolution. The student's father "got into it" with the faculty member, who held firm (and was supported by the college). The class was described as advancing a "scientific approach to the theory of evolution as consistent with Biblical faith." This particular teacher would not include intelligent design or creationism on the syllabus of a biology class. Likewise, at Calvin, a parent complained about the teaching of Darwin in a science class and demanded to know, "What is Calvin's official position?"

Noting that "Oral likes freedom," a faculty member at Oral Roberts University described an energetic debate in class on stem cell research. Another there, in the humanities, worried that some students come to ORU thinking that Christian literature is what they find in Christian bookstores.

Wheaton College faculty members noted that their beliefs needed to remain in accord with the core values of the institution, but they were free to talk openly about any subject. They noted that biology classes "were driven by doing careful science" and that evolution was taught using the same texts found in secular universities. (In fact, one of the Wheaton professors with whom I spoke noted that she had briefly taught biology on a temporary appointment at the public institution where I had served for a dozen years, and she used exactly the same materials at both institutions.)

The same theme of promoting intellectual independence also surfaced at the Roman Catholic institutions I visited. At Villanova, for example, the vice president for academic affairs discussed a lively lecture series on science and religion, and the president noted that "saying 'you must' . . . is not Augustinian." At faculty orientation, the university offers a panel of non-Catholics to help newcomers. And faculty stressed that there is "no set of rules" governing the mix of faith with reason in teaching in the Villanova classroom.

I also heard from faculty and staff that, while religious colleges tend to promulgate stricter and clearer behavioral codes for their students, they are increasingly realistic about the psychology (and physiology) of eighteen- to twenty-one-year-old students, that they focus more on education than prohibition, and that they encourage students to discover and enact their own ethical standards for righteous living. At Wheaton College, for example, faculty and staff spoke of how they realize college-age young people will sometimes experiment with alcohol and sexual activity and that the role of the institution is more to help them understand why such behaviors are immoral and unwise than simply to mete out harsh punishment for any infraction.

At Northwestern College, the dean of students noted efforts to avoid the "holy huddle" of isolationist and separatist tendencies. As evidenced in the following section, that exact phrase, or "Christian bubble" or some close variant, is often used by students at these institutions as well and used in a negative manner. The students, and their faculty, do not want to be protected or insulated from the issues and challenges of the larger American contemporary culture that surrounds them. Thus, the vice president for student services at the College of New Rochelle describes the environment at that Roman Catholic college as one of "tremendous freedom, not antiquated rules."

♦♦♦

Students at religious college echo their professors in rejecting the notion that they are overly protected, in either their studies or their lifestyles. "The idea is not to shelter us—this is not a 'germ-free environment,'" says a student at New Saint Andrews College.

At several schools, students made a point of mentioning their perception that not all their instructors thought or believed identically. Students at Wheaton College, as one fairly typical example, were clear that not all students or faculty there shared the "same worldview" and that, accordingly, the college "prepares you for the world." Like many of their peers, within and outside the faith-based schools, they were keenly aware that their faculty mentors "came from all these different perspectives." Students at Westmont said that they might tend to come to college with similar views, but the professors do not: there is "lots of professorial diversity." And Calvin students described spirited discussions and debates in and out of class on controversial topics such as evolution, stem cell research, and gay issues. Calvin students guessed that their peers were about 60–40 Republicans, but they thought that the faculty was more liberal than the student body.

Students at Northwestern College observed that "faith should not be blind" and echoed their faculty about avoiding the "Christian bubble." They noted that different members of the faculty hold different views on subjects such as Darwinian evolution. And, they asserted, "God wants us to wrestle with doubt."

Noting that some students do hide in their "Christian bubbles," a young man at Oral Roberts University spoke of how most students want to be equipped to go into the wider, secular world. "After four years of questioning, you are solid in what you believe." Another student there noted how different views of human creation are presented in class and felt it is up to the students themselves to decide, for themselves, what to believe about evolution.

Similarly, even in colloquialisms, Villanova students, echoing some of their peers at evangelical colleges, spoke of getting "outside the Christian bubble." They also emphasized the diversity within contemporary Catholicism.

♦♦♦

As part of my study of religious colleges and universities, I interviewed a number of parents whose children were currently attending, or had recently attended, religious institutions. This was by no means a scientifically selected random sampling: for example, I tended to let the parents themselves decide if the schools where their sons or daughters were studying were "religious" (although I did ask what schools they were). Most of those I spoke with were themselves employed in education, but only a few were college teachers. Among the colleges attended by their progeny were Montreat, Elon, Xavier, Catholic University, Saint Benedict, Taylor, Bethel, Northwestern College, Guilford, Evangel, Avila, Belmont Abbey—a pretty good range of evangelical and other Protestant, Roman Catholic, and Quaker institutions. I asked these parents (and, in one case, grandparents) several questions about their experience (see the appendix). Of particular interest in the context of Christian colleges as sheltered environments was a series of questions regarding why and how the colleges were chosen: what other institutions were considered; was the decision primarily a parental choice, that of the student, or a shared decision; how important were academic factors, and how important extracurricular ones, in the choice; was the Christian character of the college a major factor in the students' experiences there; and did the school live up to expectations or was it a disappointment?

The spectrum of other institutions considered by the students who eventually matriculated at religious colleges was spectacularly wide: it included the Air Force Academy, the University of Kentucky, Liberty University, the University of North Carolina at Greensboro, Davidson College, the University of Wisconsin, Marquette, St. Scholastica, cosmetology school, and community colleges. The list includes large and small, public and private, religious and secular, prestigious and obscure.

When I asked who was primarily responsible for the final choice of institution attended, it was the parents' perception that in no case was that decision primarily theirs, and in most cases they said it was their child's choice rather than a shared one. Some of the comments on this issue were instructive: "It was her choice: we were happy about it"; "absolutely her choice"; "As parents we did not direct. We are Christians and hoped our kids would be, but you can't direct them. College choice is their choice. We wanted a place that would open doors for the rest of their lives." In at least one case, parents actively discouraged their student from choosing a Bible college, in favor of a more liberal arts–oriented Christian institution.

Generally, in this small and nonscientific sample, parents were happy with the choice of a Christian college by their offspring. Their students liked their classes and professors and made good and lasting friendships.

In a few cases, parents expressed surprise that the level of student life was not as exemplary as they had hoped or anticipated. One spoke of students drinking to excess and "running wild" at a religious college. Another noted that some parents apparently sent their kids to religious colleges not because the students were solid in their faith and morally upright but "because they needed extra guidance and help." One parent complained about the strict antidancing regulations at her daughter's college. Overall, however, most felt that their students had been well prepared for their careers and future lives. Some were going on to graduate school, others were entering careers such as fitness consultants, organic gardeners, and high school teaching. Tellingly, when I asked parents if they thought they might make a financial contribution to their child's Christian college after their son or daughter graduated, most said they would (or had already done so).

When I asked these parents if they thought the fact that these were religious colleges made a big difference in their students' instructional and social experiences, the answers were generally affirmative but not strikingly so. For example, one parent said that "the teachers at 'X' college were more caring and interested in character development." Another responded, "Not much. There was prayer in some classes, and teachers did discuss Christian implications of what was being covered." Similarly, another parent responded, "Yes, but not significantly; some classes began with prayer; there was a connection between subject and faith." But another parent felt that his child had "the same" experience she would have had at a public institution, and one felt that what differences there were had more to do with campus size than religious orientation.

Are religious colleges and universities protected islands of particularist doctrines and conservative behaviors? It is clear that they are more directive when it comes to many issues of student lifestyles —drinking, smoking, sex, drugs, dress, and the like. And it is the assumption of most of these institutions that faculty and staff share the core theological and behavioral perspective of the dominant campus culture, especially in denominational institutions. (Some would make the same assertion of secular campuses—that everyone on a secular campus is expected to believe in Darwinian evolution and that nonbelievers would be punished, or not tolerated.)

But students, faculty and staff, and parents reject soundly the image of the Christian college as an isolated and protected safe haven. Students recognize the diversity of beliefs and approaches of their professors and believe they are being encouraged to explore and think for themselves. The parents with whom I spoke did not unilaterally pick Christian colleges for their students and did not seem to expect such places to control rigidly the beliefs or thinking of their young women and men, or to treat them like children. And faculty and administrators saw their job not as indoctrination but exploration. They affirm that their mission is to help students break free of unexamined ideas and beliefs, to come to grips with complex and controversial issues, and, most of all, to learn to think for themselves.

Student Satisfaction

Measurements of student satisfaction are increasingly common in an era of mandated assessment but remain somewhat elusive sources of information. Like political polling, much depends on what questions are asked, who is doing the asking, and how the queries are phrased. Moreover, results will vary from institution to institution and, to some extent, from year to year. Given all these caveats, though, there is some worthwhile information available about how students at religious colleges see their experiences there. Because some consortia of collegiate institutions have been especially interested in collecting data about their students and programs, there is some revealing aggregated information, especially about the CCCU institutions, which have been particularly aggressive in pursuing this activity.

♦♦♦

Annually, the CCCU conducts a "Student Satisfaction Inventory" (SSI) for its member institutions. This instrument has been structured primarily to enable individual members to ascertain where they are perceived by their students as doing well, and where they need to improve. Thus, the SSI first asks students what they find important about their college experiences, then asks them to assess their satisfaction in those areas of importance. With this information in hand, the SSI can tell each participating institution which areas its students value most highly, and think they are doing well, and which areas of high expectations show gaps between student aspirations and their perceptions of institutional performance. In addition to the individual reports, there is also an annual summary of SSI information for the whole field, and this is of considerable interest to the students of Christian colleges.

In the most recent data, here, in rank order, are the top items that students at CCCU schools said were "most important" to them:[25]

The content of the courses within my major is valuable.
The instruction in my major field is excellent.
Nearly all of the faculty are knowledgeable in their field.
The quality of instruction I receive in most of my classes is excellent.
Tuition paid is a worthwhile investment.
I am able to experience intellectual growth here.
My academic advisor is knowledgeable about requirements in my major.
It is an enjoyable experience to be a student on this campus.
I am able to register for classes I need with few conflicts.
Being on this campus is contributing to my spiritual growth.
Adequate financial aid is available for most students.
My understanding of God is being strengthened by classroom and/or campus experiences.
There is a good variety of courses provided on this campus.
The campus is safe and secure for all students.
Faculty are fair and unbiased in their treatment of individual students.

Six of these fifteen top items in student importance are directly focused on the students' academic experience (e.g., courses, instruction). These include the top four student priorities. Other items (e.g., faculty are fair) might well have primarily academic weight for many students. Two items ranked tenth and twelfth are religious: contributions to spiritual growth and understanding of God.

What are the areas, then, where students are most satisfied? Here, again, are their top fifteen responses, in rank order—I use boldface for those items that correlate with the list of most important:

Nearly all the faculty are knowledgeable in their field.
This institution has a good reputation within the community.
This campus provides adequate opportunities for involvement in ministry.
Males and females are treated with equal respect on this campus.
On the whole, the campus is well-maintained.
I am able to experience intellectual growth here.
The campus staff are caring and helpful.
My academic advisor is approachable.

Students are made to feel welcome on this campus.
Faculty care about me as an individual.
Faculty are usually available after class and during office hours.
It is an enjoyable experience to be a student on this campus.
My academic advisor is knowledgeable about requirements in my major.
My understanding of God is being strengthened by classroom and/or campus experiences.
The campus is safe and secure for all students.
There is a commitment to academic excellence on this campus.

Here, three items, including two on the list of "most important" issues, focus directly on the students' classroom experience (intellectual growth, commitment to academic excellence, faculty knowledgeable). Students are particularly satisfied with warm interactions on campus (equal respect, helpful and caring, approachable, feel welcome, care about me, faculty available, enjoyable experience).

When students were asked what about their campus experiences was least satisfying, they listed only two items that also ranked on the top fifteen most important issues, and these had to do with the value of the investment of tuition and the availability of financial aid. Not shockingly, parking and food lead the list (in this, Christian colleges seem to mirror exactly their secular peers):

The amount of student parking space on campus is adequate.
There is adequate selection of food available in the cafeteria.
There are a sufficient number of weekend activities for students.
Adequate financial aid is available for most students.
Billing policies are reasonable.
Channels for expressing student complaints are readily available.
I seldom get the run-around when seeking information on this campus.
Student activities fees are put to good use.
Residence hall regulations are reasonable.
The intercollegiate athletic programs contribute to a strong sense of school spirit.
Security staff respond quickly in emergencies.
Living conditions in the residence halls are comfortable. . . .
Freedom of expression is protected on campus.
Tuition paid is a worthwhile investment.
My academic advisor helps me set goals to work toward.

Students are least satisfied by a number of campus activity and living situations (parking, food, activities, runaround, athletics, security, comfort, free expression). Their top fifteen complaints include none that are explicitly religious, and none that are directly focused on classroom work (although the "free expression" and "advisor sets goals" items come close).

To refine this information into a simplistic conclusion, then, CCCU students, in the aggregate, are satisfied with the intellectual and religious opportunities afforded them by their Christian colleges, opportunities that they described as highly valued and important to them.

◆◆◆

In 2003, at the annual meeting of the Critical Issues Conference of the Comprehensive Assessment Project of the CCCU, Dr. Laurie Schreiner, codirector of the assessment project, gave an introductory paper that summarized some significant cross-institutional information about student satisfaction at Christian colleges.[26] Dr. Schreiner looked at four pieces of data: the 2002 CIRP survey (conducted by the Higher Education Research Institute at UCLA) of nearly thirteen thousand first-year students at CCCU institutions; the 2002 CCCU "College Student Survey" of six thousand graduating seniors; and the 2001 SSI, which included some twenty thousand CCCU students and data from the 2000 National Survey of Student Engagement (NSSE) in which sixteen CCCU institutions provided information from first-year and senior students. She viewed this information in the context of a survey conducted by Maguire and Associates that looked at more than two thousand prospective students and their parents who had expressed interest in a CCCU institution.

The Maguire research yielded some disturbing results, which Schreiner sought to test. It showed that "the more important academic excellence was to a prospective student, the less likely he or she was to enroll in a CCCU institution." In particular, these prospective students expressed concern about: the level of academic excellence and the intellectual life on campus, and "the level of open inquiry encouraged on campus versus a narrow or close-minded religiosity that stifled intellectual inquiry and debate."[27] Schreiner's goal was to test these perceptual conclusions of prospective students and parents against reality.

Professor Schreiner's study utilized Alexander Astin's conceptual framework of "inputs-experiences-outputs." It examines what was the situation of the students at CCCU schools when they began, what happened to them while they were there, and what was their status when they left.

Among the students, 72.2% listed religious orientation as important or very important in their decision to enroll, and 53.1% gave academic reputation the same weight. At private nonreligious institutions, academic reputation is listed by 61.9% of entering students. So, more than half the CCCU students value academic repute highly, but that is a significantly smaller number than at more secular schools. CCCU students had higher grades in high school than did their secular private college peers: 55.2% had averages at or above A– compared to 44.6%. However, they were less ambitious in their educational goals: 62.8% said their intention was to pursue graduate studies; that figure was 76.1% outside the faith-based colleges. The gain from first to fourth year in graduate school aspirations is higher in the CCCU contingent, although the actual percentage that does pursue this avenue remains smaller than at other private colleges.

Students at CCCU schools are slightly more satisfied with their contact with faculty, but the difference is not dramatic: 86.8% compared to 83.9%. However, they are less likely to have spent time discussing academic issues with faculty: CCCU students on average spend less than an hour a week doing so, while their private college peers spend one to two hours. They are similarly less likely to do research with faculty, to publish with faculty coauthors, and to talk about coursework. They are, however, more likely to discuss their courses with fellow students, to study with other students, and to do group projects in class.

The NSSE reveals that CCCU students engage in more active learning behaviors in their first year than their peers, but that the differences disappear by the fourth year. Active learning includes such activities as tutoring, community-based projects, and asking questions in class. They find the level of academic challenge higher than do students at other private colleges, and they also rate higher in their sense that faculty respect differences in students talents and learning styles.

The Student Satisfaction Inventory shows that CCCU students are significantly more satisfied than students at other private colleges with the promptness of feedback, but that they are less likely to have the opportunity to submit multiple drafts of writing projects.

CCCU students spend about the same amount of time studying out of class as their non-CCCU colleagues (six to ten hours per week), but, because they are taking slightly higher course loads, fewer hours per course.

However, they are spending more time working, doing volunteer activities, reading, and praying. They spend less time in party-type socializing.

In terms of outputs, the Student Satisfaction Inventory shows that CCCU students are significantly more satisfied with their intellectual growth, course content, quality of instruction, academic advising, and faculty expertise. They report slightly lower satisfaction in general education, social science, and humanities courses. They report greater gains than students elsewhere in knowledge of a particular field and in learning about people of different cultures or races but are less likely than students at other institutions to report much stronger abilities in some key academic areas: problem-solving, foreign language, and writing and math skills.

Dr. Schreiner sums up her information: "CCCU students are very satisfied with their academic experience—significantly more so than are students at other private colleges. . . . Some indicators of a quality learning experience are more evident on CCCU campuses than on other private college campuses. . . . The areas where our students report lesser gains are relatively few and the differences fairly small."[28] She makes a number of suggestions as to where CCCU institutions could be working harder to do better (e.g., active learning, time on task, higher expectations). She concludes that "Christian higher education has a strong academic foundation, with enormous potential to impact the world. . . . Christian colleges are too often viewed as nice places to send your daughters, places where they will be safe and grow spiritually and personally. . . but not necessarily places where they will be challenged and equipped to take on the world on its playing field."

♦♦♦

The National Survey of Student Engagement (NSSE) has filled an important gap in our knowledge of the effects of the college years on college students. It has reinforced some intuitive perceptions of college life and shifted our thinking about other issues. Generally, the NSSE has reinforced the positive contributions of smaller campuses to student engagement, and, as the work of many higher education researchers has shown, engaged students are successful ones.[29] A sufficient critical mass of Christian colleges has participated in the NSSE to constitute a distinct and significant subgroup. In 2007 twenty-five CCCU institutions participated in the survey, with 8,929 students responding.[30] Below, I have also included data from twenty-four Roman Catholic institutions.[31] Comparative data are available for these institutions in relation to the Carnegie baccalaureate–liberal arts (BA-LA) schools (111 colleges and universities and more than 33,000 respondents; denominated below as "Liberal Arts"—these are the nation's leading liberal arts colleges) and the complete survey universe (585 institutions with nearly 300,000 students covered). Here are some of the results:[32]

ACADEMIC CHALLENGE

CCCU students, and those in Catholic colleges, both in the first year and as seniors, believe that the level of academic challenge at their schools is higher than average but lower than the Carnegie BA-LA colleges. Academic challenge includes items such as preparing for class, number and length of assignments, coursework that emphasizes synthesis and making judgments, working harder than anticipated, and campus environment that emphasizes academic work. The actual numerical scores (with a range of 1–100, higher numbers indicating greater engagement) are:

	First Year	Senior Year
CCCU	53.5	57.9
Catholic	53.2	57.2
Liberal Arts	55.9	59.8
All NSSE	51.7	55.6

ACTIVE AND COLLABORATIVE LEARNING

Included in this item are queries about asking questions and participating in classes, making presentations, working with other students on class projects, teaching other students, service learning, and working with classmates on assignments. In this area, the Christian College students begin ahead of the BA-LA schools, the Catholic colleges, and the entire NSSE sample, and in the senior year are tied with the liberal arts institutions and remain ahead of the all-NSSE group. The Catholic institutions fall below the CCCU schools and the liberal arts colleges in the senior year, but do better than the national average:

	First Year	Senior Year
CCCU	45.2	52.9
Catholic	42.6	51.9
Liberal Arts	44.8	52.9
All NSSE	41.2	50.1

STUDENT-FACULTY INTERACTION

In this scale, the CCCU sample again scored better than the national average in both the first and the last year, but below the Carnegie baccalaureate group. Catholic colleges score higher than the CCCU schools, below the liberal arts colleges, and above national averages in the first year. They are exactly equal to the CCCU respondents in the senior year. Questions in the student-faculty interaction area focus on discussing grades or assignments with instructors, talking about career plans with a faculty member, discussing classes with faculty outside of regular class hours, working with teachers on nonclassroom matters, prompt response from faculty, and student-faculty research projects.

	First Year	Senior Year
CCCU	34.4	43.5
Catholic	34.9	43.5
Liberal Arts	37.0	50.0
All NSSE	32.8	41.2

ENRICHING EDUCATIONAL EXPERIENCES

Here, there is a considerable jump between first-year and senior students, in all the sample groups. That is surely in part because this area measures experiences likely to occur during the course of students' collegiate lives. These include independent study, various co-curricular activities, internship-type experiences, culminating senior experiences, community service, volunteer work, and participating in learning communities, as well as conversations with students of different religious, political, and personal values or of different races. Although students in all categories improved dramatically, those in the liberal arts and CCCU groups improved significantly more than the Catholic colleges or the overall sample:

	First Year	Senior Year
CCCU	29.2	44.8
Catholic	28.1	40.3
Liberal Arts	30.1	49.6
All NSSE	27.1	39.9

SUPPORTIVE CAMPUS ENVIRONMENT

In this category, both first-year and senior students at Christian colleges ranked their experience significantly higher than their peers at either the liberal arts institutions or the entire national sample. Students at the Catholic schools evaluated the campus environment below those at the Christian colleges and the liberal arts schools but above the national average in both first- and last-year samples. This category includes questions about providing academic support services, helping students cope with nonacademic responsibilities, the opportunity to thrive socially, and quality of relationships with other students, faculty members, and administrative personnel. Note that, while remaining high, on this scale, students' ranking of their experience drops somewhat during their college years and drops slightly more at the CCCU schools than elsewhere:

	First Year	Senior Year
CCCU	67.7	64.5
Catholic	61.8	60.8
Liberal Arts	64.2	62.0
All NSSE	59.8	56.9

In summary, on the five major areas of the NSSE, the general ranking that students give to their colleges and universities tends to put the Carnegie baccalaureate liberal arts colleges at the top, followed by the evangelical institutions from the CCCU, followed by the Roman Catholic schools (with the evangelicals and the Catholics generally close together), and all three clusters well ahead of the national average, for both first-year and senior-year students, in all five overarching areas surveyed.

ISSUES OF FAITH

The twenty-five CCCU institutions added to their surveys a series of questions involving faith and values. Students were asked to rank (on a scale of 1–5, with 5 indicating strong agreement) a series of sixteen queries about faith issues. In general, these scores stayed level over the college career, with some moving up or down one or two tenths of a point. This seems to indicate rather clearly that four years at a Christian college neither dramatically strengthens nor significantly weakens the religious faith of students. It would be worth asking these same questions of students at secular institutions, to see if that level pattern would hold true there. The questions, followed by the scores of first-year, then senior respondents:

Question	First Year	Senior Year
I have a personally meaningful relationship with God.	4.5	4.4
My relationship with God contributes to my sense of well-being.	4.5	4.5
The way I do things from day to day is often affected by my relationship with God.	4.3	4.2
Even if the people around me were opposed to my Christian convictions, I would still hold fast to them.	4.5	4.4
I feel like I need to be open to consider new insights and truths about my faith.	4.2	4.3
General education courses at this college/university help students develop good values.	3.9	3.7
Courses in my major have helped me think about how values relate to my future profession.	4.1	4.3
When appropriate, professors here take time to talk about their values and personal beliefs in class.	4.2	4.2
Faculty here interact with students outside of class in ways that help us clarify our personal values.	3.8	3.9
There is an environment on this campus that encourages me to develop values which reflect on my faith in Jesus Christ.	4.3	4.0
This college/university has helped me to "live out" my values through community service or ministry.	3.9	3.7

Question	First Year	Senior Year
This college/university has helped me to critically evaluate whether or not my behavior is consistent with Christian values.	4.1	3.9
This college/university encourages students to worship God in meaningful ways.	4.4	4.1
As a result of my experience at this college/university, I am more aware of what my personal values are.	4.2	4.2
As a result of my experience at this college/university, my values are more consistent with a Christian world and life view.	3.9	3.8
This college challenged me to critically evaluate and reconsider values that I have always held.	3.8	3.9

Of the sixteen questions, nine show very slight declines, three stay exactly level, and four rise. The three questions that focus on the faculty show improvement in two cases, and level results in the third.

◆◆◆

Taken altogether, the data in this section on student satisfaction already represent a startling condensation of mountains of raw data into a relatively few conclusions. That said, it might be worth concluding by (like Mapquest!) going back even one level further and seeking the global perspective. This information seems to lead to these very general conclusions:

- Students at religious colleges and universities value highly the academic side of the college experience and are quite satisfied with it.
- If those students are less satisfied with any aspect of their experience, it is the daily business of campus life—parking, food, security, and the like.
- Students at religious colleges pick those colleges first because of their religious emphases, but more than half of them consider academic opportunities highly important in collegiate selection.
- Students at religious colleges seem to be well qualified in comparison to their peers at nonreligious institutions, but to be less academically ambitious and to devote less time to scholarly pursuits.

- Professors and student-faculty relations are rated very highly by these students.
- Religious colleges' students are more satisfied overall than the average at contemporary American colleges and universities and less satisfied than their colleagues at the top tier of private liberal arts institutions.
- It would be hard to make the case from this information that a baccalaureate experience at a Christian college significantly strengthens students' faith, but neither does such an education seem to weaken it dramatically.
- Finally, it appears that the differences between young women and men who choose religious institutions (Protestant or Catholic) and those who find themselves in secular colleges and universities are considerably less impressive than the similarities. They seem to have the same complaints and the same satisfactions, and their progress through the four years of the collegiate experience is generally parallel.

A Spiritual Quest?

Alexander Astin and his colleagues at the "Spirituality in Higher Education" project of the Higher Education Research Institute at UCLA have amply documented the spiritual hunger of today's college students.[33] In the words of their first research report,

> The study reveals that today's college students have very high levels of spiritual interest and involvement. Many are actively engaged in a spiritual quest and in exploring the meaning and purpose of life. They are also very engaged and involved in religion, reporting considerable commitment to their religious beliefs and practices.
>
> As they begin college, freshmen have high expectations for the role their institutions will play in their emotional and spiritual development. They place great value on their college enhancing their self-understanding, helping them develop personal values, and encouraging their expression of spirituality.[34]

As noted earlier, Astin's research indicated that three-quarters of college students are searching for a meaning and purpose in life, and that eight in ten believe in God. This level of interest in spiritual and faith issues has implications in the classroom. When such students study cosmology, they want to think about more than the comparative mechanics of the big bang or steady state theories: they want to think about the possibility of a Creator. When they study Shakespeare, they want to learn more than the sources of *Hamlet* or the date of composition of *King Lear* or the rhyme schemes of *A Midsummer Night's Dream*: they want to consider what Shakespeare teaches us about being a child and a parent and how beauty nourishes our souls.

At public and secular colleges and universities, students have opportunities to pursue their spiritual quest for purpose and meaning: there are residence hall and beer bar bull sessions, as well as on-campus groups such as the Fellowship of Christian Athletes or InterVarsity Christian Crusade or Hillel or the Yoga Club or the Lutheran Campus Ministries, and many schools have chaplains. In addition, there are off-campus churches and groups that focus on matters having to do with the meaning of human development. What they are *not* likely to get at such schools is significant in-class focus on issues beyond the cognitive, beyond what Astin calls the "outer life." Although faculty members themselves commonly have lively religious and spiritual lives, less than a third of them (30%) believe that "colleges should be concerned with facilitating students' spiritual development." And most college juniors reported, according to the HERI study, that "their professors have never encouraged discussions of spiritual or religious matters, and never provide opportunities for discussing the meaning or purpose of life."[35] A recent writer on college students' spirituality and their sexuality notes that "one of the things I saw at other [nonreligious] campuses was such a yearning to express the personal, [for students] to express themselves—and meeting up with such roadblocks."[36]

But at Protestant religious colleges, 68% of faculty members agree with the notion that they should be engaged in facilitating students' spiritual development, and at Roman Catholic schools, the figure is 62%. And their institutions proclaim their accord with this premise. Thus, for example, Oral Roberts University speaks—often—about "whole-person education" and in fact has that phrase inscribed on the medallion at the entrance to the campus.[37] Westmont describes itself, on the first page of its admissions view book as nurturing students "spiritual maturity."[38] Calvin College describes itself as fostering "thoughtful, passionate Christian commitments."[39] And the College of New Rochelle "seeks to challenge students to achieve the full development of their individual talents and a greater understanding of themselves. . . . It provides opportunities for spiritual growth in a context of freedom and ecumenism."[40]

Many of us outside the orbit of religious colleges chaff at dress or be-havior codes for students at such schools, but those codes, restrictive and old-fashioned as some of us find them, make it clear that the colleges *care* about the dress and the behavior of their students, as well as their intel-lectual development. They care about the students as whole people, with inner and outer lives, not just as cognitive units.

It is my belief that those of us who work in, and love, the world of nonre-ligious contemporary American higher education need to think seriously and long about these issues. How can we meet our students' hunger for spiritual development, for religion, for seeking the meaning of their lives, and how can we do that while staying true to our nonsectarian character? I do not believe this is an impossible or an unpleasant quest. And I am convinced it is a desirable one. Certainly, those in our community who choose to opt out of the discussion should have the perfect freedom to do so. But is the obverse not also true? Should not those who wish to opt in also have that opportunity? What might be some of the things we could talk about and consider doing, if we choose?

We might want to ask if it is really necessary for faculty at nonreligious colleges to scrupulously avoid mentioning their own religious convictions in and out of class. Surely few of us continue to subscribe to the profes-sorial myth of dispassionate objectivity: indeed, one of the gifts of post-modernism is our heightened awareness of the fact that there is always a dialogue between the object being perceived and the perceiver. If a faculty member is noncoercive about her or his beliefs, does not try to evangelize, why not reveal those convictions? Many faculty members feel perfectly free to express partisan political convictions on campus, and most man-age to do so without suggesting they will give bad grades to students who disagree with them. Is it wrong for a Christian physicist to say she believes that God is behind the big bang, while noting that her students certainly don't have to share her belief? Similarly, isn't it equally okay for an atheist biologist to try to make the case for nontheistic evolution when the class gets to Darwin, while also reassuring his students that they certainly are entitled to differing opinions? One of the most memorable moments of my undergraduate career, and that of generations of students at Grinnell College, was Professor Kenneth Christensen's famed lecture on why he was an atheist. I think it could be equally memorable for some modern version of Dr. Christensen to conclude a biology class with a lecture on why she was a believer.

In religious studies or philosophy courses, perhaps we should not just ask about the history and belief structure of world religions or philosophical systems but also allow students to talk about how they react to those systems, not to guide them to personal convictions but to offer the freedom to explore them in class discussions, papers, and office hours. Students should not be forced to reveal or discuss their private religious convictions in a classroom setting, but neither should they be forced to conceal them, it seems to me. If Christian college students, at a secular institution, want to spend a few moments talking about how their study of Judaism in class has affected their spiritual growth (or Jews their study of Islam), that seems a valid and validating learning experience.

It is my belief that the two most important issues in contemporary American higher education (and they are not unrelated) are environmentalism and internationalism. Both have a special relevance to the confessional colleges. I am not persuaded it is possible to do justice to either issue without touching on matters of the spirit. Those who believe that God made the world have a faith-based obligation to cherish that gift. That means teaching about environmental issues; it means preparing students for careers and further study in "creation care"; and it certainly means turning our colleges and universities into models of thoughtful and creative sustainability. And those who believe that God made all the world's people have a faith-based obligation to cherish those gifts as well. Are we teaching the languages and cultures of the world's most populous nations? Are our students seeing those places firsthand, and are we inviting to our campuses students and teachers from India, China, Brazil, Indonesia, and Russia. The Christian Missionary tradition has led young people from Christian colleges across the world and that is a wonderful beginning. But I don't think the nineteenth- or even twentieth-century missionary impulse is enough for the twenty-first century. How do we ask students to learn to grapple, for example, with religious and political upheaval in Tibet, which requires a deep level of intellectual and emotional understanding of contemporary Chinese secularism and Tibetan Buddhism? Today's students are going to have to deal with Chinese people, for example, not just as potential converts but as bosses, colleagues, customers, and clients. As with environmental issues, the answer is in the combination of course work and practical experience.

An intriguing development in the nonreligious colleges and universities is the reintroduction of creedal or covenantal statements. As we have seen, many of the Christian colleges retain a strong student (and often others) "pledge" practice. In such a model, the institution states key elements of its value and belief system, sets forth behavioral expectations based upon those creedal elements, and asks students to "sign on" (at least metaphorically but often literally), indicating their understanding of, and willingness to abide by, those institutional values and behaviors. While nonreligious institutions have often had codes regarding academic ethics (often called honor codes), a relatively recent, somewhat curious trend has seen those codes expand beyond academic integrity to larger ethical issues. This trend began with the increased sensitivity of institutions to issues of "hate speech," racism, and sexism, which became more rather than less of an issue as most institutions aggressively sought to diversify their student bodies and overall campus populations. Thus, students who had initially been asked to pledge not to plagiarize came to be asked also not to engage in discrimination or insulting behaviors. An illustration of the earlier, wholly academic pledge is Eastern Kentucky University's pledge, signed by students, which deals only with cheating, plagiarism, and fabrication and which simply affirms that the signers "understand, accept and will uphold the responsibilities and stipulations of the Eastern Kentucky University Honors Code and Academic Integrity Policy."[41] An expanded pledge, in the private sector, is Connecticut College's, which includes pledging "to take responsibility for my beliefs, and to conduct myself with utmost respect for the dignity of all human beings."[42] The University of South Carolina goes considerably further with its Carolinian Creed:

> The community of scholars at the University of South Carolina is dedicated to personal and academic excellence.
>
> Choosing to join the community obligates each member to a code of civilized behavior. As a Carolinian . . .
>
> I will practice personal and academic integrity;
>
> I will respect the dignity of all persons;
>
> I will respect the rights and property of others;
>
> I will discourage bigotry, while striving to learn from differences in people, ideas and opinions;
>
> I will demonstrate concern for others, their feelings, and their need for conditions which support their work and development.
>
> Allegiance to these ideals requires each Carolinian to refrain from and discourage behaviors which threaten the freedom and respect every individual deserves.[43]

And at private Eckerd College, each student signs an honor pledge, which deals with academic integrity, *and* the "Shared Commitment," which states a series of principles (e.g., the responsibility to pursue personal and academic growth and excellence and to learn from human differences) and a sequence of behavioral expectations, including the prevention of academic dishonesty but also the prevention of personal violence, bigotry, and disruptive intoxication.[44] Nonreligious colleges can learn from our faith-based colleagues the potential benefits of such public declaration and affirmation of core community values.

Alexander and Helen Astin note that, as our institutions "have become larger, more acquisitive, and increasingly impersonal," faculty "hesitate to discuss issues of meaning, purpose, authenticity, and wholeness with our colleagues."[45] Here, I believe, is an invitation to a potentially rewarding and wholly innocuous opportunity. Why not invite interested faculty to have such discussions? Often, campus centers for teaching and learning organize faculty discussion groups on a huge range of topics, such as contemporary developments in China or conducting successful discussion classes. Certainly one or more options could encourage faculty members to explore together their "inner" lives and the issues they are grappling with there: for example, how to balance professional advancement with family obligations and aspirations, understanding and becoming comfortable with the stages of an academic career, relating to students as the age differential between faculty and student lengthens, being a helpful mentor to new colleagues, and responding to issues students raise regarding spirituality.

Often secular colleges and universities are very reluctant to invite to campus, in any sort of official capacity, believing spokespersons for religious groups, to speak about their beliefs. I would propose that it is perfectly appropriate, and would be very popular with students, to do exactly the opposite: to invite as many such proponents (including some who wish to argue against all religions) on as many occasions as possible. Why not an annual lecture series on the varieties of religious belief? For an outside speaker to say "this is what I believe" does not violate the separation of church and state and should be wholly noncoercive to an audience.

I had the opportunity as the chief executive of a public college to co-sponsor with the director of student counseling a lecture series called "Spiritual Pathways" in which members of our own community outside the predominant Lutheran, Catholic, or agnostic traditions had an opportunity to explain the elements of their faith traditions and to talk about how they tried to practice their religion in a culture where they were a tiny minority. Our speakers included Jews, Muslims, Wiccans, Hindus, gay Christians, and Native Americans. There were a few objections that this purely optional series violated the tenets of the separation doctrine but many more expressions of enthusiasm about opening the possibility of interfaith dialogue and understanding. Too often, colleges and universities, especially in the public sector, respond to the religious diversity carefully cultivated in our student bodies by a kind of "hands off" attitude: because there are so many differences, we won't pay attention to any faith, or anyone's. Actually, diversity can give us a chance to act in an exactly opposite fashion: to show that we care about different faiths and belief structures, that we welcome many, and that we seek to learn about each of them and to cherish their adherents.

Similarly, we should let students who have strong religious beliefs, or serious religious questions, or passionate antireligious stances have official, sanctioned campus forums in which to address their convictions. Let the students speak to, and listen to, each other's religious or spiritual perspectives: they will, generally, like it, learn from it, and grow through it. I don't believe that officially sanctioned student religious clubs should have the right to exclude other students from membership or attendance (and there are legal issues about using public funding in such ways at state institutions), but I also think they should have the prerogative of proclaiming their beliefs, celebrating them, sharing them, and learning more about them.

One definition of a "Christian" college, often criticized now as only partial, is of an institution in which learning takes place within a "Christian" atmosphere. Often, the pledges and statements of community behavioral expectations of these colleges will speak to this characteristic: for example, Wheaton College's Community Covenant asks all who study and work at the college to "'put on' compassion, kindness, humility, gentleness, patience, forgiveness and supremely, love."[46] I do not realistically imagine that everyone at Wheaton always treats everyone else there with kindness, humility, or patience. But, in our often-testy world of higher education, just to affirm that this is the way we *should* behave seems to me valuable. Too often, contemporary academic culture seems to value arrogance and impatience. We are easily provoked, over intellectual or governance differences. We divide into camps, we take sides; like too many of our politicians, we sometimes define who we are by who we are against. We have much to learn from institutions that ask their members to treat each other as fellow children of God. There is, it seems to me, a secular way of doing this. We can ask what the core humane values that animate our public and secular institutions are, and what standards of interpersonal interaction those values ask us to maintain. All colleges and universities, for example, must value honesty as we devote ourselves to seeking the truth. We could be much better at treating each other as truth-telling seekers, or at least as folks who sincerely tried to speak the truth as they understood it. All colleges and universities, by their very nature, value reflection and careful thought: do we provide ourselves opportunities for such reflective thinking, and do we reward those who find such opportunities? In sum, we can learn from religious institutions how to try to build a community that articulates and tries to live up to a coherent structure of humane personal and interpersonal ethics.

Religious colleges and universities make much of their efforts to integrate faith and learning. For those of us who are at non-faith-based institutions, this is not, obviously, an option. But, to use Astin's language, we can probably do more to integrate the outer life of objective learning and the inner life of the spirit: the life of creativity, of joy and despair, of personal attachments, of human growth, of commitment, of morality, of behavior in the world. Again, we certainly cannot indoctrinate our students. But neither should we build, then defend, an artificial wall between knowledge and behavior. How can a professor of climatology not connect the scientific data of the classroom to a concern for global environmental issues? Surely many teachers of sociology will seek to link information about the workings of race in contemporary culture with a consideration of justice? Should not the economist discuss with her class the waste and cruelty of poverty, as well as the statistics about its frequency? The Shakespearean is teaching only partially if he does not ask his class what is admirable and what tragic in the character of Hamlet. Certainly the current trend toward service learning is a step in the right direction, for all of us, in its effort to bring together real-world problems and opportunities with classroom study.

Secular institutions should not, certainly, mimic the religious colleges' frequent tradition of including prayer in class time or indulging in public worship on any occasion. But finding times and places where students, faculty, and staff can be quiet together and find and listen to their inner voices is surely inoffensive, and it equally surely speaks to students' yearning for opportunities for spiritual reflection. We live in a noisy and busy world, and it is astonishingly rare for us to stop talking long enough to reflect seriously. Today's college students and, increasingly their younger professors, are electronically linked to each other and the world most of their waking hours. It is remarkable how difficult it is for such students to just sit quietly together for some substantial period of time. But it is often the case that they find such experiences very rewarding. We have our "moments of silence," but most of them are, in fact, "moments." A decade at a Quaker college taught me how powerful silence could be, not just for Friends, and not just for believers, but for all humans. We should think about giving our students, and each other, a chance to learn that lesson, too.

In their study of encouraging authenticity and spirituality in college students, Chickering, Dalton, and Stamm observe: "An important aspect of educating for spirituality, authenticity, and meaning is the relationship colleges and universities have with the larger communities of which they are a part. Can we really strengthen spiritual growth, authenticity, purpose, and meaning if institutions, administrators, faculty members, student affairs professionals, and students are not seriously engaged with larger societal issues . . . local, regional, national, and global?"[47] It seems clear to me that one of the reasons that service learning and volunteerism have become so popular with undergraduates is that they speak directly to students' yearning for spiritual growth. Encouraging people to work physically for the values they are discovering, they proclaim, is reinforcing. It allows those values to be held with greater conviction. Seeing everyone within the campus community—college presidents and professors, cooks and maintenance people—similarly translating their convictions into actions is a powerful and convincing message that beliefs count; that mature, thoughtful individuals are engaged in the issues of their worlds intellectually and in action. Early in the twenty-first century, a college president of a historically Protestant liberal arts college in the upper Midwest caused a storm by posting an antiwar yard sign outside his campus home. Some supporters of the college thought this was an inappropriate act of partisanship. But most of the students at that college (and I) thought it was a demonstration that the college presidency is an opportunity to model and lead not just in politics but in values; to show that a campus chief executive can have a function even more important than that of "executive": spiritual leader. A moving photo of that event showed the rather austere, commanding tall figure of the president surrounded by a crowd of undergraduates, who were hugging him.

On my campus visits, I was struck by the variety of physical places for religious activities at evangelical and Catholic colleges, and how much they seemed to be used. Certainly, chapels and sanctuaries are used often for formal liturgical worship, but for many more hours of the day, they are open and available for student prayer—or meditation or, in many cases I observed, study. Most nonreligious colleges have small lounges and public areas galore—often, for example, on each floor and in each area of residence halls. I wonder if we might make a few such spaces available for quiet meditation. Given what we know about student desires and interests, perhaps they should have places where the physical surroundings are conducive to thoughtful reflection, as well as spaces for eating, studying, and hanging out with friends.

♦♦♦

William Perry's influential model of cognitive development suggested that individuals move from a dualistic absolutism to a wholehearted and assertive adolescent relativism, to a mature position that combined relativistic openness with personal commitment. That model can be applied to cultures as well as people, I suspect. The culture of American higher learning began in a clear and simple kind of religious, absolutist dualism: there was right and there was wrong, saved and damned, enlightened and beclouded. For two centuries, virtually all colleges, college students, college professors, and college presidents were Christian, and no one really gave much thought to other possibilities. American culture as a whole put Protestant Christianity in a position of insurmountable privilege. "Historically, even public institutions, although founded as nonsectarian, were distinctly Protestant institutions."[48] In 1887, the president of the University of Michigan could explain why he would not hire a non-Christian to teach history at that state institution: "I would not wish a pessimist or an agnostic or a man disposed to obtrude criticisms of Christian views of humanity or of Christian principles. I would not want a man who would not make historical judgments and interpretations from a Christian viewpoint."[49] But at or around the time of the great national trauma of the Civil War, our national and educational worlds began to become more complex, more diverse, more multifaceted. Propelled by the Morrill Act, public higher education began to move away from its direct religious links. Jews, Muslims, atheists, and individuals of every conceivable religious background, or none whatsoever, went to college, taught college, and administered colleges. Nationally, by the end of the twentieth century, the United States of America could elect a Roman Catholic president and a Jew could become a major party candidate for vice president. Were 1850–1960 our national sophomore years? In the twenty-first century our national culture is far more overtly religious than it was twenty-five or fifty years ago. We ask political candidates questions about their most personal faith beliefs, and religious organizations have been known to endorse candidates, or at least the positions taken by some of them. And colleges, and the students, faculty, and staff who populate them, no longer universally see secularism as either inevitable or necessarily desirable. Nor can we afford to see deep religious conviction as incompatible with the highest academic aspirations and standards.

Although there are surely some fundamentalists among us who would be happy to see our national and educational culture move back to the simple dualism where we began, they are not, I suspect, a very large segment of the educational establishment, or of the population of our religious colleges. Instead, perhaps we are moving into a mature period of relativistic commitment. Collectively, we seem to be saying that it is fine to have all sorts of colleges: denominational, nondenominational Christian, Roman Catholic, nonsectarian, secular, private, public. In terms of institutional plurality, we are relativists. But we have also, I hope, decided that it is enriching the already dense texture of twenty-first-century American higher education for our institutions to be tolerant and committed places, and that commitment can be a religious one. Our nation's tapestry of postsecondary learning is great in part because of its rich and varied textures. We make room for Wheaton College as well as the University of Illinois, Notre Dame and Grinnell, George Fox and CUNY, and Yeshiva and Maharishi International University, and Saint Cloud State and Calvin. "E Pluribus Unum" does not suggest homogenization but the unified strength of many, of diversity. Our religious colleges today are a valuable, strong, and significant segment of our collegiate community. We can learn from them, we can teach them, and we can embrace them as our brothers and sisters.

For Institutional Site Visits

1. How would you describe the religious mission of your college or university?
   —Denominational affiliation or association?

2. Please describe the relationship between faith and learning here:
   —Can there be Christian literature courses? Psychology? Chemistry? Physics?
   —Do students learn about other religions? How?
   —Would students learn about controversial issues, e.g., about the theory of evolution in a Biology course?
   —Number or % of required classes in Religion?

3. To what extent must students / faculty / administrators / staff be members of and/or in harmony with the religious tradition here?

4. Is chapel or some form of regular worship required?

5. Do you feel there is an institutional stance on political issues—e.g., stem cell research, gay marriage / domestic partnerships?

6. How has your institution changed over the past decade or so? Do you feel pressures for greater secularization or for greater religiosity?

7. How would you describe student behavior codes and behavior expectations? Examples?

8. Could you describe the governance processes here? Role of the faculty, the administration, the affiliated denomination (if applicable).

9. What would you say are your peer institutions?

10. Have you ever felt uncomfortably constrained by the religious character of this college or university?

11. Why did you choose to come here?

12. Do you feel "protected" here? Safe? Isolated? Embraced? Free? (For students especially)

Thanks for your cooperation!

For Parents

1. Tell me a bit about your children. How many are there? How many went to Christian colleges? Did any go to other sorts of colleges or universities?

2. Let's talk about your son(s) or daughter(s) who did attend a Christian college. What institution was chosen? Did she or he attend (or is she or he planning to attend) all four years there?

3. When considering college choice, what other institutions did you look at?

4. Would you say that the choice of the Christian college was primarily a parental choice, that of the student, or were you all equal partners in the decision?

5. How important were academic factors in the decision (choice of major, scholarly reputation, etc.)? Which?

6. How important were extracurricular factors (residential life, athletics, safety, etc.) Which?

7. How has the college lived up to your expectations and those of your son or daughter?

8. Are there any ways in which you have been disappointed?

9. Do you think the specific Christian character of the college has been a major factor in your child's experience there? How?

10. Do you imagine you might make a donation to the college after your daughter or son has graduated?

11. What is your child's plan for life after graduation; what is he or she doing now?

12. Do you think the character of the classroom interaction between teachers and students was different at a Christian college than it would have been at another institution? How?

13. Do you find that the college seemed to relate to students differently than you would expect other sorts of institutions might? How?

14. What did you think of your student's acquaintances and friends at college?

15. Any other thoughts?

Thanks for your cooperation and assistance!

Notes

Chapter 1
An Agenda for the Study of Religious Colleges and Universities

1. An effort to clarify the nomenclature regarding "Christian College" is presented at the end of this chapter.

2. For an impassioned defense of the censorship of *The Vagina Monologues* at Catholic institutions, see Patrick J. Reilly, "Are Catholic Colleges Leading Students Astray?" *Catholic World Report,* March 2003, 38–46.

3. Paul Bramadat, *The Church on the World's Turf* (New York: Oxford University Press, 2000), 147.

4. Kyle Lynch-Klarup, "Christian Faith at Grinnell," *Exit 182,* Fall 2007, 4.

5. The response to Astin and the HERI project has not, however, been universally positive. In particular, some critics find irritating the differentiation between "spiritual" and "religious" and view with some contempt those who describe themselves as "spiritual but not religious." For example, Naomi Schaffer Riley, in *God on the Quad: How Religious Colleges and the Missionary Generation Are Changing America* (New York: St. Martin's Press, 2005), describes the heroes of her book, the "missionary generation," as those who "refuse to accept the sophisticated ennui of their contemporaries. They snub the 'spiritual but not religious' answers to life's most difficult questions. They rebuff the intellectual relativism of professors and the moral relativism of their peers" (5).

6. "Why Spirituality Deserves a Central Place in Liberal Education," *Liberal Education* 90, no. 2 (Spring 2004): 34–41.

7. "Spirituality and the Professoriate," Spirituality in Higher Education project, HERI, UCLA, Los Angeles, [2006]. Obviously, these groups overlap—for example, some of the Baptists and the "other Christian" groups are also self-identified as "born again."

8. Stephen Prothero, "Worshiping in Ignorance," *Chronicle of Higher Education,* 16 March 2007, B6–B7.

9. Scott Jaschik, "Not So Godless after All," *Inside Higher Ed,* 6 October 2006. See also Christine Hartelt, "Student Spirituality Spurs Change," *Administrator* 18, no. 1 (January 1999): 1–3.

10. Reported in *Inside Higher Ed* by Scott Jaschik, 20 November 2006.

11. See L. S. Hulett, "Being Religious at Knox College: Attitudes toward Religion, Christian Expression, and Conservative Values on Campus," *Religion and Education* 31, no. 2 (2004): 41–61.

12. Bramadat, *The Church on the World's Turf,* 18.

13. *Minneapolis Star-Tribune,* 15 January 2006, A-5.

14. *Minneapolis Star-Tribune,* 20 January 2002.

15. The Council for Christian Colleges and Universities (CCCU) describes itself as a group of 101 "intentionally Christ-centered institutions in the US and Canada."

16. Scott Jaschik, "Growth in Canadian Christian Colleges," *Inside Higher Ed,* 17 October 2007.

17. www.wheaton.edu.

18. Note, though, that, in the class that entered in 2008, Baylor paid new first-year students to retake the SAT and improve their scores: Scott Jaschik, "Baylor Pays for SAT Gains," *Inside Higher Ed,* 15 October 2008.

19. This information on the academic qualifications of entering first-year students comes from the Web sites of the respective institutions.

20. John Russell, "Funding the Culture Wars: Philanthropy, Church and State," National Committee for Responsive Philanthropy, Washington, DC, 2005, 3.

21. See Ben Gose, "Charity's Political Divide," *Chronicle of Philanthropy* (electronic version), 5 December 2005, http://philanthropy.com.

22. See www.sheldonjackson.edu; Beth McMurtrie, "Accreditation Is at Risk for Small Alaska College," *Chronicle of Higher Education* (electronic version), 23 February 2001, A39, http://chronicle.com, and "Regional Accreditors Penalize 16 Colleges," *Chronicle of Higher Education* (electronic version), 28 February 2003, A31, http://chronicle.com. Also Scott Jaschik, "Sheldon Jackson Suspends Operations," *Inside Higher Ed,* 2 July 2007. The official Department of Education report is Control Number ED-OIG/A09F0020, Office of the Inspector General, United States Department of Education (24 February 2006).

23. For example, what percentage of classes enroll fewer than twenty students (good); what percentage more than fifty (bad). One might ask why not twenty-five and sixty, or eighteen and thirty-five?

24. *U.S. News* Web site, www.usnews.com.

25. Alas, the discourse is often less than civil and rational, on both sides. See, for example, the anti-Creationist blog "Pharyngula," http://scienceblogs.com/pharyngula, or the creationist Web site, creationscience.com.

Chapter 2
Contexts Historical and Denominational

1. Francis Oakley, *Community of Learning* (New York: Oxford University Press, 1992), 145.

2. John R. Thelin, *A History of American Higher Education* (Baltimore: Johns Hopkins University Press, 2004), xiii.

3. A helpful general volume, now slightly out of date, is William C. Ringenberg, *The Christian College: A History of Protestant Higher Education in America* (Grand Rapids, MI: Eerdmans, 1984). A thirty-six-page introduction to this volume is

contributed by Mark A. Noll and represents an intellectual history of American Protestantism and its colleges.

4. William C. Ringenberg, "The Old-Time College, 1800–1865," in Joel A. Carpenter and Kenneth W. Shipps, eds., *Making Higher Education Christian: The History and Mission of Evangelical Colleges in America* (Grand Rapids, MI: Eerdmans, 1987), 77.

5. The material on colonial colleges is from Arthur M. Cohen, *The Shaping of American Higher Education* (San Francisco: Jossey-Bass, 1998); Sheldon S. Cohen, *A History of Colonial Education, 1607–1776* (New York: John Wiley, 1974); and the current Web sites of the nine institutions. See also Samuel Schuman, *Old Main: Small Colleges in Twenty-First Century America* (Baltimore: Johns Hopkins University Press, 2005), esp. chap. 2.

6. Arthur M. Cohen, *Shaping of American Higher Education*, 17.

7. John D. Pulliam, *History of Education in America*, 4th ed. (Columbus: Merrill, 1987), 36.

8. Douglas Sloan, *The Great Awakening and American Education* (New York: Teachers College Press, 1973), 12.

9. Arthur M. Cohen, *Shaping of American Higher Education*, 9.

10. From *New England's First Fruits*, 1643, cited in ibid., 64.

11. See, for example, James Axtell, *The School upon a Hill: Education and Society in Colonial New England* (New Haven: Yale University Press, 1976).

12. Student behavior codes had, of course, been strict at the time in Europe.

13. Richard Hofstadter and Wilson Smith, eds., *American Higher Education*, 2 vols. (Chicago: University of Chicago Press, 1961), I:2.

14. Sheldon S. Cohen, *History of Colonial Education*, 137. See Axtell, *School upon a Hill*, for a more skeptical interpretation.

15. Sheldon S. Cohen, *History of Colonial Education*, 100.

16. Cited in Sloan, *Great Awakening*, 178 and 186.

17. Sheldon S. Cohen, *History of Colonial Education*, 168.

18. Brown University Web site, www.brown.edu/web/about/history.

19. Arthur M. Cohen, *Shaping of American Higher Education*, 19.

20. Thelin, *History of American Higher Education*, 41.

21. Donald G. Tewksbury, *The Founding of American Colleges and Universities before the Civil War* (New York: Teachers College Press, 1932), 28.

22. Arthur M. Cohen, *Shaping of American Higher Education*, u62.

23. David Breneman, *Liberal Arts Colleges: Thriving, Surviving or Endangered* (Washington, DC: Brookings Institution Press, 1994).

24. Ringenberg, *Christian College*, notes that many of the earlier state universities had religious practices and assumptions that would today seem out of place at public institutions.

25. The information on pre–Civil War affiliations is from Tewksbury, *Founding*.

26. Donald Scott, "Evangelism, Revivalism, and the Second Great Awakening,"

National Humanities Center, Teacher Serve, Web site, www.nhc.rtp.nc.us/tserve/ tserve.htm.

27. Tewksbury, *Founding*,1.

28. See, for example, David B. Potts, *Wesleyan University, 1831–1910: Collegiate Enterprise in New England* (New Haven: Yale University Press, 1992).

29. Encyclopedia Africana Web site, www.africana.com.

30. Pulliam, *History of Education in America*, 68. Thelin, *History of American Higher Education*, 70–73, takes a somewhat more nuanced and skeptical view of the case.

31. Arthur M. Cohen, *Shaping of American Higher Education*, 60.

32. See, for example, Thelin, *History of American Higher Education*, for the demythologized version.

33. Pulliam, *History of Education in America*, 70.

34. Ilstu.edu Web site.

35. Burton R. Clark, *The Distinctive College: Antioch, Reed, and Swarthmore* (Chicago: Aldine, 1970), 172.

36. Arthur M. Cohen, *History of Colonial Education*.

37. Lawrence A. Cremin, *American Education: The Metropolitan Experience, 1876–1980* (New York: Harper and Row, 1988), 248.

38. George A. Baker, *A Handbook on the Community College in America* (Westport, CT: Greenwood Press, 1994), 7–10.

39. Carnegie Classification 2000 Web site, www.carnegiefoundation.org/ classifications/.

40. Breneman, *Liberal Arts Colleges*, 20.

41. Douglas Sloan, *Faith and Knowledge: Mainline Protestantism and American Higher Education* (Louisville: Westminster John Knox Press, 1994), 72.

42. Ibid., 203–4.

43. For example, James Tunstead Burtchaell, *The Dying of the Light: The Disengagement of Colleges and Universities from Their Christian Churches* (Grand Rapids, MI: Eerdmans, 1998); George M. Marsden *The Soul of the American University* (New York: Oxford University Press, 1994); and Sloan, *Faith and Knowledge*.

44. Sloan, *Faith and Knowledge*, 206.

45. Burtchaell's history of Davidson College, for example, in *The Dying of the Light* chronicles the successful anti-Presbyterian activism of both students and faculty.

46. For example, Christopher Jencks and David Riesman, *The Academic Revolution* (Garden City: Doubleday, 1969), 238ff.

47. See particularly Burtchaell, *The Dying of the Light*; Marsden, *The Soul of the American University*; George M. Marsden and Bradley J. Longfield, eds., *The Secularization of the Academy* (New York: Oxford University Press, 1992); Philip Gleason, *Contending with Modernity: Catholic Higher Education in the Twentieth*

Century (New York: Oxford University Press, 1995); and Sloan, *Faith and Knowledge.* See below for scholars who question the "secularization" hypothesis.

48. Thelin, *History of American Higher Education,* 148.

49. This and the subsequent historical information about Cornell College is from the two-volume *Cornell College: A Sesquicentennial History* (Cedar Rapids, IA: WDG Publishing, 2004). Volume 1 (1853–1967) is by C. William Heywood; volume 2 (1967–2003) was written by Richard H. Thomas. Both were members of the History Department at Cornell; Dr. Thomas also served as the college's chaplain. Candor compels me to note that I was a (very young) member of the Cornell College faculty from 1969 to 1976.

50. Private communication with the author, 2 March 2007.

51. Cornell College Web site, "Cornell Perspectives on Religious Heritage and Spiritual Life," www.cornellcollege.edu/chaplain-and-spritual-life/.

52. This and the following material are taken from the Naropa University Web site, www.naropa.edu.

53. See Web sites shambhala.org/teacher/chogyam-trungph.php and home-planet.nl for different perspectives on this intriguing figure. There is also a good Wikipedia entry on Chogyam Trungpa.

54. A twist on the traditional "Athens-Jerusalem" formulation of Christian colleges.

55. See Maharishi University of Management Web site, www.mum.edu.

56. There is a somewhat humorous Parsons College alumni Web site, www .parsonscollege.org/.

57. Elizabeth Redden, "A New Campus, According to Ancient Principles," *Inside Higher Ed,* 28 January 2008.

58. Tina Hesman, "Maharishi U. Curriculum Includes Study of Meditation," *St. Louis Post-Dispatch,* 25 March 2005.

59. 19 December 2006.

60. www.mum.edu/nsse.html.

61. www.mum.edu.

62. See Jencks and Riesman, *Academic Revolution,* for a discussion of Brandeis and Yeshiva and some consideration of why America's Jewish community has tended to prefer "universities and colleges where they were not a majority, or failing that where their majority was unofficial" (318–19).

63. Yeshiva University Web site, www.yu.edu.

64. Compare Yeshiva's "Maccabees" to the Wake Forest "Demon Deacons," the Elon College "Christians," and, my personal favorite, the Guilford College "Fighting Quakers."

65. http://unicomm.byu.edu.

66. Reinhard Maeser, *Karl G. Maeser: A Biography* (Provo: Brigham Young University Press, 1928), 79.

67. "Aims of a BYU Education" at http://unicom.byu.edu/president/ aimsprintable.html, p. 1.

68. Larry Lyon, Michael Beatty, and Stephanie Mixon, "Making Sense of a 'Religious' University: Faculty Adaptations at Brigham Young, Baylor, Notre Dame and Boston College," *Review of Religious Research* 43, no. 4 (June 2002): 326–48.

69. Ibid., 339.

70. http://honorcode.byu.edu.

71. Naomi Schaefer Riley, *God on the Quad: How Religious Colleges and the Missionary Generation are Changing America* (New York: St Martin's Press, 2005), 23. The chapter is entitled "An Oasis in the Desert."

72. Information on BYU-Hawaii is from its Web site, byuh.edu.

73. www.graceland.edu/about-us/mission/.

Chapter 3
Three Roman Catholic Colleges and Universities

1. See Kathleen A. Mahoney, *Catholic Higher Education in Protestant America: The Jesuits and Harvard in the Age of the University* (Baltimore: Johns Hopkins University Press, 2002).

2. Christopher Jencks and David Riesman, *The Academic Revolution* (Garden City: Doubleday, 1969), 234–36.

3. For the complete text on the Internet, see consortium.villanova.edu/excorde/ landlake.htm. See also, for a forty-year retrospective, Elizabeth Redden, "Academic Freedom, Faith and Nuance," *Inside Higher Ed,* 4 February 2008.

4. "The Land O' Lakes Statement" from the Web site of *This Rock* 16, no. 9 (November 2005), a special edition entitled "Colleges: Catholic and No Longer Catholic," www.catholic.com/magazines/thisrock.asp.

5. Richard Byrne, "For Catholic Educators, Eagerness and Angst Attend Pope's Visit," *Chronicle of Higher Education* 54, no. 31 (11 April 2008): A-1ff.

6. See Joseph M. Herlihy, "Reflections on *Ex Corde Ecclesiae*," in Paul Dovre, ed., *The Future of Religious Colleges* (Grand Rapids, MI: Eerdmans, 2002), 283–303.

7. John Wilcox and Irene King, *Enhancing Religious Identity: Best Practices from Catholic Campuses* (Washington, DC: Georgetown University Press, 2000).

8. www.images.villanova.edu/seallegend/.

9. See, for example, the *Catholic Encyclopedia* which is also on the Web at www .newadvent.org/cathen.

10. The Order of St. Augustine has an extensive Web site at www.osanet.org.

11. "Augustinian Spirituality" at the Order of St. Augustine Web site.

12. This paragraph is derived from the university's Web site, www.heritage .villanova.edu/history.html.

13. A substantial minority of the board are members of the Order of St. Augustine. They are required by board bylaw to vote unanimously on matters that might alter the mission of the University.

14. Conversation with the director of the course, Dr. John Doody.

15. As is common, students in some preprofessional areas such as engineering and nursing have slightly altered requirements.

16. Villanova University, "Guide for Faculty Search Committees—Mission Centered Hiring," draft 5, nd, p. 7.

17. These observations are based on two research visits to the College of New Rochelle: one in 2004 and another in the winter of 2007.

18. See, for instance, the "President's Message" on the CNR Web site, www.cnr .edu, by Dr. Stephen Sweeny, who has been at the college since 1977.

19. James Burtchaell, *The Dying of the Light: The Disengagement of Colleges and Universities from Their Christian Churches* (Grand Rapids, MI: Eerdmans, 1998), 663. Burtchaell devotes considerable attention and invective to the College of New Rochelle as one of three Roman Catholic institutions that he seeks to demonstrate have lost their Catholic character. The other two are St. Mary's College of California and Boston College.

20. College of New Rochelle Mission Statement, 1991, CNR Web site.

21. Dr. Ann Raia, on the CNR "Faculty Profiles" Web site.

22. Burtchaell, *The Dying of the Light,* 661.

23. Ibid., 649, 666.

24. "Ursuline Heritage" on the CNR Web site.

25. On 9 February 2007. Our meeting was facilitated by Dr. Ann Raia, a long-time teacher at CNR and a longtime friend of mine.

26. "Ursuline Heritage," CNR Web site.

27. Thomas Aquinas College Web site, www.thomasaquinas.edu, "A Brief History of Thomas Aquinas College," from which the historical sketch that follows is also drawn.

28. Candor compels me to note that I was also working at St. Mary's College at this time, although not in the Integrated Liberal Arts program. I was a young instructor, between MA and PhD degrees, and only in the most tangential way aware of the discussions taking place around me that led to the founding of Thomas Aquinas College.

29. Burtchaell, *The Dying of the Light,* 708.

30. I asked about the inclusion of authors and works as exemplars of falseness and if students were informed that this was the reason for inclusion. The response was that students were meant to discover the errors of those texts independently, without prior prejudicial warning.

31. 2007 *College Bulletin,* 4.

32. Ibid., 36.

33. Ibid., 37.

34. *Alumni News,* Winter 2007.

Chapter 4
Pro Ecclesia, Pro Texana

1. One has to wonder, in an era of animal rights activism and heighted mascot scrutiny, whether this arrangement has much of a future.

2. It is worthwhile (and impressive) to compare the Armstrong Browning Library at Baylor to the Wade Museum at Wheaton College with its collection of books and artifacts connected to C. S. Lewis and his contemporaries.

3. Baylor University Vision 2012 Web site, www.baylor.edu/vision/index.php?id=9690.

4. Imperative III, www.baylor.edu/vision/index.php?id=9696.

5. Wacotrib.com (Web version of the *Waco Tribune* newspaper), 7 May 2008.

6. Discussed at length, for example, in Theodore M. Hesburgh CSC, ed., *The Challenge and Promise of a Catholic University* (Notre Dame, IN: University of Notre Dame Press, 1994).

7. But note that it has emerged that Baylor has been paying prospective first-year students to retake the SAT and, thus, to raise their scores.

8. Robert B. Sloan Jr. "The Baylor Project," in Barry G. Hankins and Donald D. Schmeltekopf, eds., *The Baylor Project: Taking Christian Higher Education to the Next Level* (South Bend, IN: St. Augustine's Press, 2007), 325. Several others with whom I spoke reiterated this hiring priority listing.

9. Conversation with the president and with the provost.

10. Donald D. Schmeltekopf and Dianna Vitanza, eds., *The Baptist and Christian Character of Baylor* (Waco: Baylor University, 2003).

11. For example, James Burtchaell, "The Decline and Fall of the Christian Colleges," part 1, *First Things* 12 (April 1991): 16–29, or George Marsden and Bradley Longfields, eds., *The Secularization of the Academy* (New York: Oxford University Press, 1992).

12. See, for example, Elizabeth F. Farrel, "Baylor U. Removes a Web Page Associated with Intelligent Design from Its Site," *Chronicle of Higher Education*, 4 September 2007. In another well-publicized and controversial series of events, the Baylor University athletic program was involved in a series of infractions that were uncovered after a star basketball player was murdered by his roommate in 2003.

13. Actually, Baylor dropped its official dress code in the mid 1990s.

14. The figure seems slightly different in different sources—another lists twenty-four fraternities and twenty sororities. At least one fraternity at the time of this writing is on suspension from Baylor. See www.baylor.edu/studies_activities/greek_life/.

15. Dr. Lilley's term as president ended in July 2008, when he was removed by the board of regents. See "Baylor Fires Its President," *Inside Higher Ed*, 25 July 2008.

16. In the 2007–8 academic year, Baylor raised the percentage of tenure denials from about 10% in the recent past, to 40%, with nine of twelve rejected candidates being rejected by the president and provost after endorsement by their departments and the university-wide faculty review committee.

17. I should note that I knew Dr. Schmeltekopf slightly in his prior post as chief academic officer at Mars Hill College, North Carolina.

18. *Christianity Today* Web site, www.christianitytoday.com/ct/2005/august /9.24.html.

19. Ibid.

20. In conversations with an outsider doing research at and about Baylor, none of these three individuals fired any shots at any of the others; there was not even any sniping. Obviously there are points of disagreement among them, but all agreed that BU valued its Baptist character and its high academic aspirations.

21. Baylor regularly updates progress on Vision 2012 on the Web site cited in note 3 (above).

Chapter 5
A Civil College

1. The Southern Baptist Convention Web site affirms as core principles, "Baptists cherish and defend religious liberty and deny the right of any secular or religious authority to impose a confession of faith upon a church or body of churches. We honor the principle of soul competency and the priesthood of believers." www .sbc.net/bfm/.

2. www.andersonuniversity.edu, "History."

3. I visited Anderson College in the midst of this transition, as a consultant to its developing Honors Program, in 1990. I was asked to assist the Honors Program make the transition from a two-year enterprise to a four-year one.

4. Within the context of the Southern Baptist Convention, the word "moderate" has an idiosyncratic definition: it is not understood to be some sort of "middle road" but the polar opposite of "conservative."

5. The other two qualities are scholarship and truth or grace. Dr. Evans P. Whitaker, Opening Convocation Address, 22 August, 2007.

6. Elizabeth Beck, "A Place of Uncommon Civility," *Sandlapper*, Winter 2007–8, 15–18.

7. Ibid., 16–17.

8. View book: *Anderson University—Knowledge for the Journey* (nd, np). "Kind" seems an unusual description, and a winning one.

9. What makes the story somewhat more memorable is that the student's mother, in India, simultaneously and with no communication, also became a Christian.

10. Anderson University view book.

Chapter 6
"At the Front Lines of the Culture Wars"

1. 2006–8 *General Catalog*, New Saint Andrews College, 17–18. This is the source for the remainder of this historical section. The same material is published separately on the college's Web site, www.nsa.edu, and has appeared elsewhere as well, for example in the *Student Handbook* and in various admissions publications.

2. Roy Alden Atwood, "The *Major* Problem with Colleges Today," published by the New Saint Andrews College Admissions Office, 2006.

3. I was able to meet with all three of the founders of New Saint Andrews College, together, in Moscow.

4. Douglas Wilson, "Strategic Education: New Saint Andrews College at the Front Lines of the Culture Wars," published by New Saint Andrews College, nd, 3.

5. *Student Handbook, 2006–2007*, 25–26.

6. Ibid., 4.

7. Ibid., 30.

8. Ibid.,27–29.

9. Ibid., 37.

10. Ibid., 6.

11. www.nsa.edu/mission/faith.html.

12. Mitchell O. Stokes, "Mathematics as a Liberal Art," *New Saint Andrews College Colloquium* 2, no 2 (Spring 2006): 2.

13. Surely there are few other administrations in American colleges or universities that define their objectives in terms of Godliness and submission.

14. *General Catalog*, 6–7.

15. Roy Alden Atwood, "Higher Education's Golden Calf," *Higher Expectations* 1, no. 1 (Fall 2006): 14.

16. Atwood, "The *Major* Problem with Colleges Today."

17. I do not think that these phrases are intended to be as Orwellian as they might sound.

18. New Saint Andrews College, 2006–7 College Directory, 3.

19. *General Catalog*, 6.

Chapter 7
"To Clear Some Part of the Human Jungle"

1. Elisabeth Bumiller, "White House Letter: President Gets Lecture from the Christian Left," *International Herald Tribune*, 23 May 2005, Internet version, www .iht.com. The remainder of this paragraph is drawn from this account, and from Thomas Bartlett, "Bush Policies Criticized at Evangelical College," *Chronicle of Higher Education* 51, no. 38 (27 May 2005): A10. Three years later, in spring of 2008, the same president had a similar experience at another faith-based institution, Furman University in South Carolina.

2. Dick DeVos Jr. lost the election in 2006; his father, Dick DeVos Sr., the founder of Amway, was a student at Calvin, but did not graduate. The family has been very generous to Calvin College.

3. *Grand Rapids Press*, 20 and 21 May 2005.

4. www.commandrang.org.

5. Material concerning the CRC is drawn from the Web site of the Christian Reformed Church, www.crcna.org, and the Web site of the Reformed Church in America, www.rca.org.

6. From the "Statement of Purpose" for Calvin's Core requirements. The Statement is an eight-page, dense, document on the Web site of the provost, www.calvin.edu/admin/provost/core_chap1.html.

7. James D. Bratt, "What Can the Reformed Tradition Contribute to Christian Higher Education?" in Richard T. Hughes and William B. Adrian, eds., *Models for Christian Higher Education: Strategies for Survival and Success in the Twenty-First Century* (Grand Rapids, MI: Eerdmans, 1997), 125.

8. A case for the disproportionate influence of Reformed, Kuyperian higher education is made by Joel A. Carpenter in "The Perils of Prosperity: Neo-Calvinism and the Future of Religious Colleges," in Paul J. Dovre, *The Future of Religious Colleges* (Grand Rapids, MI: Eerdmans, 2002),185–207. One strand of the CRC adheres to a strong pietist, and thus anti-Kuyperian, philosophy.

9. From the "Statement of Purpose" for Calvin's Core requirements. The remaining citations in this paragraph are to the same document.

10. Ibid.

11. See Calvin College Web site, www.calvin.edu.

12. James D. Bratt and Ronald A. Wells, "Piety and Progress: A History of Calvin College," in Hughes and Adrian, *Models*, 144.

13. Chapter 5, "Core Virtues," available at www.calvin.edu/admin/provost/core/chap_5.html. Such long and careful descriptions are, it seems to this observer, a characteristic of Calvin.

14. Calvin College, *Facts 2006–2007*, brochure, 11.

15. Calvin College, "Calvin Distinctives: Spirited Community" Web site, www.calvin.edu/about/distinctives.

16. "Concerned Women for America" Web site, 10 December 2003, www.cwfa.com; "Student Editor Apologizes" by Robert Knight. The additional material in this paragraph comes from the same source.

17. Calvin College, *Multicultural Resources*, brochure, 4.

18. Elizabeth Redden, "When Identity Trumps Diversity," *Inside Higher Ed*, 4 January 2008. This issue was also the subject of several stories in the Grand Rapids press.

19. MLive.com, 20 May 2008.

20. "Retirement Tributes," *Calvin Spark*, Summer 2007, 56.

21. Calvin College, "Handbook for Teaching Faculty," chap. 3, sec. 6.

22. The churches in "ecclesiastical fellowship" include a handful of international denominations in places like South America and the Netherlands, as well as American denominations including the Associated Reformed Presbyterian Church, the Evangelical Presbyterian Church, the Reformed Church in America, and the Reformed Presbyterian Church in North America.

23. Conversation with Dr. Claudia Beversluis, Provost, July 2007.

24. "Equality Ride Visits Calvin," *Calvin Spark*, Summer 2007, 17.

25. Cornelius Plantinga Jr., "Educating for Shalom: Our Calling as a Christian College," Calvin College Web site, "Our Calling," www.calvin.edu/about/shalom .htm.

Chapter 8
Swedes and the City

1. www.northpark.edu.

2. See the university's history Web site, www.northpark.edu/home/index.cfm? NorthPark=About.Abt_History, as well as the Wikipedia history of North Park University, "The Beginnings of a Covenant School."

3. For some discussion of the naming of buildings "Old Main," see S. Schuman, *Old Main: Small Colleges in Twentieth Century America* (Baltimore: Johns Hopkins University Press, 2005).

4. North Park University view book, 2006–7, 11.

5. Leland Carlson, *A History of North Park College* (Chicago: North Park College, 1941), cited at www.northpark.edu.

6. *North Park Press* (Student Association Publication) 87, no. 23 (4 May 2007): 3.

7. www.northpark.edu.

8. www2.northpark.edu/library/general/policies/gencoldev.htm.

9. Interview, 7 May 2007.

10. *North Parker* 67, no. 2 (Spring 2007).

11. Ibid., 13.

12. "The Value of a North Park Education," North Park University, 2006. I would define "tuition discount" differently—as the percentage or dollar value differential between the listed tuition rate and the average paid by all students with financial aid factored in. Thus, if the published tuition is $20,000 and the average aid package is $5,000, then the tuition discount is 25% or $5,000. And I would affirm that it is not just the "unwitting" who pay the full price, but rather most students whose family income is assessed by the FAFSA as sufficient to pay the full charge.

13. www.northpark.edu/en/about/exploring-north-park-university/facts-at-a-glance.asp.

Chapter 9

Friends and/or Friendly?

1. Candor compels me to note that I spent a decade as the chief academic officer at another Friends institution, Guilford College in North Carolina.

2. A "yearly meeting" is, in Quaker parlance, more of a description of an organization (a collection of churches or meetings) than of an actual annual event, although yearly meetings do have yearly meetings.

3. As is the case with so many other denominations, the subtleties of Quaker divisions can be a bit baffling. The three subgroups of Friends in the United States are the most "conservative," the Evangelical Friends International, with which the Northwest Yearly Meeting and George Fox University are affiliated. This group tends to blend traditional Quaker values and practices with those of contemporary Evangelical Protestantism. The Friends United Meeting is the more centrist of the American Quaker organizations. The third group, the Friends General Conference, is the most politically and socially liberal, but, in an unusual pattern, it is the most "conservative" liturgically, practicing "unprogrammed" worship, with no formal clerical role. Evangelical Friends International groups often call themselves "churches"; Friends General Conference bodies refer to themselves as "meetings."

4. Rob Felton, "Our Foundation," *George Fox Journal* 2, no. 1 (Spring 2006).

5. George Fox University "Statement of Faith," www.georgefox.edu/about/beliefs/faith.html.

6. www.georgefox/edu/about/beliefs/mission.html.

7. George Fox University Community Lifestyle Statement, www.georgefox.edu/about/beliefs/lifestyle.html.

8. www.georgefox.edu/about/beliefs/values.html.

9. OregonLive.com, 4 April 2007.

10. Arthur O. Roberts, "Friends and Their Colleges," *Quaker Life* 37 (Fall 1996): 4, 10.

11. The Stevens Center, a new facility housing a number of administrative and student services offices clustered around an open atrium, is as handsome an academic building as any I have seen.

12. These estimates came from the campus Office of Student Life.

13. One suspects that this link between the Society of Friends and the Southern Baptists might not be particularly convincing to more conservative believers of either persuasion.

Chapter 10

An Island of Piety . . . in a Sea of Riches

1. Westmont's campus suffered serious damage in the November 2008 "Tea Fire," including the destruction of several academic buildings and much campus landscaping.

2. "Five Great Reasons to Choose a Christian College," Westmont College Admissions Office, nd.

3. www.westmont.edu.

4. "Staffing Westmont to Carry Out Its Mission Most Effectively," nd.

5. Conversation with Warren Rogers, Interim Provost.

6. These interviews took place in January 2007 on the campus of Westmont College. I also visited the college and interviewed students, faculty, and administrators in 2004.

Chapter 11
"Expect a Miracle"

1. There seems to be an unspoken, but rarely broken, rule that that these signature structures appear at least once every three years on institutional holiday cards.

2. See, for example, Carl Lounsburg's review of Peter Williams, *Houses of God,* which appeared in the *Winterthur Portfolio* 33, nos. 2–3 (1998): 195–97, which describes the prayer tower as "exuberant."

3. Oral Roberts University Web site, "What We're About," www.oru.edu/aboutoru/what_we_are_about.php.

4. William C. Ringenberg, *The Christian College: A History of Protestant Higher Education in America* (Grand Rapids, MI: Eerdmans, 1984), 191.

5. Indeed, one standard reference work treats them together in an article on "Pentecostal and Charismatic Christianity," in *The Encyclopedia of Religion,* 2nd ed., Lindsay Jones, editor in chief (Farmington Hills, MI: Thomson Gale, 2005), vol. 10.

6. For example, the first section of the student honor code is entitled "A Whole Person Education for your Spirit, Mind, and Body," 1. The honor code is contained in a sixteen-page booklet, which sets forth at some length the premises upon which it is based.

7. "Oral Roberts University: Vision, Mission, Values, Learning Outcomes" from the Office of the Vice President for Academic Administration.

8. *Q and A about ePortfolio* (nd).

9. Oral Roberts Institutional Research Office.

10. There was no equivalent welcome for Muslim students, or those from other faith traditions.

11. *Student Honor Code,* 5–6.

12. *Student Honor Code.*

13. "Christian bubble" was a phrase I encountered often among students and faculty at the Christian colleges I visited.

14. *Student Honor Code,* 6.

15. Information about faculty and student denominational affiliations was provided by the Oral Roberts University Institutional Research Office.

16. This account of the autumn 2007 crisis at Oral Roberts University is drawn from a number of print, and some personal, sources. Most prominently, it is derived from several stories in *Inside Higher Ed* and in the daily newspaper, the *Tulsa World,* from the October–November 2007 period.

17. April Marciszewski, *Tulsa World,* 22 November 2007.

18. Justin Juozapavicius, "Oral Roberts Univ. to get $70M Gift," Associated Press, 28 November 2007.

Chapter 12
A Christian Walk Up North

1. See the college's Web site, nwc.edu/display/50.

2. William C. Ringenberg, *The Christian College: A History of Protestant Higher Education in America* (Grand Rapids, MI: Eerdmans, 1984), 159.

3. View book, Northwestern College, 14.

4. The Graduate Center offers two degrees, master in organizational leadership and of theological studies. The Christian Center for Communications in Quito is a three-year collegiate program that trains Latin American students in Christian broadcasting and journalism. Instruction is in the Spanish language.

5. For an interesting comparison between teaching at a small Christian college in Minnesota and at the huge University of Minnesota, Twin Cities, that argues that there is greater academic freedom at the former, see Mary Ellen Ashcroft, "Risky Business? Teaching Literature at a Christian Liberal Arts College," *American Experiment Quarterly* 2, no. 4 (Winter 1999–2000): 15–29.

6. All these statements are available at the Northwestern College Web site, www.nwc.edu. The doctrinal statement is in eight sections, supplemented by biblical references, including the Scriptures, the Godhead, the Father, the Son Jesus Christ, the Holy Spirit, the Salvation of Man, the Church, and the Responsibility.

7. FAQs about the new declaration of Christian community at www.nwd.edu/display/5605.

8. Northwestern's recent revision of the declaration followed chronologically and, to some extent, duplicates the highly publicized revision of Wheaton College's Community Covenant.

Chapter 13
"For Christ and His Kingdom"

1. The Marion E. Wade Center is named for the founder of the ServiceMaster Company. The center was conceived by Wheaton College professor of English Dr. Clyde S. Kilby in 1965. The Wade Center occupies a 2001 building adjacent to the campus of the college, and today comprises some twelve thousand books and sixty-five thousand pages of letters, as well as memorabilia such as Lewis's wardrobe,

Charles William's bookcases, Tolkien's writing desk, and Dorothy Sayers's wall tapestries. It has a small museum space and handsome reading room, as well as archival storage space. The college publishes a small brochure about the Wade Center, simply entitled *The Marion E. Wade Center,* and additional information is available at www.wheaton.edu/learnres/wade. See the discussion in Chapter 4 of the Armstrong-Browning collection at Baylor.

2. A now somewhat dated history of the college is Paul M. Bechtel, *Wheaton College: A Heritage Remembered, 1860–1984* (Wheaton, IL: Harold Shaw Publishers, 1984). This history, obviously, was written for the college's 125th birthday. Another noteworthy historical perspective on the college is afforded by a book entitled *Stones of Remembrance* (Wheaton, IL: Wheaton College, 1995), a collection of memories and devotional essays written by members of the Wheaton College community, arranged with one essay for each day of the year. For example, the entry for 26 September cites Psalms 37:5 and is written by Dr. Orley R. Herron, '55, who himself served as a college president at Greenville College in Illinois and is a recollection of Wheaton president Dr. V. Raymond Edman.

3. See Clyde S. Kilby, *A Minority of One: A Biography of Jonathan Blanchard* (Grand Rapids, MI: Eerdmans, 1959).

4. Bechtel, *Wheaton College,* 14.

5. PCA Historical Center, www.pcahistory.org/findingaids/buswell.

6. William C. Ringenberg, *The Christian College: A History of Protestant Higher Education in America* (Grand Rapids, MI: Eerdmans, 1984), 174.

7. James Oliver Buswell Jr.'s grandson is the well-known violinist James Oliver Buswell IV.

8. Earle E. Cairns, *V. Raymond Edman: In the Presence of the King* (Chicago: Moody Bible Institute, 1972), 97.

9. Duane Litfin, *Conceiving the Christian College* (Grand Rapids, MI: Eerdmans, 2004).

10. The faculty member, Assistant Professor of Philosophy Joshua Hochschild, left Wheaton in the spring of 2005. The story was fully covered in the *Wall Street Journal,* 6 January 2006. A similar controversy erupted in 2008 when a longtime, well-regarded English professor filed for divorce, and the professor choose to resign rather than discuss the reasons for his marital failure with the appropriate college officials, as required (William McGurn, "What's So Odd about Religious Colleges?" *Wall Street Journal,* 20 May 2008, A 15).

11. The complete statement is available at www.wheaton.edu/welcome/mission .html.

12. 14 November 2003, www.cnn.com.

13. See www.answersingenesis.org/pbs/nova/0928ep7.asp.

14. See, for example, Beth McMurtrie, "Critics Say the Oaths at Some Religious Colleges Are Intellectually Confining," http://chronicle.com/free/v48/i37/ 37a01201.htm; John Owens, "Schools Faith-Based Doctrines Raise Concerns, Risk

Backlash," *Chicago Tribune*, 6 October 2002, Education Today section, 1; Carmen Greco Jr., "Wheaton Professor's Firing Rallies Students," *Wheaton Daily Herald*, 22 February 2001, 1.

15. When I visited Wheaton I had the opportunity to visit the dining facilities and would happily agree with their high ratings.

16. Michael S. Hamilton and James A. Mathisen, "Faith and Learning at Wheaton College," in Richard T. Hughes and William B. Adrian, eds., *Models for Christian Higher Education: Strategies for Survival and Success in the Twenty-First Century* (Grand Rapids, MI: Eerdmans, 1997), 263.

17. www.wheaton.edu/reslife/policy.

18. I have not included the scriptural references that undergird the various statements of the community covenant. For the complete document, as well as explanatory remarks by President Litfin, see www.wheaton.edu/welcome.cov/comcov .html.

19. This discussion, and the account of Wheaton's revivals, is drawn largely from Timothy Beougher and Lyle Dorsett, eds., *Accounts of a Campus Revival: Wheaton College, 1995* (Wheaton, IL: Harold Shaw Publishers, 1995). Ringenberg discusses revivals at Wheaton and elsewhere in *The Christian College*, 201–2.

20. Beougher and Dorsett, *Campus Revival*, 85.

21. I am grateful to Merilee Melvin, formerly Wheaton's vice president for alumni relations and now executive assistant to the president for discussing the college's missionary alumni with me.

22. David M. Howard, *From Wheaton to the Nations* (Wheaton, IL: Wheaton College, 2001).

23. It is possible that they were careful in part because the director of student activities remained in the room during our conversation, although his presence seemed in no way intimidating nor censorious.

Chapter 14
What Can We Learn?

1. George D. Kuh and Robert M. Gonyea, "Spirituality, Liberal Learning and College Student Engagement," *Liberal Education*, Winter 2006, 40–47.

2. Wheaton College Web site, www.wheaton.edu.

3. Calvin College Web site, www.calvin.edu.

4. *Calvin College Faculty Handbook*, 3.6. The four denominations in ecclesiastical fellowship with the CRC in North America are the Associate Reformed Presbyterian Church, the Evangelical Presbyterian Church, the Reformed Church in America, and the Reformed Presbyterian Church of North America.

5. *New Saint Andrews College 2006–2008 General Catalog*, 6, 8.

6. North Park College Web site, www.northpark.edu.

7. New Saint Andrews College Statement of Faith and Student Code of Conduct.

8. The two extreme positions on the issue of student homosexuality were both taken by Roman Catholic institutions.

9. These, and the following statistics come from the 2006 survey, available at www.nacubo.org.

10. In the interests of some economy of endnotes, I simply observe here that all the sources mentioned in this section are fully documented in the essay on sources.

11. This is an accurate citation of an institutional recruiting brochure. I have kept the institution anonymous.

12. See WashingtonPost.com, 3 August 2005.

13. *Time* magazine, 10 March 2008, 41.

14. *Council for Christian Colleges & Universities*, Washington, DC, 2007–8, brochure.

15. www.cccu.org.

16. *Best Semester: The Off-Campus Study Magazine*, no. 1 (Fall 2007). Published by the CCCU.

17. A recent article highlighted the CCCU's success in helping Christian colleges grow more diverse, finding that the number of CCCU colleges where African American enrollment is at more than 10% has tripled in the past ten years: Elizabeth Redden, "Christian Colleges Grow More Diverse," *Inside Higher Ed*, 15 August 2008.

18. The history of the Council for Christian Colleges and Universities has been written in two volumes by James A. Paterson. The first covers the first twenty-five years of the organization (1976–2001), *Shining Lights: A History of the Council for Christian Colleges and Universities* (Washington, DC: CCCU, 2001); the second, the subsequent five-year period, *Shining Lights and Widening Horizons* (Washington, DC: CCCU, 2006).

19. www.georgefox.edu/about/mission_vision_value/index.html.

20. www.wheaton.edu.

21. www.stcloudstate.edu.

22. Wheaton College Community Covenant.

23. Westmont College Student Handbook; Community Standards.

24. www.calvin.edu; www.nwc.edu.

25. Stephanie Juillerat (CAP Project Researcher for the CCCU), *Student Satisfaction Inventory: Executive Summary*, 4 February 2008, Council for Christian Colleges and Universities.

26. Laurie Schreiner, "Making the Case for Academic Excellence in Christian Colleges," www.cccu.org/resourcecenter.

27. Ibid., 1.

28. Ibid., 6.

29. See, for example, Ernest J. Pascarella and Patrick T. Terezini, *How College Affects Students: A Third Decade of Research* (San Francisco: Jossey-Bass, 2005);

George D. Kuh, John H. Schuh, Elizabeth Whitt, and Associates, *Involving Colleges* (San Francisco: Jossey-Bass, 1991); Alexander Astin, *What Matters in College: Four Critical Years Revisited* (San Francisco: Jossey-Bass, 1993).

30. The responding institutions are Abilene Christian, Anderson, Bethel (MN), California Baptist, Covenant, Dordt, Eastern Mennonite, Gordon, Grace, Houghton, John Brown, Judson (IL), Malone, Messiah, Milligan, Northwestern (IA), Seattle Pacific, Southern Nazarene, Southern Wesleyan, Trinity Christian, Trinity Western, Warner Pacific, Waynesburg, Westmont, and Whitworth.

31. The Catholic results are from the 2006 administration of the survey, the remainder of the figures are from 2007. Catholic participants are Belmont Abbey, Chaminade, Clarke, Edgewood, Fontbonne, Gwynedd Mercy, Lewis, Madonna, Mount Marty, Mount Saint Mary's, Neumann, Niagara, Rivier, Sacred Heart, St. Ambrose, St. Francis, Saint Xavier, Siena, St. John's University (NY), the College of St. Scholastica, University of St. Francis, University of St. Thomas (TX), Viterbo, and Walsh.

32. These results come from the Westmont College analysis of the NSSE, compiled by William A. Wright, associate provost, January 2008, and available at the Westmont College Web site.

33. Including an update presentation at the January, 2008 annual meeting of the Association of American Colleges and Universities in Washington, DC.

34. See www.spirituality.ucla.edu.

35. HERI 2004–5 Faculty Survey.

36. Donna Freitas, cited in Elizabeth Redden, "Sex and the Soul," *Inside Higher Ed,* 15 April 2008.

37. "Living a Life of Honor," Oral Roberts University, Tulsa OK, nd.

38. Westmont College view book, "Grow Deeper," 1, nd.

39. Calvin College Mission brochure, Grand Rapids, MI, nd.

40. College of New Rochelle Mission Statement, www.cnr.edu/CNR/missta .html.

41. Eastern Kentucky University web site, www.academicintegrity.eku.edu.

42. http://aspen.concoll.edu/camelweb/index.cfm?fuseaction.

43. www.sc.edu/words/item.php?wid.

44. www.eckerd.edu/section.php?fhonorpledge.

45. Alexander and Helen Astin, in Arthur Chickering, Jon Dalton, and Liesa Stamm, *Encouraging Authenticity and Spirituality in Higher Education* (San Francisco: Jossey-Bass, 2006) viii–ix.

46. www.wheaton.edu/welcome/cov/comcov.html.

47. Chickering, Dalton, and Stamm, *Authenticity and Spirituality,* 175.

48. Ibid., 75.

49. Cited by C. Stephen Evans in "The Christian University and the Connectedness of Knowledge," in Donald D. Schmeltekopf and Dianna M. Vitanza, eds., *The Baptist and Christian Character of Baylor* (Waco: Baylor University, 2003), 23.

Essay on Sources

Because of the widespread interest in religion and religious colleges and the strong feelings aroused by these institutions, much has been written about them, both from within and from without. Indeed, one of the surprises of writing *Seeing the Light* was my discovery of the sheer volume of scholarship on, or related to, this subject. There is a very large range of perspectives on religious universities and colleges, and consequently a wide breadth of conclusions have been affirmed concerning them. These extend from the most dire of Jeremiads to the most assertive of hegemonic claims. Given the daunting volume of scholarship and of advocacy regarding religious higher education, I make no effort to undertake a comprehensive survey of the literature. Many works that I cite elsewhere in *Seeing the Light* are not noted here, including some significant studies. It is useful, however, to look at major themes in this literature and at a few of the most important and/or vigorous voices that addressed the topic in the reasonably recent past. The goal of this review is to develop some sense of the varied theoretical perspectives that have evolved in the understanding and assessment of religious colleges.[1]

Advocates and Appreciators

In this first section, I have combined two sometimes distinct but often blended groups of writers. First, there are those who directly and overtly seek to make the case for religious institutions. These commentators assert the superiority of religious institutions and often, as well, are critics of other (secular) colleges and universities. Second, some writers, while not taking the position of overt advocacy, praise some element(s) of religious higher education or write to communicate one or several aspects of its success.

Perhaps the most widely known, probably the most vigorous, and arguably the most strident recent work on religious colleges is Naomi Schaefer Riley's *God on the Quad: How Religious Colleges and the Missionary Generation Are Changing America.*[2] Riley comes not from the world of higher education but from that of journalism. She is a contributing writer at the *American Enterprise*, has written for the *Wall Street Journal, National Re-*

view, the *New York Times*, and *First Things*, and has served as the editor of *In Character*, published by the John Templeton Foundation. Riley's own educational credentials are outstanding: she is a magna cum laude graduate of the class of 1998 at Harvard University and has received a number of important and impressive fellowships. The major themes of *God on the Quad* are these:

- Students who bring a faith, in particular a Christian faith, to most colleges and universities in America today are "a beleaguered minority, both in the classroom where their beliefs are derided . . . and in their extracurricular lives."[3]
- Religious colleges (Riley finds more than seven hundred such institutions) reject and offer an antidote to both the "intellectual relativism of professors and the moral relativism" of students.[4]
- Graduates of such institutions are the nation's best hope of returning "an ethical perspective back into their professions, their schools, their communities and their government institutions."[5]
- Enrollment and other indicators of success at such colleges and universities have jumped remarkably.

Riley's attack on secular education (of which, of course, she is herself a product) is vigorous. She focuses especially on "diversity," which she sees as robbing institutions of particularity, identity, and mission, and on "post-modernism," which, she argues, is stripping nonreligious institutions of any ethical grounding, indeed, of any shared notion that there is such a thing as objective "truth." She argues that "promiscuity, or at least 'sexual awareness,' has become part of a college education promoted by the administration at secular schools."[6] It is primarily at the religious colleges, she suggests, that students are freed from the constant pressure of peers—and, at least tacitly, of administrators, faculty, and institutional culture—to experiment with sexual wantonness and mind-altering drugs. She agrees with one faculty member at a Christian college who affirmed that at secular colleges students come "to class stoned at eleven in the morning."[7] And, she believes, secularist students and faculty are dominated by a politically leftist agenda, a "monolith of liberal faculty and administrators."[8]

Riley calls the graduates of religious colleges "Gen M" or (as per her subtitle) "the missionary generation." In an interview in the *National Review*, she praises this "small but increasingly influential group," who "snub the 'spiritual but not religious' attitude."[9] Actually, an extensive, careful, and scholarly study by Christian Smith with Melinda Denton, reported exhaustively in his book *Soul Searching*, convincingly refutes the thesis that many American young people embrace spirituality but spurn religion.[10]

God on the Quad defines religious institutions by characteristics such as the religiosity of students, whether faculty must sign a profession of faith, the extent to which teachers must be of the institution's denomination, if chapel attendance is required, and the strictness of behavioral codes. The institutions profiled in chapter-long depth in the book are Brigham Young, Bob Jones, Notre Dame, Thomas Aquinas, Yeshiva, and Baylor. Many others are mentioned more than casually; Riley visited about twenty religious institutions while preparing her book.

Chapters are devoted to the issues of feminism, race, student life, political activism, the integration of faith and learning, and the question of how members of minority faiths are treated at religious campuses (better, Riley concludes, than religious people are treated at secular campuses).

As a work of journalism and not scholarship, *God on the Quad* is unabashedly partisan, which is the source of both its keen readability and its weaknesses. Riley's work is without nuance. In her effort to make her case as strongly as possible, she often seems to overstate the virtues of religious institutions and the vices of secular ones. Thus, for example, she speaks of the "spiritually empty education of secular schools . . . the sophisticated ennui . . . the intellectual relativism of professors and the moral relativism of [students]." Surely not all secular schools are spiritually empty, nor all professors there intellectual relativists. Similarly, she cites as "the typical model of college-student behavior" years of "experimenting with sex or drugs," and she castigates the "androgynous culture of the secular world," while making clear her contempt for the "diversity mantra—so deep-seated in today's institutions of secular higher education."[11] *God on the Quad* is not a work of objective research and thoughtful conclusions: rather, it is a potent work of advocacy.

The popular periodical press also has discovered the success of religious colleges, as well as the growth of religion in secular institutions, and frequently comments upon it (often with a somewhat naive note of surprise). Thus, for example, an article "Searching, Learning, Faithful" in the *Minneapolis Star-Tribune* notes how Minnesota mainline Protestant private colleges such as St. Olaf and Macalester are rediscovering their religious roots and comments that students who are taught to question virtually everything in class can feel grounded when they go to chapel.[12] *USA Today* reports on the growth of Council for Christian Colleges and University (CCCU) colleges from 1990 to 2005, in an article entitled "Christian Colleges Rebound."[13] It describes this trend as a turnaround and comments that from 1960 to 1979 some 120 Christian colleges went out of business. The *Chronicle of Higher Education* has frequently featured articles on the resurgence of collegiate religiosity, for example, "Colleges and Piety," which reports that "many students today see off-campus religious groups as havens from a college life that seems to shun piety."[14]

From the faculty perspective, Mary Ellen Ashcroft writes about how she believes she found truer academic freedom at a small Christian college than at a large, secular, state university, in "Risky Business? Teaching Literature at a Christian Liberal Arts College."[15] Like Riley, she believes that currently most higher education bows to a Marxist ideal, worships critical theory over literature itself, and is dominated by deconstructionist attacks on objective or universal truth. A valuable collection of essays that generally focus on the life of the mind at Christian colleges is the compilation of the Hester Lecture Series of the Association of Southern Baptist Colleges and Schools entitled *Faithful Learning and the Christian Scholarly Vocation.*[16]

The familiar theme is that students, faculty, administrators, and staff who are serious, practicing Christians are the victims of discrimination in public and secular institutions. In a good illustration of casual attacks on the liberal, atheistic academy, newspaper columnist Shaunti Feldhahn writes that "our culture is led and populated by those who have had Biblical skepticism drummed into them by humanistic college professors. If a student manages to arrive at college with literal views of the Bible intact, his 'naiveté' is quickly attacked by professors—classroom sages who are overwhelmingly humanistic and liberal in their own world views."[17] Page Smith's popular attack on higher education in the 1980s, *Killing the Spirit*, castigates what he calls the "spiritual aridity" of American universities.[18] Often reported are efforts to seek legal redress for such discrimination. Thus, *Inside Higher Ed* reports on one law case in which a faculty member at the University of North Carolina at Wilmington complained to U.S. District Court that he was denied promotion to full professor as a consequence of discrimination against him as a "devout Christian Republican." *Inside Higher Ed*, however, has reported that religious faith is actually considerably stronger than many think among both students and faculty. So, for example, 17% of the faculty at *secular* institutions describe themselves as "born again."[19] The *Chronicle of Higher Education* published a review article entitled "Missing from Campuses: Religion."[20] John Schmalzbauer argues that academic professionals now "are more open to religious perspectives than has been acknowledged."[21]

In response to the resurgence of interest in religion by students, even Stanley Fish has observed that if you "announce a course with 'religion' in the title, . . . you will have an overflow population." Fish goes on to predict that religion will succeed high theory and race, gender and class as "the center of intellectual energy in the academy."[22]

A useful summary of various taxonomic systems used to classify church-related American higher education is offered by David S. Guthrie.[23] He describes four such studies, by Patillo and McKenzie, Pace, Cunningim, and Sandin.[24]

In a scholarly vein, Robert Benne has made the case for religious, Christian colleges. In *Quality with Soul: How Six Premier Colleges and Universities Keep Faith with Their Religious Traditions*, he profiles Calvin, Wheaton, Baylor, Valparaiso, St. Olaf, and Notre Dame.[25] Although he notes pressures toward the secularization of religiously founded liberal arts colleges, he argues that the schools that have clung to their Christian tradition are prospering, academically and materially, for having done so. Benne suggests that, to maintain and renew their church ties, religious colleges need:

- A strong founding church
- Formal governance links (e.g., trustees) with their denomination
- Officially endorsed and institutionally important chapel programs
- Multiple opportunities for student religious formation
- A strong and comprehensive theological vision
- People (e.g., faculty) who are embedded in the college's church tradition

Benne offers suggestions for how a college that has slipped into secularism might "come back." Such a strategy would, for example, assure that the president and dean are "on board," and that the Religion Department has at least one strong member who speaks for the founding tradition. Similarly, a collection of essays from a 1985 conference on "The Task of Evangelical Higher Education" at Wheaton College includes a variety of thoughtful pieces such as Virginia Brereton's on the historical role of Bible schools, Thomas Askew's on evangelical colleges from World War II to the mid-1980s, and Alvaro L. Nieves's essay on "Minorities in Evangelical Higher Education."[26]

In an article entitled "The Christian University: Defining the Difference," Mark Schwehn seeks to define the differences between Christian and nonsectarian institutions. He notes cultural changes that have led to a revival of interest in Christian colleges, among them: interest in the process of secularization; a more nuanced sense of public discourse on religion; and discussions of pluralism. Dualistic models have been replaced with more complex understandings of the range of religiosity within institutions, he believes.[27]

An important document is the 2006 draft of the *Wingspread Declaration on Religion and Public Life: Engaging Higher Education*.[28] This report on a July 2005 conference asserts that the academy must examine how it teaches religion and how welcoming it is to students' religious views. Today's citizenry is inept in engaging the religious perspectives of others and is increasingly intolerant. Religion should be taught across the curriculum, as an important, albeit often contentious, part of intellectual life. Each higher education institution should examine its mission in light of the contemporary yearning of college students for purpose and spiritual meaning.

A number of studies have reported on the successes of particular Christian colleges. One balanced and thoughtful study is Hanna Rosin's *God's Harvard*, which examines Patrick Henry College, outside Washington, D.C.[29] Hughes and Adrian's *Models for Christian Higher Education* offers essays on two colleges each from seven faith traditions (e.g., James Bratt on Calvin College and the Reformed tradition), seeking to answer the question of how Christian colleges can both be first-rate academic institutions and nurture faith commitments.[30] An essay by William Adrian concludes that such coexistence is, in fact, possible. The *Chronicle of Higher Education* reported on Kings College, which is located within the Empire State building in New York City, noting that it was "fending for itself in the heart of Manhattan."[31] Right-leaning columnist Katherine Kersten praised President Dennis Day of the University of St. Thomas for disciplining an unmarried couple leading a student travel program.[32] James Kennedy and Caroline Simon devote an entire book to the study of Hope College's "middle way," which is "neither sectarian nor indifferent to its Reformed Christian identity . . . neither wholly mainline nor wholly Evangelical."[33]

A work written primarily for students explaining and advocating Christian higher education is Cornelius Plantinga Jr.'s *Engaging God's World: A Christian Vision of Faith, Learning and Living.*[34]

Several studies have examined the relationship between Christian higher education and particular subject matter areas, for example Stanton L. Jones, "A Constructive Relationship for Religion with the Science and Profession of Psychology."[35] Accounts of religion-based controversy at colleges and universities appear on virtually a daily basis. For example, one conflict at one specific institution concerned the efforts of the athletic program at Iowa State University to hire a spiritual adviser for the football team.[36] A similar concern surfaced when Medgar Evers College of CUNY tried to create a religious studies major, which struck some as particularistic and evangelical, rather than scholarly and objective.[37]

C. John Sommerville forecasts the decline of the secular university, arguing that secularism, which at the beginning of the twentieth century seemed to hold great intellectual promise, has become exhausted. Christian scholars are now called to consider how to reenter the discussion of the directions for American higher learning.[38] This theme is echoed in Rodney Stark's ominously titled "Secularization, R.I.P." Stark argues that secularization theory, as promulgated by scholars for more than a century, has never been consistent with empirical reality. He finds in secular scholarship "utterly failed prophecies and misrepresentations of both present and past."[39] Gertrude Himmelfarb asserts that the post–World War II secular American university has abandoned faith, reason, and the search for truth in order to become an agent of social reform, especially (in the mid-1990s) in the areas of race, class, and gender.[40]

The Pessimists

Many advocates of the mission of America's religious colleges have perused the history of those institutions, as outlined earlier, and reached a gloomy conclusion. They perceive that since their founding, many, perhaps most, religious private colleges and universities have lost their spiritual core identities. The colleges, these pessimists believe, first lost their denominational connections, then their Christian character, and have now become not just nonsectarian but wholly secular institutions. This thesis is perhaps most powerfully stated by James Burtchaell in the aptly titled

The Dying of the Light: The Disengagement of Colleges and Universities from Their Christian Churches.[41] Burtchaell's work, which is comprehensive in scope and magisterial in both length and tone, is echoed by several other students of American religious colleges and disputed by others. Burtchaell profiles seventeen institutions, representing seven denominations, which he feels have lost, or are losing, their Christian character in order to survive fiscally and flourish in secular academe. About some of these colleges and universities, he is caustic; about others, he is more charitable: his most positive comments concern the two evangelical schools on his list, Azusa Pacific and Dordt. The complete list is:

Congregationalist	Dartmouth, Beloit
Presbyterian	Lafayette, Davidson
Methodist	Millsaps, Ohio Wesleyan
Baptist	Wake Forest, Virginia Union, Linfield
Lutheran	Gettysburg, St. Olaf, Concordia (IL)
Catholic	Boston College, College of New Rochelle, Saint Mary's College of California
Evangelical	Azusa Pacific, Dordt

Burtchaell prefaces his study of these seventeen schools by observing that "the story in these stories is more melancholy than the author had expected. Most of these colleges no longer have a serious, valued, or functioning relationship with their Christian sponsors of the past."[42] At times, the vigor of Burtchaell's argument is such as to give some offense: for example, speaking of the "descending religious history of the college" at Lafayette, he notes that between the wars there was an unofficial limit of 15% on Jews and Catholics which, when dropped, resulted in an instant increase within the student population to 28% Jews and 38% Catholics. Burtchaell notes disapprovingly that today Catholics and Jews form the two largest cohorts in the student body and that the chairman of the board and the president of the college are Jews.[43] He is especially venomous when discussing the Catholic colleges, where he himself spent most of his career, castigating "the failure of nerve, the deviance of purpose and the degradation of public discourse which has drawn these schools, severally, to abandon their calling to be ministries of the Catholic Church."[44] I note elsewhere his unusually negative description of the College of New Rochelle.[45]

Burtchaell sees a number of causes and markers on colleges' roads to secularism. Often, fiscal pressures play an important part, as when the federal government threatened to withdraw support for sectarian institutions, or when institutions faced enrollment crises that seemed solvable only by opening admission to a more diverse student body. He notes, as well, the faculty, and later administrative and even board belief that the pathway to academic prestige led away from church ties. His work attempts to trace the steps in the evolutionary (or devolutionary) route of collegiate secularism. Finally, Burtchaell laments, it is active Christians, not hostile secularists, who have led this movement of colleges away from their churches.

While *The Dying of the Light* is, perhaps the most dramatic and provocative iteration of the thesis of the secularization of religious colleges, it is hardly the only such statement. A key early sounding of the secularization alarm (and perhaps even more imperial in tone) was the young William F. Buckley's *God and Man at Yale*.[46] Buckley famously argued that Yale is supported by Christian individualists and then "persuades the sons of those supporters to be atheistic socialists."[47] Another important voice in the "secularization theory" discussion is that of George Marsden. In an early review of Burtchaell, Marsden found *The Dying of the Light* a remarkable series of case studies combined with insightful analysis—but noted that the results suggested greater certainty than he observed and that Burtchaell might be unduly fatalistic about the possibilities of at least some institutions defying the trend toward secularization.[48] Marsden's own views are expressed in the subtitle of his book, *The Soul of the University: From Protestant Establishment to Established Nonbelief,* and he also takes a pessimistic stance in *The Outrageous Idea of Christian Scholarship*.[49] Although Marsden believes that Christian faith is an alternative to hollow secularism and simplistic fundamentalisms, he finds that "our dominant academic culture trains scholars to keep quiet about their faith as the price for full acceptance in that community."[50]

Julie A. Reuben's *The Making of the Modern University: Intellectual Transformation and the Marginalization of Morality* is a more general work than *The Dying of the Light,* and, while it comes to much the same conclusions, its authorial voice is quieter.[51] She is concerned with the separation of values and facts, knowledge and morality. She studies how eight top universities lost the nineteenth-century faith in "unity of truth." Reuben finds that early nineteenth-century scientific discoveries led to growing doubt of the total compatibility of science and religion (e.g., geological discoveries concerning the Earth's origins), and this, in turn, led to "un-sectarianness," not irreligiousness. "By the end of the nineteenth century, educational leaders presented nonsectarianism as an essential feature of university government."[52] Increasingly, moral considerations were understood as tainting objective scientific research. Efforts at moral instruction moved from the curriculum to extracurricular moral guidance.

In his history of Christian higher education, William C. Ringenberg devotes a chapter to "The Movement toward Secularization," noting that "over the last century, American higher education in general has changed its spiritual direction to the point that it now exerts a primarily negative effect upon the spiritual development of its students."[53] (Note that the research of the Higher Education Research Institute yields quite a different conclusion.)

Nathan Hatch calls for a higher education that "is unflinching in its commitment both to Christian values and to serious learning;" while he warns that "the gentle lamb of toleration often returns as the wolf of relativism."[54]

In "Christian Higher Education: An Historical and Philosophical Perspective," Beatty, Buras, and Lyon similarly found that colleges are tied to religious communities with "increasingly slender threads."[55] They study Baylor University and its Baptist links as an illustration of the "two spheres theory," in which religion and the academic are seen as separate and disconnected. Such a view, they believe, is inherently unstable, and a stepping-stone from a religious to a secularized view of the university. They note that the dangers of this view are especially strong for institutions that have national academic aspirations. Russell Kirk, whose primary interest is the political alignments (and decline) of higher education, rather than the religious, notes that "as the proportion of students enrolled in independent colleges steadily diminished after the second world war relative to the proportion enrolled in state universities,—why, the Christian character of the higher learning in America diminished also."[56]

Reflecting on the founding of the Association of American Colleges in 1915 and its early focus on private, Christian colleges, Fredrick Rudolph concluded that "the era of the small Christian college as the defining institution of American higher education had ended."[57] Even at that time, too few students and too little money, the dissolution of the traditional curriculum (e.g., the presidential capstone course on "natural philosophy" and the evidences for Christianity), and the growth of nondenominational institutions all had a negative impact on religious higher education.

Robert Benne, as noted earlier, believes that some institutions have "kept faith with their religious traditions" but that many have become only mildly connected. He observes a diminishment, a "darkening" in both the religious ethos and the religious people of many private, church-related colleges and universities, with the faculty especially becoming increasingly secular. Most such institutions, he finds, "became generic liberal arts colleges in which their religious heritage played a very small role—a flavor in the mix, a social ornament, or a fragile grace note."[58] Benne suggests a typology of collegiate religiosity that descends from "orthodox" to "critical mass" to "intentionally pluralist" and finally to "accidentally." The first two of these categories have as their organizing paradigm a Christian vision; the second two are structured according to secular sources.[59]

Douglas Sloan's *Faith and Knowledge: Mainline Protestantism and American Higher Education* is also firmly in the "secularization theory" camp.[60] He affirms the Christian roots of America's colleges and universities, noting that "the history of American higher education, until well after the middle of the nineteenth century, can scarcely be understood apart from the history of American Protestantism,"[61] which he detailed in an earlier work, *The Great Awakening and American Education.*[62] But that link disintegrated in the mid-twentieth century: "By the end of 1969, along its entire front, the major twentieth-century engagement of the Protestant church with American higher education had collapsed, and its forces were in rout."[63] Sloan sees the mainline Protestant colleges as maintaining the "two realm" theory that separates the truths of Christian faith from those of the academic intellect, but he notes the rise of the evangelical colleges, beginning in the late 1960s and 1970s.[64]

Cherry, Deberg, and Porterfield take something of a middle ground.[65] On the one hand, they deny the secularization thesis, but their examination of four (unidentified) colleges suggests that pluralism, more than either sectarianism or secularism, defines religion on American campuses today.

Mark V. Edwards, writing when he was president of St. Olaf College, disagrees with the secularization pessimists. He notes that "critics such as James Burtchaell . . . have simply not indicated realistically how, in the face of massive changes in society, church and human knowledge, church-related colleges could have maintained their traditional church-relatedness in all its nineteenth- or early-twentieth-century glory."[66] Edwards remarks on Burtchaell's "condescendingly sardonic" tone and his emphasis on the role of self-deception and "presidential hubris." He argues that today's Christian colleges are Christian in the callings of faculty and students and in the Christian context surrounding the academic enterprise —"and God can be trusted to preserve the colleges of the church in the form and way that God wills."[67] Other voices have also been raised to contest the secularization theory of Burtchaell and his allies. Even as thoroughly secularized a college as Grinnell recognizes and honors its roots as an (abolitionist) Congregationalist school. George Drake, a Grinnell graduate, former president and current faculty member, notes "what we are today is very definitely the product of a Christian past."[68]

Mark Noll offers perhaps the most nuanced view of the secularization-thriving controversy. He remarks that, "to at least some degree, the secularization of American higher education was a gift from God."[69] He believes that there is now more Christian scholarship of a higher order in America than ever before. While the future is imperfect, not all prospects are negative. Strategies for the future of Christian higher education, he believes, need to be based on a complex understanding of an often-messy past.

Catholic and/or University?

A variant or subset of the issue of the continued religiosity of religious colleges is the question of whether Roman Catholic colleges and universities have remained Catholic. The traditional Catholic colleges and universities have both defenders and critics, and a group of "new Catholic" institutions has been created in recent years, grounded commonly on the assumption that the "old" institutions have lost sight of their traditional Catholic missions. We have noted already James Burtchaell's harsh criticisms of three "old" Catholic institutions, Boston College, the College of New Rochelle, and St. Mary's College ("They have compromised the Catholic character of the three institutions; more soberly said, they have doomed it").[70] A multifaceted, largely positive, but not uncritical survey of this issue is provided by *The Challenge and Promise of a Catholic University*, edited by Theodore M. Hesburgh, CSC, surely a dominant figure in twentieth-century Catholic education.[71] The book is a series of essays by various authors that focuses largely on Notre Dame, but the issues it raises, and the analyses of them it offers, are easily generalized.

Father Hesburgh notes in his introduction that a Catholic university is different from the Catholic Church, that it has a freedom that state institutions lack, and that it must be governed internally (these observations, particularly the first and the third, are not uncontroversial). To be "Catholic," a university must put philosophy and theology at its center. He observes that Catholic educators "cannot be satisfied with medieval answers to modern questions" and offers his vision of Notre Dame as a "living witness to the wholeness of truth" and the Catholic university as a "bridge or mediator in a crossroads of ideas."[72] Many of the contributors focus particularly on their subject matter areas, but many also make useful observations regarding the Catholicity of Catholic higher education generally. Thus, for example, Harold Attridge believes that the mission of a Catholic university is to find the place where faith and reason are in harmony,[73] a theme echoed in the essay of Ralph McInery. Similarly, Provost Timothy O'Meara believes that what is Catholic about a Catholic university is "faith seeking understanding,"[74] and John Van Engin also points to the link between believing and learning. Fredrick Crosson finds that a Catholic university "aspires to determine what is true about nature and society and art and God."[75] Lawrence S. Cunningham echoes Father Hesburgh on the freedom found in a religious institution—for example, the freedom to begin class with prayer, a theme as well in the essay of Sonia Gernes. Cunningham believes that "the work of the University at its deepest level is the drive towards God who is the source of all truth."[76] Fernand N. Dutile writing about the law school believes that "faith has nothing to fear from ideas."[77] Richard P. McBrien argues that what makes a university Catholic is that it identifies itself with the Catholic tradition, it lives by Catholic values, and a critical mass of the faculty and administration are committed and active Catholics. Several authors, including Wilson D. Miscamble share the perception that it is Catholic faculty, administrators, and students who make a university "Catholic." Richard A. McCormack has a slightly different set of criteria. He believes that the measure of a Catholic university is in its graduates, who should have a Catholic vision, a thirst for knowledge, and sensitivity to justice. George Marsden, from whom we have heard before, states that seeking to serve both the church and the public has led inevitably to secularization, and that Catholic schools face "immense pressures to be less Catholic if they are to be widely accepted."[78] He argues for "diversity" *between,* not within, universities. Likewise, Marvin R. O'Connell bemoans secularization and the drive to be another Harvard, while Robert E. Rodes Jr. denies the desirability of a Catholic university living in mutual tolerance with a secular society. In his "Afterword" to the volume, Father Hesburgh reiterates the themes of human service, liturgical community, the special interest in philosophy and theology, and the interaction of faith and reason.

Another very helpful overview of Notre Dame as a representative Roman Catholic university is "The Intellectual Appeal of Catholicism and the Idea of a Catholic University" by Mark W. Roche, dean of arts and sciences at the university. He makes the case for four particularly Catholic traits in higher education: universality, sacramental vision, the elevation of reason, and a stress on unity.[79]

There has been a considerable amount of fairly contentious writing surrounding these issues, largely but not exclusively in Catholic sources. So, for example, Nathan Hatch, former provost at Notre Dame and later president at Wake Forest, contends that the Vatican distrusts American Catholic higher education, which consists of some 230 institutions and 600,000 students.[80] He believes the Land O'Lakes Statement has been successful: schools are better as schools and still have a moral dimension, a "holistic nurturing of students."[81] On the other hand, as the *Chronicle of Higher Education* reports, the Cardinal Newman Society and its leader, Patrick Reilly, are trying to make Catholic colleges Catholic again, having "stoked a feeling among many Catholics that Church affiliated colleges have lost their way."[82] Mr. Reilly himself writes on the provocative topic, "Are Catholic Colleges Leading Students Astray?"[83] He decries performances of *The Vagina Monologues* at Catholic colleges. He reports with indignation that students at American Catholic colleges *during their student years* become increasingly pro-abortion (57%) and in favor of gay marriage (71%). These figures, he states, are higher than at non-Catholic religious colleges. The same occurrence is reported by Burton Bollag, who notes that Ave Maria University chancellor Joseph D. Fessio is bitterly critical of institutions such as the University of San Francisco and reports on the creation of new, "neo-conservative" Catholic institutions which promote conservative campus life and traditional Catholicism.[84] Bollag also notes that other Catholic institutions see the "new Catholic" colleges as "holier than thou." He cites as examples of such schools Campion, Holy Spirit

College, New Catholic University, and Southern Catholic College, as well as pizza plutocrat Thomas S. Monaghan's Ave Maria in Florida. Thomas Aquinas College fits this category. In 2005 a senior Vatican official speaking at Notre Dame reported that the church planned to avoid maintaining ties to institutions that have become too secular. He was widely believed to be speaking for the then new Pope Benedict XVI.[85] In a different twist, in 2006 Georgetown University, which has a mainline Protestant chaplain, as well as a rabbi and imam on the payroll, insisted that it would not grant any institutional recognition to evangelical groups such as InterVarsity Christian Fellowships.[86] Faculty voices have been raised at some Catholic colleges in opposition to what is seen as a move to increase the religious identity of the institution—for example, when the Ave Maria Law School of Michigan planned to join with Ave Maria University in Florida.[87]

In many books and articles, including Robert Benne's *Quality with Soul,* the question of whether the University of Notre Dame can simultaneously retain its essential Catholic character and count itself among the ranks of America's premier research universities is raised.[88] Also in a larger study, Cherry, Deberg, and Porterfield profile an anonymous eastern Jesuit university and the tension there between religiosity and academic freedom.[89] The issue of Catholic identity and academic excellence is also addressed in several places by David Riesman.[90] Stephen Steinberg's *The Academic Melting Pot* is a careful history of the very different higher education pathways of Jewish and Catholic immigrants to America in the early twentieth century.[91] He notes that the former group included a large proportion of individuals in managerial positions, and with considerable education, whereas Catholic immigrants tended to have less of an educational background. Moreover, the church in the early twentieth century distrusted nonparochial education. This led to a slower integration of Catholics into full participation in American colleges and universities, but, by the 1960s, Steinberg finds, they had achieved proportional representation.

After a full and careful history of Catholic education in America, Philip Gleason's *Contending with Modernity: Catholic Higher Education in the Twentieth Century* focuses directly on contemporary issues.[92] Gleason notes that as early as the late nineteenth century, Catholic University of America was embroiled in liberal-conservative strife, in which modernist "Americanism" contended with traditional Catholicism. Today, he finds, it is not that Catholic educators do not want to remain Catholic—it is that they are not "sure what remaining Catholic means."[93] Writing about the

College of Saint Benedict and Saint John's University, two Benedictine college presidents conclude that for those who recognize the presence of God in the world, secularization can equal sacramentalism.[94]

Evangelicals and Contemporary Conservative Christianity

There has been steady and voluminous writing about evangelical Christianity in America, from the historical, theological, and cultural perspectives. Much of this scholarship, journalism, and opinion is fascinating reading but only tangentially related to higher education. I have already cited in the first part of this essay discussions that include advocacy for evangelical institutions and comments on their successes. A few additional works that touch on evangelicalism generally and educational issues are worth noting.

One particularly winning look into contemporary evangelical culture is *Mine Eyes Have Seen the Glory* by Randall Balmer.[95] This is a thoughtful but not particularly scholarly set of portraits of a wide range of evangelical people and institutions: a megachurch, a Christian film maker, a summer camp, churches, missions, a bookseller's convention, camp meeting, revival, rock band, artists, and the like. Balmer, who was the host of a popular TV show about evangelicalism based on this book, has written and taught extensively on religious issues, especially the rise of contemporary evangelical Protestantism. In *Mine Eyes Have Seen the Glory*, he discusses several educational institutions. The first of these is the Dallas Theological Seminary, which sees itself as defending evangelicalism and fundamentalism against the onslaught of modernity. The seminary teaches a pure evangelical theology, focusing upon biblical inerrancy, dispensationalism, and premillenialism (the beliefs that human history is divided into seven "dispensations," the last of which is the second coming; the world is degenerating, great suffering is ahead; the born-again will rise soon to be with Jesus). It teaches, as well, a very traditional view of the role of women, focusing upon family responsibilities. Balmer's discussion of another educational institution, Multnomah School of the Bible in Portland, leads to a discussion of evangelical Bible colleges. Multnomah offers two and four-year degrees, all of which focus upon Bible studies, but also has programs in other areas such as music and Christian education. There are courses in New Testament, Greek, the English Bible, missions, and the like. Balmer believes that this school, with its limited curriculum and literalist, dispensationalist theology, is one of a dying breed of Bible institutes, created in the model of Moody's Bible Institute in Chicago after 1925.[96] Now many such institutions are seeking accreditation and teaching other subjects. Thus, for example, the Bible Institute of Los Angeles has become Biola University. Many Bible colleges have evolved into Christian liberal arts colleges (e.g., Westmont, in this study). These postsecondary institutions share a strong emphasis on apologetics, stressing biblical inerrancy. They seek reasoned, logical arguments, as distinct from the ecstatic emotionalism of Pentecostalism. But, Balmer believes, they remain separatist and traditionalist, for example, holding to the subserviency of women. In support of that observation of persistent separatism, Balmer cites the president of Multnomah: "I resist moving towards an environment where the academic reigns."[97] *Mine Eyes Have Seen the Glory* also describes the Oregon Branch of Trinity College of Deerfield, Illinois (subsequently connected to Houghton College in western New York as its "Oregon Extension").[98] At this institution, Balmer found an outdoor-oriented community, with a clear anticonsumerist, antisuburban and antiprosperity slant on theology. It inclined toward the left-wing evangelicals at Trinity Evangelical Divinity School, expressing its goal as saving evangelicalism from itself. Balmer contends that evangelicalism is "the most resilient and influential movement in American history."[99] He defines the basics of that movement as an emphasis on personal conversion, the importance of scripture, and an expectation of apocalypse, as well as, for many, an unambiguous morality based upon conviction. He notes how American evangelicalism has built and maintained a network of institutions, including schools and colleges, that often escape the notice of casual, nonevangelical observers. *Mine Eyes Have Seen the Glory* leaves the reader with a detailed and humanized image of evangelicalism as a complex, varied, evolving set of beliefs, practices, individuals, and institutions.

In *Thy Kingdom Come: How the Religious Right Distorts the Faith and Threatens America—an Evangelical's Lament,* Balmer takes a more personal stance.[100] He argues that the religious Right has entered into an unholy union with the political Right and hijacked evangelical Christianity. In an interview about this book, Balmer observes that reactionary zealots "have taken the gospel, the 'good news' of the New Testament, which I consider lovely and redemptive, and turned it into something ugly and punitive." He goes on, "I suspect that when Jesus asked us to love our enemies, he probably didn't mean that we should torture or kill them."[101]

A few more general studies of contemporary religion, especially evangelical Protestantism, include Carroll Colleen's *The New Faithful: Why Young Adults are Embracing Christian Orthodoxy,* which focuses on how college-age men and women are attracted to Christian worship and hunger for religious truths.[102] (A similar outcome, but with a different religion, is reported in Lynn Davidmann's *Tradition in a Rootless World: Women Turn to Orthodox Judaism.*)[103] Evangelical Christians in general, and evangelical Christian colleges in particular, are taking an increased interest in environmental issues, which they call "creation care." This concern is reported in E. J. Dionne Jr.'s "Climate Right for New Moral Issue," which tells of the stance of the National Association of Evangelicals against global warming and Cindy Crosby's "Christian Colleges' Green Revolution."[104] Speaking especially strongly on this issue is Reverend Richard Cizik, the National Association of Evangelical's vice president for Global Affairs.[105]

An important study is Robert Wuthnow's *Struggle for America's Soul: Evangelicals, Liberals and Secularism.*[106] Wuthnow finds that "virtually all surveys and polls, whether of the general public, college students, church members or clergy, show inverse relations between exposure to higher education and adherence to core religious facts, such as the existence of God, the divinity of Christ, the divine inspiration of the Bible, life after death, religious conversion and the necessity of faith in Christ for salvation."[107] The "struggle" of his title is that between liberal and conservative Protestantism. In *Class Matters,* a book compiled from a *New York Times* series, one chapter discusses, in some depth, the "expanding beachhead of evangelicals in the American elite," noting, for example, that "since 1985, the percentage of incoming freshmen at highly selective private universities who said they were born-again . . . rose by half, to 11 or 12 percent each year."[108]

Mark Noll's very thoughtful book *The Scandal of the Evangelical Mind* is, in effect, a study of why evangelicals do not write many very thoughtful books: he claims that "the scandal of the evangelical mind is that there is not much of an evangelical mind."[109] Noll traces the unfortunate influence of dispensationalist fundamentalism on evangelical intellectual life, noting the evangelical impulse to action over reflection. He is especially saddened by the anti-intellectualism evangelicals exhibit in the area of science (e.g., "creation science"). Although his study is not an optimistic one, he does conclude on a note of hope that evangelical Christians might come to study God's world, as well as his biblical word.

There has been considerable public interest in the legal efforts of religious institutions, including colleges and universities, to free themselves from what they view as restrictive laws and regulations. Fairly typical of this genre is "Christian College Sues Colorado Commission," in the *Chronicle of Higher Education*, which reports that Colorado Christian University sued the state higher education coordinating board over a rule that denies state aid to students at "pervasively sectarian" institutions.[110] In "Big Win for Religious Colleges," *Inside Higher Ed* reports on a California case in which the state supreme court ruled that sectarian colleges can use government bonding to fund facilities that serve primarily nonreligious purposes.[111] Earlier, it reported on a suit filed by Geneva College, of the Reformed Presbyterian Church, against the state of Pennsylvania regarding its right to publish advertisements for faculty positions that say "the inability of an applicant to articulate a personal faith commitment to Jesus Christ and to be supportive of a Reformed worldview will have a direct impact on employment consideration."[112]

Skeptical college professors critical of the role of Christianity in American history are among the subjects of Steven Keillor's *This Rebellious House: American History and the Truth of Christianity*.[113] Keillor teaches at Bethel College in Minnesota and writes in a log cabin in northern Minnesota, somewhere that is not Lake Wobegon.

We have already cited works by George Marsden, retired from Notre Dame, which discuss the secularization of Christian colleges. But many of his books on evangelicalism and fundamentalism provide important background for understanding those institutions, beginning with his rewritten PhD thesis, *The Evangelical Mind and the New School Presbyterian Experience*. This volume discusses the church's tendency to embrace American nationalistic and middle-class values and to move from Calvinism to a less intellectual conservative Christianity during the nineteenth century.[114] Among the other useful works by this important author are *Fundamentalism and American Culture*, and *Understanding Fundamentalism and Evangelicalism*.[115] Another prolific writer on topics concerning higher education and contemporary religion is Tim Stafford, author of "Campus Christians and the New Thought Police," in *Christianity Today*, to which he is a frequent contributor on this and similar topics.[116]

A noteworthy historical document is "The Christian Ideal of Education," a presentation from the first meeting of the Association of American Colleges by William Fraser McDowell, a bishop of the Methodist Epis-copal Church. McDowell asserted that the reason for the church to found colleges is to train a Christian ministry and laity as well. Church colleges exert a Christian influence on students by "the teaching of the various subjects . . . from the Christian point of view and in the Christian atmo-sphere."[117] Henry Churchill King, then president of Oberlin College re-sponded to McDowell at that 1915 meeting, focusing upon the methods of attaining such a Christian education. King states his belief that the aim of education is "to share in the great intellectual and spiritual achievements of the race."[118]

In *The Naked Public Square: Religion and Democracy in America*, Rich-ard John Neuhaus, the founder of the journal *First Things* argues against the exclusion of religion from American political life—perhaps an issue that seemed to need more argument in 1984 when the book first appeared than it does today.[119]

A particularly charming look at contemporary evangelicalism is Mark I. Pinsky's *A Jew among the Evangelicals: A Guide for the Perplexed.*[120] The author is the religion editor for the *Orlando Sentinel,* and he reports that he found much more thoughtful variety among evangelical Christians in his travels in the Southeast than is commonly suspected by nonevangelicals. And, he notes, both those groups tend to feel persecuted by each other. An appreciative look at contemporary evangelical culture, again noting its variety and range, is Alan Wolfe's "The Opening of the Evangelical Mind," focusing especially on Wheaton College. Wolfe notes that "the rest of America cannot continue to write off conservative Christians as hope-lessly out of touch with modern American values."[121]

Student Spirituality

An important and relevant current conversation is that concerning stu-dent spirituality. The focus of *Seeing the Light* is religious colleges and universities, not religious students, but it is obvious that it is the exis-tence of the latter that makes possible the success of the former. I have already cited the work of Alexander and Helen Astin, and the Higher Edu-cation Research Institute (HERI) project on "Spirituality in Higher Educa-tion."[122] Astin defines the "spiritual" as that which is interior, subjective, qualitative, affective, and values oriented, from which individuals derive a sense of self and a meaning or purpose in life. He argues that, if we do not understand ourselves, "how can we ever expect to understand others?"[123] Colleges and universities need to put more emphasis on the interior lives of students, he affirms, but have tended to encourage fragmented and inauthentic lives. The HERI survey of 2004 overturned some widespread public perceptions of college students and professors.[124] It looked at 112,000 students from 236 colleges, and found that contemporary college students are keenly interested in spiritual issues: about three-fourths of them say they are searching for meaning and purpose in life, 80% believe in God, and two-thirds pray. Faculty members, too, consider themselves to be spiritual beings (more than 80%) and 64% say they are religious. In spite of this student and faculty interest, colleges and universities tend to keep spiritual issues strictly within the extracurriculum, a tactic that frustrates students' desires to relate their spirituality to their classroom work. Reporting on Astin's work, Thomas Bartlett pays particular attention to the strong correlation between religious values and political beliefs on issues such as same-sex marriage.[125] A report of ten nonsectarian colleges meeting with the HERI project to discuss their efforts to respond to student spirituality issues is found in *Inside Higher Ed* in May 2007.[126] A good overview of the HERI project up to spring 2007 is found on its Web site, and entitled "Overview of the National Institute on Spirituality in Higher Education."

Rob Capriccioso reports the National Survey of Student Engagement finding that "students who frequently engage in spirituality-enhancing practices also participate more in a broad cross-section of collegiate activities." He also reports that students at faith-based colleges have "far fewer serious conversations with students whose religious, political and personal beliefs and values differ from their own."[127] Jon C. Dalton has created an "Inventory for Assessing the Spiritual Growth Initiatives of Colleges and Universities," which includes items such as "the institution promotes public dialogue and debate about its mission and core values."[128] Kelly Denton-Borhaug, the chaplain and a professor of religious studies at Goucher College, has reported on a study of the spirituality of Goucher College students. She find that those students describe themselves as highly spiritual but not very religious (a position that, as we have seen, irritates James Burtchaell and Naomi Riley).[129] The Council for Christian Colleges and Universities has surveyed student satisfaction and academic achievement at member institutions and found it higher than at nonreligious private schools.[130]

One indication of the interest in spiritual issues of contemporary college students (and college-age young people generally) is the phenomenal success of the books of Frank E. Peretti (discussed in Balmer's *Mine Eyes Have Seen the Glory*).[131] *This Present Darkness,* the first and most popular of these works, has sold in excess of 2.5 million copies. In a casual survey, I recently asked students (mostly not students of religion or literature) in four honors classes at a Research I public university how many had read any of these works. In each class, at least some (around 20% on average) had.

Obviously, student religious organizations are correlated to students' interest in spiritual issues. Perhaps the most important collegiate student religious club is the InterVarsity Christian Fellowship (IVCF), which has organizations on some 560 campuses worldwide and claims a student membership of thirty-five thousand.[132] Paul Bramadat has studied, from an "outsider's" perspective, the IVCF at McMaster University in Canada.[133] He concludes that the group is thriving. It sees itself as a fortress of religion in a secular university because "the secular university classroom is an environment that typically privileges . . . at least a general indifference to the possibility of God's relevance to most academic matters."[134] Bramadat comes to a position of respect for the IVCF students, noting that evangelical students are not "illiterate hillbillies" and that "most IVCF participants I met struck me as no less sane, healthy, contented and well adjusted than the non-Christian students I have met."[135] A similar study looks at the persistence of an evangelical outlook among college students.[136] Its authors, Phillip Hammond and James D. Hunter, note that some one hundred evangelical colleges and universities have been created as one mechanism for helping college-going evangelicals to maintain their faith. Even more noteworthy, however, they also observe that evangelical students, at secular schools, find that their theological ideas are often under attack, but more often than not, such attacks cause those beliefs to grow stronger. On the other hand, Elizabeth Redden reports on efforts to measure the spiritual growth of students at Christian colleges, the Faithful Change Project, which found a significant difference in the changes of students' sense of their relationship with God between Catholic and Protestant colleges, on the one hand, and nonsectarian institutions on the other.[137]

Various Topics

There has been, of course, substantial writing, on important topics, that falls wholly or partially outside the categories somewhat arbitrarily covered thus far. Again, this scholarship and journalism is so extensive that only a sampling of some of the most persistent and significant work can be attempted.

For more than a half century, the relationship between professorial academic freedom and faith-based colleges and universities has been much discussed. The 1940 *Statement of Principles on Academic Freedom and Tenure* of the American Association of University Professors (AAUP) is a document of deep and continuing influence in the American higher education community. Its discussion of academic freedom includes what has become known as the "limitation" clause: "Limitations of academic freedom because of religious or other aims of the institution should be clearly stated in writing at the time of the appointment."[138] In 1970 the association issued a set of "Interpretative Comments" (longer than the original statement), including this comment on the limitation clause: "Most church-related institutions no longer need or desire the departure from the principle of academic freedom implied in the 1940 *Statement*, and we do not now endorse such a departure." In 1988 an AAUP subcommittee reiterated the right of religious institutions to require doctrinal fidelity, but suggested, disparagingly, that "the necessary consequence of denying to institutions invoking this prerogative the moral right to proclaim themselves as authentic seats of higher learning." And again in 1996, the organization reaffirmed that faith-based schools could seek faithful teachers, but noted that such schools "are usually not institutions of a kind to which the academic freedom provision of the 1940 Statement apply."

In William Van Alstyne's *Freedom and Tenure in the Academy,* two chapters present contrasting responses to the "limitation clause," one by Michael W. McConnell and a response by Judith Jarvis Thomson and Mathew W. Finkin.[139] Peter J. Hill discusses how the professional listing of job openings by the American Economic Association forbids advertisements that list explicit religious requirements—such as the one Hill sought to publicize at Wheaton College.[140] Kenneth Elzinga argues to the contrary that faculty ranks at Christian colleges should be "dominated by a faculty who are followers of Jesus."[141] George Marsden, comparing his experiences at Calvin and at the University of California at Berkeley, finds a freer, less constrained discussion of religious issues at the former and argues, with some humor, that the AAUP's consignment of religious institutions to second-class status, in comparison to public and secular ones, is exactly backward.[142] Robert Sandin, former provost at Mercer University, summarizes this theme in "To Those Who Teach at Christian Colleges."[143]

Another important topic, and one which figures to some extent in almost all of the works above on religion and higher learning, is that of the relationship between faith and learning. Some writers argue that faith issues can only deflect the pure academic search for truth; some argue that true wisdom can come only when these two realms converge; and some argue that, while both are important, they need to be kept distinct. Beaty, Buras, and Lyon, in their historical survey of Christian higher education, explain how an early assumption that reason and the church were linked, and "the best of science would always fit neatly with the best of theology," has now evolved into the "two spheres model," in which the curriculum was seen as the realm of reason, and the extracurriculum the proper venue for religion.[144] A thoughtful and humane volume by Douglas and Rhonda Jacobsen of Messiah College focuses on differing ways in which faith and learning can be integrated within different educational and faith traditions.[145] Beginning in the late 1980s, the HarperCollins publishing house produced an entire series on various academic disciplines, Through the Eyes of Faith, including works on literature, biology, music, sociology, business, psychology, and history.[146] Not surprisingly, an independent research study commissioned by the Council for Christian Colleges and Universities suggested that recent graduates of religious institutions responded particularly favorably to those courses in which "values" issues were directly engaged in class.[147]

At least two scholarly disciplinary journals focus explicitly and primarily on such integration: *Faith and Philosophy* and *Fides et Historia*. Catholic institutions in particular, perhaps because of the continuing influence of the Thomistic belief that right reason and right religion will inevitably reach identical conclusions, have been particularly engaged in this issue. Gleason's *Contending with Modernity*, for example, devotes considerable attention to the topic as do several of the essays in Hesburgh's *The Challenge and Promise of a Catholic University*. In many ways, Marsden's influential book *The Outrageous Idea of Christian Scholarship* is an argument for the integration of religious faith into learning, as is Alexander Miller's aptly titled *Faith and Learning*.[148] In *The Making of the Modern University*, Julie Reuben points out that "the separation of knowledge and morality was an unintended result of the university reforms of the late nineteenth century."[149] But Mark Schwehn argues that Christian universities today still can and must connect the emotional, spiritual, and intellectual.[150] A grim look at this subject is found in Douglas Sloan's *Faith and Knowledge:*

Mainline Protestantism and American Higher Education. Sloan believes that the tumultuous events of the 1960s severed thoroughly the link between churches and their colleges and destroyed, in the mainline Protestant institutions, a sense that faith and knowledge could or should be linked. Today, accordingly, we are left with ways of knowing that are mechanistic, which have no room for values, meaning, or purpose. At about the same time that the mainline institutions abandoned the effort to link faith and knowledge, during the second half of the twentieth century, he says, the evangelical colleges and universities came out of the shadows and embraced it. Sloan goes so far as to suggest that "the faith-knowledge issue turned out to be the most important issue of the modern age. . . . early in its twentieth-century engagement with higher education, mainline American Protestantism seems to have had a dim awareness that this might be the case."[151] Several of the papers in Andrea Sterk's compilation from the Lilly Seminar in Religion and Higher Education deal with the faith-learning continuum.[152] Nicholas Wolterstorff's contribution asserts that scholarship rooted in religion still has an important place in the academy; James Turner answers the question, "Does religion have anything worth saying to scholars?" in the affirmative; and Jean Bethke Elshtain writes about how her teaching does, and should, reflect her religious perspective.[153] Nicholas Wolterstorff's *Reason within the Bounds of Religion* is a carefully argued philosophical investigation of two issues for Christian scholars: what to investigate and what views to hold.[154]

A special section of the *Chronicle of Higher Education* in 2004 explored "Religion and Culture: Views of Ten Scholars."[155] Some of the pieces focus upon topics directly linked to higher education (e.g., Robert Wuthnow's "Still Divided, After All" argues that fundamentalism continues to flourish on American campuses) and others are more general (e.g., Jean Elshtain's "God Talk and American Political Life" discusses the contemporary entwining of religion and civic life).

Finally, there are a number of personal stories in the literature, difficult to classify but sometimes of keen interest. Here is a sampling:

- Elizabeth Redden reports in *Inside Higher Ed* on how Spring Arbor College in Michigan dismissed John/Julia Nemecek, its former associate dean of adult studies for cross dressing. She/he is suing the college, which, in turn, argues that this behavior violates its Christian ideals.[156]

- Melanie Springer Mack writes about how she discovered that as a woman teaching at a conservative Christian institution it was assumed she would quit her job when she became a parent. She alleges that the Bible was (and is) used to justify gender discrimination and that Christian colleges need to work to stop deifying stay-at-home moms and demonizing those who work.[157]
- Cary Nelson, the national president of the AAUP narrates how he was "kicked out" of a (noncollegiate) class he was teaching at a Christ-centered substance abuse program by the clergyman in charge. He affirms that "many religiously oriented colleges and universities would never conduct business so crudely. But some do."[158]
- Jacob Reitan, the leader of the Soulforce Equity Ride for gay rights was arrested (nonviolently) at Liberty University. His group planned to visit eighteen Christian Colleges, and at ten of the eighteen, the schools agreed to his visit. Some, like Bethel in Minnesota, facilitated discussions between the college community and the task force.[159]
- In *Exiles from Eden*, Mark Schwehm writes about "religion and the academic vocation in America."[160]

The preceding sketch, while exhausting both to write and to read, is far from exhaustive. Both religion and higher education are topics of long and keen interest, and when combined, they have generated a massive ongoing bibliography. After even a partial and hasty sketch of that bibliography, it is refreshing to recall that even the best scholarly writing about colleges and universities is just a dim reflection of the institutions themselves and their people. Those of us who write about these fascinating places would be wise to recall Shakespeare's and Nabokov's description of a similar literary and astronomical phenomenon: "the moon's an arrant thief, / And her pale fire she snatches from the sun."[161] If this study has been, in any way, illuminating, it is in its reflection of the light that burns in its subjects.

NOTES

1. In this survey, I pay very little attention to issues outside the United States or to writings more than twenty-five years old. Carol Geary Schneider points out how the events of 11 September 2001 significantly changed the role of religion in

American higher education in "When 'Understanding' Is Not Enough," *Liberal Education* 87, no. 4 (Fall 2001): 2–4.

2. Naomi Schaefer Riley, *God on the Quad: How Religious Colleges and the Missionary Generation Are Changing America* (New York: St. Martin's Press, 2005). For a slightly different perspective, see also her "Conservatives, Too, Are Politicizing Campuses," *Chronicle of Higher Education*, 18 March 2005, B-20.

3. Riley, *Quad*, 1.

4. Ibid., 5.

5. Ibid., 6.

6. Ibid., 169, 67. As one who has served as a senior administrator at three schools Riley would clearly classify as "secular," I must protest that I have never myself promoted promiscuity, or seen such advocacy in any of my peers! Dinish D'Souza launched a similar, and similarly popular attack, in *Illiberal Education* (New York: Free Press, 1991). In the same vein, Alan Wolfe notes, "Parents dissatisfied with binge drinking, fraternities and the peer pressure to which young people are so vulnerable are increasingly looking to Evangelical colleges as an alternative"; "The Potential for Pluralism," in Andrea Sterk, ed., *Religion, Scholarship, and Higher Education: Perspectives, Models and Future Prospects,* Essays from the Lily Seminar (Notre Dame, IN: University of Notre Dame Press, 1999), 30.

7. Riley, *Quad*, 214.

8. Ibid., 238.

9. *National Review Online*, 11 January 2005, www.nationalreview.com. See also Carroll Colleen, *The New Faithful: Why Young Adults Are Embracing Christian Orthodoxy* (Chicago: Loyola Press, 2002), for a similar view of twenty-first-century young adults, here from a Catholic journalist who worked as a speechwriter for President George W. Bush; James Dobson, *From the Edge: A Young Adult's Guide to a Meaningful Future* (Dallas: Word, 1995).

10. Christian Smith, with Melinda Denton, *Soul Searching: The Religious and Spiritual Lives of American Teenagers* (Oxford: Oxford University Press, 2005).

11. Riley, *God on the Quad*, 67. Is it petty to point out that as a Jewish female, Ms. Riley would herself probably not have gone to Harvard University prior to that institution's reciting the "diversity mantra" beginning in the mid-twentieth century?

12. Martha Sawyer Allen, "Searching, Learning, Faithful," *Minneapolis Star-Tribune*, 26 January 2002, B5–B7. See also Mary Jane Smetanka, "Christian Colleges Pull More Students," *Minneapolis Star-Tribune*, 15 January 2006, A1, A5.

13. G. Jeffrey McDonald, "Christian Colleges Rebound," *USA Today*, 14 December 2005, Web site, www.usatoday-com/news/religion.

14. "Colleges and Piety," *Chronicle of Higher Education Review*, 16 December 2005, B5.

15. Mary Ellen Ashcroft, "Risky Business? Teaching Literature at a Christian

Liberal Arts College," *American Experiment Quarterly* 2, no. 4 (Winter 1999–2000): 15–29. See also Jean Bethke Elshtain, *Who Are We?* (Grand Rapids, MI: Eerdmans, 2000); Parker Palmer, *The Courage to Teach* (San Francisco: Jossey-Bass, 1998) and his *Let Your Life Speak* (San Francisco: Jossey-Bass, 2000). A case for Christian liberal learning in the Wesleyan tradition is made by college president V. James Mannoia Jr. in *Christian Liberal Arts: An Education That Goes Beyond* (Lanham, MD: Rowman and Littlefield, 2000).

16. Douglas V. Henry and Bob R. Agee, *Faithful Learning and the Christian Scholarly Vocation* (Grand Rapids, MI: Eerdmans, 2003). See also R. J. Nash, *Spirituality, Ethics, Religion and Teaching: A Professor's Journey* (New York: Peter Lang, 2002).

17. Shaunti Feldhahn, "The Bible Stands as the Ultimate Truth," *Asheville Citizen Times*, 16 July 2007, B5. This piece notes how at Cornell, "166 leading professors" had a liberal-conservative ratio of 27 to 1, without citing any source, or describing what constitutes a "leading" faculty member at Cornell.

18. Page Smith, *Killing the Spirit: Higher Education in America* (New York: Viking, 1990), 20. Similar reports of controversy include Scott Jaschik, "Academic Freedom and Evolution," *Inside Higher Ed*, 10 December 2007, and "Purge at Ave Maria Law?" *Inside Higher Ed*, 6 August 2007.

19. Scott Jaschik, "Not So Godless after All," *Inside Higher Ed*, 9 October 2006. See also Bruce Kuklick, "Devout Profs on the Offensive," *Chronicle of Higher Education*, 4 May 1994, A18.

20. "Missing from Campuses: Religion," *Chronicle of Higher Education*, 21 January 2005, B2.

21. John Schmalzbauer, *People of Faith: Religious Convictions in American Journalism and Higher Education* (Ithaca: Cornell University Press, 2003), xiii.

22. Stanley Fish, "One University, Under God," *Chronicle of Higher Education*, 1 July 2005, C1–C4. See as well his "Why We Can't All Just Get Along," *First Things* 60 (February 1996): 21. For a somewhat amusingly outdated approach, see Merrimon Cunningim, *The College Seeks Religion* (New Haven: Yale University Press, 1947), and Charles McCoy and Neely McCarter, *The Gospel on Campus* (Richmond, VA: John Knox, 1959).

23. David S. Guthrie, "Mapping the Terrain of Church-Related Colleges and Universities," in his *Agendas for Church-Related Colleges and Universities, New Directions for Higher Education* 79 (Fall 1992): 3–28.

24. M. M. Patillo Jr. and D. M. McKenzie, *Church-Sponsored Higher Education in the United States* (Washington, DC: ACE, 1966); C. R. Pace, *Education and Evangelism* (New York: McGraw-Hill, 1972), R. Sandin, ed., *HEPS Profiles of Independent Higher Education* (Lake Forest, IL: Higher Education Planning Services, 1991), vol. 1, no. 1; M. Cunningim, "Categories of Church-Relatedness" in R. Parsonage., ed., *Church-Related Higher Education: Perceptions and Perspectives* (Valley Forge, PA: Judson, 1978).

25. Robert Benne, *Quality with Soul: How Six Premier Colleges and Universities*

Keep Faith with Their Religious Traditions (Grand Rapids, MI: Eerdmans, 2001). See also, for example, his "Recovering a Christian College," *Lutheran Forum* 27 (1993): 58–66. Useful historical and philosophical essays are included in Stanley Hauerwas and John H. Westenhoff, eds., *Schooling Christians: "Holy Experiments" in American Education* (Grand Rapids, MI: Eerdmans, 1992). Although dated, Arthur Holmes, *The Idea of a Christian College* (Grand Rapids, MI: Eerdmans, 1975), remains a worthwhile and thoughtful study of the cultivation of faith integrated with learning. A worthwhile general study is Martin Marty, *Education, Religion and the Common Good* (San Francisco: Jossey-Bass, 2000).

26. Joel A. Carpenter and Kenneth W. Shipps, eds., *Making Higher Education Christian: The History and Mission of Evangelical Colleges in America* (Grand Rapids, MI: Eerdmans, 1987).

27. Mark Schwehn, "The Christian University: Defining the Difference," *First Things* 93 (May 1999): 25–31.

28. *The Wingspread Declaration on Religion and Public Life: Engaging Higher Education* draft, 24 January 2006. This document is easily found on multiple Internet sites, including that of the Society for Values in Higher Education (SVHE), www.svhe.org.

29. Hanna Rosin, *God's Harvard: A Christian College on a Mission to Save America* (Orlando, FL: Harcourt Books, 2007).

30. Richard T. Hughes and William B. Adrian, eds., *Models for Christian Higher Education: Strategies for Survival and Success in the Twenty-First Century* (Grand Rapids, MI: Eerdmans, 1997). Some similar studies of particular institutions include Victor Kazanjian, "Beyond Tolerance," a conversation about religious life at Wellesley in *Spirituality and Higher Education* (electronic version) 3, no. 4 (August 2007), www.spirituality.ucla.edu/newsletter; Robert Kiely "Out of the Closet and into the Classroom, the Yard and the Dining Hall: Notes on Religion at Harvard," *Liberal Education* 87, no. 4 (Fall 2001): 24–30; Thomas LeDuc, *Piety and Intellect at Amherst College, 1865–1912* (New York: Columbia University Press, 1946); Mark A. Noll, *Princeton and the Republic, 1768–1822* (Princeton, NJ: Princeton University Press, 1989); Ella Powers, "Speech Hits Sore Spot at Dartmouth," *Inside Higher Ed,* 26 November 2007.

31. Sarah Hebel, "An Evangelical College Fends for Itself in the Heart of Manhattan," *Chronicle of Higher Education,* 17 June 2005, A17.

32. Katherine Kersten, "St. Thomas Leader Courageously Took Principled Route," *Minneapolis Star-Tribune,* 22 April 2006, B1–B2.

33. James Kennedy and Caroline Simon, *Can Hope Endure? A Historical Case Study in Christian Higher Education* (Grand Rapid, MI: Eerdmans, 2005), 3.

34. Cornelius Plantinga Jr., *Engaging God's World: A Christian Vision of Faith, Learning and Living* (Grand Rapids, MI: Eerdmans, 2002).

35. Stanton L. Jones, "A Constructive Relationship for Religion with the Science and Profession of Psychology," *American Psychologist* 49 (March 1994): 184–99.

36. Elia Powers, "When Prayer Reaches the Locker Room," *Inside Higher Ed*, 28 June 2007; follow-up story on 29 June 2007.

37. Jennifer Epstein, "At CUNY, Religious Studies or Religion?" *Inside Higher Ed*, 27 June 2007.

38. C. John Somerville, "The Exhaustion of Secularism," *Chronicle of Higher Education*, 9 June 2006, B6–B7.

39. Rodney Stark, "Secularization, R.I.P.," *Sociology of Religion* 60, no. 3 (1999): 249–73.

40. Gertrude Himmelfarb, "The Christian University: A Call to Counterrevolution," *First Things* 59 (January 1996): 16.

41. James Burtchaell, *The Dying of the Light: The Disengagement of Colleges and Universities from Their Christian Churches* (Grand Rapids, MI: Eerdmans, 1998). Burtchaell repeats his major theses in much shorter fashion in "The Decline and Fall of the Christian Colleges," part 1, *First Things*, no. 2 (April 1991): 16–29. See also David Dockery and David P. Gushee, eds., *The Future of Christian Higher Education* (Nashville: Broadman and Holman, 1999); Jon H. Roberts and James Turner, *The Sacred and the Secular University* (Princeton, NJ: Princeton University Press, 2000). See as well Gertrude Himmelfarb's "The Christian University: A Call to Counterrevolution," *First Things* 59 (January 1996): 16; Harry Smith, *Secularization and the University* (Richmond, VA: John Knox, 1968); and Eric O. Springsted, *Who Will Make Us Wise? How the Churches Are Failing Higher Education* (Cambridge, MA: Cowley, 1988).

42. Burtchaell, *The Dying of the Light*, xi.

43. Ibid., 153, 170, 177.

44. Ibid., 563.

45. I should note that Burtchaell discusses at length St. Mary's College of California during the 1960s, which he terms "a long season of difficulty and decline at St. Mary's" (ibid., 676), leading to the founding of Thomas Aquinas College in Santa Paula. I myself taught briefly (and enjoyably) at St. Mary's in the 1960s and visited Thomas Aquinas while doing research for *Seeing the Light*.

46. William F. Buckley, *God and Man at Yale* (Chicago: Henry Regnery, 1951).

47. Ibid., lix–lx.

48. George Marsden, "Dying Lights," *Christian Scholar's Review* 29 (Fall 1999): 100ff.

49. George Marsden, *The Soul of the American University: From Protestant Establishment to Established Nonbelief* (New York: Oxford University Press, 1994); *The Outrageous Idea of Christian Scholarship* (New York: Oxford University Press, 1997); and also his *The Secularization of the Academy* (edited with Bradley Longfields) (New York: Oxford University Press, 1992).

50. Marsden, *Outrageous Idea*, 7.

51. Julie A. Reuben, *The Making of the Modern University: Intellectual Transformation and the Marginalization of Morality* (Chicago: University of Chicago Press,

1996). Robert E. Roemer, "The Possibility of Denominational Higher Education," *Educational Theory* 26, no. 1 (Winter 1976): 93–106, approaches the subject from the perspective of Talcott Parsons's theories.

52. Reuben, *The Making of the Modern University*, 87.

53. William C. Ringenberg, *The Christian College: A History of Protestant Higher Education in America* (Grand Rapids, MI: Eerdmans, 1984), 114. A portion of this important survey appeared in slightly different form as "The Old-Time College, 1800–1865," in Carpenter and Shipps, *Making Higher Education Christian*, 77–97.

54. Nathan O. Hatch, "Evangelical Colleges and the Challenge of Christian Thinking," in Carpenter and Shipps, *Making Higher Education Christian*, 155–77.

55. Michael Beaty, Todd Buras, and Larry Lyon, "Christian Higher Education: An Historical and Philosophical Perspective," *Perspectives in Religious Studies* 29 (1997):145.

56. Russell Kirk, *Decadence and Renewal in the Higher Learning* (South Bend, IN: Gateway Editions, 1978), 63.

57. Fredrick Rudolph, "Reflections on the Challenges to the Church-Related College," *Liberal Education* 90, no. 1 (Winter 2004): 35.

58. Benne, *Quality with Soul*, 35.

59. Ibid., 49.

60. Douglas Sloan, *Faith and Knowledge: Mainline Protestantism and American Higher Education* (Louisville: Westminster John Knox Press, 1994). Sloan is more optimistic in "Faith and Knowledge: Religion and the Modern University," in Paul J. Dovre, ed., *The Future of Religious Colleges* (Grand Rapids, MI: Eerdmans, 2002), 3–34. This volume is a collection of papers presented at the Harvard Conference on the Future of Religious Colleges, October 2000. The conference focused on five organizing questions: the place of religiously informed scholarship, the inevitability of the trend toward religious disengagement, the reversibility of the disengagement of colleges and churches, the viability of religious college missions, and whether public policy is a friend or enemy toward religious institutions. A shortened version appeared in *Liberal Education* 87, no. 4 (Fall 2001): 18–24.

61. Sloan, *Faith and Knowledge*, 1.

62. Douglas Sloan, ed., *The Great Awakening and American Higher Education* (New York: Teacher's College Press, 1973).

63. Sloan, *Faith and Knowledge*, 206.

64. Ibid., 228.

65. Conrad Cherry, Betty Deberg, and Amanda Porterfield, *Religion on Campus* (Chapel Hill: University of North Carolina Press, 2001).

66. Mark V. Edwards, "Christian Colleges: A Dying Light or a New Refraction?" *Christian Century*, April 1999, 459.

67. Ibid., 463.

68. Doug McInnis, "Rooted in Spirituality," *Grinnell Magazine*, Spring 2004, 16. A student at Grinnell observes in the same article, "My sense is that there are

a lot more religious students at Grinnell than there are students who feel comfortable talking about religion" (17).

69. Mark A. Noll, "The Future of Religious Colleges: Looking Ahead by Looking Back," in Dovre, *The Future of Religious Colleges*, 73–94.

70. Burtchaell, *The Dying of the Light*, 708.

71. Theodore M. Hesburgh, CSC, ed., *The Challenge and Promise of a Catholic University* (Notre Dame, IN: University of Notre Dame Press, 1994). The 2004 HERI survey of "The Spiritual Life of College Students" finds that self-identified Catholic students are the largest single denomination of contemporary students: 28% describe themselves as Catholic, 17% as mainline Protestant, 26% are "born again," and 17% answer "none." In *Cultivating Humanity* (Cambridge, MA: Harvard University Press, 1997), Martha Nussbaum has some positive things to say about Notre Dame's linking of scholarship and faith.

72. Hesburgh, *Challenge and Promise*, 8–9.

73. Ibid., 13.

74. Ibid., 257.

75. Ibid., 58.

76. Ibid., 61.

77. Ibid., 81.

78. Ibid., 191.

79. Mark W. Roche, "The Intellectual Appeal of Catholicism and the Idea of a Catholic University," in Dovre, *The Future of Religious Colleges*, 163–84. For an introduction to the controversy concerning *Ex Corde Ecclesiae* and the Mandatum, see chapter 3.

80. Nathan O. Hatch, "Intellectual and Moral Purpose Still Meet at Catholic Universities," *Chronicle of Higher Education*, 6 May 2005, B16–B17. See also David O'Brien, *From the Heart of the American Church: Catholic Higher Education and American Culture* (Maryknoll, NY: Orbis, 1994); John Tracy Ellis, "American Catholics and the Intellectual Life," *Thought* 30 (Autumn 1955): 351–88; and Stephen Steinberg, *The Academic Melting Pot: Catholics and Jews in American Higher Education* (New York: McGraw Hill, 1974).

81. Hatch, "Intellectual and Moral Purpose," B17.

82. Thomas Bartlett, "Bully Pulpit," *Chronicle of Higher Education*, 30 June 2006, A6.

83. Patrick J. Reilly, "Are Catholic Colleges Leading Students Astray?" *Catholic World Report*, March 2003, 38–46.

84. Burton Bollag, "Who Is Catholic?" *Chronicle of Higher Education*, 9 April 2004, A26–A29.

85. Scott Jaschik, "'Evangelical' Pruning Ahead?" *Inside Higher Ed*, 3 November 2005. See also Elizabeth Redden, "A Challenge to Catholic Colleges," *Chronicle of Higher Education*, 5 February 2007.

86. Scott Jaschik, "Georgetown Rejects Evangelical Groups," *Inside Higher Ed,* 28 August 2006.

87. Katherine Mangan, "Conflict over Relocation Divides a Catholic Law School," *Chronicle of Higher Education,* 18 May 2007.

88. Benne, *Quality with Soul,* 124.

89. Cherry, Deberg, and Porterfield, *Religion on Campus.*

90. For example, David Riesman, "Reflections on Catholic Colleges, Especially Jesuit Institutions," *Journal of General Education* 34, no. 2 (Summer 1982): 109.

91. Steinberg, *The Academic Melting Pot.*

92. Philip Gleason, *Contending with Modernity: Catholic Higher Education in the Twentieth Century* (New York: Oxford University Press, 1995).

93. Ibid., 320.

94. Emmanuel Renner, OSB and Hillary Thimmesh, OSB, "Faith and Learning at the College of St. Benedict and St. John's University," in Hughes and Adrian, *Models for Christian Higher Education,* 24–46.

95. Randall Balmer, *Mine Eyes Have Seen the Glory: A Journey into the Evangelical Subculture in America,* 4th ed., rev. (New York: Oxford University Press, 1989, 2005). See as well Tom Krattenmaker, "A Force for Good," *USA Today* (electronic version), 12 November 2007, blogs.usatoday.com/oped/2007/11/.

96. Balmer, *Mine Eyes,* 134. Ringenberg, *The Christian College,* 157–73, has a substantial discussion of the evolution and character of the Bible colleges.

97. Balmer, *Mine Eyes,* 142.

98. Trinity began in the late nineteenth century as part of the Norwegian-Danish Evangelical Free Church, and had, at points in its history, connections with the Swedish Evangelical Free Church and is, therefore, a very distant relative of North Park College in Chicago.

99. Balmer, *Mine Eyes,* 290.

100. Randall Balmer, *Thy Kingdom Come: How the Religious Right Distorts the Faith and Threatens America—An Evangelical's Lament* (New York: Basic Books, 2006).

101. Pamela Miller, "Church and State," interview with Randall Balmer in the *Rio Rancho (New Mexico) Journal,* 21 October 2006, 3.

102. Carroll Colleen, *The New Faithful: Why Young Adults Are Embracing Christian Orthodoxy* (Chicago: Loyola University Press, 2002).

103. Lynn Davidmann, *Tradition in a Rootless World: Women Turn to Orthodox Judaism* (Berkeley: University of California Press, 1991).

104. Cindy Crosby, "Christian College's Green Revolution," *Christianity Today* 25 (25 May 2007); see also the CCCU Web site, www.cccu.org.

105. E. J. Dionne Jr., "Climate Right for New Moral Issue," a *Washington Post* editorial reprinted in the *Albuquerque Tribune,* 18 March 2007.

106. Robert Wuthnow, *The Struggle for America's Soul: Evangelicals, Liberals and*

Secularism (Grand Rapids, MI: Eerdmans, 1989). Also relevant is his "Religious Loyalty, Defection and Experimentation among College Youth," *Journal for the Scientific Study of Religion* 12 (1973): 157–80. See too Melinda Bullar Wagner, *God's Schools: Choice and Compromise in American Schools* (New York: Rutgers University Press, 1990).

107. Wuthnow, *The Struggle for America's Soul*, 145.

108. Laurie Goodstein and David D. Kirkpatrick, "On a Christian Mission to the Top," in *Class Matters* by the correspondents of the *New York Times* (New York: Henry Holt, 2005), 74, 81.

109. Mark Noll, *The Scandal of the Evangelical Mind* (Grand Rapids, MI: Eerdmans, 1994), 3. See also George Marsden's "Why No Major Evangelical University? The Loss and Recovery of Evangelical Advanced Scholarship," in Carpenter and Shipps, *Making Higher Education Christian*, 294–304. On evolution, see Ronald Numbers, *The Creationists* (New York: Knopf, 1992).

110. Sara Hebel, "Christian College Sues Colorado Commission," *Chronicle of Higher Education* 7 January 2005.

111. Scott Jaschik, "Big Win for Religious Colleges," *Inside Higher Ed,* 5 March 2007.

112. Elizabeth Redden, "Religious Freedom or Bias," *Inside Higher Ed,* 20 December 2006.

113. Steven Keillor, *This Rebellious House: American History and the Truth of Christianity* (Downers Grove, IL: InterVarsity Press, 1996).

114. George Marsden, *The Evangelical Mind and the New School Presbyterian Experience* (New Haven: Yale University Press, 1970).

115. George Marsden, *Fundamentalism and American Culture* (New York: Oxford University Press, 1980) and *Understanding Fundamentalism and Evangelicalism* (Grand Rapids, MI: Eerdmans, 1991).

116. Tim Stafford, "Campus Christians and the New Thought Police," *Christianity Today* 36 (1992): 15–20.

117. William Fraser McDowell, "The Christian Ideal of Education," January 1915, reprinted in *Liberal Education* 90, no. 1 (Winter 2004): 28.

118. Henry Churchill King, "Methods of Its Attainment," January 1915 (response to William Fraser McDowell), reprinted in *Liberal Education* 90, no. 1 (Winter 2004): 30.

119. Richard John Neuhaus, *The Naked Public Square: Religion and Democracy in America* (Grand Rapids, MI: Eerdmans, 1984).

120. Mark I. Pinsky, *A Jew among the Evangelicals: A Guide for the Perplexed* (Louisville: Westminster John Knox, 2006).

121. Wolfe, "Opening," 2. See also his "Scholars Infuse Religion with Cultural Light," *Chronicle of Higher Education,* 22 October 2004, B6–B7.

122. Alexander Astin and Helen Astin, "Spirituality and the Professorate," HERI, Los Angeles, 2006; Alexander Astin, "Why Spirituality Deserves a Central

Place in Liberal Education," *Liberal Education* 90, no. 2 (Spring 2004): 34–41; Alexander Astin, "The Spiritual Life of College Students," HERI, Los Angeles, nd. For an exhaustive survey of the more general literature, see Ernest J. Pascarella and Patrick T. Terenzini, *How College Affects Students: A Third Decade of Research* (San Francisco: Jossey-Bass, 2005).

123. Astin, "Why Spirituality," 36.

124. See, for example, the public perception of college professors reported in the Zogby International poll released 10 July 2007, www.zogby.com/news/ReadNews.dbm?ID=1334.

125. Thomas Bartlett, "Most Freshmen Say Religion Guides Them," *Chronicle of Higher Education*, 22 April 2005, A1, A40.

126. Elizabeth Redden, "Adding Spirituality," *Inside Higher Ed*, 8 May 2007. For a contrarian point of view, see Robert J. Nash, "Understanding and Promoting Religious Pluralism on College Campuses," *Spirituality in Higher Education* (electronic version), 4 August 2007, www.spirituality.ucla.edu.

127. Rob Capriccioso, "Praying for College Success," *Inside Higher Ed*, 7 November 2005.

128. Jon C. Dalton, "Inventory for Assessing the Spiritual Growth Initiatives of Colleges and Universities," Florida State University, nd, 8.

129. Kelly Denton-Borhaug, "The Complex and Rich Landscape of Student Spirituality: Findings from the Goucher College Study," *Religion and Education* 31, no. 2 (Fall 2004), www.umi.edu/ioc/jrae/fall2004. See also Elizabeth Redden "More Spiritual, but Not in Church," *Inside Higher Ed*, 18 December 2007. Stephen Prothero finds that contemporary college students suffer from "religious illiteracy" in "Worshiping in Ignorance," *Chronicle of Higher Education*, 16 March 2007, B6–B7; Kathleen A. Mahoney, John Schmalzbauer, and James Youniss, "Religion: A Comeback on Campus," *Liberal Education* 87, no. 4 (2001): 36–41.

130. Laurie A. Schreiner, "Making the Case for Academic Excellence in Christian Colleges," Critical Issues in Christian Higher Education Conference, 20 June 2003.

131. Frank E. Paretti, *This Present Darkness* (Wheaton, IL: Crossway Books, 1986). See Michael G. Maudlin, "Holy Smoke! The Darkness Is Back," *Christianity Today* 15 (1987): 58–59.

132. Ringenberg, *The Christian College*, 147–57, notes how IVCF replaced the dominant YMCA and YWCA organizations beginning around 1925. Currently, Hillel claims 500 chapters, and there appear to be about 350 Newman Centers worldwide.

133. Paul Bramadat, *The Church on the World's Turf* (New York: Oxford University Press, 2000). For more on InterVarsity Christian Fellowship, see also Melvin Donald, *A Spreading Tree: A History of Inter-Varsity Christian Fellowship, 1928–1987* (Richmond Hill, Ontario: IVCF of Canada, 1988); Samuel Escobar and Mary Fisher, "IVCF's Urbana '90: A Student Missionary Convention and Missiologi-

cal Event," *Missiology* 19 (1991): 333–46; Gail Frankel and W. E. Hewitt, "Religion and Well-Being among Canadian University Students: The Role of Faith Groups on Campus," *Journal for the Scientific Study of Religion* 33 (1994): 62–72; Stephen Hayner, "Challenges Face New IVCF President," *Christianity Today* 32 (1988): 55–56; Paul Little, *How to Give Away Your Faith* (Downers Grove, IL: InterVarsity Press, 1988). Other related works include Charles Minneman, ed., *Students, Religion and the Contemporary University* (Ypsilanti: Eastern Michigan University Press, 1970); Gary E. Madsen and Glenn Vernon, "Maintaining the Faith during College: A Study of Campus Religious Group Participation," *Review of Religious Research* 25 (1983): 127–41; Bruce Shelly, "The Rise of Evangelical Youth Movements," *Fides et Historia* 18 (1986): 45–63; and Kenneth Sidey, "Twentysomething Missionaries: IVCF's Urban Missions Conference," *Christianity Today* 35 (1991): 52–55.

134. Bramadat, *The Church*, 142.

135. Ibid., 147, 71.

136. Phillip Hammond and James D. Hunter, "On Maintaining Plausibility: The Worldview of Evangelical College Students," *Journal for the Scientific Study of Religion* 23 (1984): 221–38.

137. Elizabeth Redden, "Spiritual Accountability," *Inside Higher Ed,* 1 February 2007. In this study, students at the religiously affiliated institutions reported a much higher incidence of strengthening their religious beliefs during college than those at nonsectarian/secular schools.

138. This, and further interpretative statements, are from the official AAUP Web site, www.aaup.org. For a tangential article on this issue, see Thomas Bartlett's "Give Me Liberty or I Quit," *Chronicle of Higher Education,* 19 May 2006, A10–A12, concerning a dispute between faculty members and the president at Patrick Henry College in which faculty members were punished for not including mention of the Bible in a lecture on St. Augustine, and for criticizing a student citation of scripture as simplistic.

139. William W. Van Alstyne, ed., *Freedom and Tenure in the Academy* (Durham: Duke University Press, 1993). The articles are "Academic Freedom in Religious Colleges and Universities," by Michael W. McConnell, 303–24, and "Academic Freedom and Church Related Higher Education: A Reply to Professor McConnell," by Judith Jarvis Thomson and Matthew W. Finkin, 419–29. McConnell is a prominent conservative judge, Thomson a moral philosopher and defender of abortion rights and Finkin a law professor.

140. Peter J. Hill, "My Religious College, My Secular Profession," *Academe,* January–February 2006, www.aaup/pubsres/academe/2006/JF/Feat/hill.htm.

141. Kenneth G. Elzinga, "Christian Academe vs. Christians in Academe," *Inside Higher Ed,* 30 September 2005, reporting on an address at Abilene Christian University.

142. George M. Marsden, "Liberating Academic Freedom," *First Things* 88 (December 1998): 11–14.

143. Robert T. Sandin, "To Those Who Teach at Christian Colleges," *New Directions for Higher Education* 79 (Fall 1992): 43–54; a useful collection of miscellaneous essays such as Gordon Van Harn's discussion of the covenantal relationship between colleges and their churches and Sandin's advice noted above.

144. Beaty, Buras, and Lyon, "Christian Higher Education," 156. See also Caroline J. Simon, Laura Bloxham, and Denise Doyle, *Mentoring for Mission: Nurturing New Faculty at Church Related Colleges* (Grand Rapids, MI: Eerdmans, 2003); Kenneth W. Shipps, "Church-Related Colleges and Academics," *New Directions for Higher Education* 79 (Fall 1992): 29–42; Douglas Sloan, "Faith and Knowledge: Religion and the Modern University," in Dovre, *The Future of Religious Colleges*, 3–34, and his *Faith and Knowledge* (Louisville: Westminster John Knox, 1994); as well as a collection of essays edited by John Paul VonGrueningen entitled *Toward a Christian Philosophy of Higher Education* (Philadelphia: Westminster Press, 1957).

145. Douglas Jacobsen and Rhonda Hustedt Jacobsen, *Scholarship and Christian Faith: Enlarging the Conversation* (New York: Oxford University Press, 2004). The volume includes six supplementary essays, as well as an introduction by Martin Marty.

146. HarperCollins, various authors and dates, 1989–2002.

147. Conference for Christian Colleges and Universities, "What Matters in College after College," a 2001 study conducted by Hartwick-Day, Inc.

148. Marsden, *The Outrageous Idea*, e.g., 3; Alexander Miller, *Faith and Learning* (New York: Association Press, 1960).

149. Reuben, *The Making of the Modern University*, 4.

150. Schwehn, "The Christian University."

151. Sloan, *Faith and Knowledge*, 237.

152. Sterk, *Religion, Scholarship, and Higher Education*.

153. The following are all included in Sterk, *Religion, Scholarship and Higher Education*: Nicholas Wolterstorff, "Scholarship Grounded in Religion," 3–15; Mark Ammerman, "Sociology and the Study of Religion," 76–88; Clark E. Cochran, "Institutions and Sacraments," 128–41; Mark A. Noll, "Teaching History as a Christian," 161–71; Robert Wuthnow, "Teaching and Religion in Sociology," 184–92; and Jean Bethke Elshtain, "Does or Should Teaching Reflect the Religious Perspective of the Teacher?" 193–200.

154. Nicholas Wolterstorff, *Reason within the Bounds of Religion*, rev. ed. (Grand Rapids, MI: Eerdmans, 1984).

155. "Religion and Culture: Views of Ten Scholars," *Chronicle of Higher Education* 22 October 2004, B7–B13.

156. Elizabeth Redden, "Gender Change Costs a Dean a Job," *Inside Higher Ed*, 6 February 2007.

157. Melanie Springer Mack, "Confined by the Stained Glass Ceiling," *Chronicle of Higher Education*, 4 November 2005, B24.

158. Cary Nelson, "Kicked Out," *Inside Higher Ed*, 22 December 2006.

159. Kay Miller, "Compassion Crusader," *Minneapolis Star-Tribune*, 13 March 2006, E1, E10.

160. Mark Schwehm, *Exiles from Eden: Religion and the Academic Vocation in America* (New York: Oxford University Press, 1993).

161. *Timon of Athens*, IV, iii.437–38; *Pale Fire* (New York: Vintage, 1989).

Index

319

University of Pennsylvania, 22, 25–26
University of Richmond, 55, 60
University of Seattle, 143
University of South Carolina, 95, 97, 251
University of Southern California, 60, 91
University of St. Thomas (Minnesota), 178
University of Tennessee, 28
University of Texas, 87, 88, 169
University of Tulsa, 172, 173
University of Vermont, 28, 30
University of Virginia, 32, 172
University of Wisconsin, 172
University of Wisconsin, Marquette, 234
University of Wisconsin, Stevens Point, 202
University of Wisconsin, Superior, 17
Ursuline colleges, 63–70
U.S. News rankings, 14–15

Vagina Monologues, The (Ensler), 5
Valparaiso University, 15, 129
Vanderbilt University, 19, 87, 169, 205
Vanguard University, 221
variety of Christian institutions, 213–21; biblical interpretation among, 219–20; denominationalism among, 215–16; fiscal health among, 220–21; internal or external focus of, 216–17; pledges among, 218–19; size of, 214
Vassar College, 27, 29, 30
Vassar, Matthew, 30
Villanova University, 19, 52–62, 214, 227, 232, 233
Vision 2014 plan, Anderson College, 99–100
Vitanza, Dianna, 85

Wall, Barbara, 57–58
Walsh, Diana Chapman, 7
Walvoord, Barbara E., 9
Warren Wilson College, 19
Washington and Jefferson College, 14

Washington and Lee College, 27
Washington College, 27
Washington State University, 105, 116
Washington University (Missouri), 87, 169
Webster, Daniel (Dartmouth College case), 30
Westchester Community College, 67
Western Oregon University, 204
Westmar College, 204
Westmont College, 2, 14, 17, 73, 86, 88, 130, 134, 145, 189, 195, 196, 207, 209, 214, 216, 220, 230, 231, 233, 248, 273n1; profiled, 155–62
Wheaton College, 1, 12, 14, 28, 87, 88, 124, 129, 130, 143, 145, 146, 147, 153–54, 157, 162, 169, 173, 180, 187, 189, 215, 220, 221, 222, 227, 228, 229–30, 231, 232, 233, 253, 257, 275–77; profiled, 191–210
Wheaton, Warren L., 191
Wheelock, Eleazar, 26
Wheelock, John, 30
Whitaker, Evans, 100–101
Whitworth University, 153
Wilberforce University, 30
Wilcox, John, 51
Willamette University, 14
Williams, Roger, 26
Williams College, 21
William Smith College, 42
Wilson, Douglas, 106
Wilson, Gordon, 113
Winter, David, 155
Winthrop College, 97
Wolf, Helen, 64, 69

Xavier University, 234

Yale University, 22, 24–25, 32, 172, 202
Yeshiva University, 41–44, 220, 257
Young, Brigham, 45